CURRICULUM
AND
INSTRUCTION
IN THE
ELEMENTARY
SCHOOL

CURRICULUM AND INSTRUCTION IN THE ELEMENTARY SCHOOL

Frederick A. Rodgers
University of Illinois

Macmillan Publishing Co., Inc.
New York
Collier Macmillan Publishers
London

Copyright © 1975, Macmillan Publishing Co., Inc.

Printed in the United States of America

All right reserved. No part of this book may be reproduced or
transmitted in any form or by any means, electronic or
mechanical, including photocopying, recording, or any
information storage and retrieval system, without permission in
writing from the Publisher.

Macmillan Publishing Co., Inc.
866 Third Avenue, New York, New York 10022

Collier-Macmillan Canada, Ltd.

Library of Congress Cataloging in Publication Data

Rodgers, Frederick A
    Curriculum and instruction in the elementary school.

    Includes bibliographical references and index.
    1. Education, Elementary—United States—Curricula.
2. Elementary school teaching.   I. Title.
LB1570.R63   372.1'1'02   74–12594
ISBN 0-02-402610-7

Printing: 1 2 3 4 5 6 7 8   Year: 5 6 7 8 9 0

Preface

Teaching children at the elementary school level is basically concerned with a particular act, with a specific class in a given time and space. The instructional program of the elementary school has to accommodate the variety of specific conditions that characterize schools across the country. In order to accomplish this task the curriculum must relate to societal reality while providing children with the opportunity to gain and practice transferable skills and intellectual processes. The relationship between curriculum and instruction at the elementary school level determines the extent and quality of life children experience as pupils and sets the stage for the types of choices available to them as adults. The influence of the elementary school is pervasive and vital to all who serve and are served by it.

The purpose of this book is to relate elementary education to the quality of life sought and expected by the majority of our citizens now and in the future. In pursuing this purpose the writer has attempted to show the relationship between elementary education and qualitative aspects of present-day living as opposed to focusing on preparation for the next level of education. This focus is intended to enable preservice and inservice teachers to develop sensitivities and feelings that will enhance more qualitative and effective human relationships as professional educators. Teachers who study this text should come to believe in a concrete way that the *now* relationships they share with others must be grounded in desirable, satisfying, and qualitative human interaction experiences.

Another goal of the book is to relieve teachers from some of the "rat race" notions in learning. This is accomplished by focusing on the basic and critical components of classroom teaching that affect the type and quality of

v

learning that can be accomplished under different conditions. The *quality* of the instructional program experienced by children is stressed over the *quantity* of exposure to content and activities. Emphasis is also directed toward the way schools must contribute more to improving children's understanding of their daily life experience by helping them to pursue a more critical approach to social reality. It is hoped that this pattern will enable teachers to change their view of education from something you strive for as an end to one that characterizes education as a means for achieving basic understanding and making personal choices. In short this is a process wherein the teacher is concerned both with how children "learn to learn" and how to make that learning enjoyable and meaningful.

This book is intended for use in preservice and inservice education programs for both inexperienced and experienced teachers, supervisors, and administrators. It can also be profitably used in programs preparing people for paraprofessional roles in schools or other educational settings.

The first major concern of the book deals with the social and educational setting of the elementary school, making use of social and educational indicators which point to developments, trends, and conditions in society and within the elementary school that, on the one hand, are intended to:

a. provide opportunity for the fullest development of the individual
b. foster more effective human relations
c. extend pupil participation in the learning situation and in other matters affecting them.

On the other hand, these same developments are, at least in part, having the counter effect of

a. alienating the individual
b. destroying personal relationships
c. limiting participation.

Selected trends, developments, and conditions (social and educational) are identified and briefly analyzed. These developments and conditions have produced conflicting results, which are discussed in relation to the alienation and participation of individuals and groups. For example, technological advance, intended to free the individual for greater self-enhancement and participation in the good life, is also accompanied by the dangerous potential of man's enslavement by the machine and the impersonalization of relationships.

The implications of these developments and their impact upon the role of the elementary school—its function, program, policies, and procedures—are examined.

The second major concern of the book deals with the elementary school as an idea, an institution, and a concept. The elementary school is described as an operating unit with a specific purpose in our society. There is a description of the curricula and instructional program of the elementary school and the structure that is employed to carry out their functions. This section is intended to provide the reader with a good review of the elementary school and its program.

The third major concern of the book deals with specific aspects of the instructional program of the elementary school. This section outlines and discusses the major goals of the instructional program and some of the patterns that are required to reach them. Much emphasis is placed on what children have to learn and on concepts children need to acquire to become effective and happy participants in our society. Critical aspects of classroom teaching are also explored in this section.

The fourth major concern of the book deals with the instructional support systems of the elementary school. In this section the means of achieving the goals of the elementary school are explored. Primary focus is on the instructional materials and resources employed by teachers to aid children in their learning. Different aspects of the professional staff of the elementary school are covered in this section.

The fifth major concern of the book deals with issues that are likely to face the elementary school of the future. Many of the issues covered are presently part of the concerns of the elementary school scene. This section is intended to serve as an early indicator of those factors that are likely to influence the goals that elementary schools will pursue systematically.

F. A. R.

Acknowledgments

==========

A project such as this one requires the assistance and cooperation of many people. Although it is not possible to thank personally all who had a hand in the completion of this book, I wish to express my appreciation to everyone who aided in any way.

There are a few individuals who should be offered special thanks. One such person is Professor John E. McGill, a friend and colleague. During the early stages of this book's development, Professor McGill was coauthor; we worked together to conceptualize the total project. As time passed it became clear that Professor McGill had too many other obligations to continue as a coauthor. However, Professor McGill wrote the first drafts of Chapters 2 and 4 and made valuable contributions to other sections of the book. Although some revision of his work has been made, the essentials of his ideas remain intact.

This section would not be complete if I failed to express my deep appreciation to my wife and sons for cooperation and understanding during some of the more difficult periods of this project. My wife, Arnetta, also provided valuable assistance by providing helpful comments on parts of the manuscript. My family must take a major share of the credit for the completion of this effort.

I think it only appropriate to express special appreciation to Diane Campbell who painstakingly typed and retyped the myriad versions of the manuscript.

Even though I have responded to the critical comments of my colleagues and have used some ideas presented by others, I take the full responsibility for the interpretations given to ideas that are included here.

F. A. R.

Contents

4

Perspectives of Curriculum, Instruction, and Organization   95

6

8

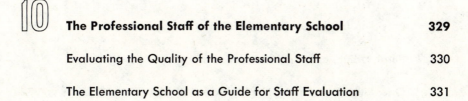

Social Indicators and Elementary Education

As social patterns change, it becomes necessary to develop more refined techniques to describe the social setting that embraces human activity. If we are to formulate an effective and reasonable social policy to deal with mounting human problems, we need a more exacting picture of social reality. The highly speculative sociological and philosophical armchair analysis of society no longer provides the precision necessary to plot social trends and formulate relevant solutions to diagnosed problems. It is evident that more sensitive social indicators are required if we are to acquire a direct measure of social welfare that allows one to discern whether changes are in the desired direction (improvement in the quality of life) while other social factors maintain a reasonable balance.

In recent years, we have witnessed the development of more refined and systematic procedures for collecting and analyzing information relative to social developments and their impact on the quality of life. As a consequence, better social indicators that define and illuminate trends and conditions critical to social development are now becoming more readily available. When these social indicators are studied in relation to the minimum requirements expected for each citizen, it will be possible to determine more precisely the effects of social action programs. Some of the information concerned with general society resulting from these social indicators should point up significant trends and developments that have profound implications for elementary education.

It is our contention that an analysis of selected social indicators will reveal the trends in our social setting that provide the environmental press (the influence one's surroundings exert on his actions and op-

1

portunities) that shapes the pattern of elementary education. Taken separately, social indicators do not furnish a complete and rational picture of society and the forces that shape it. However, when certain social indicators are studied in terms of the interrelationships among the social indicators themselves and how they relate to the cultural and political traditions in our society, they bring into sharp focus aspects of our daily living patterns that affect feelings of positive involvement, participation, contribution, and self-worth. This kind of information, as it is collected and analyzed, can be utilized as a basis for shaping elementary education in a pattern that maximizes the development of the individual intellectually, morally, socially, and psychologically. As the use of social indicators is refined as a means for making decisions about the nature and direction of elementary education, the refinement should contribute substantially to the establishment of a more rational basis for formulating the instructional and curricular patterns*† to be employed in the elementary school. Using this latter notion as a point of departure, a group of selected social indicators are discussed in relation to their effects on elementary education now and in the future.

Knowledge Explosion

It is commonly accepted that human affairs presently, and probably more so in the future, are greatly influenced by the overall "knowledge production" in our society. The impact of discovery, invention, and "socially new knowledge" upon human affairs is positively correlated with the amount and type of knowledge that is available to large segments of our society. Not only do we have a general knowledge explosion but we also have a chain reaction of such explosions in present and ever-proliferating special areas of concern to scholars and other producers of information. This situation has the negative effect of making more information available than can be handled by members of special groups and the general public, of making some knowledge obsolete before it can be prepared for dissemination, and of restricting a larger segment of available knowledge to private use by special groups. We are now in the curious

* Stan Dropkin, et al., eds., *Contemporary American Education: An Anthology of Issues, Problems, Challenges,* 2nd ed. (New York: Macmillan, 1970).

† J. Minor Gwynn and John B. Chase, Jr., *Curriculum Principles and Social Trends,* 4th ed. (New York: Macmillan, 1969).

position of producing useful knowledge that renders past, present, and other new knowledge obsolete before it is known to, or tried by, a large number of the general public.

When one considers the critical nature of knowledge as a type of production of human activity, it is evident that our approach to knowledge determines the validity of the importance we attach to its influence and impact upon society. As cybernetic control has been increasingly integrated into our industrial process, economic growth has become less dependent upon direct human activity or labor. As the society becomes less dependent upon the physical activity or labor of its members, industrial productivity diminishes as a primary societal activity. In the face of a completely automated system similar to the one we are experiencing,

> the basic (wealth) resource input is *information*—programming-machine performance. The machines and, increasingly, the material resources forming them and their products are "produced" by other information inputs and recycled and restructured through further information. The only nonexpendable and "value" component in the whole process is man, in his organized and accumulated knowledge and in his role as defining the value of the activity by the degree to which it assists or constrains his human functions.[1]

It is clear that the ways we devise to deal with and process accumulated knowledge determine the quality of life that can be formulated on the basis of this knowledge. The amount and type of knowledge to which we are exposed will definitely influence our ability to use it for effective decision making.

Another way to view the knowledge explosion is to think of it as a growing knowledge industry. If knowledge is thought of as a growth industry, its impact on the total development of society can be partially assessed in terms of general trends and predictable directions. This phenomenon is easily comprehended when one considers the following analysis by W. O. Baker as he suggests that in 1965 the knowledge industry accounted

> for about $195 billion of our GNP, and employment of 24 million persons, some third of all nonfarm workers . . . (with growth) about a 43% expansion in the last five years . . . rise in real income is 40% from knowledge gain (21% from education of the labor force, 19% from R & D), compared to 14% from capital investment (plant and equipment).[2]

There is little doubt that the knowledge industry adds tangible results to the development of economic, intellectual, and personal factors affecting human activity. However, we will have to continue to devise better ways to make this knowledge contribute to the quality of life in areas related to both the economic and transeconomic aspects of human activity.

In the main, the knowledge explosion has created an information crisis. As more knowledge is made available, its volume creates an "informational retrieval" problem. This crisis, according to Bertram M. Gross, can be thought of as "the overproduction of information relative to the capacity for the storage, analysis, and distribution to point of need."[3] Whenever ideas represented in the new knowledge are cluttered to the extent that information does not flow freely, critical problems are created regarding the assembling and dissemination of information to those who need it at a time that it is most useful to their decision making and activity. As knowledge continues to expand[4,*] the problem of rational and realistic information retrieval for specific purposes at different periods by select groups will continue to be one of the troublesome side effects of the knowledge explosion pattern.

When elementary education is viewed in relation to the problems inherent in and resulting from the many facets of the knowledge explosion that we are presently experiencing, it is clear that the development of curriculum and instructional practice warrants careful consideration. It also suggests that our solutions must be related to specific problems associated with different aspects of the knowledge explosion. We can no longer afford to note that a knowledge explosion exists and respond by making minor adjustments in the ongoing curriculum pattern that is common to the elementary school. There is ample evidence available to indicate that it is essential that our new curriculum patterns be shaped by conclusions derived from a careful and systematic analysis of the knowledge explosion as it relates to the requirements of elementary education. If we do not discover and implement approaches to aid pupils

---

* According to W. O. Baker in "Communications Science—Today and Tomorrow" (*Science and Society: A Symposium,* Xerox Corporation, 1965), certain aspects of the knowledge industry have grown tremendously in the last four decades. Since 1930, research and development have grown at an expanding rate (fifteenfold); publishing and printing (tenfold); entertainment—includes broadcasting, movies, plays, concerts, phonograph records, and spectator sports (2.4-fold); information machines—typewriters, copying systems, and computers (fourteenfold); professional services—accounting, architecture, medicine, legal information for businesses and other organizations (threefold); communications—as a knowledge purveyor (threefold); education (fourfold). In some instances selected aspects of the knowledge industry indicated have grown twice as fast since 1965. This tends to add more credibility to the contention that the problems related to the retrieval of information during a period of accelerated expansion of the knowledge explosion are acute.

in their attempts to retrieve specialized knowledge that will enable them to solve social problems, we will run a high risk of educating dysfunctional literates and drowning in a sea of nonusable knowledge.

In the content areas of elementary education, the explosion of knowledge presents us with a number of problems related both to the selection of content and to the development of appropriate instructional practices. It is evident that coverage of all knowledge is not possible and, moreover, undesirable. For example, much of the knowledge that is produced for consumption is an outcome of "pure" rather than "applied" research.* This suggests that the dominance of pure research leads to the overproduction of new knowledge without an intended function. In addition, the improvement of the quality of life is not a guiding value of pure scientific research even though this might be the ultimate result of such research. The impact of the pure researchers on the schools was tremendous during the 1960s, and much new knowledge was introduced that could not be directly related to social problems. The emphasis during this period centered on teaching children to think and act like scientists. In effect, this notion became a curricular objective. When knowledge for its own sake and knowledge production procedure† became a curricular objective, questions concerning societal relevance were raised more frequently by laymen and professionals alike. Knowledge that fails to help children solve practical problems is not thought of as being as useful or meaningful for achieving the purposes of the elementary school. The form and substance of knowledge in the elementary school are critical considerations that determine the extent to which necessary objectives can be achieved.

Since we cannot respond to all the new knowledge that is and will be available, our strategy of content selection must take into account the fact that the discovery of new knowledge occurs in many different places and is collected and produced by many different kinds of specialists. We must also deal with the fact that different kinds of specialists study the same or similar problems. Therefore, it is essential to look at the different kinds of methods employed to discover new knowledge. Knowledge must also be considered in relation to the delivery system employed to dissem-

---

* The distinction intended between pure and applied research treats the former as research that does not consider uses of its results outside the domain of science, whereas the latter deals with the use of research to solve a problem. Although it is possible that some pure research can be readily applied to the solution of a practical problem, the intent of pure research is not application outside the profession. In short, a related way of distinguishing between pure and applied research lies in the distinction between trying "to answer a question" and trying "to solve a problem."

† The process or method employed to create new or rearrange old knowledge.

inate and process it and in relation to how the media influence its acquisition and acceptance.

When knowledge is being considered for the elementary curriculum, it must be selected on the basis of its critical relationship to human activity acquiring such things as food, shelter, and personal protection. This notion assumes that we have a realistic view of human activity and of how information is likely to influence its development and direction. Our selection and use of sources and resources will influence how well the available knowledge parallels and helps us to understand the complexity of human activity in a changing environmental setting. As we consider elementary education, the impact of knowledge on our choices and priorities cannot be underestimated or overstated.

Urbanization

Since the 1950 Census the pattern of urbanization in America has had profound effects on the development and implementation of curricula and learning experiences in elementary education. The 1950 Census revealed that there were one hundred and fifty metropolitan cities with populations of one hundred thousand or more, and that for the first time in the history of America, about half of the total population resided in the combined metropolitan areas comprising this group. Since that time, the process of urbanization has accelerated as demonstrated by the fact that the rate of population change in metropolitan areas from 1950 to 1960 was twice that of the preceding fifty years. At the present time more than 70 per cent of the citizens of the United States reside in urban areas. This pattern of the percentages of people becoming city dwellers is similar to that of other industrial countries. However, it should be noted that half of the world's largest cities are located in the underdeveloped countries. All indicators suggest that this trend toward urbanization is likely to continue at an expanded rate. Presently, urbanization has advanced to the point where more than two thirds of the schoolchildren and schoolteachers in America are located in metropolitan area schools. The pattern of urbanization we are presently experiencing has created some acute problems that threaten to cancel out the positive effects of a well-conceived conception of elementary education as a viable institution in our society.

In addition to the critical problems related to supplying the simplest of services in metropolitan areas, the problems related to providing relevant educational experiences have proliferated to crisis proportions in many urban centers. Faced with high rates of intra- and intercity mobility, growing slums, overcrowded and outdated schools, increased juvenile antisocial behavior, heavy unemployment and underemployment, expanding welfare roles, and deteriorating social-service delivery systems, the central cities are caught in a viselike grip of steady decline. If there is to be any hope of slowing the pace of decline and reversing the present trends, schools must remain—or become—viable institutions for initiating and sustaining positive social changes. For schools to provide viable alternatives to decay, patterns must be devised to help educators deal with problems created by and associated with the existence of urbanization. This development can be affected by researching, analyzing, and rationalizing solutions to influence negative conditions in urban area schools. It would be a much needed improvement if we had more examples of how known ideas are employed to extend and expand the quality of our lives.

Now—midway in the 1970s—we must be attuned to the fact that in urban industrial societies the city is the primary center of human occupation. Since agriculture accounts for no more than 5 per cent of the Gross National Product (GNP) of the United States, it appears that our population is committed to a basically new form of human settlement. This new form will influence our lifestyles in accordance with patterns that are easily predicted by us at the present time. Yet, schools are expected to furnish the necessary learning experiences that will enable young people to cope effectively with the situations they will face as adults. The ability of schools to deliver this kind of education is going to depend largely upon the amount of knowledge educators have about the effects of urbanization upon human activity and associations, as citizens and institutions interact in a democratic society.

In this discussion, the term "urbanization" ". . . refers to the proportion of the total population concentrated in urban settlements, or else a rise in this proportion."[5] Urbanization is not synonymous with the growth of cities even though they often occur together. Thus, cities can grow without experiencing urbanization if the rural population grows at the same, or at an accelerated, rate thus keeping the proportion of the population living in these different areas in relative balance. Although urbanization is increasing, on the whole, it is possible and highly probable that the trend will subside in some areas at the same time that cities continue to grow in size. The important factor to remember here is that once urbanization has advanced to a given stage over a period of time, human activity and association will be determined by the specifics of the pattern of urbanization experienced.

In order to make our discussion of urbanization more manageable as it relates to elementary education, we limit the communities to be included in this discussion to those with populations of one hundred thousand or more. This will give us a meaningful basis for distinguishing between the proportion of the population classified as "urban" or "rural" in the official population statistics. This pattern of classifying a proportion of the population as "urban" or "rural" leaves us with the knotty problem of establishing boundaries when the existence of political boundaries are diminished by the pattern of human settlement such as that noted for New York City and northeastern New Jersey or Los Angeles and its surrounding communities. When the pattern of urban sprawl is not properly accounted for in a population statistic, there is a tendency to underestimate the proportion of the city population and exaggerate the proportion of the rural population. This can lead to an understatement of the extent of the influence of urbanization on the area under consideration and cause planners to focus narrowly on the resulting problems. In a real sense, this is the crux of the problem facing educators in urban areas. Our limited knowledge and understanding of the factors of urbanization affecting schooling have fostered approaches to education that run counter to the trends of human development and activity.

The patterns of migration determine the rate, extent, and specific characteristics of urbanization evident in different areas of the country. Even though urban areas share many common characteristics related to absolute size in numbers, density, and heterogeneity of their respective populations, these factors combine in different ways to form an environmental press that distinguishes one urban community from another. In general, however, as each of these characteristics becomes more pronounced there is increased incidence of the following aspects of the community.

1. There is a noticeable increase in the complexity of the occupational structure and the patterns of social stratification. Among the majority of the work force, the division of labor is characterized by narrow specialization. On the other hand, as specialization increases, lines of social distinction are more sharply drawn and considerably more complicated.

2. There is an increase in the extent and kinds of mobility patterns. A high rate of intra- and intercity and neighborhood mobility is reflected in most urban schools. Part of the rapid mobility rate in urban areas is attributable to the increased opportunity for social mobility.

3. As urbanization increases, the nature of social interaction is

less intimate and the forms of interaction are altered. Members of the urban population tend to join voluntary associations that focus on the special interests and needs of individuals. Group associations are not limited to a particular geographical location.

4. There is a complex distribution of an urban population because of the presence of more complicated zoning regulations. The lines between ethnic neighborhoods are more sharply drawn revealing recognizable and distinct differences in lifestyles.

5. Urbanization tends to contribute to increased differentiation of the social roles persons play in their daily activities. This leads to the development of divergent styles for acting out specific roles and greater difficulty in integrating the many different roles one must play. Therefore, many of the contacts between urban dwellers become anonymous and unrelated to role demands because acquaintances who are significant in their primary life activities do not influence most social segments of personal behavior.

6. Social tolerance in urban areas is highly correlated with increased specialization and anonymity. The urban dweller tends to use a broad basis for judging behavior because of the fact that he is exposed and therefore accustomed to a wider range of social expression of behavior. The conditions for social change in urban areas are particularly good when one notes the rapid shifts in personal tastes and patterns of consumer consumption.

7. Tolerance for bizarre behavior results from urbanization. There is much more deviation from commonly held social values and less concern for acceptable social standards. Standards for individuals are more closely related to subgroup associations and often run counter to standards set by the larger community.

In summary, the extent to which any one of these factors operates in a given urban area is a function of how the size, density, and heterogeneity factors interact with one another.

The mobility pattern of a community exerts short- and long-term influence upon the problems facing social institutions in urban areas. In earlier years, increases in urbanization resulted from the movement of large segments of the population from rural to urban areas. For example, more than twenty-seven million people moved from farms in the United

States between 1920 and 1959. During this same period of time, approximately eight million immigrants entered the United States and more than two thirds of this group settled in urban areas. These two groups presented very different as well as related social problems to different urban centers. In one sense, the assimilation of different cultural groups into the urban fabric was one of the major problems. Both groups had to learn the ways of the city and often they did not have the necessary educational background, language facility, and skills required to support themselves. One of the major responsibilities facing social institutions in urban areas during that period dealt with survival and financial security.

Even though the general characteristics described previously for inmigrants to urban areas during the period between 1920–1959 define the group generally, the description is not adequate for understanding the nature of the problem. When the total group is viewed in shorter time spans, a very different view of the population characteristics related to selected mobility patterns in urban areas emerges. As a case in point, an analysis of the 1955–1960 migration data for New York City[6] reveals the following:

1. Nonwhite migrants to New York City from other parts of the United States show a *higher* average level of schooling than the resident population of the city—*both white* and *nonwhite*.
2. These differences in educational attainment can be explained in considerable measure by the younger age distribution among the nonwhite migrants.
3. Similarly, white inmigrants average higher educational attainment levels than white or nonwhite residents.
4. Among inmigrants of both color groups a considerably larger proportion originated from metropolitan areas, thereby contributing to the educational differences favoring migrants.
5. The average educational attainment level of outmigrants exceeded that of inmigrants.

As this information indicates, the inmigrants to New York City during the latter part of the 1950s were very different from those of earlier years and they presented a very different set of social problems for the city's social institutions, most especially its schools.

At the present time, more than 70 per cent of America's people live in a metropolitan area with a population of fifty thousand or more which is increasing in size at different rates related to Census regions and divisions.[7] However, the resulting population characteristics of this growth are related to a mobility pattern that is much different from the patterns of earlier years. At this point in our history, the farm proportion of our population is approximately 5 per cent. This means that the growth in urban populations in the future will have fewer inmigrants from rural areas. The urban inmigrant population of urban areas will comprise individuals from other metropolitan areas who are seeking more opportunity by moving from place to place in short periods of time.[8]* This trend is on the increase and exerts a decided influence on the character of many urban communities and multiplies the complexity of problems facing the social institutions and human associations involved.

It is clear that an increase in urbanization changes patterns of human activity and alters social associations and institutional relationships regarding the delivery of social services to an urban population. Even after urbanization stabilizes, problems created by the increased population will remain and become more complex owing to inclusion and interaction of other important factors. The characteristics of the mobility in a given urban area determine the nature of the resulting problems and the direction of the focus to bring about effective solutions. Under these conditions, urbanization breeds a type of centralization that does not provide for individual expression because urban areas are too often characterized by governmental functions that are increasingly distant from their constituencies. Urban areas are often caught up in a morass of their own bureaucratic structures, lack the necessary funds needed to supply essential services, must operate without the support of significant members of the financial power structure, and are devoid of meaningful goals.

Specialization resulting from urbanization fosters pluralism but limits intergroup exchanges and makes members of a population feel estranged from each other. Increased specialization contributes to increases in social mobility and sharply drawn lines of social stratification. Tight social stratification is reflected in the housing patterns that are evident in an urban area. These housing patterns are highly correlated with certain types of social problems, as individuals join together in special interest groups to achieve certain goals that are in conflict with those of other groups who are competing for the same meager resources. There is growing evidence that the boundaries between different special interest groups have hardened to a point of open and bitter conflict.

As urban conditions have deteriorated with the onslaught of social patterns resulting from urbanization, improvement in city living

---

* According to data shown in the 1970 *Statistical Abstract of the United States,* approximately 20 per cent of the resident population moved between 1968 and 1969. Of that 20 per cent approximately 12 per cent and 7 per cent moved within and outside the same county, respectively.

seems rather remote. In most urban areas, the downward turn of most economic conditions for an increasing number of city dwellers negates the effects of improvements in providing basic social services. This, in part, is related to the fact that ineffective and wasteful communication patterns between governmental agencies in many urban areas do not permit operating units to maximize their use of scarce resources for delivering needed services. It is evident from the sharp increase in negative social indicators that describe the typical urban setting of today that the quality of life promised by the urban setting is not forthcoming for the majority of its inhabitants. All indicators suggest that these conditions will get worse before they get better.

Urbanization as a phenomenon is not the real problem but is an expression of a more basic problem—rapid human multiplication. It is a painful fact that as the human population expands there will be an expansion of cities whether rates of urbanization increase, decline, or stabilize. Continued city growth will lead to greater density and an increase in the social problems resulting from this condition. It appears that low-density living in the future will be a costly commodity—both in terms of its negative and positive consequences. In this sense, urban planners must begin to think in terms of planning for population growth and the rate at which this growth should take place in given areas. Our programs in elementary education must help educators and the youth they teach to understand the processes and problems produced by urbanization if they are to cope effectively with future social problems. The different aspects of urbanization will play an important role in influencing the quality of life possible for future generations.

Technological Advance

Technological advance has had, and continues to have, a profound effect upon the style and quality of life experienced by the vast majority of the population. These technological advances have tended to have first-, second-, and third-order consequences for altering the structure of society and rearranging social interaction patterns between individuals, groups, and institutions. One example of how the orders of consequences resulting from technological advance affect the pattern of society is

the development of the internal combustion engine and its use in the automobile. First-order events include road-network-development effects on over-all human mobility, on industry, and the like; second-order might be the more delayed effects on various human institutions—for example, the family, community structure, and the *urbs;* other orders would go on through up until today, including, on the negative side, air pollution, traffic fatalities and congestion.[9]

The effects of the order of consequences emanating from the development of television, supersonic jets, computers, nuclear power, rockets, insecticides, and plastics will influence the structure of society in much the same way as the automobile. For some technological advances the order of consequences is known only wholly or in part at the first or last stage. Increasingly, we are not advised of the possible consequences of technological advances. We have come to the realization that the by-products (both social and material) of technological advances might yield consequences that are counterproductive and ultimately threatening to the population. At this point in our history we must approach the consequences of technological advances with a more critical eye, evaluating their possible effects upon the quality of life in America and the world.

Technological advances are altering our lifestyles at an increasingly quickened pace because of prior technological breakthroughs, instrumentation, and integrated management techniques. For example, the development of the computer resulted from technological advances, which, at the same time, made it possible to invent new, and update old, technology at an exponential rate of growth. The rapid improvement of the computer itself has accelerated this process at a rate beyond the comprehension of the majority of our population. Instrumentation as a factor in technological advance exerts a variety of specific influences on our society and the rate of technological growth. The type of instrumentation employed determines the research areas that will be selected for funding and continued support; increases precision in the use and development of quantitative and nonquantitative data needed for scientific advance; influences the deployment, allocation, and technological displacement of personnel at all levels; affects the kind of education and training required; affects the *internal* organization of the scientific communities; and alters *external* relationships between the scientific community and governmental units at all levels. Instrumentation employed in our technology is changing many social patterns beyond the scope and understanding of the general citizenry, and the condition is growing at a fast rate. There is little doubt that instrumentation in technological advance will manifest itself in many radical changes in our society.

Changes in our approach to management have contributed greatly to the advancement and delivery potential of our rapidly developing technology. If one considers the fact that advance in technical instrumentation often spurs discovery in "pure" science and that discovery in "pure" science paves the way for development of technical instrumentation, then we see that the integration of the management process to deal with this emerging relationship was inevitable. This view of management treats the relationship between basic research and technical advancement as permanent "capital" gain to be nurtured and expanded for the benefit of society and the people directly involved. This kind of management ushered in the development and use of operations research and systems analysis as a coordinated approach organized innovation.* As these new management techniques have been employed, there has been a vast decrease in the time lag between basic research and the introduction of the resulting technology for the general public consumption. In addition to the serious social consequences that result—the rapid introduction of new and radically different technology into society—there can also be an increase in environmental deterioration because adequate testing, monitoring, and forecasting techniques are not employed and are not available in some instances. Technological advancement must be given more consideration in relation to negative ecological effects that occur when they are put to greater use by more people. This aspect of technological advance must be a major concern in the future.

Technological advancement has also led to greater dependence on large-scale government funding for continued development and growth. As a consequence,

> the new technologies resulting from these developments have made government, industry, and society in general, more dependent upon science. This interdependence is further compounded by the degree to which science is increasingly turned to by government—both for expert guidance in policy-making and planning and for associated "legitimizing" function which science now wields as a major institution.[10]

Our society is (and becoming more so) fully permeated by science and technology to the extent that the consequences of the changes they initiate in our daily lives have raised serious questions concerning our ability to cope with or direct the resultant effects. Technological advancement has presented us with the dilemma of being ". . . confronted with changes in social and cultural forms which are unaccountable in terms

---

* The program-budgeting and cost-benefit analysis (also known as program-planning-budget system, PPBS) system employed earlier by the Defense Department is a case in point.

of past traditions. . . ."[11] and the change and instability of societal forms have become the new "norm."

As technology advances, the resulting industrialized mass production accelerates the obsolescence of notions related to the nature of wealth-goods-use value. Previously, the use of land, labor, and artifacts was the basis for "capital" that is utilized as the foundation for wealth inputs and realized outputs in the general economy. As automation or cybernetic control has been introduced into the industrial process, the value orientation of man regarding his relationship to the work ethic has been altered. It is agreed that:

> For the first time, man could produce utility objects in huge numbers with a precision and use—life greater than any produced previously— in a fraction of the time and with swiftly decreasing investment of human energy. . . . [D]irect human-labor input in production has even less relevance to economic growth; industrial productivity itself loses its main role as primary societal activity, as society moves farther from marginal survival for most toward possible material abundance for all its members.[12]

As this trend becomes more pronounced in our industrial activity, the effects of automation growth on restructuring our value orientation toward basic institutions and human activity will become a crucial social indicator for guiding focus in elementary education. Since the individual's relationship to the means and ends of production is a basic value of our democratic way of life, this relationship must be of central concern in any conceptual scheme or organization slated to provide educational experiences for our youth.

One other area of concern initiated by technological advance deals with problems of choice and constraints. As technology increases the availability of social or human services, accessibility and choice to the general public is implied. However, there is some evidence that advertising practices and design characteristics of new products severely limit the "choice" or "alternate life strategies" that remain open to individuals who partake of the fruits of our technological society. In some instances, it appears that man has become a slave to the machine instead of the opposite pattern that was intended. When this occurs, technological advancement is more closely related to "constraints" than to alternative "choices" for human activity. Technology must serve society by enhancing freedom of choice regarding various modes of operation and living styles. It is becoming increasingly evident that a systematic approach to the study of the effects that technological advancement has upon "choice" and "constraints" available to individuals in our society is a concern that should be given much more attention in elementary education. Students must evaluate technology in terms of the increased threat to their individuality and human associations.

As we attempt to study and consider the effects of technological advancement upon the value orientation of individuals and groups in our society, it is evident that we must become more adept at dealing with the long-term and qualitatively different changes they motivate in our way of life. In short, we must be able to distinguish between controlled and uncontrolled changes, desired changes, and how changes desired will be influenced by technological means and ends. As specific goals are set for our technology, we must become capable of evaluating the future social and human consequences of the results before we initiate the effort. When there is a narrowing interval between scientific discovery and technological implementation, the increased rate of change in social patterns requires a more adequate assessment of the impact of qualitative changes upon human interaction. If we continue to introduce new technology without social innovation to parallel a particular advance, we run the risk of shaping our value orientation in a pattern that might be inconsistent with our democratic way of life and its requisite advantages. As we increase our knowledge and skill in keeping technological advancement in workable proportion to social innovation, we are in a better position to aid the citizen in governing his lifestyle. Further, we are able to lessen our increasing dependence upon a small number of highly trained professionals who develop and operate the functional technology.

Changes in technological advancement have had a profound influence on practices and possibilities in the instructional program at the elementary school level. However, the availability of new technology is no guarantee that the technology will be employed as an integral part of the instructional program. Or if employed that it will be used appropriately and more effectively than the currently used techniques and materials at the elementary school level. The place of new technology in the elementary school program is discussed in greater detail later.

Poverty

The relatively recent realization that poverty is persistent and real to a sizable minority of the population in America has proven to be quite revealing to the general public and somewhat troublesome to existing political structures and philosophies. The existence of poverty has become even more abhorrent when one considers the fact that poverty and widespread affluence are generally juxtaposed in this country in an uneasy coexistence. Since the "rediscovery" of poverty in America, it has become apparent that the present nature of this condition is qualitatively different from the historic concern with physical survival and pauperism that characterizes low-income societies, and earlier economic declines (Great Depression of the 1930s) in the United States. As we view poverty in its present context, we become painfully aware of the inequalities that continue to exist for the most deprived groups in our society during times of great prosperity and economic expansion. Despite all efforts to eradicate poverty affecting those at the bottom of the economic ladder in America, the proportion of national income earned by this group has remained negatively disproportionate to that of *the upper* economic groups and relatively stable during the last twenty years. On the other hand, the upper economic group has experienced a relationship that is opposite to those in the lower group. If this condition is allowed to continue, new types of social separation and stratification are likely to emerge as a force having a significant negative effect on the quality of life in our democratic society.

There is little disagreement over the importance of focusing attention on the problems of poverty in America in our basic approach to designing programs in elementary education. If there is any disagreement in this area, it is related to issues concerned with the definition of poverty in an industrialized society. Since poverty in America has many aspects, it is essential that we approach the subject in accordance with a pattern that allows us to view the problem within the context of elementary education as a basic concern and value orientation.

Inherent in a definition of poverty are concepts of disparity and inequality. In fact, the fundamental essence of all poverty is inequality. Therefore, any approach attempting to eliminate discernible inequalities must go beyond seeking a minimum level of incomes, assets, and basic services, and must deal with the more elusive issues of personal satisfaction and self-respect, social mobility, and democratic participation in decision making. It is clear then that

> income alone is an inadequate indicator of level of living. Movement along varied dimensions of well-being is not always synchronized—advance or loss along one dimension does not necessarily mean that similar movement occurs on the other dimensions.[13]

When we deal with poverty, we are dealing, essentially, with the quality of life of individuals and not with a set standard for all.

In general, a definition of poverty will vary in accordance with the value orientation of those involved. We recognize the factors of absolute poverty (starvation, death from exposure, and loss of life) that result from the total lack of resources and generally discard this notion as a viable concept of poverty in the United States at this period in our history. Although poverty exists in the United States, being poor in America today is different from being poor in the Far East (or in this country during the early 1930s for that matter).

The basic characteristics of poverty today are related to differences in the

> total amounts of consumable resources available in relation to the population, the distribution of control over resources within the social structure, the cultural standards of value and adequacy, the proportion of the society's membership whose level of disposable resources stands below such standards, and degree of contrast in welfare between higher and lower socioeconomic strata.[14]

It is clear, then, that to evaluate poverty only on an absolute scale would involve failure to deal with some of its characteristics that exist on a continuum related to a variety of quantitative and qualitative criteria subject to influences caused by societal fluctuations. Given this situation, it is possible for poverty to expand and contract at various times, depending upon the existence of different conditions and situations.

Since a large proportion of the conditions used to define poverty are associated with the establishment of an income level that differentiates between the poor and the nonpoor, there are essential elements that are necessary to establish the definition of the line to be employed. Two of the elements of reference in this instance are stability and source of income. Income is related to present and future life conditions whereas the source of income encompasses social honor and feelings of self-respect and accomplishment.

A person's level of income can be defined in at least three ways. The *first* definition involves income as it relates to estimates of a cost-of-living budget. The *second* defines an adequate level of existence as it relates to the median family income in America. A *third* definition of income deals with an evaluation of the proportion of the total national income that is earned by various percentages of groups at the bottom of the population. Each of these definitions used to evaluate one's condition of poverty is useful to the extent that it allows one to make certain statements about the differential effects of poverty upon the lifestyles of different groups in our society.

The budget-oriented approach to defining the poverty level depends upon the delineation of an "adequate" level of income. This immediately raises the issue of "adequacy for what and for whom." In this sense, adequacy can range from a focus on survival to one that deals with providing motivation and means for upward social mobility. Since the budget-oriented approach is subject to these vastly different kinds of fluctuations, it offers too much range for the focus that is necessary to deal adequately with the reality of poverty in America. The evidence suggests that the use of a comparative approach to defining poverty in the United States is more appropriate because it enables one to judge the conditions of the poor in relation to the changing conditions of our rising expectations for an ever-increasing standard of living.

One way to employ the comparative approach in judging the character and scope of poverty is to use the median family (four people) income as a standard for judging the adequacy of a family's budget. It has been suggested by some researchers[15] that the poverty line should be fixed at 50 per cent below (one half the median family income) the median family income and that the poverty line for the poorest group be fixed at about 25 per cent of the standard (median family income). This approach clearly establishes the condition of poverty as being relative to the conditions evident at different levels in society. If the standard of 50 per cent of the median of the family income had been employed in 1968, the poverty line would have been at $4,308. Generally speaking, this result can be interpreted to mean that approximately 18.4 per cent of the families in the United States in 1968 were living in poverty. If one were to go one step further and show the trend[16] using the median, it is particularly revealing to note that the percentage of the poor did not decline significantly between 1947 and 1960 (see Table 1.1).

Table 1.1 shows that the number of families with incomes of less than $3,000 declined from 33.9 per cent to 22.1 per cent, and that families with incomes of less than one half of the median increased from 19.0 per cent to 20.2 per cent. This finding indicates that efforts to eliminate poverty prior to the 1960s were unsuccessful. Unfortunately, the great push to eliminate poverty during the 1960s failed to alter the pattern to any significant degree when one notes that approximately 18.4 per cent of the families earned less than one half of the median income in 1968. According to this standard, the proportion of our population living below the poverty level has remained almost unchanged for more than twenty years. The prospects for altering this pattern seem quite remote unless there is a radical change in social policy and practices.

Another way to view poverty is to think of it as the proportion of national or net income obtained by defined levels of the population.

Table 1.1
Percentage of U.S. Families Classified as Poor by
Relative and Absolute Standards, 1947–1960

Year	Median Income (1959 Dollars)	Less Than One Half of the Median*	Less Than $3,000 (1959 Prices)	Less Than $2,000 (1959 Prices)
		Percentage of Families with Income		
1947	3,957	19.0	33.9	19.1
1948	3,868	19.4	34.7	19.8
1949	3,807	20.1	35.9	21.3
1950	4,036	20.0	33.0	19.8
1951	4,164	19.0	30.9	17.9
1952	4,277	19.0	29.3	17.8
1953	4,627	19.9	27.1	16.8
1954	4,530	20.7	28.7	18.1
1955	4,817	19.9	25.9	16.0
1956	5,129	19.5	23.6	14.2
1957	5,148	20.0	23.5	14.2
1958	5,143	19.9	23.8	14.1
1959	5,417	19.9	22.7	13.4
1960	5,547	20.2	22.1	13.2

* Estimated by interpolation.

Source: Victor R. Fuchs, "Toward a Theory of Poverty," in Task Force on Economic Growth and Opportunity, *The Concept of Poverty* (Washington, D.C.: Chamber of Commerce of the United States, 1965).

Table 1.2 shows the percentage of income obtained by families divided by quintiles and the top 5 per cent. It is interesting to note that the income earned by the bottom quintile has remained between 4 and 6 per cent since 1950.

Even though the share of the income received by families in the lowest quintile increased by 27 per cent from 1950 to 1968, the corresponding share received by the highest decreased by only 5 per cent. The families in the lowest quintile did not improve economically at the expense of families in the highest quintile to any significant degree. This fact is even more disturbing when one notes that total personal income increased by more than 200 per cent from 1950–1968. It is obvious that

Table 1.2

Distribution of Total Money Income Received by Each Fifth and the Top 5 Per Cent of Families 1950–1968 Compared with Total Personal Income

		Census (Total Money Income)						
Year	Total	Lowest Fifth	Second Fifth	Middle Fifth	Fourth Fifth	Highest Fifth	Top 5 Per Cent	Personal Income (Billions)
1968	100.0	5.7	12.4	17.7	23.7	40.6	14.0	687.9
1967	100.0	5.4	12.2	17.5	23.7	41.2	15.3	629.4
1965	100.0	5.3	12.2	17.6	23.7	41.3	15.8	538.9
1964	100.0	5.2	12.0	17.7	24.0	41.1	15.7	
1960	100.0	4.9	12.0	17.6	23.6	42.0	16.8	401.0
1955	100.0	4.8	12.2	17.7	23.7	41.6	16.8	310.9
1950	100.0	4.5	12.0	17.4	23.5	42.6	17.0	227.6

Source: Adapted from Tables 480 and 489 of the Statistical Abstract of the United States, 1970; 316 and 323.

the families in the different quintiles continue to receive a similar (and seemingly unchanging) share of the total personal income even when the economy, as a whole, grows rapidly.

Our discussion of poverty in terms of income has revealed that there are many ways to identify people who live in conditions of poverty. It is agreed that relative rather than absolute poverty is probably a more meaningful evaluation of poverty in America. The data that have been presented suggest that the elimination of poverty for large numbers of Americans is still far from being a reality. As long as poverty conditions exist, it is not possible to eliminate the vast inequalities that continue to exist between different segments of our population. If we are unable to reduce significantly poverty conditions for all citizens, it will not be possible for selected groups to develop stable life patterns that ensure life-long security, to acquire personal assets, to partake of basic services, to become socially mobile and well-educated, and to attain a reasonable level of status and satisfaction. We must begin to focus more realistically on the factors and conditions of poverty as we deal with young children in our elementary schools. Through the use of an elementary curriculum that takes into account the persistent (and sometimes negative) life patterns that characterize different cross sections of our population, it is possible to acquaint children with life as it exists. If elementary education is to be meaningful to tomorrow's youth, it must deal realistically with the social problems and moral issues associated with poverty in America.

Impact of Modern Media

Modern media are exerting an ever-increasing influence upon lifestyles worldwide. More and more, our decisions, emotional well-being, values, and approaches are being influenced by ideas encountered through such modern media as newspapers, television, radio, recordings (records, tapes, and video tapes), film, filmscripts, magazines, newsletters, movies, and books. The format and technology of a medium may be inconsistent with the patterns people employ to draw personal conclusions and make decisions. At this point media can change the meaning and intent of data for a particular person or group of people. Even though some forms of modern media influence segments of our population differentially, they all have a profound effect on the total fiber and development of our society. Since the impact of any medium is dependent upon the interaction patterns among the socioeconomic backgrounds, ages, ethnic backgrounds, personal identifications, time orientations, modes of presentation, educational backgrounds, social experiences, traditional practices, and future aspirations of the receivers, it is essential that a more systematic approach to the study of modern media's impact on learning become an integral part of elementary education.

There is no gainsaying that modern media have effectively replaced the school as the primary presenter and keeper of the largest share of knowledge to be learned and used. In fact, the onslaught of modern media has contributed to a diminution in the influence of the school as a source of knowledge. Because most of the information that is presented via modern media is more current than similar or related content used in schools, students and citizens alike are confronted with conflicts in knowledge that were limited to a privileged group of intellectuals not too many years ago. This situation inevitably leads to the readers' rejection of material presented by both the media and the school because the information they present is contradictory in terms of conclusions drawn and their own experience. In this instance, both the media and the school come to lose their importance and effectiveness as media of communication because their chosen audiences no longer accept the information that is being presented. It becomes the responsibility of the school in educating youth to evaluate what is learned via media, by helping learners to develop and employ criteria for judging conflicting information on similar subject matter, and by noting gaps and discrepancies related to time, place, and interpretation.

By all indicators, Americans are provided with more information via newspapers, magazines, and broadcasting (television and radio) than citizens of any other country. Thus, Americans are afforded an opportunity to become involved in the affairs of other men. Ideas that become the fodder for change are more accessible than ever before, and the power of the people has been greatly expanded because they are armed with more knowledge to effectively challenge traditional practice and unsubstantiated assumptions often used as the basis for public policy. However, the usefulness of the knowledge provided through media is very much dependent upon our ability to evaluate and understand the various media that play such a critical role in communicating the ideas and concepts that shape our cultural patterns and our common style of living.

In the main, modern media have not provided the kind of information that the average layman needs to make intelligent personal decisions. One reason might be that modern media have not been overly concerned with providing knowledge apart from entertainment. Another reason for this gap is that the total amount of knowledge gained since 1940 is greater than that gained in all the years of human history up to that time. Most of this knowledge gain was in specialized areas. When one considers that knowledge in physics has doubled in the last decade and that physics is not the leader in the development of new learning, the charge and the challenge to modern media become readily apparent. Accompanying the growth of new knowledge is a type of specialization dependent upon language that is increasingly esoteric and decreasingly comprehensible to the layman. At this point, modern media must bridge the communications gap between the specialists and the average learner. Even though the media have been handling this task more adequately of late, the new knowledge available far exceeds media's efforts to present this information in an intelligible form. Modern media have thus not fulfilled their potential as a major source for interpreting new ideas to the average layman.

A closer look at the forms of modern media that are most utilized by the general public reveals some interesting facts. Even though newspapers are physically larger than they were in the past, an average of fifty-six pages in 1969 compared with twenty-two pages in 1945, the average amount of nonadvertising space has declined from 48.5 per cent in 1945 to 38 per cent in 1969. It appears that the trend toward the growth of new specialized knowledge has not prompted a parallel growth in the space that newspapers devote to these concerns. This situation reflects the fact that publishers dictate space usage in most newspapers. Advertising is considered to be more important than news and this trend appears to be gaining increasing acceptance.

In contrast with this, the composition of most mass magazines is determined by the editor rather than the business manager or the publisher. The advertising-editorial ratio in mass magazines is very different as this statement suggests:

> In a survey of fifty of the largest national magazines for 1965, for example, well over half the space was devoted to editorial content. In some magazines, including some of the largest, the ratio was as high as 70 per cent editorial. Only sixteen had less than 50 per cent and one less than 40 per cent.[17]

These data suggest that mass magazines try harder to educate the public than do newspapers if we consider the amount of space devoted to nonadvertising content as the gauge. Since newspapers are more readily available, actively sought, and used by a larger percentage of the general population than most magazines with widespread circulations, newspapers must begin to play a larger role in educating the general public regarding new developments and learning. Although there are a few notable exceptions, generally the quality of information programs broadcasted via television and radio is superficial and episodic. More specifically, television programming is vastly one-sided toward providing entertainment as opposed to information. A study completed in the mid 1960s revealed that approximately two thirds of the television stations devoted between 78 and 80 per cent of their programming time to entertainment. Data collected further indicated that approximately 85 per cent of the network-affiliated stations allotted 78 per cent of their time to entertainment, 6 per cent to news, 2 per cent to education, and 1.4 per cent for discussion-type programs. The evidence strongly suggests that a similar situation exists in radio programming. The broadcasting industry falls short, considerably, as a source for educating the general public on the important issues, new ideas, and changing cultural patterns that influence our citizens daily. The broadcasting industry must become more responsive to the need of helping to educate young people and adults alike, if this form of the media is to become effective in helping people make meaningful decisions.

When modern media are considered in relation to elementary education, there are many issues to be resolved and questions to be answered. As elementary schoolteachers become more aware of the different types and concerns of modern media, they should also become better able to assess how the school should structure its activities and offerings in order to best utilize the knowledge gained by students through the media and the opinions they have formed.

There is little disagreement with the conclusion that there should be an increase in the quantity and quality of social information reported via modern media. Further, this information should be reported as impartially as possible. Whenever information is not reported impartially, schools should assume a greater responsibility for helping young people to deal effectively with this state of affairs. If this latter goal is to be accomplished, we need to know more about the impact that modern media generally have on audiences. Teachers must be prepared to deal with the fact that reporting the dramatic (so commonly practiced by most media) often distorts the receiver's view of reality and this, in turn, can initiate a belief that the media initially sought to prevent. It is essential that teachers become aware of the influences of modern media upon how well they will be able to communicate valid and rational ideas to their students. Modern media provide learners with a view of reality that increasingly offers a serious challenge to the information dispensed by teachers; and this trend is bound to accelerate in the future. This fact suggests that teachers should reconsider the influences of modern media upon learners in formulating an instructional strategy.

Finally, modern media should be considered in terms of their contributions to, and contradictions of, the idea of freedom of speech. Since most media in the United States are privately controlled and operated for profit, there is a great opportunity to enhance freedom of speech for a few but to seriously curtail or eliminate this freedom for vast numbers of our citizenry. In a sense, freedom of speech is not present when citizens are denied the right to give their views via the means available to those who have access to the communication media. As modern media expand, it is becoming increasingly difficult to speak to the concerns of selected and sizable minorities in our society. When the means for communicating ideas, issues, and opinions to the public are controlled by a small number of individuals who are guided to a large degree by special interests, the freedom of speech of the public is diminished and subject to the direction of the controlling group. Elementary education must help students to deal with the problems modern media are causing regarding the changes in an individual's ability to exercise his freedom of speech to influence decisions that affect his life.

Social Control

Emerging and redefined values appear to be a rejection of traditional means of social control.* As new groups using new modes to deal with new issues increase the rate and expand the degree of participation in societal processes, notions about the nature of social control become revised. In the main, however, social control is defined by the large proportion of the general population that subscribes to the values, attitudes, and accompanying practices that are universally accepted by the culture as basic to its survival. The existence of social control is determined by the covert and overt behavior patterns that members of the culture exhibit with regard to the official rules of conduct (laws) that characterize the society in question. Behavior deviances from the official rules of conduct are an indication of decreasing social control.

One of the basic assets of our democratic way of life is our ability to provide for the greatest level of individuality while maintaining and ensuring the necessary social control required to enhance the existence of all society's members and our ability to foster the continued development of society. In this sense, social control in a democracy is largely dependent on individual control of one's behavior. As individual control deteriorates in this country, the level of social control shows a parallel decline. If we are to understand how the elementary school can enhance the existence of social control, we must acquire more information about the underlying factors influencing the deviance of individuals from acceptable modes of behavior by ignoring official rules of conduct. One point of departure for the study of this problem is to study the impact of crime on our society and how the existence of crime is related to social control.

A criminal act is primarily an individual act of social deviance. When the number of these antisocial individual acts increase to a certain level, there is a real threat to our ability to maintain the degree of social control that is necessary to further the growth and development of society. Citizens in any society do not want to become victims of criminal acts or to live in constant fear of crime. If crime is allowed to exist and expand unchallenged, the basic assumptions underlying a civilized society will be open to serious question. No society can claim to be a civilized social unit if personal gain and aggression replace respect for the rights

---

* Social control is the spectrum of modes whereby social systems induce or ensure normal compliance on the part of their members.

of other people. Therefore, any increase in crime threatens social control in a society and ultimately will have a negative effect on the society's well-being as a healthy and viable social system.

Crime can be viewed in terms of the work load, size, and activity of the police force, the amount of harm that befalls the victims, and the prevalence of overt and covert (supportive attitudes) criminal behavior. In order to assess the impact of crime on undermining social control, it is necessary to view the prevention and control of crime in terms of the factors indicated previously.

Serious crime (criminal homicide, assault, rape, and different varieties of theft) has been on the increase in America at an average yearly growth rate of approximately 9 per cent since 1958. According to the President's Crime Commission in 1965, this reported increase is only a fraction of the actual crimes (with the exception of criminal homicide) that were committed. Because of the circumstances surrounding many criminal acts, many crimes are not reported. Therefore, the average annual increase in the incidence of crime is probably much greater than the percentage that is recorded.

Any increase in the level of crime carries with it many negative consequences. Increased crime contributes to the tax burden of every member in a community because local police force activities are sharply expanded. In addition, increased crime contributes to a restriction or curtailment of the individual movement of all citizens. Victims of crime often lose valuable work time as a result of personal injury, and sometimes the families of victims become wards of the state when the victim is injured permanently or killed. Also, the loss of valuables by some members of our society represents a large amount of work over long periods of time. The negative human and social consequences of crime suggest that the very existence of a society is seriously threatened if crime is not effectively controlled.

Since the majority of crimes are committed by the young with limited knowledge and experience, harsher punishments are not likely to serve as an effective deterrent. The actions of youthful offenders are likely to be influenced more by the social circumstances governing their socialization than by abstract rules of social conduct. Young people who grow up in less than ideal circumstances are likely to view the existing social order as restrictive and oppressive and which should be opposed at any cost. This point is adequately highlighted in the following statement:

> What this means is that the social context of poverty and the poorer prospects for those who grow up in it, *both* tend to make socioeconomic deprivation a major cause of crime. A crime prevention strategy which

focuses only on punishment, prosecution, and policing is therefore not only insufficient in terms of the theory that is used to justify it, but in addition neglects the cultural factors that must be taken into account.[18]

It is apparent that criminal behavior results from values and perceptions gained through exposure to deviant social environments and groups. In this sense, crime must be viewed, in part, in terms of social control as it relates to the context of the act and the circumstances that fostered this social deviation.

When some of the causes of crime are analyzed, it is clear that social control requires the consent of the controlled. When individual or group-held attitudes toward official rules of conduct are used as a justification of antisocial behavior, we must take a critical look at the objective circumstances of those who take part in criminal activity. If the lack of individual opportunity is a major contributor to the increase of crime, our approach to social control must help eliminate this condition. Social control is required to maintain a healthy social organism, and the existence of high levels of crime tends to erode social control. If we are to maintain the level of social control that is essential to fostering the highest levels of individuality, then we must approach the study of crime or social deviance in a broader context. Elementary education can help young people understand the facets of crime as a springboard toward developing accurate concepts concerning social control in a democracy.

Environmental Conditions

Economic development and social welfare are highly correlated with the management of the natural environment and the production of raw materials. Throughout human history forging an adequate subsistence out of the natural environment of land, water, and minerals has remained the central economic problem. Although the majority of the world's people continue to live at low material levels, people in the United States and a few other countries have developed the technology to utilize resources at a constant and unbelievable rate. Unlike past concerns with the available quantity of raw materials, the present and future worry is centered on the qualitative problems associated with how the use of natural resources affects our life space. According to Joseph L. Fisher,

More and more people are concerned with water pollution, air pollution, pesticides and radioactive fallout, solid wastes, the preservation of

areas for outdoor recreation and for open space, the design and arrangement of both the urban and rural landscape, noise, the use of the
radio spectrum, and other qualitative elements or attributes of the natural environment.[19]

At every level of our society widespread attention is being focused on the
aesthetic, social, and ethical results of the ways in which our natural
environment is being utilized. There is uniform consensus that man must
learn to live in harmony with the natural environment if he is to survive
and continue to share the fruits of a good life.

Elementary education must become more concerned with the relationship between the quality of life and how we use our natural environment. It is apparent that youth will need to learn how our lifestyles
affect the quality of the natural environment which, in turn, affects the
quality of life that is possible. If future adults are to learn how to make
better use of our limited resources, they will have to be taught about the
interrelationships between man and his environment. Since youth should
be exposed to this concept early, the program in elementary education
can be organized and implemented to deal with the study of this vital
area.

Because of our present technological approach to processing raw
materials, there is widespread pollution resulting from a variety of resi-
due. Pollution results from our industrial processing, packaging, transport-
ing goods, marketing products, and discarding related wastes. Air, water,
and land pollution are interdependent and are often caused by the
actions of people who appear unrelated. Even though the average person
does not pollute intentionally, he does so in the normal use of basic
goods and services. This condition results from the fact that:

> The total weight of materials taken into the economy from nature must
> equal the total weight of materials ultimately discharged as wastes plus
> any materials recycled.
>
> This means that, given the level and composition of the re-
> sources used by the company, and the degree of recycling, any reduc-
> tion in one form of waste discharge must be ultimately accompanied
> by an increase in the discharge of some other kind of waste. For ex-
> ample, some air pollution can be prevented by washing out the parti-
> cles—but this can mean water pollution, or alternatively solid wastes.[20]

It is apparent that our technological approaches to meeting basic human
needs have become associated with our worst environmental problems.
The complexity of this problem multiplies as our population increases
and urbanization grows. We seem to be caught in a viselike cycle that
dictates that any increase in our population sufficient to require an ex-

pansion of our industrial production is likely to cause a parallel increase in pollution resulting from both industrial and household wastes.

Since pollution is already a significant problem, all young people should be exposed to critical aspects of the problem in an intellectually honest fashion so that they will be in a better position to affect public policy governing the elimination or curtailment of pollution.

Environmental pollution is not necessarily an intentionally initiated act on the part of most members of our society. It results from our approach to industrial production and from the need to provide basic services to an ever-increasing population. Since an individual citizen is not likely to get a complete picture of the different facets of pollution, it is now necessary for representative governments to pinpoint the nature of the problem and devise a pattern for implementing solutions. This approach to environmental protection requires some form of social management so that human activity in one area will not cancel out attempts to curtail pollution in other areas. Since our very existence may be dependent upon how well we manage social behavior and economic activity, our real test is related to how well we correlate this concept with our notion of democracy and individual freedom. It is entirely probable that the pollution of our environment will bring about changes in our interpretations of individual freedoms as a first step to conserving the ecological balance so necessary for preserving human life and maintaining a high standard of living. Schools must prepare youth to deal with the social issues and consequences of the destruction of our natural environment by polluting waste materials. By so doing, schools can play a crucial role in helping future adults to face one of mankind's greatest challenges—conserving our natural environment.

Health

The presence of good health and the expectation of a long life are two of the fundamental requirements for human achievement, enjoyment, and happiness. It is essential that we appraise factors that affect changes in the health status and life expectancy across and within different groups in society if young people are to be helped to formulate realistic decisions concerned with public policy in this area. As technology has advanced to the point wherein the production of basic goods and services requires less human labor and time, man has acquired more free time than ever to do some of the things that were only dreams for the average man of yesteryear. However, man will not be able to take advantage of this increase in free time if he does not enjoy good health and a long life. A program in elementary education should be concerned with health problems associated with group, lifestyle, and age differences. Children should learn how changes in public policy and socioeconomic conditions, as well as medical breakthroughs can influence the health status of the total population to some extent and greatly improve the health status of selected groups. Because health tends to deteriorate with age, it is appropriate for the elementary schoolteacher to explore issues related to health on a systematic basis. This section deals with some of the factors influencing the general health status of members of the population.

During the twentieth century, great strides have been made in improving health and life expectancy for all members of our society. However, the most dramatic developments in these areas have differential effects upon younger age and selected ethnic groups. Since the turn of the century, the life expectancy at birth in the United States has advanced from 47.3 in 1900 to 70.5 years in 1967, which represents an average gain of 23.2 years. On the whole, whites gained more than nonwhites, women gained more than men, and young people gained more than mature adults. In 1900, the number of expected years of life for nonwhites at birth was 33.0 years, which was 14.6 years below that of whites. By 1967, nonwhite life expectancy had risen to 64.6 years, which was still 6.3 years below that of whites. Women lived an average of 2 years longer than men in 1900 and in 1967 the spread had grown to 7 years. By 1967, the number of expected years of life remaining at 5 increased by 12 years; at age 25 an increase of about 12 years was noted, and at age 65 the increase had declined to a little less than 3 years. These figures suggest that lifestyle and modern medicine have benefited youth and females more when comparisons are made within groups and benefited whites more when comparisons are made across groups. Societal benefits that increase life expectancy do not appear to be evenly distributed within and across ethnic groups. In this sense, every citizen does not have equal access to a similar life expectancy.

Health data suggest that the American people have not fully utilized existing medical and technological knowledge to maximize a healthier existence and longer life expectancy. This is evident in the fact that nonwhites experience a life span that is shorter than that of whites and at least fifteen nations have a longer life expectancy than do Americans at birth. Likewise, the relative rank of the United States among other nations has worsened progressively in recent years. Consider the following remark concerning our rate of infant mortality:

In 1950 the United States ranked fifth; in 1955 we ranked eighth; and we fell to twelfth by 1960. While many other countries were making great progress in the reduction of infant mortality, the United States rate declined sluggishly. At least five countries also have better maternal mortality rates than the United States.[21]

It is difficult to explain these data when one notes that the United States is reported to be the leading nation in biomedical science and technological development.

Medical records indicate that we have almost eliminated or greatly reduced the incidence of some diseases whereas other diseases seem to be on the increase. This, in part, explains why we have not been able to make great studies in increasing life expectancy in recent years. Also, some of the prevalent diseases (ulcers, diabetes, cirrhosis of the liver, hypertension, defective hearts) are closely related to our lifestyle, and a dynamic, pressured, and competitive economy. As long as these conditions exist, it is unlikely that we will be able to increase our life expectancy.

Since the United States is among the leading nations with the highest ratio of dentists and physicians (fourth) and professional nurses (third) to the total population, our poor showing in relation to other nations on life expectancy, infant and maternal mortality, and higher incidences of other common diseases cannot be attributed to a short supply of highly trained medical personnel. Likewise, our medical shortcomings cannot be blamed on a decrease in the expenditures allotted for medical services because the proportion of the personal consumption expenditures going for health care rose from 4.6 per cent in 1950 to 7.2 per cent in 1968, or from $8.8 billion to $38.6 billion.[22] The United States is unsurpassed by any nation on the basis of the proportion of resources allotted to pay for medical services. If the lack of resources (both human and material) is not the cause for our poor health showing, then we must look elsewhere for explanations for why we are not healthier. Recent data documenting the relationship between the physical environment, our lifestyle, and our health status appear to offer part of the explanation for the present state of health experienced by our population.

Many factors will affect the health status of our population in the future. The nation's health picture will be closely tied to the future pattern of population growth. A fast rate of population growth is likely to decrease the ratio of medical personnel to population, place considerable pressure on available medical facilities, and lower the standard of living that is so essential to maintaining a high level of medical services. On the other hand, a slow rate of population growth is likely to increase the mean age of our population resulting in a larger proportion of mature (over sixty-five years of age) citizens who tend to require more medical services. Even with a moderate rate of population growth, there is likely to be a bipolar distribution (more very old and very young citizens) of our population with a resulting increase in the solidification of generation gaps in many areas of social interaction and exchange. If we are to maintain an acceptable level of mental health, adjustments in our social institutions will be required to accommodate changing characteristics of our population. Since a larger proportion of our population is living past sixty-five years, we will have to find a way to alter concepts that make longevity dysfunctional in our institutional patterns.

There is universal agreement that good health is positively related to human achievement and enjoyment. It is critical to the growth and development of our country that the highest level of health for all citizens be sought and maintained. Discrepancies in the health status recorded for selected groups in our society should be adjusted to the point that every citizen has an equal opportunity to be a healthy individual insofar as his condition is dependent upon characteristics that are subject to human manipulation and control. The health of citizens in the United States should be given higher priority in the educational program of our youth. Elementary education lends itself to this concern because it is never too early to acquaint children with the importance of a healthy emotional state and physical body as a prerequisite condition for a happy and productive life.

Political Activeness

Recently, there has been increased attention focused upon the extent to which members of the population are accorded civil liberties guaranteed by our Constitution. The sharp increase in court cases and resulting decisions involving, clarifying, and defining our individual liberties give substance to the idea that people are more prone to become involved in the political and legal processes that affect their lives collectively and individually. This political activity is likely to be guided by our judgments concerning moral values that can lead to certain conflicts. Since political realism acknowledges and adapts to the limitations of morality in political life, it can be concluded that there is not a sharp separation between politics and morals. One author commented on the problem as follows:

> There is room for the moral judgment of political action, provided that the moral principles are not kept and used as pure abstractions; provided that our judgment takes into account the indescribable complexities of social life; provided that our thinking is far removed from utopian commitments and fanatic claims; provided, in a word, that our judgment proceeds from humility in the face of the complexity of forces, recognition of the small role left for creative action, and obligation to try to accommodate and harmonize competing values.[23]

During a period of fluctuating values, it is difficult to attain a realistic fix on a core of values that characterize the beliefs of an individual. Without this it is highly improbable that traditional politics will be able to deal with the expanding number of individual concerns. Thus, there is an increasing need to expand old, and formulate new, patterns that contribute to and foster democratic participation by individuals who want to influence the public policy that affects their way of life.

Most citizens agree that there should be more democratic participation in the organized institutional structures of our society. This development is partly an outgrowth of concern about the perceived deterioration of the viability and stability of the family as a unit in the structure of society. If institutions are taking over more functions that were formerly reserved for family socialization patterns, then individual citizens should be able to influence or control elected or hired representatives who are charged with the major responsibility of making decisions affecting their lifestyles. This view is the essence of present notions defining democratic participation.

A review of the philosophical support for our democratic society reveals that democratic participation is a crucial value. At this point, we seem to be going through a crisis in participation as selected groups (ethnic minorities, youth, women) expand their perception of themselves as being powerless to control those who make decisions affecting them. Since "participatory democracy" is not an absolute, some citizens are allowed to participate in every society; however, no society allows equal participation by all citizens. This being the case it is not possible to solve all of the problems of participation for all times and all places. Issues of participation arise continuously as societies evolve and face new challenges and conditions.

According to Harold Lasswell, the issues of participation can be summarized as follows: *Who* participates, about *what* and *how?* In contemporary America a participation crisis has arisen because all three of these issues are being raised simultaneously:

> new people want to participate, in relation to new issues, and in new ways. The question of who ought to participate has been raised most

strikingly by Southern Negroes; but in colleges, students want to participate and, in welfare agencies, clients want some voice. At the same time, participation is demanded in relation to a wider range of issues or governmental activities: the subjects of administrative programs demand chances to participate within such programs; parents demand more voice in school planning; and students demand more voice in deciding what they are taught.[24]

It is clear that much of the present controversy highlighted by many protest and special interest groups is related to the process of determining who participates in making decisions that are relevant to them.

Many problems are associated with democratic participation. One is related to what should be the disposition citizens take regarding the patterns of participation (public elections) provided by the society. Also, it appears that participation is highly related to education and income, that different groups participate in government according to patterns determined by their life situations, and that feelings of personal involvement are fostered both through formal and informal patterns. These factors outline some of the problems that are related to participation in democracy as they are related to (1) definition, (2) delineating important social goals, (3) pinpointing the different facets of participation, (4) determining the effectiveness of participation from the standpoint of the participant and the decision maker, and (5) specific problems associated with the current crisis in participation. As we view elementary education for present and future youth, it is imperative that realistic consideration be given to the problems of democratic participation. In some quarters, it is believed that this is probably one of the most important tasks the elementary school will have to perform in the future.

Social Mobility and Leisure Time

Social mobility is very closely associated with the availability of leisure time in our society. This relationship results from the fact that as people advance in social status a greater proportion of their earnings is not required for fulfilling basic human needs. Further, an advance in responsibility and rank is accompanied by a different role expectation in one's lifestyle. The socially mobile usually can afford (and therefore know about) different patterns associated with leisure time. During the past two decades, leisure time has been extended to groups that did not have it previously. Increased production with less manpower, rising income, and a shorter work week have made it possible for people at different levels in the social structure to enjoy more free time. Even though the availability of leisure time has been extended to a greater variety and number of people, it has not always been accompanied by increased opportunities for upward social mobility. The program in elementary education should explore this relationship between social mobility and leisure time.

Since social mobility is associated with increased production, and societal advance and the effective use of leisure time are associated with the emotional well-being of the population, it is essential to the future of our society that young people be exposed to these problems early in their educational experience.

We are well acquainted with the fact that complete equality of opportunity has not been possible in our society and that the success of one group does not guarantee that it will support other groups seeking more opportunity and better living conditions. In some instances, ethnic factors have operated to increase the opportunity for some ethnic groups in some occupational groups (policemen, firemen, sanitation workers, teachers, skilled trade areas), whereas in other instances these ethnic factors have operated to exclude members of some groups. This relationship seems to persist even when members of an excluded or included ethnic group do or do not acquire the skills (or education) needed to handle a particular job. Factors other than individual efforts and abilities operate to determine the nature of the opportunity that is available to a given group.

Evidence suggests that an advanced education, a high income, or a white-collar job do not guarantee a greater opportunity to achieve some of the highest levels of responsibility in public life and private enterprise. Even though the occupational status of parents appears to be playing a lesser role in determining the occupational status of their offspring, the occupations of parents can still be of considerable advantage—or disadvantage—to their children. The expansion of educational opportunity has contributed to the chances of selected groups to increase their social mobility upward. Data suggest that:

> There is some tendency for sons of those of high education and status to obtain more education than others (an extra year of schooling for the father means on the average an extra 0.3 or 0.4 of a year of education for the son), and this additional education brings somewhat higher occupational status on the average. However, the variations in education that are not explained by the socioeconomic status are much larger. Thus, on balance, increased education seems to have increased opportunity and upward mobility.[25]

It is apparent that increased opportunities in education are likely to yield greater upward social mobility but probably not to the extent claimed by some educators.

There are dramatic exceptions to the notion that opportunity is generally available. Many of these exceptions result from covert and overt ethnic discrimination and the patterns that enable parents to pass their accomplishments on to their offspring. A high status individual of one ethnic group is unlikely to be able to pass his achieved status on to his children especially if this high status is associated with a salaried position. In a salaried position the opportunity to accumulate material wealth that can be transferred from one generation to another is slight or nonexistent. Too often a high status position ensures a good life for the holder but makes no promises to his children. As long as members of a selected ethnic group are primarily dependent upon a salary as a sole source of support they will be unable to ensure a status level for their offspring. However, even after noting these shortcomings, we must also state that there is increased opportunity for a sizable majority of our population to utilize their talents to improve their occupational status and access to upward social mobility. Far too many people are still denied true equality of opportunity. The elementary school should strive to eliminate the barrier of a man's ethnic origin as a determining factor affecting his full participation in the society.

Summary

In this chapter we have discussed some of the social problems that are critical today and will probably become more so in the future. We have chosen to study social trends by utilizing data gathered from many sources covered under a number of different topics. The topical pattern proved to be convenient for grouping closely related problems. However, it is evident that all social problems are interrelated and that they must be approached on a very broad scale if progress toward achieving viable solutions is to be made. Throughout this chapter, it has been the author's contention that an analysis of data presented by social indicators is the most appropriate approach to determining the nature, direction, and concerns of elementary education. As such, social indicators should be the foundation blocks for guiding curriculum development at the beginning level of our formal educational efforts.

The results documented by every social indicator available to us reveal that society is undergoing rapid and largely uncontrolled change. Evidence suggests that public schools will have to play a greater role in helping young people understand the nature and possible effects of social trends and developments if they are to become and remain a vital force in our society. This is doubly important when one considers the fact that education itself is such a crucial contributing factor in initiating and shaping the direction of social change we are, and will continue to be, experiencing. It is clear that the role of elementary education in this process must be understood and molded to help all citizens achieve the promise of the good life expected in a democratic and prosperous state.

At this period in our history, it is not possible for a citizen to learn how to cope with our rapidly changing society through the experience of living. This is because changing lifestyles do not require the same response to certify accomplishments or that accomplishments of recent years are no longer sought by the majority of the population. In this kind of situation, information (both specialized and general) becomes the most important input in making it possible to take advantage of, and live with, new developments in human existence. Consequently, the school is presented with an unprecedented challenge to prepare citizens to function effectively within the boundaries of our democratic tenets on a stage that presents rapidly changing social scenes. In this sense, elementary education is faced with a totally new and expanded body of knowledge. We feel, however, that this new content is likely to be more beneficial in the long run because it is concerned directly with problems that really exist in society without forcing upon them an unnatural* instructional pattern to make them more acceptable to the general public. Children taught in this fashion are likely to see the school as more relevant and as an integral part of life as it exists for most people.

Since an approach to the development of curriculum in elementary education through the use of social indicators requires the application of skills of critical thinking, problem analysis, and research, greater demands will be made upon students in terms of increased emphasis on intellectual growth and the development and use of intellectual processes in learning. As the use of the intellect becomes the dominant factor in shaping human activity, the elementary school must enable young learners to adapt to this situation without loss to their individual development. As success and social position become more associated with a special

---

* Unnatural here refers to presenting information to children in a clean and formal version that does not relate to the inconsistencies that govern the reality of the experience being studied. In the former sense we are talking about how the courts work and in the latter sense we are talking about the transcript of a trial.

type of education, the elementary school must begin to prepare young people to take an active role in the intellectual world of the future. New and different pressures will be directed at learners at an earlier age as mass social changes are reflected in the development of mass education. Most social indicators suggest that these pressures are likely to expand much more rapidly in the next few years.

There is general agreement that the elementary school is the most appropriate starting point if young people are to develop attitudes that will allow them to alter their behavior patterns as adults. The elementary school is still our most crucial socializing and humanizing institutional force, and must become more so in the future. The program of mass education in elementary education with its intellectual and technological dimensions dares not neglect the personal and social needs of the individual, his potential, his uniqueness, his group associations, and his emotional stability in a mass and rapidly changing society. If elementary education fails to help young people to think realistically and critically about these concerns, it will cease to adapt to the demands of the future by preparing citizens to join in the procession of progress.

References

1. John McHale, "Science, Technology, and Change," *The Annals,* 373: 131 (Sept. 1967).
2. W. O. Baker, "Communications Science—Today and Tomorrow," *Science and Society: A Symposium,* Xerox Corporation, 1965, as quoted by John McHale, "Science, Technology, and Change," *The Annals,* 373:134 (Sept. 1967).
3. Bertram M. Gross, "Operation Basic: The Retrieval of Wasted Knowledge," *The Journal of Communications,* 12:67–83 (June 1962).
4. Baker, op. cit.
5. Kingsley Davis, "The Urbanization of the Human Population," in Dennis Flanagan (ed.), *Cities* (New York: Knopf, 1968), pp. 4–5.
6. Eleanor Bernert Sheldon and Raymond A. Clazier, *Pupils and Schools in New York City* (New York: Russell Sage Foundation, 1965), pp. 10–11.
7. U.S. Bureau of the Census, *Statistical Abstract of the United States: 1970,* 91st ed., Washington, D.C.: 1970, p. xii.

8. Ibid., p. 33.

9. McHale, op. cit., p. 137.

10. Ibid., p. 123.

11. Ibid.

12. Ibid., pp. 130–131.

13. S. M. Miller, Martin Rein, Pamela Roby, and Bertram M. Gross, "Poverty, Inequality, and Conflict," *The Annals,* **373**:19 (Sept. 1967).

14. Charles A. Valentine, *Culture and Poverty* (Chicago: U. of Chicago, 1968), p. 13.

15. Miller, op. cit., p. 20.

16. André Fontaine, "The Mass Media—A Need for Greatness," *The Annals,* **371**:78 (May 1967).

17. Ibid.

18. *Toward a Social Report* (Washington, D.C.: Department of Health, Education, and Welfare, 1969), p. 63.

19. Joseph L. Fisher, "The Natural Environment," *The Annals,* **371**:128 (May 1967).

20. *Toward a Social Report,* op. cit., p. xvii.

21. Ibid., p. 7.

22. *Statistical Abstract of the United States,* op. cit., p. 314.

23. Milton R. Konvitz, "Civil Liberties," *The Annals,* **371**:39 (May 1967).

24. Sidney Verba, "Democratic Participation," *The Annals,* **373**:54 (Sept. 1967).

25. *Toward a Social Report,* op. cit., p. xvi.

2

Educational Indicators and the Elementary School

The elementary school is a uniquely American institution; its unique characteristics have been identified and attested to by American educators and historians as well as by social science scholars from other lands. Similarly, the American elementary school has been a dynamic and changing institution responsive from its very beginning to the social and political ideas of our developing society and progressive social changes. The development of the elementary school in this country has continued to be shaped by the fundamental educational ideas and beliefs that gave rise to its birth and impetus to its growth. Its progress has been influenced by a steady input of new educational ideas, new knowledge unearthing human and social needs, and the changing directions and emphasis of our society.

In Chapter 1, several social indicators derived from an analysis of information describing current developments and conditions in our society were examined for the implication they hold for future developments in the elementary school. That the present elementary schools will be influenced by, and must be responsive to, the social directions indicated in the mass of information now available on social trends and conditions is hardly debatable. The elementary school is a vital part of our society. At the same time it is an institution in itself. It has its own history, traditions, concepts, and commitments that have significantly influenced its evolution and development for more than a century that characterize its present status and give direction to its future. In addition, the social

41

indicators and their implications for the future development of elementary education are educational indicators. As the term is used in this chapter, educational indicators are derived from five sources. The first source is information reaffirming the basic and historical concepts and commitments that have had a significant impact in shaping the present elementary school. The second source derives from current educational developments and trends in the elementary school. A third source is the moral and value orientation that characterizes the American. The fourth source grows out of the third and deals with the legal requirements that enforce social contracts and ensure fair play and equal protection under the law. The fifth and last source is associated with the continuing and future needs of our society.

Educational indicators are rooted in real situations; they are the benchmarks of what is real and true about the elementary school. The concept of educational indicators is a comparatively new but important one to education. Even now education needs more systematic systems and procedures for gathering abundant and precise information about educational activity, its many dimensions and effects. Much more information is needed about what is actually going on in schools, the status, impact, quality, and value of current educational innovations and developments, the quality of the educational innovations and developments, and the quality of the educational processes employed to achieve their stated purposes. Such information would provide us with a more substantial basis for making educational policy and program decisions, for solving educational problems, and for singling out significant trends from the morass of fads and fashionable ideas in the marketplace. Moreover, such data would be useful in improving the setting and the context of the present offerings, pinpointing the desirable directions of educational change and plotting the future directions of the elementary school.

Educational indicators, like social indicators, are concerned with improving the quality of life through the use of knowledge and information to guide human activity and decision making. The uniqueness of educational indicators for the elementary school is related to attempts at gathering information on the processes and outcomes of elementary education. As such, social indicators reveal the presence or absence of a particular attribute categorized as either a process or outcome. However, the attributes should define and describe the realities in the lives of children that can be consciously altered to improve the quality of their life experiences now and in the future. In this sense educational indicators are not necessarily dependent on prespecified goals. However, educational indicators might be instrumental in assisting educational personnel and laymen in determining where they are in relation to the many alternatives that might have been—or may be—chosen as means and goals. As long as there are multiple publics concerned with educational endeavors, the permutations resulting from possible selections and pairings of differing means and goals are unlimited. They are also, therefore, unintelligible to most professional educators for communicating and comparing educational efforts to multiple publics, and for making program decisions and monitoring the effects of those decisions. Educational indicators will help elementary school personnel make decisions and monitor programs because they tend to identify significant variables related to process, organizational characteristics of a school's environmental contexts, outcomes, and the side effects of achieving certain outcomes under varying conditions.

When one attempts to monitor the program of the elementary school, some use of educational indicators is necessary, because educational indicators are either measures of a particular phenomenon or, at least, are a surrogate of a phenomenon difficult to measure. For example, one of the expected outcomes of attending elementary school is that children will enjoy the experience. As it is not possible to measure enjoyment directly, a reasonable surrogate of the phenomenon, one that is easier to measure, has to be studied. Surrogate measures of pupil enjoyment might include the analysis of stable sociometric patterns that are evident in classrooms, the rate of voluntary involvement in class activities, the specificity of information given to parents about class events and activities, the number of days absent, and the frequency of self-initiated activity in school. All of the foregoing phenomena can be thought of as surrogates of enjoyment or phenomena characterizing the psychological state of elementary schoolchildren. One other point to remember is the notion that the surrogate phenomenon should be acceptable as evidence of the reality of the existence of the phenomenon (in this instance, enjoyment) to be measured because of the difficulty or impossibility of portraying the reality in question directly. Educational indicators are expected to provide indications of that reality.

It is clearly evident that there are many phenomena* that represent the concerns, commitments, means, and goals of the elementary school for which there are no adequate measures or ways to monitor operationally. These phenomena include instructional practices, organizational patterns, social practices, instructional materials and resources, physical facilities, characteristics of student populations, social conditions, social demands, and multiple publics to be served. Since most of these

* Harold Full, ed., *Controversy in American Education: An Anthology of Crucial Issues,* 2nd ed. (New York: Macmillan, 1972).

phenomena defy direct measurement, any educational indicator utilized to provide some kind of measurement of developments in each area must be sensitive to the particular phenomenon of reference in terms of program purposes. As long as the conduct of educational programs in the elementary school has a variety of effects on all who are involved that extend beyond specific and distinct student outcomes, educational indicators can be helpful in assessing the features of the associated educational processes that have profound influence on program effects and outcomes. If educational indicators are to be expected to improve the nature of decision making and program monitoring in the elementary school, they must satisfy the following criteria:

1. *Feasibility of data collection*—educational indicators must be available and usable with minimal effort. Wherever possible, indicators should be aggregates of data collected for other purposes. Indicators should be easily interpreted within the
2. *Sensitivity*—the educational indicator chosen must be tested context of the regular operation of the elementary school. and evaluated for its sensitivity as representative of the reality for which it is a surrogate. In instances where the educational indicator is a direct measure of reality the sensitivity might be assumed.
3. *Significance*—the educational indicators must be regarded as significant to the elementary school's program effects and outcomes and to the needs and requirements of the multiple publics related to the program.

Our purpose here is to explore the significant concerns, commitments, trends, means, and goals that influence the processes and effects of the elementary school's programs. Hopefully, these educational indicators may be used as a basis for program monitoring that will make decision making about overall effects of educational activity and practice more effective. The sources of educational indicators for the elementary school serve as the structural bases for the remainder of this chapter.

Basic and Historical Concepts and Commitments of the Elementary School

The basic and historical concepts and commitments of the elementary school have shaped the present-day elementary school and are likely to direct the focus of this institution in the future. Because certain basic and historical concepts and commitments continue to play such a critical role in the organization and conduct of the elementary school, it is possible to utilize these phenomena as bases for selecting appropriate educational indicators. The basic and historical concepts and commitments of reference include concerns for universal education, democratic citizenship, total development of children, foundational learnings, and parental involvement. Each of these concerns is discussed in relation to some educational indicators that will enable professional personnel and multiple publics to monitor the programs of the elementary school to determine the extent to which basic and historical concepts and commitments are being realized.

Universal Education

One of the characteristics of the elementary school that marks it as a peculiarly American institution is its commitment to universal education. Although the commitment characterizes our entire common (public) school program, the elementary school is the oldest of our institutions providing universal education. Caswell and Foshay note:

> The American Elementary School as we now know it is only about a century old. Yet it would be difficult to imagine the American scene without it. Nobody intended that it should be so but as a social institution the American elementary school is probably the most extensive social experiment ever undertaken. No previous society has deliberately attempted the education in the same way of its total population six to fourteen years of age.[1]

Now, more than a century later, the modern elementary school remains committed to the concept of universal education. Commitment is one thing; but the question of whether or not we have achieved universal education is also important. The response to this question must be in the affirmative. Not only has the percentage of school-age children who are actually enrolled in elementary school increased over the years but the number of years of schooling received by each generation has also increased. The rate of illiteracy in the United States is down to 2.4 per cent in the total population. Among young Americans, aged fourteen to twenty-four, the rate of illiteracy is about one half of 1 per cent. A marked increase in specialized programs for exceptional children, including the mentally handicapped, has contributed to the increase in the percentage of school-age children attending the elementary school. School transportation systems have brought schooling to still other children. Moreover, our present-day commitment to universal education has long been fixed in legislation establishing compulsory school attendance. The elementary school's commitment to universal education is thus both real and historic; the achievement of this goal is a virtual reality. At present, more than 36 million American children are attending elementary schools; of these, about 33 million are enrolled in public elementary schools.

In recent years, the concept of universal education has been extended downward to include younger children. Kindergarten education, once available only through permissive legislation, is rapidly being mandated as a part of the elementary school. Recent developments in early childhood education, such as Operation Headstart, public and private nursery schools, and day-care centers indicate this downward trend. Research dealing with the successful impact of formal instruction on intellectual growth and learning in the very young suggest even further extensions of the concept of universal education to include educational programs for three- and four-year-olds as a part of the public elementary schools. In a report on the origins and characteristics of educational innovations, Orlosky and Smith characterize nursery schools as "a change that has successfully been installed and is sufficiently present that instances of change are obvious."[2]

All present indications are that our commitment to universal education in the elementary school persists. Only its meaning has been broadened to include the commitment to educational opportunity for younger children and special, deviant groups who have heretofore not been accommodated in the public elementary school.

Based on the experience of private nursery schools and of Follow-Through and Headstart programs, specialists in early childhood education indicate that educational programs for younger children (ages two to five) are generally more effective when they are accompanied by educational programs for the parents of the children involved. The inclusion of parents of younger children as intimate partners in the educational process is also important from the standpoint of social and emotional development. Since the value of the home experience, as it relates to the positive development of children, is almost universally accepted in our society, meaningful cooperation between parents and professional staff appears likely to contribute positively to the learning experiences of young children.

For the future elementary school, the implications of the broadened concept of universal education now with us are manifold. Special programs for the young and the parents of the young will be needed, as will more functional housing to accommodate and facilitate these programs. Far more specialized and auxiliary services, dictated by increasing human variability as well as by the special needs of younger learners and other deviant groups, will be required. Greater individual school autonomy will be necessary to enable schools to develop special programs that are responsive to the unique populations served. These will include urban education programs, career education programs, and parent education programs. The future elementary school must become an expansionary institution giving continuous attention to special programs and curriculum adaptations to meet the ever-changing needs of the children and the community it serves.

Educational Indicators for
Universal Education

Many educators could monitor the extent to which the elementary school remains committed to universal education. One such indicator includes data collected by the Bureau of the Census on school enrollment by race, sex, and age. These data are contained in the *Digest of Educational Statistics* for 1972. See Table 2.1 for a modified version of one table.

Table 2.1 shows the percentage of children enrolled at the elementary school level in various age groups. The percentage of children enrolled at the different age levels can be utilized as an educational indicator of the elementary school's commitment to universal education. It is evident that the majority of the preschool age (three and four years) children are not served in the regular school system. However, the trend is moving in that direction. By 1971, service to nursery school age (five and six years) children was moving quickly toward universality. Universal education for elementary school age (seven to thirteen years) children was, for all practical purposes, a reality by 1971 although there was a slight drop in the percentage of children enrolled in 1970. As an educational indicator the percentage of children enrolled in the elementary school at various age levels suggests the extent to which this institution universally

Table 2.1
Per Cent of the Population 3 to 34 Years Old Enrolled[1] in Schools by Race, Sex, and Age: United States, October, 1971

Age	Total		White		Negro and Other Races Total	
3 and 4 years	$[15.6]^3$	21.2		20.9	22.5	21.5
5 and 6 years	$(77.7)^2$	91.6	(82.0)	91.9	90.2	(73.3) 89.8
7 to 9 years	(99.5)	99.1	(99.7)	99.1	99.0	(99.3) 99.0
10 to 13 years	(99.3)	99.2	(99.5)	99.2	98.9	(99.0) 98.8

1 Includes enrollment in any type of graded public, parochial, or other private school in the regular school system. Includes nursery schools, kindergartens, elementary schools, high schools, colleges, universities, and professional schools. Attendance may be on either a full-time or part-time basis and during the day or night. Enrollments in "special" schools, such as trade schools or business colleges, are not included.
2 Parentheses contain percentages for 1960. Taken from Table 160 in U.S. Bureau of the Census, *Statistical Abstract of the United States: 1971*, 92nd ed. (Washington, D.C.: 1971), p. 108.
3 Brackets contain percentage for 1968. Taken from Table 37 in *Digest of Educational Statistics* (Washington, D.C.: Department of Health, Education and Welfare, National Center for Educational Statistics, 1969), p. 31.

Source: Adapted from Table 6 in *Digest of Educational Statistics* (Washington, D.C.: Department of Health, Education and Welfare, National Center for Educational Statistics, 1972), p. 1.

educates those in selected age groups. This educational indicator confirms that the elementary school is still committed to the universal education of children served in the traditional age groups (seven to twelve years) and is approaching a similar position with nursery and preschool age groups. Although universal education for the preschool group may not occur quickly in the very near future, the trend toward universality is unmistakable.

An educational indicator that monitors the extent to which elementary school buildings are built or adapted to accommodate and facilitate newer programs for young children and parents would be a list of new school plant construction or conversions to implement new programs. Many community schools that enable parents to utilize the schools themselves and work with them are being constructed around the country. The model community school in Flint, Michigan, is a good example of a school plant designed to implement a particular program. The increase in the number of such schools is an indicator of the extent to which school plants are more closely correlated with programs that are more responsive to the increasingly heterogeneous groups of children being served by the elementary school.

Other educational indicators can be utilized to pinpoint the effects of the elementary school's continued commitment to universal education. Since the move toward universal education in the elementary school takes in more children who are different in a variety of ways, data that provide a demographic profile of the students served make good educational indicators of the effects of moving toward universal education. These data are available and can be easily adapted to the requirements of the elementary school.

Education for Democratic Citizenship

Directly related to the concept of universal education is the elementary school's commitment to the development of effective citizenship for a democratic society. Prior to the inclusion of citizenship education as a major concern of the elementary school, its primary goals were literacy and moral or character education. In the early 1800s, citizenship education was included in the program in the form of courses in history and geography. Later, civics and government were introduced into the curriculum. It is no accident that this development was concurrent with the early development of our republican type of government and our great experiment in democratic rule. Thomas Jefferson, as well as many of his contemporaries in politics and education, referred repeatedly to the need for an enlightened citizenry if our democratic approach to government was to be successful. The oft-spoken phrase that education is the foundation of democracy is most pertinent here. And if it is so, and we have since come to realize that it is, then the elementary school is certainly the cornerstone of that foundation.

From the earliest beginnings to the formal introduction of citizenship education courses in the 1800s and up to the present day, the elementary school and its purposes have become increasingly aligned and identified with the goals of our society: the ideals, values, and tenets of democracy and democratic behavior. However, in more recent years, this commitment of the elementary school has been implemented through a multifaceted approach as compared to the nineteenth-century approach of including single, isolated courses in history, civics, and government as the means of developing good citizenship. This multifaceted approach characterizing the present-day elementary school views democratic citizenship education as a function of the total instructional program wherein all subject areas contribute, and wherein children develop as citizens through involvement and experience in the activities, relationships, and values that comprise the social system(s) of the school.

One implication for the elementary school, as it moves forward in the years ahead, is thus very clear; it must continue to relate instruction in all subject areas to effective citizenship. For example, history must be used to teach and develop understanding of our democratic heritage—or developing literacy through the communication subjects. But more important, the elementary school must move to democratize its own social system. Our understanding of the educative process today leaves little doubt that children learn not only what they are taught but also by how they are taught and from what they experience in interaction with school norms, rules, procedures, and in relationship with people in school, their attitudes, values, and behaviors. Joyce,[3] in his book *Alternative Models of Elementary Education,* makes the point that the school's social system may be a far more educative force than the curriculum itself.

To make the elementary school more democratic than it has been or is thought to have been in the past will require that faculty and students together determine, plan, and establish an educational environment, social as well as physical, emotional as well as intellectual, wherein the values, attitudes, and procedures that guide human behavior and characterize human relationships are consistent with the democratic ethic.

Educational Indicators for Democratic Citizenship

An educational indicator of the elementary school's influence on democratic citizenship can be described on at least two levels. One level deals with the relationship between children in the classroom and in the school. At the classroom or school level such indicators include results of sociometric tests applied to classroom or school elections, or any activity requiring students to make selections from among their peers, the observed behavior of children in play situations, the noting of children who took part in activities controlled by the actions of their peers, and the noting of the frequency with which the majority of students are allowed to make independent decisions. At another level, the school management and community levels, an educational indicator of democratic citizenship might be the elementary schools' official rules concerning student conduct and independent choice. School management indicators might include such things as dress codes, rules for using common facilities, specific suggestions for the use of the school day, and the nature of grievance procedures employed. Community indicators might include the number and percentage of parents regularly involved in school activities (social, curricular, governance, and so on), the percentage of citizens participating and voting in local elections (emphasis on those elections that are closely associated with educational issues), and the percentage of citizens participating and voting in national elections. Educational indicators of democratic citizenship at the community level for monitoring the effects of the elementary school are indirect at best. One would have to assume that a good program in the elementary school for improving democratic citizenship will have a positive effect on those qualities and actions in the surrounding community. Of course, the reverse of that pattern might also be true. The real point to be made here is that there are some educational indicators that can be utilized to judge the effectiveness of the elementary school in fostering and developing democratic citizenship.

Total Development of Children

During the past two centuries the functions that the elementary school has served in the education of children have multiplied. From the earliest schools of the colonial period, when these functions were confined to moral education and the teaching of reading and writing, to the "little red schoolhouse" with its emphasis on the Three R's, the elementary school has arrived at its present-day comprehensive program of educational opportunities and services. Over the years, many critics and observers of elementary education have interpreted and commented on the expanding functions of the elementary school. Some have viewed it as uncontrollable, undirected expansion and described it as without an apparent direction or focus. Others have viewed it as a kind of residual growth resulting when the school almost automatically inherited the responsibility for attending to the needs and problems of students that other social agencies and units failed or declined to meet. Still others, primarily critics, viewed the expanding functions of the elementary school as an intentional move on the part of educators to usurp responsibilities belonging to others; a sort of self-aggrandizement to enhance the power of the educational establishment in our society. Although these views and interpretations are interesting, and may even contain a few kernels of truth, the expansion of the elementary school's program and the many functions it now serves rests on a much sounder basis and results from ideas and developments of much greater substance. Early recognition of the relationship of body and mind—in every-day language the healthy body-healthy mind idea—is but a part of the more complex and significant concept of the "whole child."

The whole-child concept has had a tremendous impact on the development of the elementary school. In the last century alone understanding based on research findings in physiology, psychology, and human growth and development and the expositions in the works of Dewey, Parker, Hall, and Jersild have extended the whole-child concept, its meaning and application, in the elementary school. Three very important meanings were derived from this concept to influence the elementary school. First, the elementary school is and must be concerned with the development of the entire child, not just with certain, selected aspects of the child's growth. The interrelatedness of all aspects of growth is well established through physiological studies and accounts for the elementary school's recognition of the importance of total development and its commitment to the development of well-rounded persons.

A second and very significant meaning is that in any situation the total organism responds; the whole child learns. In fact, it is impossible for the school to provide experiences that affect only isolated aspects of growth or development. When a child is involved in intellectual activity, his whole being is involved; he thinks with feeling; his emotional reactions stimulate his thoughts and his entire psychological organism is readied for effective action or adjustment to the demands of the situation. Any number of studies in medicine, physiology, and psychology have demonstrated the fact of total response by the human organism even though any individual situation or experience may appear overtly to stimulate some particular aspect of the organism's development—be it intellectual, emotional, or psychomotor.

A third and closely related meaning that the whole-child concept has for the elementary school is the indisputable fact that the whole child comes to school. He cannot leave his feelings, his physical stature, his social competencies, or his emotional weaknesses at home and out of his or his teacher's way so that the school might seek to provide only for his intellectual growth. The child comes to school as a whole, complex being, and he responds and develops as a total organism in each and every learning experience comprising the school's program.

There is no way for the elementary school to divorce its curriculum, instructional program, and activities; indeed, the total operation of the school cannot be separated from the reality of the whole-child concept.

Since the elementary school can neither discard nor retreat from its commitment to the whole-child concept, we must consider the steps that the school has taken to provide for the total development of children. Throughout its history, up to the present time, the primary emphasis of elementary school instruction has focused on intellectual development. Concern with the teaching of basic skills and the acquisition of facts, information, and understandings has been foremost. Because of the interrelatedness of the different aspects of growth, such emphasis contributes to total development. Skill in language is basic to successful and satisfying social interaction. Knowledge that turns the unknown into known eliminates fear and contributes to emotional stability and maturity of the learners. However, other steps, more directly related to specific aspects of growth, such as the wide range of auxiliary personnel and services commonly found in elementary schools have been taken. The work of school nurses, as well as selected health services, psychological services, school lunch and milk programs, guidance activities, social workers, and special physical education programs and activities are noteworthy examples. In addition, the current thrust toward increased individualization of instruction serves to sensitize the classroom teacher to pupil needs in all areas of growth.

What about the elementary schools of the future? What further responses will be required to enhance the quality of education in providing for the total development of children? Medical science and research indicate the promise of longer life, but also relate good nutrition and health in the early years to the quality of life in old age. Science and technology are paving the way to a shorter work week and increased leisure time. Conflicts in human relations are apparent in increasing divorce rates, the generation gap, the breakdown of family structures, and racial violence. Mental health problems and needs are at a point of national crisis. Rapid social change and the press of social conditions affect the school behavior of children and are reflected in the increased social and emotional problems and needs of young children. In the years ahead, the elementary school must give more attention to social and emotional development in children. A better job of diagnosing individual social and emotional needs must be done. Specialized personnel, services, and programs in greater number and diversity than currently exist must be available. Whereas present elementary school programs assign major emphasis (sometimes an almost exclusive emphasis) to academic growth, future programs must be better balanced in their attention to, and provision for, all academic, social, emotional, and physical aspects of development.

Educational Indicators and the Total Development of Children

Educational indicators illustrating the extent of the elementary school's involvement in operating programs that cater to the total development of its children are not easily identified, although they do exist. One such indicator might be the percentage of elementary schools that employ organizational or instructional schemes that make other factors such as interests, social and emotional needs, and pursuit of independent activities, rather than intellectual development, the central focus of their activities. Another indicator is the percentage of auxiliary personnel (school nurses, guidance counselors, social workers, psychologists, and so on) at the elementary school level. One might also want to view auxiliary personnel on a per total staff or per student basis. Other indicators might include the percentage of schools having school lunch rooms, maintenance health services, and psychological services for students and their families. The number and percentage of children referred for personal counseling can also serve as an educational indicator in this area.*

Foundational Experience and Learning

Another tradition or basic characteristic that has had a marked influence on the elementary school and is unlikely to be forsaken in its future development is that of providing for foundational experience and learning in the academic, physical, and social-emotional development of children. No other institution of our society has been charged with, or has accepted the responsibility for formal and systematic development of

* Although evidence suggests that the total development of children should become the concern of the school, other factors are likely to exert great influence on whether this can become a reality. For instance, the rising costs of existing school services are causing many communities to pull back and eliminate programs in this area. It seems unlikely that these communities will want to reinstate these programs at this point. In addition, there are many who feel that these problems are private matters to be purchased by individuals as needed or desired. In either event, focus on the total development of children in the elementary school is likely to gain in importance in the very near future, but the road to full implementation will encounter many challenges and difficulties.

the intellectual capacities and potential of all children. From its very beginning the elementary school has provided instruction in the Three R's; it has evolved as the place where children not only learn and develop their skills and abilities to read, write, and cipher but also as the place where their abilities and capacities to think critically, analytically, and creatively are developed. No other unit or agency of the society has undertaken such a mission for all the children of the society. Similarly, insofar as young learners are concerned, no other institution has sought to provide or transmit a common body or background of significant, though ever-changing, knowledge derived from the organized and scholarly disciplines that make up the world of knowledge. The general education* of children in the skills and subject matter of the so-called common branch subjects is indeed traditional and foundational not only to continued learning and personal development but also to effective participation in society. This unique characteristic and function of the elementary school has two major dimensions. First, its emphasis has been on general education rather than on specialized training. Children may study and explore the world of work. In so doing they acquire information, career awareness, essential skills, and attitudes toward work. Although these are important experiences that may be useful and applicable in later life, such learning experiences do not constitute training for specific vocations.

Second, the school's emphasis in general education has been on intellectual development despite commitment to the whole-child concept. However, this emphasis on foundational learning in the academic domain should not prevent the elementary school from recognizing that it also provides children with their first formal and standardized group experience outside the home. For the majority of children, the elementary school (including public and private nursery schools) provides them with their first formal involvement in group activity with other children of similar age—yet different in every other respect. Consequently, the school's role and contribution to the early development of children's feelings, attitudes, and sensitivities toward others with all their differences, are foundational indeed.

---

* A more detailed discussion of the general education function of the elementary school is provided in Chapter 3.

Educational Indicators and Foundational Learnings

An educational indicator that shows the effects of the elementary school on foundational learnings might be achievement data on the basic skills mastery of elementary schoolchildren. These might include samples of written work from students in elementary schools in different parts of the country or a list of the number, types, and checkout frequency of books in the school or local library used by elementary schoolchildren. These might serve as educational indicators for this area. Another indicator would be the percentage of elementary schools having libraries and trained librarians. Surveys showing the percentage of children's independent reading preferences and personal recreational interests at the elementary school level can be used as an educational indicator of emphasis on foundational learnings. These are just a few samples of the educational indicators that might be employed.

Close Relations with the Home

More than at any other level of the public educational system, the elementary school has historically, and with much success, sought and maintained close communication and cooperation with the homes and families of children attending the elementary school. This close relationship between the home and the elementary school is almost a natural one. Parents, proud of their precious offspring and wanting only the best for them, entrust their children to the elementary school for a major portion of the day. They want their children to get off to a good start and have definite ideas of what they should derive from school and how they should be treated. Parents hold high aspirations for their children and are greatly concerned about their successes in school.

The elementary school has long recognized the importance of close relations with the home. Through the home the school receives a continuous flow of information that assists teachers in the better understanding of children's interests, needs, problems, and backgrounds. The school looks to the home for support and reinforcement of its total program and teaching effort.

Relations with the home have been developed and maintained primarily through the vehicle of parent-teacher organizations, room-mother assignments, parent-teacher conferences, involvement of parents in school projects, volunteer activities, and special programs designed to attract parents to the school.

The elementary school of the future will need to maintain, extend, and revamp these relationships if it is to remain effective in meeting the needs of children by making the best use of home support. Even closer and more cooperative relationships will need to be established. As younger children, three- and four-year-olds, begin to attend school, parents and teachers will need to work together in planning programs and services for both younger children and their parents. This is understandable because the family is still expected to be the dominant force in the lives of children at this age. The only way the elementary school can deal with its concerns and commitments to three- and four-year-olds, while taking into account parental desire to have strong, substantive input concerning the nature of programs and instructional approaches, is to establish a close relationship with the home that becomes an integral part of the program. This step should contribute greatly to the effectiveness of the elementary school in formulating and implementing a meaningful program for three- and four-year-olds.

Elementary schools have the obligation of working directly with parents in improving the educative environments of the home, and providing for a variety of needed family services when the lack of these services adversely affects the school's program. The intensification of individualized instruction related to the highly personal needs of children will require closer communication with the home than ever before. The elementary school's relations with the home must approach a true partnership.

Educational Indicators and Home Relations

Educational indicators that give some information about the effects of the elementary school on home relations include the percentage of schools that have organized parent programs, the percentage of standing school committees in which parent members have equal participation rights, the number of informal visits parents make to individual classrooms, the number of schools having rules and procedures that facilitate parental involvement, and the percentage of schools having facilities that enable parents to compete in activities of their choice or for the school. The main objective in trying to find an educational indicator that provides information about the effects of the elementary school on home relations is to determine the extent to which the relationship between the home and the school is part of an intentional and formal program. Because some elementary schools have good relations with parents of children served by the formal program, this confuses the issue associated with the presence of a structured home relations program. As long as the reader keeps this factor in mind, the indicators discussed previously will provide adequate information about the extent to which elementary schools are trying to develop good home relations with parents.

Trends and Educational Indicators

In a sense, the trends that have characterized the recent elementary school scene represent generalized educational indicators of the impact of the elementary school on the quality of life that children experience while they are in school. Even though these gross indicators cannot be measured, they can be described theoretically and operationally. It is also possible to determine the extent to which these gross educational indicators are present in the schools. If we consider the special sensitivity that trends have for monitoring elementary school programs when used as educational indicators, we can discuss how major educational trends extant in today's elementary school can be employed as additional indicators that have significant meaning for the future elementary school.

Two major trends in elementary education are apparent in the developments of the recent period of curriculum reform (1950–1970). The first of these involves the updating of subject matter in the subjects comprising the curriculum. In his 1964 analysis of school curriculum reform, Goodlad noted that "the strengths of the current curriculum reform movement lie in its efforts to update content and to identify subject-matter elements thought to be of lasting value, as well as in its emphasis on inquiry in teaching and learning."[4]

This trend is partially grounded in the tremendous explosion of new knowledge discussed in Chapter 1. This avalanche of new knowledge has caused the elementary school to retreat from the long-entrenched concept of the systematic coverage of organized knowledge. The reality of the knowledge explosion has rendered this concept inoperable and resulted in efforts to find new approaches to select and update subject matter. In the last two decades we have witnessed these efforts in the steady increase of experimental curriculum projects concerned with the revision and reorganization of elementary school subjects. For example, since the movement began in 1951 with the University of Illinois Committee on School Mathematics under the leadership of Max Bieberman, more than a dozen major programs in the "new math" have been developed. Cook and Doll[5] report that in 1970 there were nearly seventy social studies projects in existence. At the present time, in the elementary schools alone, there are twelve major elementary school science projects, and although some are of recent vintage, each offers a different program. Just how many of our eighty-five thousand public elementary schools have been involved in, or had their programs influenced by, these curriculum reform projects is not precisely known. One estimate is set at 85 to 90 per cent.

Most of these projects stressed the importance of understanding the structure of the discipline and its methods of inquiry as fundamental to updating content and the reorganization of elementary school subjects. New subject matter was selected on the basis of its significance to the discipline and took the form of major principles and generalizations— what J. Myron Atkin[6] referred to in the University of Illinois Elementary School Science Project as "pervasive concepts" and "ideas with mileage."

As an educational indicator, what does this trend in the reselection and updating of subject matter suggest and imply for the future elementary school? One implication is quite clear. The elementary school will need to solve the problem of selecting those basic concepts to be included in the elementary school subjects from an almost endless number of important concepts that are significant in the many disciplines that are the basis of elementary school subjects. To make such a selection, the function and the purpose of elementary education will need to be studied and analyzed and clearer statements of aims will have to be formulated. Only then will the elementary school have a valid basis for making choices essential to updating and reorganizing elementary school content.

Most efforts to update content have focused on single subjects that are separate and isolated from other subjects. This has had the effect of fragmenting the elementary school program. Content revision has been an important and valuable accomplishment, but the task of once again fashioning these separate subjects into a viable and integrated educational program, consistent with its mission, still remains. When a large number of the elementary schools become involved in large-scale curriculum reform or adoption, the growth and strength of the trend is an educational indicator for judging some of the effects these schools are exerting on the students served.

A second related trend, also a consequence of the curriculum-reform movement, is the present and pronounced emphasis on the development of thinking skills and abilities. The development of thought processes such as conceptualizing, logical reasoning, generalizing, and valuing, as well as the skills of inquiry have become learnings in the content of the elementary school. Emphasis on concept formation, modes of inquiry, interpretation of data, value analysis, and discovery is apparent in the many programs and materials adopted by the elementary school in different subject areas. Although such an emphasis on process learnings needs little documentation, the American Association for the Advancement of Science program in elementary science—a process approach—along with the Taba Social Studies curriculum with its attention to concept formation, interpretation of data, and the analysis of feelings are typical. Similar emphasis is found in materials prepared by Simon to develop the skills and abilities in the valuing process. The processes of inquiry and discovery are basic in new math and anthropology-centered social studies programs. The emphasis on process learnings is also reflected in Russell's call for process-oriented elementary schools to accomplish the primary task of education, the development of thinking. In their book *Process as Content: Curriculum Design and the Application of Knowledge,* Parker and Rubin offer this proposition:

> The substance of our proposition is that process—the cluster of diverse procedures which surrounded the acquisition and utilization of knowledge—is, in fact, the highest form of content and the most appropriate base for curriculum change. It is in the teaching of process that we can best portray learning as a perpetual endeavor and not something which terminates with the end of school.[7]

The development of thought processes in the elementary school may be more a function of how teaching is organized and carried on than a function of the subject matter taught. Critical thinking can be generated in one teaching situation; shifted in another. The future elementary school must pay more heed to the fact that the how of teaching can and does make a real difference. In the continuing in-service education of teachers, more intensive study and analysis of teaching strategies and styles is warranted if teaching is really to make a difference.

Hollis Caswell[8] once identified the "either . . . or" dichotomies among the major problems and issues facing elementary education. His point is pertinent here. Should priority be given to process learnings and the how of teaching, or should more importance be attached to what (that compendium of information of a particular course or grade level) is taught?

Such a question demands that the elementary school establish a basis for selecting content samples (elements of subject matter) that are worth learning that also can serve as effective vehicles for developing thought processes. When a large percentage of the schools began to critically analyze and reconstruct their basic mode of instruction, that act represents an educational indicator of the possible effects elementary schools are having or would like to have on the pupils who attend them.

Individualized Instruction

A third trend of major proportions and one of increasing momentum in today's elementary schools is the individualization of instruction. The basis for this trend is rooted in the many individual differences found in learners. These differences are manifest in the learner's interests and needs, his abilities, achievements, rate of growth and learning, his cultural background—in fact in every aspect of his being, behaving, and becoming. They are documented in our empirical knowledge and in research on human growth and development. Although movement from teaching an entire class through a variety of grouping procedures to the present-day emphasis on individualized instruction has been slow, it has also been steady. As an innovative trend, Orlosky and Smith described the practice of individual instruction as another one "that has successfully been installed and sufficiently present that the instances of change are obvious."[9] With the idea of providing each child with a unique educational program, many nationwide projects are in operation to provide schools with programs, materials, and services toward that end. IPI (Individually Prescribed Instruction), IGE (Individually Guided Education), IDEA (The Institute for the Development of Educational Activities), and PLAN (Program of Learning According to Needs) attest to the attention showered on this important educational development. The agendas of national education conferences, the programs of state and county institutes, and the activities of preschool and in-service educational workshops offer evidence of the educators' interest in this current development.

The present state of interest and commitment to individualized instruction and the extent of its use in the public schools point to the individual learner as the primary focus in the organization of teaching and instruction for many years to come.

Central to providing individual instruction is the diagnosis of individual learning needs. Equally important is the development of learning activities and materials to meet those needs. These two elements, diagnosis and prescription, are fundamental to individualized instruction and are destined to become even more critical operations in the teaching-learning process. Future elementary schoolteachers will need to develop a diagnostic orientation in their view of teaching. And even more important, they will need to increase their own skills and abilities in the development and uses of diagnostic techniques.

With individualized instruction on the increase, the elementary school must be prepared to provide the wide variety of human, material, and technological resources that are essential to its effective operation. Drastic changes in the ways in which time and space are used will be necessary to accommodate learners pursuing individualized studies at different rates and with different needs in space, time, and resources.

It is unlikely that the current or future elementary school will find it possible to meet all of the individual needs of all of its learners. Yet steps to expand the personal, material, and mechanical means of teaching and to reorganize the time, space, and learning environment and materials must be taken. An even more important step will require the development of teachers' skills and sensitivities that will provide for the learners' unique needs. The trend toward individualization is an educational indicator of the elementary school's attempts to foster the effects suggested by this instructional approach.

Open Education

In some ways the trend toward open education is related to the current emphasis on individualized instruction. Both attach importance to individual needs; both seek to provide learning experiences related to these needs in an environment that is more suitable and adaptable to the learner's style. Yet in another respect there is a significant difference. Individualized instruction runs the risk of being highly prescriptive and at times is organized in rigid sequence. Although this is not necessarily the case, prescriptive sequencing is related to the operational requirement that some notion of direction and intent become part of the total program. We do not intend to compare and contrast these two major developments. Suffice it to say here that there is a little of each in the other.

Open education is discussed under many different headings such as the open classroom, open schools, and the open curriculum. The term *open education,* as used in this chapter, has three major aspects to it. First it is characterized by an open curriculum, which means the absence of any predetermined, prescribed body of content that must be taught to all learners at the same specified time and in prearranged sequences. Second, open education is conducted in a setting containing more open space than the conventional classroom, one in which the organization of space can be suited to the needs and activities of learners. Finally, open education is characterized by the openness in human relations, the interactions and interrelationship that take place among and between people learning and living together. A very insightful description of open education is offered by T. Manolakes.

> Open education is a whole variety of related approaches—not a neat package. Informal education might be viewed as a developing continuum. The beginnings can be small with no fanfare or publicity—a matter of time and evolution rather than flashy revolution. Open education can begin in many forms: modification of physical arrangements of classrooms, modifications in the use of time, or modifications or substitutions in some aspects of the classroom program such as in writing or science. But probably more important than these changes is a developing conviction on the part of teachers that they can depart from textbook and coverage requirements; that they can make use of their own talents and still help children to learn, and that, given proper conditions, children will learn quite well without coercion.[10]

Open education as a variety of related forms that can begin in many forms is well under way in the American elementary schools. The reader is once again referred to a report on educational changes by Orlosky and Smith, who characterize the open classroom as a "change that has been successfully installed and is sufficiently present that instances of the change are obvious."

Will open education become the norm in our public elementary schools? Present-day emphasis on open education and its successful implementation to date gives every indication that our schools are headed in that direction. With regard to such prospects, Manolakes[10] believes we can "evolve our own lasting model of humane schooling." He then goes on to state: "For the near future the best thing that we can do to encourage this educational approach is to view it as an alternative to our formal programs and not a panacea for all our educational problems."

As a trend, open education is an educational indicator of the direction in which many of the nation's elementary schools are going. The adoption of open education programs is a statement about what most elementary schools are trying to do to shape the learning experience of pupils.

Multimedia and Educational Technology

The explosion of knowledge about which so much has been written has been accompanied by a major revolution in the multimedia and technical means of processing knowledge. Such events as these have given rise to still another major development now extant in elementary schools. This refers to the seemingly never-ending flow of new instructional resources, namely printed materials, educational kits, equipment, and technology designed to support and enhance the teaching-learning process. The availability and use of new instructional material and equipment was stimulated by the National Defense Education Act of 1958, which provided federal funds for a wide variety of teaching aids and materials in the areas of reading, language arts, and foreign languages. The many curriculum reform projects undertaken during the 1950s and 1960s generated new text materials, trade books, educational kits, and other specialized materials that were introduced into the schools. For example, in the mid-1960s more than two hundred different kinds of programmed texts and workbooks were available and in use in the schools. The market in text and trade books including text-related workbooks and paperbacks flourished in response to the introduction of new curriculum content. The updating of subject matter and the school's turn to multimedia approach in teaching characterized curriculum development during that period. The Elementary and Secondary Education Act of 1965 poured additional funds into the instructional resources of the schools and provided for their effective organization, management, and use through instructional materials centers, satellite centers, trained personnel, and teacher education.

The availability of all of these media and technical means for reaching and teaching children have both accompanied and facilitated new approaches such as individualized instruction and the use of educational gaming techniques; new instructional programs such as environmental studies and economic education; new facilities such as classroom learning stations, language labs, and instructional materials centers. Impetus for the open education movement has been provided through such enriched resources.

Very few elementary schools remain untouched and free from the impact of the many developments that have made an increasing array of instructional resources that are more readily available and accessible. The present situation, in terms of educational technology, is a good indicator of the future instructional pattern that can be expected in the elementary school. Nothing at the present time suggests that the availability or flow of instructional materials in support of educational programs will subside. Spokesmen for publishers, school architects, and technologists assert their present capacities and readiness to meet and accommodate any new ideas and future needs of public education in the way of materials, facilities, and equipment. The extent to which multimedia and educational technology become a part of the instructional pattern in the elementary school is an indicator of how the elementary school will be changed and how these changes are likely to affect the children they serve. The use of instructional materials and resources is discussed in detail in Chapter 11.

Elementary School Organization*

The organization of the elementary school consists of a plan and procedures by which children are admitted to and progress through the years covered by the elementary school. The format and procedures also provide for their organization and distribution as individuals and groups for purposes of instruction.

Until very recently, the plan and procedures most commonly followed in the elementary school were based on the grade standard practice. Under this practice, pupils were admitted at a specific age, usually specified in legislation or the state code of education. Fixed tasks and standards of accomplishment were assigned to each grade level and upon meeting these standards the student advanced to the next grade or level. One year at each level was considered normal progress. Some children progressed more rapidly through what was called acceleration. Other children who failed to meet grade level standards, called repeaters, were detained, usually for a second year at the same grade level

* Elementary school organization is discussed in detail in Chapter 9.

before advancing. Under this plan most of the children in the same grade level were of the same age.

For purposes of instruction, pupils were organized in different ways. The most common way, known as the self-contained classroom organization, grouped children according to age and grade level. Each group was then assigned a specific room and teacher responsible for its total classroom learning program.

Another organizational plan was called departmentalization. Under this plan, children were grouped according to age and grade level and assigned to a different teacher for each subject. Under this arrangement, a group would be taught reading by one teacher, and then move to another room and another teacher for arithmetic. Sometimes the children would stay put in one room while the teachers would move from one class to the next. When the number of children at the same age and grade level was large enough to require two groups, they were divided according to ability—with a fast and slow group. Such a division was possible under the self-contained arrangement whereby each group was assigned to a single teacher. But it was much more common under departmentalization and was really an early form of modern-day "tracking."

Of these arrangements the self-contained classroom is by far the most common. Departmentalization in the earlier years of the elementary school is disappearing. However, some features of departmentalization have reappeared in recent years. For example, some groups of children are regrouped from one subject to another according to ability in each subject and assigned to a teacher who is best suited to work with a group at a specified level.

In recent years, there have been many changes and modifications in school organization at the elementary level. Some of these changes relate to how children are admitted to, and progress through, the school. For example, in some schools admission policies have been made more flexible. Kindergartens, prekindergarten programs, and nursery schools have rendered rigid age admission requirements untenable. In some instances, grades have been eliminated and progress is through levels; for example, Level I, Level II, Level III; or through units, such as nongraded primary units and intermediate units. Changes are also under way in the plans and procedures for organizing pupils for purposes of instruction. Interage grouping, introduced experimentally in the 1950s, is again becoming prominent. Sex-based grouping (boys and girls), employed in some school situations, is being tried on the basis that, in early years, development is more advanced in girls than in boys. Large groups of children, around one hundred, with an interage composition, are organized and assigned to a team of teachers (usually four or five) under a multiunit organization.

All of these examples are offered as evidence of the many new twists and features that are a part of present-day trends involving organizational changes. Underlying each change are attempts to achieve greater individualization of instruction and more effective utilization of teachers, their specialized skills, and competencies.

Organizational trends are educational indicators that help one to assess the changes that are occurring in elementary schools and how these changes are likely to affect the quality of life, instruction, and learning of those who serve and are served. As educational indicators, organizational patterns outline the flow of resources and manage the time that is available to all parties in the school. An accurate picture of organizational patterns provides a meaningful educational indicator for making certain judgments about the elementary school.

Summary

This chapter introduced the idea of educational indicators and how they relate to the elementary school. These educational indicators were used to provide us with a degree of reality in terms of valid benchmarks that characterize the existence of the elementary school. Educational indicators, as viewed in this chapter, were intended to reveal a meaningful look at the reality of what is happening in schools, the status, impact, quality, and value of current educational innovations and developments, and the quality of the educational processes employed to achieve stated purposes. In this sense, educational indicators are basically concerned with improving the quality of life through the use of knowledge and information to guide human activity and decision making. At the elementary school level, educational indicators are used to gather information on the processes and results of elementary education that reveal the presence or absence of particular attributes that define and describe children, both as persons and as learners. Used this way, educational indicators might be employed profitably to improve the quality of elementary school education. Additionally, educational indicators can be extremely helpful in assessing the features of the associated educational processes that have profound influence on program effects.

References

1. Hollis Caswell and Wells Foshay, *Education in the Elementary School* (New York: American Book, 1957), p. 1.
2. Donald Orlosky and B. Othanel Smith, "Educational Change: Its Origin and Characteristics," *Phi Delta Kappan* 53:412–414 (March 1972).
3. Bruce Joyce, *Alternative Models of Elementary Education* (Waltham, Mass.: Blaisdell, 1969).
4. John Goodlad, *School Curriculum Reform* (New York: The Fund for the Advancement of Education, 1964), p. 65.
5. Ruth C. Cook and Ronald C. Doll, *The Elementary School Curriculum* (Boston: Allyn, 1973), p. 277.
6. J. Myron Atkin, "Teaching Concepts of Modern Astronomy to Elementary School Children," *Science Education,* 45:54–58 (Feb. 1961).
7. I. Cecil Parker and Louis J. Rubin, *Process as Content: Curriculum Design and the Application of Knowledge* (Chicago: Rand McNally, 1969), p. 1.
8. Op. cit.
9. Op. cit. p. 412.
10. Theodore Manolakes, "The Open Education Movement," *The National Elementary Principal,* 52:15 (Nov. 1972).

3

The Elementary
School: A Conception

At a time of rapid and dramatic social change, the public school system is not only feeling the impact of these sweeping social changes but is also examining and analyzing them for the meanings and implications they hold for the future development of public schools. As an integral part of the society, public education is just as much in a state of revolution as is the total society. It is indeed a most perplexing and critical time for public schools and professional educators.

It seems hardly necessary to document the sweeping changes, social, scientific, and technological that have occurred since Sputnik. One only needs to recall the tremendous explosions in knowledge and population growth or remember the seething and militant activism of minority groups seeking equal rights and opportunities. Sweeping and extensive scientific and technological developments in space exploration, communication, health, and medicine touch our lives daily. Urbanization with the problems it presents, war with the issues it raises, the environment with the concerns it generates, youth culture, drug abuse, inflation, crime, automation, and racism are but a few of the many conditions indicative of the tempest, turmoil, and change under way in our society.

In these recent years of accelerated change and social turmoil, public education has been the object of both criticism and reconstruction. It has been condemned as an illegitimate institution—either as unresponsive to the needs of society and individuals, or as irrelevant in such responses as it has made to meet these needs. It has been criticized as contributing to—and failing to solve—the problems of poverty, racism and racial integration, urbanization and inner-city ghettos. It has been held responsible for its shortcomings in educating future leaders as well as in training workers to meet ever-changing and unpredictable manpower needs. It has been criticized for fostering permissiveness and generating the activism of youth engaged in riotous, rebellious behavior. It has been charged with the failure to resolve many value conflicts and rebuild a core of values essential to developing harmony among various groups in the American community.

In the face of all the charges, criticisms, and condemnations directed at public education, there have been numerous efforts to reconstruct the public schools. Some movements, such as the free school, have even sought to find alternative arrangements with which to replace the public school system. Reconstruction efforts, however, have been the more numerous—many organized agencies, from the public and private domain, namely, state and federal offices of education, industry and foundations, universities, and countless other groups and individuals, have injected and inoculated the educational bloodstream of the public schools with research funds, experimental programs, and educational innovations. Packaged curricula, new materials, educational hardware, and specialized personnel—all designed to save and reconstruct the public schools—have been introduced. The full measure of the effectiveness of this reconstruction effort is yet to be determined; its overall impact has never been fully assessed. Yet many believe that some educational progress and improvement during this most recent period of curriculum reform is discernible. The subject matter taught is judged to be more significant and up to date. The media explosion has made it possible to use more exciting and effective materials of instruction. New buildings of more functional design are better equipped with the educational hardware of the electronic age. And teachers are receiving better training than ever. The extent to which such apparent improvements are the results of the curriculum-reform movement or the slower process of educational evolution is not readily discernible.

Despite any claims of recent progress in specific schools and specific programs, there are educational observers who are cautiously doubtful that any major and substantial changes have resulted during the last twenty years that have permeated—or will last in—public education throughout the country. To many observers, the reality, substance, and durability of educational changes in our schools are minimal and almost insignificant when compared to the broad-scale investment and effort to redirect and reconstruct public educational programs.

In the "Educational Supplement" to *The New York Times* (January 8, 1973), Dean J. Myron Atkin of the University of Illinois compared our recent approach to strengthen education to the model employed to develop and implement changes in agriculture and medicine. He wrote:

> Millions of dollars have been spent to apply the model to education. But the results are meager and the public's sense of crisis about the schools has not diminished. We might profit by some reflection before we invest still more money.

The elementary school as an integral and vital unit in the educational ladder of the public school system has been affected or unaffected no more or no less than the total public school system. Subjected to many efforts at curriculum reform and organizational modification, the elementary school, in terms of program, teaching methods, and organization remains very much as it was in the late 1940s. One prominent American educator offers the opinion that had a classroom teacher of the 1940s pulled a Rip Van Winkle and awakened today, that teacher could pick up right where he fell asleep, unaware of any major curriculum or basic institutional changes.

In writing about the past fifteen years of curriculum reform in an article addressed to elementary school educators, John Goodlad states:

> we have been virtually inundated with efforts of almost every conceivable kind to inject into the schools some ingredient of change or innovation, inoculations presumed to be for the health of the elementary school.

He then reports as follows:

> But in our studies reported in *Behind the Classroom Door,* and in the studies of others who have looked carefully and deeply at the schools during this period of change, it becomes increasingly clear that these inoculations, these injections, have not been markedly effective.

Goodlad concludes:

> In spite of both substantive and political proposals for change, however, many of our schools go on very much as before.[1]

But just where is the elementary school today? Where does it stand? What is its status? Some educators see it as existing in a state of flux; a school in transition. Bombarded as it has been during the past fifteen years by a battery of educational ideas and innovations, it is in process of assimilating them, working them through, and implementing them. And by so doing, it is consolidating the gains that have accrued in recent years. These same educators believe that present-day assessments of the impact and results of all of these recent changes were either premature or conducted too hastily to reveal the full impact of the educational reform period. They insist that dramatic changes are a likely consequence as the elementary school moves through this transitional period.

Still other educators, appreciative of the substance and value of many of the more recent innovations and educational ideas, regard many of the efforts to change the elementary school as abortive. Newer materials and content, their use demanding new teaching methods and approaches, have instead been adapted to older and more traditional teaching styles and rendered almost ineffective in accomplishing change. New patterns of school organization have been adopted, but only the name has changed. Individualization of instruction, in many instances, has boiled down to an entire class working individually on the same dittoed exercise sheets. These educators point to new ideas adopted to fit old patterns, their innovative qualities aborted and lost in the status quo of the elementary school.

Still other educators see the elementary school in a dire state of confusion and contradiction; confusion in the curriculum reflecting a confusion as to the purpose of the elementary school; contradiction reflected in the side-by-side presence of the new and the old. New math programs in one school, or one classroom, the old math in another school, or in the classroom next door. The curricula of many schools present a hodgepodge of the open classroom in one school, a highly subject-centered organization in another, and a combination of separate subjects (such as mathematics) and broad fields approach (such as social studies) in still another. This third group of educational observers expresses a broader concern in their questions about what is happening to the elementary school. Whether the elementary school is in a state of transition, flux, or even revolution, it is concerned about the lack of clarity in its purposes, contradictions and inconsistencies in its policies, programs, procedures, and organization.

The situation facing the elementary school is very difficult and complex. If, in fact, the elementary school is in a state of transition, then what is it likely to become? If it is in a state of flux, in the process of becoming some kind of conglomerate, what will evolve? Such questions present at least two alternatives. The first assumes that the directions of the future elementary school are known and are clear, and that given time to absorb the impact of the last decade of changes and attempted changes, it will gradually evolve and progress to become what it was intended to become. The second alternative is that even now when the elementary school is in a state of change, or a picture of confusion and contradiction, it is time to consider, suggest, and hopefully to build a viable conception of the elementary school. This by no means is a simple task. To predict what the elementary school will become is one thing; to project what it should become is another; both are difficult—and would be made even more difficult if such efforts at prediction or projection were fully descriptive and detailed. And yet there is a critical need to examine some conceptions of the elementary school of the past and present, even if such attempts to do so are confined to the major components in a skeletal description of the future elementary school.

One can think of the elementary school in terms of the grade levels covered, the characteristics of the children served, the content to be taught, and the primary method of instruction employed. Each of the areas would present a different view of what the elementary school is like. Even when taken together they do not define the elementary school as an idea or concept, for they only reveal its organization, the groups it serves, the material to be learned, and the means for achieving goals. However, these separate descriptions do not tell what the elementary school is. They do not provide one with a concept of the elementary school.

In order to derive this conception, a view of its historical development would place it in appropriate perspective as an institutional entity. The heritage of the elementary school can be traced to three main sources: (1) practices central to the Greek way of life, (2) techniques and rules developed by Romans to conduct their affairs throughout the world, and (3) beliefs guiding the lifestyles of Christians. The Greeks furnished us with their ideals of personal and political freedom along with a knowledge of and an appreciation for literature, art, and philosophy, and a desire for creative expression. From the Romans, we inherited an understanding of law and its role in the social order and individual rights, of government and its role in ordering and coordinating critical social functions, and of practical arts and their role in improving the output and effectiveness of social functions. Our Christian heritage provided us with many of the current civilization ideals related to the interactions between individuals and groups as they participate in various social functions. In summary, it appears that the Christians synthesized the cultural ideas of the Greeks and the systems of law and government created and employed by the Romans, and provided all subsequent generations with a foundation upon which a way of life could be developed, one that highlights notions of respect for individual and group rights of all people.

The first organized, systematic, and recurring effort to provide instruction for young children in America grew out of church needs and took the form of private instruction in reading and religion carried on in the home or taught by the master of apprentices. In the larger New England towns, the Latin grammar schools prepared boys to enter the English College* in which ministers were prepared for the churches, or the colony college in which nonministerial students continued their scholarly pursuits. It is apparent that from the very beginning the education of young children was viewed as providing the necessary foundation for vocational training or intellectual activity within a social context. That tradition is still very much an integral part of elementary schooling.

The beginnings of elementary school education were strongly rooted in the private sector of the total society. As American society became more complex and differentiated, education necessarily increased in importance as a public concern and responsibility. In a real sense, the public education of young children resulted from a need to institutionalize instruction for those who were expected to further the development and improve the maintenance of an increasingly complex society. The public elementary school was built on the traditions set in the private education of young children and on the demands of a developing and growing societal structure. A brief discussion of the historical development of the public elementary school is a first step in trying to provide a meaningful and functional conception of this school as it presently exists.

The Development of the
Public Elementary School

The public elementary school was the direct result of the failure of private instruction to meet the educational needs of the community and the general welfare of the society. As the social functions in the community became more complex and differentiated, it was apparent that the voluntary efforts to promote general education fostered the

---

* The first English College was Harvard, endowed in 1636, and the second was Yale, which was endowed in 1701.

teaching of puritanical religious beliefs, but failed to teach the information required to take advantage of the new opportunities in the wilder-
ness. In order to deal effectively with the sins of omission and the vital
needs of commission, the legislature of Massachusetts enacted a law
compelling appropriate individuals to fulfill their teaching obligations
as they related to the general education of the community's youth. This
act, popularly known as the Massachusetts Law of 1642, made the following provisions when it

> directed the officials of each town to ascertain, from time to time, if
> parents and masters were attending to their educational duties; if all
> children are being trained "in learning and labor and other employ-
> ments profitable to the Commonwealth"; and if the children were
> being taught "to read and understand the principles of religion and
> the capital laws of the country." The officers were empowered to im-
> pose fines on those who failed to give proper instruction . . . and the
> courts were insistent that the towns be compelled to obey the law.[2]

This law turned out to be a precedent that has endured until the present
and forms the basis for one of the primary concerns of the present-day
elementary school. That concern is that all children of both sexes must
be taught to read for their own benefit and so that they will be able to
contribute to the general welfare of the community.

Using the 1642 law as a starting point, the legislature of Massachusetts passed a law in 1647 that provided for the hiring of teachers
and the establishment of an elementary school system.[3] At this point
elementary school education became compulsory and could be enforced
because laws passed previously—in 1634 and 1638, respectively—had au-
thorized the levying of taxes to meet all town expenditures. Since elementary schools were considered a responsibility of townships containing
more than one hundred households, they were included as part of the
town expenditures. This provision for the financing of schools ensured
the continued existence of the elementary school and service to the
majority of young children residing in each town. This situation still
characterizes the elementary school.

There is one other idea that has characterized the elementary
school since its inception. That idea is the belief that the elementary
school serves the state and the general welfare when it provides a sound
education for the individual child. This view is effectively presented by
Cubberley when he asserts the following:

> It is important to note here that the idea underlying all this legislation
> was neither paternalistic nor socialistic. The child is to be educated,

not to advance his personal interests, but because the state will suffer if he is not educated. The State does not provide schools to relieve the parent, nor because it can educate better than the parent can, but because it can thereby better enforce the obligation which it imposes.[4]

Even though the dichotomy between education *for the good of the state* and *for the good of the individual* is not as great now as it was because an equal amount of emphasis is being placed on the latter focus as an appropriate concern of the elementary school, the former focus is still a primary concern of the elementary school. Elementary school education is still viewed as necessary to the survival, development, and improvement of our social institutions and the optimum promotion of the general welfare. The elementary school still remains a vital part of the supportive structure of the community and the society.

After an evolutionary development of the elementary school from its inception in the form of the Dame School,[5] the Three R's School,[6] the Latin Grammar School,[7] the English Grammar School,[8] the Primary School,[9] and the Lancastrian School,[10] the first graded elementary school was founded in 1848 at the Quincy Grammar School at Boston by J. D. Philbrick.[11] Although this graded elementary school did not closely resemble our present-day elementary school, it did evolve to approximate its form. According to Jarvis and Wootton:

> There were at least four steps in the evolution of the graded elementary school plan before it began to approximate the program that we are familiar with today. First, there was the horizontal division of the elementary program into two or more grades. The most commonly utilized method was one grade for the primary and one for the grammar school. A variation consisted of three grades; primary, intermediate, and grammar. The second phase in evolving the graded elementary school was housing these broad grade-units within the same building. The names of these broad grade-units are in common usage even today. The third step was the classification of pupils into one of the grade-units and the fourth action was to change the type of building construction which would provide several small classrooms. Within each classroom all of the subjects were taught by one teacher to the pupils who had been assigned to her.[12]

It is evident from this description that the elementary school has a long history and that it has resembled its present form for a long period of time. The ability of the elementary school to endure essentially unchanged in purpose and function is a good beginning for establishing the basis for providing a conception of this unit of instruction.

The Development of the Elementary School Curriculum

After the passage of the Massachusetts Laws of 1642 and 1647, the curriculum of the elementary school was dominated by reading. Writing was included in the 1647 law but was not much emphasized. Arithmetic gradually became a fixture in the curriculum, and by 1775 the elementary school was predominately known for teaching the Three R's. These subject areas still enjoy a central place in the elementary school curriculum today.

If one notes the elementary school curriculum shown in Table 3.1, the inclusion of subject matter (or experiences) is indicated from 1775 to 1900. It is interesting to note that the present curriculum of the elementary school was set by 1900. The elementary school curriculum covers essentially the same subject matter areas and topics that were considered important in the elementary schools of 1900. Any student of elementary school curriculum should discern that at different periods

Table 3.1

Time Allotment in the Elementary Subjects from 1826 to 1935

Dates	Three R's	Content Subjects	Special Activities
1826	91.7%	0.0%	8.3%
1856	70.1%	15.7%	14.2%
1866	63.0%	12.5%	25.5%
1904	61.8%	12.3%	25.9%
1926	51.7%	11.8%	36.5%
1935	51.3%	14.5%	34.2%

Figures are per cent of total school time. Three R's consists of reading, 'riting, and 'rithmetic; content subjects include such subjects as history, geography and science; special activities consist of music, drawing, and opening exercises, and other content not readily classified under the Three R's or content subjects.

Source: B. Othanel Smith, William O. Stanley, and Harlan Shores, *Fundamentals of Curriculum Development,* 2nd ed. (New York: World, 1957), p. 198.

since 1900 different segments of the curriculum have received greater emphasis, whereas in other time periods the emphasis has remained

Table 3.2

The Evolution of the Elementary-School Curriculum, and of Methods of Teaching

1775	1825	1850	1875	1900
READING	READING	READING	READING	READING
	Declamation	DECLAMATION	Literary	LITERATURE*
Spelling	SPELLING*	SPELLING	Selections	Spelling
Writing	Writing	WRITING	SPELLING	Writing*
Catechism	Good Behavior	Manners	PENMANSHIP*	
Bible	Manners and Morals	Conduct	Conduct	....
Arithmetic	ARITHMETIC*	MENTAL ARITH.*	PRIMARY ARITH.	ARITHMETIC
		CIPHERING	ADVANCED ARITH.	
	Bookkeeping	Bookkeeping	....	....
	GRAMMAR	Elem. Lang.	Oral Lang.*	ORAL LANG.
	Geography	GRAMMAR	GRAMMAR	Grammar
		Geography	Home Geog.	Home Geog.
			TEXT GEOG.	TEXT GEOG.*
		History U.S.	U.S. HISTORY	History
			Constitution	Stories*
				TEXT HIS.*
		Object Lessons	Obj. Lessons*	Nature
			Elem. Science*	Study*
			Drawing*	Elem. Sci.*
			Music*	Drawing*
			Phy. Exercises	Music*
				Play
				Phy. Train.*
	Sewing and	....	....	Sewing
	Knitting			Cooking
				Manual
				Training

CAPITALS = Most important subjects.
   Roman = Least important subjects.
      * = New methods of teaching now employed.
Underlined = Subjects of medium importance.

Source: Adapted from E. P. Cubberley, *Public Education in the United States* (Boston: Houghton Mifflin, 1934), p. 473.

These figures were taken from Oscar T. Jarvis and Lutian R. Wootton, *The Transitional Elementary School and Its Curriculum* (Dubuque, Iowa: William C. Brown Company, Publishers, 1966), pp. 14–15.

almost constant. At the present time, more informal or open education programs are making greater use of those specific areas listed in the bottom box in the 1900 year column of Table 3.2. However, the areas listed in the top two boxes (Table 3.2) are still considered critical to the curriculum offerings of the elementary school.

Another element in the elementary school curriculum relates to the amount of time allocated to instruction in the core subject matters, or the Three R's. In Table 3.1, one can readily observe the amount of time that the Three R's commanded for little more than one hundred years. The percentage of time devoted to teaching the Three R's decreased from a high of 91.7 per cent in 1826 to 51.3 per cent in 1935. Even though the teaching of content subjects became an important segment of the elementary school curriculum in 1856, its influence remained just about constant through 1935. The big increase in attention in the elementary school curriculum occurred in the area of special activities. This area of the curriculum fluctuated greatly at different periods and in different places. Since 1866, Special Activities command at least one quarter of the available time devoted to the elementary school curriculum.

Even though Table 3.1 showed a decrease in the percentage of time devoted to teaching the Three R's, it does not reflect the absolute amount of time given to teaching in this area. Table 3.3 shows that there was a great increase in the average number of days of schooling from

Table 3.3

Effects of Increase in Total Time Allowed for Schooling upon Amount of Time Given to the Three R's

Dates	Average No. of Days of Schooling	Average No. of Hours Per School Day, Elementary Grades	Total No. of Hours of Schooling	Percent of Time Given to Three R's	Average No. of Hours Instruction in Three R's
1826	163	6.25	1,019	91.7	934
1866	523	5.22	2,730	62.0	1,693
1926	1,360	5.07	6,895	51.7	3,565

Source: Carleton H. Mann "How Schools Use Their Time," *Teachers College Contribution to Education,* **333:** 50 (1928). This table was taken from Oscar T. Jarvis and Lutian R. Wootton *The Traditional Elementary School and Its Curriculum* (Dubuque, Iowa: William C. Brown Company, Publishers, 1966), p. 16.

1826 to 1926, which gave rise to a significant increase in the total number of hours (1,019 to 6,895) available for instruction, although the average number of hours per school day actually declined. It can be readily observed that the average number of hours of instruction in the Three R's increased almost fourfold even though the percentage of available time devoted to the area declined by forty percentage points. The teaching of the Three R's still commands a major portion of the instructional time in the elementary school curriculum.

From a historical perspective a conception of the elementary school must deal with its importance to the development, maintenance, and advancement of the society and individuals in the society. The elementary school must be thought of as the basic institution that promotes and ensures the general welfare. Another part of the elementary school conception is related to the nature of the curriculum and the time devoted to the different subject matter areas and experiences comprising the curriculum. It is apparent that these two areas form the basic foundation that begins to outline a conception of the elementary school as we know it today and as it is likely to become.

The Elementary School

Primarily, the elementary school is a social institution concerned with the basic orientation of youth to ways of knowing, ways of learning, general education, social functions of the society, the morality guiding our social functions, and the acceptable socialization experiences. The elementary school as an institution is both rational and social. As a rationally designed institution, the elementary school is expected to achieve prespecified goals of learning and individual and group behavior. And as a social institution, the elementary school is expected to affect the emotional and practical behavior of the children served. The elementary school is expected to fulfill both of these major roles in a balanced fashion as a precondition for becoming in reality what it is conceptually. Before a characterization of the conceptualization of the elementary school can be complete, a brief discussion of the components that comprise it should provide the reader with a clearer picture of the total idea intended. We now turn our attention to those components as a basis for the finer differentiation and definition of the elementary school as a concept.

Basic Orientation to Ways of Knowing

There are many ways of knowing about the world around us, both physically and spiritually. At present the empirical mode of knowing the physical world is dominant in the elementary school. This situation has given rise to the notion that knowing about man's physical world is of greater worth than knowing about his nonphysical world. Too much emphasis on the former leads children to conclude, wrongly, that reality is primarily a physical entity. Therefore, it is necessary for the elementary school to expose children to both empirical and nonempirical ways of collecting, processing, and receiving knowledge.

The elementary school attempts to do this by exposing the young child to the major epistemological methods.* The methods and their abbreviated definitions are as follows:

1. *Appeal to Authority.* Knowledge based on the authority of an expert in the field.
2. *Intuition.* Knowledge based on ultimate and noninstrumental values or supposed ultimate and ineffable truths.
3. *Formal Logic.* Knowledge based on self-evident insights of reason.
4. *Empiricism.* Knowledge based on the systematic procedures for discovering facts and data or concrete relations in nature.
5. *Pragmatism.* Knowledge based on evaluating things or processes on the basis of their palpable effects.
6. *Skepticism.* Knowledge based on the realization that all epistemological methods fail to provide a complete picture (knowledge of anything).[13]

It should be readily apparent to the reader that the effectiveness of each method of knowing for children is dependent on the nature of the entity to be known. They cannot be given a priority ordering apart from their use. Each method of knowing has superiority over another

---

* One might argue that the present elementary school fails to adequately expose learners to the major epistemological methods. However, that would not eliminate the idea as part of the conception of the elementary school. It is possible that any given institution will fail to complete activities in accord with the elements of its conception and yet not be absolved of the responsibility to do so. In this regard the elementary school is no exception.

for specific kinds of investigation and understanding. The elementary school has the task of orienting the young to these six methods of knowing, to teach them how to match the best method (or combinations of methods) to the topic of focus. This gives the young child the background needed to begin to explore his world using all of the available knowledge that may relate to the subject area of interest to him.

Some examples that illustrate how the elementary school orients young children to the methods of knowing might help the reader to recognize the extent to which the school does and should expose learners to these tools of investigation used to process certain kinds of knowledge. In the first instance, appeal to authority, young children learn to accept the conclusions of experts who have spent years studying events or phenomena whose existence cannot be substantiated by any other means of justification or substantiation. Many of the conclusions about events and activities in history and anthropology make extensive use of the "appeal to authority" method of knowing. The use of intuition in the elementary school is evident when children are encouraged to make judgments or derive meanings or ideas without employing any known process of cogitation or reflective thinking. In these instances judgments are often derived as a result of minimal cues and of awareness of the similarity of the present phenomenon to other experiences. The majority of practical judgments on complex issues and of persons* contain a large intuitive element.

Formal logic as a method of knowing in the elementary school is employed extensively in arithmetic and science as a way of dealing with abstract relations between classes and things. This method of knowing enables a child to learn how to establish criteria by which, granting the correctness of the factual data employed, the worth or validity of arguments or reasoning may be judged. The use of formal logic is concerned with whether reasoning is correct, not with the psychological conditions that lead to correct or incorrect reasoning. In that sense, it is a normative rather than an empirical way of knowing. Many of the scientific experiences and experiments utilize formal logic as a way of knowing about certain things. Empiricism is a vital part of the elementary school's efforts to introduce children to the major ways of knowing. The use of this method of knowing enables children to discover particular facts of concrete relations in nature. Elementary schoolchildren make use of this method primarily in the science and social studies areas because some of the content in these areas can be more easily processed

* As one might have already observed, intuition as a method of knowing is a mainstay in most social studies programs.

through the use of empiricism. The field trip in science and social studies is an example of how the elementary school attempts to introduce young children to empiricism as a method of knowing. Empiricism helps children learn the value of experience as a source of knowledge and to learn that a great deal of what is known originated from the personal experience of people involved in different social functions.

As a method of knowing, pragmatism is employed to help elementary schoolchildren evaluate objects and events on the basis of their palpable effects. The use of pragmatism in the elementary school is approached primarily in the area of socialization. Since one of the concerns of the elementary school necessarily deals with the socialization (establishing guidelines for children's social behavior) of young learners, pragmatism is important because it helps children to learn to test the validity of certain concepts by their practical results. It is another way of relating to children the idea that the meaning to be attributed to a certain phenomenon is derived from its practical consequences. This approach to knowing occupies a strong place in the elementary school program today.

One other way of knowing employed by the elementary school is skepticism. Even though it is not used as much as it should be, skepticism is used to help children balance their way of thinking about their world. The use of either (singularly or combined) of the ways of knowing previously discussed tends to make young children think that they have been provided with a complete knowledge of the object or phenomenon under study. Since this is not the intent of any of the methods of knowing discussed earlier, skepticism is a way of knowing that helps children to question the validity of the completeness of a particular description of reality. Helping children to employ a systematic attitude of doubt to the results obtained from other ways of knowing is a critical step in orienting them to a broadly based pattern of knowing. The use of skepticism deals with this problem in the elementary school.

One of the roles of the elementary school is to orient children to the major ways of knowing about the world. Some of these ways of knowing are employed as major patterns for dealing with both the formal and informal curriculum programs. In order to do the job properly, the conception of the elementary school must allow for helping children to develop a healthy and wholesome respect for all of the major epistemological methods rather than a faith in the absolute validity of any one or two of them. The elementary school should enable young children

> to choose authorities carefully, subject . . . [their] intuition to other methods when possible, avoid fallacies in . . . [their] reasoning, recog-

nize the limitations of the scientific method, use pragmatic evidence with prudence, and maintain enough doubt without doubting all.[14]

This way of characterizing the orientation of children to the major ways of knowing is a central component in the conceptualization of the elementary school.

Basic Orientation to Ways of Learning

The elementary school attempts to introduce many approaches to learning to the children it serves. These approaches are not always taught directly to the children as content but are communicated as an integral part of the processes used by the teacher to present the curriculum program. Since we are not concerned here with curriculum and instruction per se, they can be thought of as supplying the environmental context in which different ways of learning are utilized. Even though a detailed discussion of learning as an intellectual activity would add to this section immeasurably, it would detract from our present concern of outlining and defining the conception of the elementary school. It would be profitable for anyone aspiring to be a curriculum development specialist, to explore the study of learning as it relates to teaching as discussed in many sources such as Hullfish and Smith,[15] Glaser and Resnick,[16] Gagne,[17] Travers,[18] and Ripple.[19] For our purposes, we concentrate on the general classes of ways of learning that are the operational part of elementary schools and, as such, serve to help determine how this institution should be conceptualized.

Since the whole point of instruction is to direct the learning of students, it is only natural that elementary schoolteachers turn to a systematic study of learning to gain understanding and to improve the results of the tasks performed. When a teacher is required to turn to psychology for a scientific understanding of learning, he is immediately faced with an array of conflicting data, experimental approaches, theories, and conclusions. Since the teacher has no systematic means of scientifically formulating decisions about the limitations, overlaps, and complementarity of present data on learning, it is difficult for him to provide a clearly stated operational definition of learning on which to base his instructional decisions. Even though the precise definition of learning is probably not possible when thought of in relation to the complexity of human thinking and information processing, it is helpful to establish some general ways of learning that offer promise in an instructional setting.

In general, changes in observed behavior that cannot be attributed to either instinct or maturation can be thought of as the products of learning. Learning becomes the intellectual construct that accounts for or explains certain changes in observed behavior* resulting from direct or indirect instruction. These changes in behavior (basic understanding) are the results of learners being exposed to a stimulus and responding to it. Because children are not passive units who can only be stirred to action when stimulated from without, the stimulus employed must have meaning if it is to effect learning in the desired directions. Therefore, a totally meaningless object, event, or sensation could not serve as a stimulus required to result in learning. A stimulus need not be precise or unambiguous to be capable of carrying the meaning required to initiate learning. In that sense, the term *learning* may be applicable to any process or procedure that renders potential stimuli meaningful, changes meaning, aids discrimination with respect to possible meaning, and provides for transfer of meaning.

The elementary school orients children to ways of learning by the reorganization or reconstruction of a meaning pattern. This idea is taken from Dewey who stated that "It is that reconstruction or reorganization of experience which adds to meaning of experience, and which increases ability to direct the course of subsequent experience"[20] that characterizes the nature and intent of instruction. Instructional processes reorganize meanings and are directed by teachers who control the situational context of implementation and presentation. However, the reorganized meanings are something that happens to the learner even though the learner is not the agent controlling the reorganization of meaning. When the environment permits and encourages students to create and test meaning reflectively, the conditions for the reconstruction of experience are present. This latter characterization of learning contrasts with the imposed or induced reorganization of experience suggested earlier because the learner becomes the controlling and directing agent for such reconstruction. Emphasis on open or informal educational approaches attempt to treat learning as reconstruction. However, most programs (including those that are open or informal) combine reorganization and reconstruction of meaning as the basis for changing or providing meaning that defines learning. The following list shows the specific ways of learning that operationalize some of the ideas expressed previously.

* Observed behavior here refers to basic understandings ("meanings" rather than "kinds of behavior") discussed in more detail in a later chapter.

1. *Perception.* A psychological function that (by means of the sense organs) enables the organism to receive and process information on the state of, and alterations in, the environment.
2. *Discrimination.* The process of selecting the characteristics of stimulus situation that serve as guidelines for purposive behavior.
3. *Association.* A functional relationship between psychological phenomena established in the course of individual experience and of such a nature that the presence of one tends to evoke the other; or the establishment of such a relationship; or the process whereby the relationship is established.
4. *Memory.* The ability of an organism to store information from earlier learning processes (experience; retention) and reproduce that information in answer to specific stimuli.
5. *Problem Solving and Thinking.* The process required to reach a desired goal starting from a set of initial (cognitive) conditions. By introspection, or by the observation of behavior in solving problems, the teacher attempts to obtain information about thinking processes being used to guide activity.
6. *Language As a System.* An attempt to describe the multilevel canon of rules (grammar) that linguistic products must obey (synchronic aspects), to understand sequential regularities (syntagmatic relations) and relations or correspondences (paradigmatic relations) for linguistic units or various levels: phonemics, graphemes, significant elemental units (morphemes, words), phrase structure, sentences, and so on.
7. *Behavior Modification (Operant Conditioning).* The form of learning wherein the organism becomes progressively more likely to respond in a given situation with that response that, in previous similar situations, has brought about a rewarding or satisfying state of affairs; or wherein a stimulus having evoked a response that brings into view a rewarding stimulus or that prevents or removes an obnoxious stimulus, thereafter is more likely to evoke that response.

The elementary school has the responsibility of orienting its children to some of the primary ways of learning that are employed to process different kinds of knowledge. Introducing children to systematic and controlled perception is an important activity of the elementary school. As a way of learning, perception involves the use of input of information from the environment. Since the individual child has only a limited capacity for processing and utilizing information from the environment it is critical for him to learn ways to economically and accurately sort out relevant material. This is necessary because of the infinite nature of the available information from the environment and the finite ability of the sense organs to process it. Although the sense organs tend to receive only a limited sample of information from the environment, it is still very necessary to reduce the quantity and complexity of that information so that it can be utilized in a meaningful way. The problem is to make the senses more selective in a way that is predictable within probable limits. In this way, a child's pattern of perception determines the extent to which he can develop a working relationship with the environment. When the elementary school attempts to orient children to perception as a way of learning, it tries to deal with the information-handling aspects of perception. These are: (1) refining the selective nature of the intake process, (2) denoting ways to compress information, and (3) structuring information for achieving meaningful predictable perception. The use of sets in arithmetic and the focusing of attention on critical parts in other subjects are just two of the ways in which elementary schools presently orient children to perception as a way of learning.

Discrimination is a way of learning that teaches children to make fine distinctions between various cues that may be present. This is an especially difficult task when two cues are very similar. Different tasks vary greatly in terms of the demands placed on the learner to make perceptual discriminations and in terms of the demands placed on the learner to associate responses with readily identifiable stimuli. These two approaches to the use of discrimination as a way of learning are employed to a varying degree in many learning tasks in the elementary school.

The use of discrimination learning has had its greatest impact in the elementary school as a means of helping children acquire concepts. Whether they are concepts associated with recognizing and understanding symbols (p, d, b, g, l, ll, and so on), sounds (ph, sh, ch, st, and so on) or objects (chair, table, desk, box, and so on) children are learning to match—on the basis of specific characteristics—a given symbol with its name, a given sound with its symbol, and a given object with the specific name assigned to it. The appropriate application of discrimination as a way of learning facilitates the development of concepts.*

Association as a way of learning has been central to guiding the pattern of instruction in the elementary school for a long time. In its early history, in the elementary school, association was used to teach

---

* The process of concept formation is discussed in greater detail in Chapter 5.

children how to read by having them associate the sight of the word with the sound a sufficient number of times to establish the connections. The use of association in that manner still survives and is practiced in many elementary schools even today. The use of association as a learning pattern makes use of comparison, contrast, and past experiences of learners to establish an idea. The elementary school orients children to association as a way of learning because this pattern of learning is so critical to children's requirements to effectively process information used to achieve instructional goals outlined for this level.

Memory, as a way of learning, also has a long history in the elementary school. Although memory is no longer the primary way of learning, it still plays a vital role. Memory is important because it is necessary for young children to retain certain kinds of information that have to be employed and deployed when they are attempting to learn new content. Almost all of the work-study or basic study skills are and probably should be subjected to memory as a way of learning them because of their critical nature in affecting later learning patterns. Children attending elementary schools should memorize, or at least have a sound working knowledge of, skills (such as dictionary, library, reference, ability to read graphs and tables, and how to locate information on specific topics) that are required to process information needed to foster a certain level of understanding. Memory as a way of learning can help young children to acquire these skills that become the foundational tools for all learning in school.

Problem solving and thinking as a way of learning in the elementary school is utilized when there is a need to help children learn how to find solutions to perceived problems. As a way of learning, it is used to deal with certain kinds of problems in arithmetic, science, and the social studies. The use of problem solving helps young children to systematically collect and organize data to reach a desirable conclusion about the nature of the object being studied. The elementary school should help children utilize problem solving and thinking as a way of learning because certain phenomena in real life cannot be understood without such an approach. It is the job of the elementary school to see that the void in young children's learning repertoire is filled adequately.

When language is viewed as a system, it becomes a way of learning because it provides young learners with a pattern for analyzing information and content more precisely. Language as a system is widely used in reading programs at the elementary level because it helps many children learn how to process content with greater understanding. This might be called improving reading comprehension in some quarters or content analysis in others. In either case, language as a system is a valuable learning approach in the elementary school because it helps children to focus more attentively on the medium of communication. When the elementary school fulfills this role, it plays a critical role in the future learning possibilities of all the children that it serves.

Behavior modification (operant conditioning) as a way of learning is new to the elementary school but it has received more of the spotlight in recent years as a result of highly publicized federally funded projects in this area. Although many educators might believe that this approach to learning is much too mechanistic to be used with children extensively, behavior modification is still a pattern of learning from which young children can derive considerable profit as a result of exposure. The idea that rewards can influence the responses of an organism or person is a valuable outcome to be obtained as a result of utilizing behavior modification as a way of learning. Young children can learn how to deal with certain phenomena associated with the behavior of organisms, people, or animals when they have been properly exposed to the use of behavior modification as a technique. The elementary school is expected to orient children to ways of modifying their behavior as a way of learning about certain aspects of their world.

Previously, we have discussed in some detail some of the ways of learning that are the responsibility of the elementary school and as such are part of the school's conceptualization. The conceptualization of the elementary school includes orienting children to some of the major ways of learning. In this sense, ways of learning are central to defining the concept of the elementary school.

Basic Orientation to General Education

The elementary school is expected to orient young children to a general education that becomes the foundation for pursuing more specialized education at later stages of development. General education is a vital component of the conceptualization of the elementary school because it is the central focus of content at that level. The definition of general education is suggestive of why it is the central concern of the elementary school. In the main, "General education is the term that has come to be accepted for those phases of nonspecialized and nonvocational learning which should be the *common experience* of all educated men and women."[21] From this definition it can be readily discerned why the elementary school has a general education function.

Since the content at the elementary school level integrates the knowledge produced in the various disciplines, it is nonspecialized in character and built around basic problem themes or major social functions characterizing our society. Further, this content is not directed at any specific vocation as an end apart from general social function. And lastly, the content of the elementary school is meant to be taught to all of our young people as the basic knowledge required if one is to perform a variety of social functions in our society. It follows then that the elementary school has a major responsibility for providing general education to young children.

Given the maturity of the learners attending and the universal quality of the elementary school, it is easily understood why general education is the major focus at this level. The elementary school is expected to prepare young children for a specialized educational experience at higher levels, to develop an appreciation for the different ways of organizing knowledge, and to make choices concerning preferences for different knowledge areas. General education is the central means for achieving these goals at the elementary school level. Therefore, one of the major concerns of the elementary school is to orient young children to general education. This task becomes a part of any conceptualization of the elementary school.

Basic Orientation to Social Functions, Morality, and Socialization

In trying to conceptualize the elementary school, it is possible to lump together concerns with social functions, morality, and socialization because they are so interrelated as central ideas. The first two concerns are covered in the content areas intellectually and in the social system of the school operationally. The third concern, socialization, is covered in the way the school is operated and organized in terms of employment and enforcement of rules, procedures, and standards of behavior. The first two concerns (social functions and morality) can be interjected into the latter one (socialization) by suggesting areas of life to be utilized and rules of conduct to be practiced in school activity.

The elementary school orients children to the major social functions that characterize our society. These social functions include providing for basic human needs (food, shelter, clothing, and so on), studying the patterns of governing at different levels, understanding economic and delivery systems, and describing the roles of major institutions. In short, the study of social functions at the elementary school level is really the study of basic human activity required to maintain the society.

When the elementary school focuses on morality guiding social functions, it deals with the basic values that define our system of government and formal political activity. This concern focuses on the formal rules and procedures of our democratic society and the behavior expected of individuals. Children are taught the values that are expected and consistent with the democratic creed and constitutional laws. The elementary school is responsible for communicating the morality that should guide all social functions of young learners.

The elementary school's role in providing a basic orientation to socialization in groups is the result of how the school is organized and operated. In this role the school formulates, employs, and enforces rules, procedures, and standards that perpetuate the kind of social pattern that tends to socialize children a certain way. Through this process the elementary school provides the normative structure that creates the socialization environment determining the behavior of most of its children. The pattern of socialization that is present in an elementary school determines how children behave, what they believe, and the acceptance and mastery of technology required in the future. In this sense the socialization pattern that exists in a school operationalizes the standards (morality) of behavior expected, and introduces children to critical human activities (social functions) that must be performed if the society is to develop, prosper, and be maintained to further the general welfare of all members in the society.

Summary

The elementary school can be thought of as a social institution concerned with the basic orientation of young people to ways of knowing, ways of learning, general education, the social functions of society, the morality guiding our social functions, and the acceptable socialization experiences. This school is both rational and social in its orientation. As a rational institution it is expected to provide the child with a foundation for later learning and achieving success in some human activity. As a social institution, the elementary school is expected to expose children to a positive emotional, and meaningful socialization, experience. In conclusion, the elementary school is the social institution charged with the responsibility of beginning the formal process of preparing youth for meaningful and productive integration into the society. To the extent that it does this job well, it fulfills its role and matches its conceptualization as a social institution.

References

1. John I. Goodlad, "The Child and His School in Transition," *The National Elementary Principal,* 52:28–29 (Jan. 1973).
2. Ellwood P. Cubberley, *Public Education in the United States* (Boston: Houghton, 1934), p. 17.
3. Ibid., p. 18.
4. Ibid., p. 19.
5. Ibid., p. 27.
6. Ibid., p. 29.
7. Ibid., p. 31.
8. Henry J. Otto, *Elementary School Organization and Administration,* 3rd ed. (New York: Appleton, 1954), p. 10.
9. Ibid.
10. Cubberley, op. cit., pp. 131–132.
11. Otto, op. cit., pp. 11–12.
12. Oscar T. Jarvis and Lutian R. Wootton, *The Transitional Elementary School and Its Curriculum* (Dubuque, Iowa: Brown, 1966), p. 12.
13. Jed Arthur Cooper, "Why the Monopoly in Epistemology???" *Phi Delta Kappan,* 48:406 (April 1967).
14. Ibid.
15. H. Gordon Hullfish and Phillip G. Smith, *Reflective Thinking: The Method of Education* (New York: Dodd, 1961).
16. Robert Glaser and Lauren B. Resnick, "Instructional Psychology," in *Annual Review of Psychology,* edited by Paul H. Mussen and Mark R. Rosenzweig (Palo Alto, Cal.: Annual Review, Inc., 1972).
17. R. M. Gagne, "The Acquisition of Knowledge," *Psychological Review,* 69:355–365 (1962).
18. Robert M. W. Travers, *Essentials of Learning: An Overview for Students of Education* (New York: Macmillan, 1967).

19. Richard E. Ripple, ed., *Learning and Human Abilities: Educational Psychology* (New York: Harper, 1964).
20. John Dewey, *Democracy and Education* (New York: Macmillan, 1916), pp. 89–90.
21. *Higher Education for American Democracy: The Report of the President's Commission on Higher Education, Vol. I: Establishing Goals* (Washington, D.C.: and New York: Harper, 1947), p. 49.

Perspectives of Curriculum, Instruction, and Organization

Any discussion of curriculum and instruction in the elementary school must necessarily be prefaced by a brief review of the meaning of these terms, particularly as they are used in this chapter. The problems of the definition and meaning of these terms are very real. For example, the meanings and definitions of the term *curriculum* are various. To some it is a synonym for a written course of study or content outline in a specific subject such as arithmetic. Others use it interchangeably with educational program or instructional program. Still another group of educators assign a broader definition to mean all the experiences that children have under the supervision of the school. In his recent book on instructional theory, Hosford reports on his research of the vocabulary problem confronting education as it relates to multimeanings assigned to the term *curriculum* and notes how educational writers have redefined and used the term *curriculum* since the early 1950s. Hosford's search of the writings of prominent curriculum specialists revealed a wide range of definitions and meanings that he classified into four major groups.

Group I, as classified by Hosford[1] included all those definitions in which curriculum was viewed as everything that *happens* in school.[2]

Beauchamp's definition of curriculum as all of the experiences of children under the jurisdiction of the school exemplifies Group I.

The definitions that comprised Group II were slightly more restrictive in confining the term to mean everything *offered* by the school. Typical of this group is the definition by Saylor: "Curriculum encompasses all the learning experiences provided by the school."[3] In differentiating between Groups I and II, Hosford notes that many things that happen in school are not necessarily caused by the school.

The third set of definitions (Group III)—tabbed by Hosford as "The Planned What and How Group"—is best represented in the definition by Phenix, "Curriculum is the organized pattern of the school's educational program and describes the subject matter of instruction, the method of instruction and the order of instruction—the what, how and when."[4]

As defined by Mauritz Johnson, Jr., "Curriculum is a structured series of intended learning outcomes. Curriculum prescribes the means."[5] Johnson's definition is typical of Group IV, which Hosford calls "The Planned What Group" and excludes both instruction and teaching from the definition and meaning of curriculum.

Miel and Lewis[6] have also examined various conceptions of curriculum, its definitions and meanings, and offer their classification and clarification of different concepts of curriculum.

These two classifications of curriculum concepts provide the background for understanding this concept. The meaning of the term *curriculum* as used in this text is of the variety found in Hosford's Group IV, "The Planned What" and in Miel's and Lewis's classification of "curriculum as something intended." The definition is as follows:

> The curriculum is a plan of the intended learning outcomes organized in some fashion with implicit suggestions and directions for the learning opportunities to comprise the instructional program.

Some comments on this definition are in order to give it clarity and precision. First, the curriculum as defined is the product of a curriculum development system. It is a combination of the contributions of many different audiences, including teachers, parents, administrators, curriculum specialists, students, and other laymen and groups who have an interest and stake in the school's curriculum and are properly involved in the process of curriculum development.

This definition separates and differentiates curriculum from instruction and teaching. Instruction (or the instructional program), of which teaching is an important variable, becomes, in fact, one of the major means for implementing the curriculum. There are other means,

Table 4.1

A Classification of Concepts of the Curriculum[6]

Curriculum as Something Intended			Curriculum as Something Actualized		
Course of study	Intended learning outcomes	Intended opportunities for engagement	Learning opportunities provided	Learner's actual engagements	Learner's actual experiences
Traditional, persisting meaning					
Phenix 1958[7]	Johnson 1969[8]	Miel 1968[9]	Saylor & Alexander 1966[10]	Mackenzie 1964[11]	Caswell & Campbell 1935[12]
					Many others current

Source: From *Supervision for Improved Instruction: New Challenges, New Responses* by Arthur J. Lewis and Alice Miel © 1972 by Wadsworth Publishing Company, Inc., Belmont, California 94002. Reprinted by permission of the publisher.

for the total educational environment of the school should certainly serve to facilitate the implementation of the curriculum. Included among these other means are the supporting instructional materials and services—what Professor Norman Dodl refers to as the facilities, resources, hardware, and software of the instructional delivery system. (A fuller treatment of instructional support systems is provided in Chapters 9 and 10.)

In addition to the supporting instructional resources, both the social arrangements—what Bruce Joyce[13] refers to as the social system of the school—and the administrative arrangement, how the school is organized for instruction—are important means in facilitating the implementation of the curriculum. Each of these means is discussed later in this chapter.

Relating Curriculum to Instruction

As mentioned previously the meaning of curriculum separates and differentiates it from instruction. Yet it has major implications for instruction and for the instructional program. As Johnson states, it (the curriculum) "prescribes (or at least anticipates) the results of instruction."[14] More than that, the curriculum is a major source of input in fashioning the instructional program. Careful analysis of any single "intended learning outcome" can provide a significant base of information in making subsequent instructional and teaching decisions such as the selection of teachable content samples, instructional procedures, teaching methods, and learning activities. Moreover, the curriculum, so defined, becomes in itself a starting point, indeed a major component, in any evaluation scheme to assess whether or not one has been successful in implementing the curriculum.

One other element in our definition of curriculum merits further discussion. Recalling the definition, the reader will note that the curriculum as a plan of the intended learning outcomes requires that these outcomes be organized in some fashion. Both words *plan* and *organize* are important to this concept of curriculum. Certainly, no one would argue for a planless or disorganized curriculum even though visiting many schools makes one wonder if the lack of planning and organization in the determination of the curriculum is not reflected in a thread of disorganization apparent in the ongoing instructional program and teaching effort.

Equally important connotations of these two words indicate that choices must be made in the determination of the curriculum. Some learning outcomes—those not chosen, those not intended—can be excluded. Planning and organizing the intended learning outcomes that comprise the curriculum is a process of making choices. Certain intended learning outcomes of high priority within the functions and mission of the school can be included; others of questionable import and less relevant to the task of the school can be intentionally excluded. In recent years we have witnessed a rapidly expanding curriculum—without an apparent directive or focus—growing by an unmonitored additive process. The curriculum is more than a series of random learning outcomes; it is planned and organized, and the selected outcomes are by intent.

The Organization of Intended Outcomes

One question remains with respect to the definition of curriculum under discussion. How might the intended learning outcomes be organized? The only honest and direct response to this question is that there are several possible ways. The method chosen by a particular school or school district will necessarily reflect the dominant educational philosophy and views of teaching and learning of those who participate in the organization of the curriculum. Yet, as mentioned, there are several possible ways that could be followed, either separately or in combination with others. The organization of intended learning outcomes could be done according to:

1. The importance or the priority assigned. Conceivably some learning outcomes, for example, those in the area of skill development, might be given a higher priority than specific outcomes in the learner's production of creative products.
2. Established subject areas. According to this method, selected learning outcomes would be assigned to science, for example, and accomplished through the instructional program in that area.
3. Grade level. In this manner specific outcomes would be assigned as tasks to be accomplished by the end of grade 1, grade 2, and so on.
4. Developmental stages of learners. Through this approach selected outcomes to be achieved would be organized in accordance with the levels of development indicated in younger children, older children, and young adults.
5. The inherent difficulty or complexity or any obvious sequence in those tasks implied in the intended learning outcomes.
6. The manner in which they might be most effectively learned. Several subpossibilities are present here.
   A. Outcomes most effectively learned individually, in small group settings, in large group settings; in age-level groups, in interage groupings.
   B. Outcomes most effectively learned through direct and formal instruction, through the educative force of the school's social system, through modeling behavior, through play

activity, through extra class, or all-school learning projects.
C. Outcomes most effectively learned through programmed techniques, computer assisted instruction, and so on.

It is not possible, and probably not desirable, to predetermine the one way or combination of ways that all elementary schools should structure or organize the learning outcomes. It would be foolish even to try. Such responsibility rests with those people who are involved in the process of selecting the intended learning outcomes that comprise curriculum for a particular school or school system. Needless to say, it is also the responsibility of curriculum and instructional leadership to make clear the several possible ways of organizing the intended learning outcomes and to make certain that those involved are well informed with respect to:

1. Approaches that have met with success in other school situations.
2. Latest findings on the nature of learning, effective learning activities, teaching strategies, and educational resources.
3. Changing views and ideas about curriculum, its organization, and implementation.

Yes, there is the very real possibility that in one setting the intended learning outcomes will be organized in accordance with specific grade levels, with rigidly specified tasks and standards established at each grade level, and that a highly prescripted instructional program with commonly used content and approaches, traditional and sterile teaching performance will result.

But it is also possible that in another situation a less rigid organization will be devised, and a less prescriptive instructional program fashioned in which individualized learning styles of children and teaching styles of teachers are recognized and respected.

The Instructional Program

The foregoing discussion has focused on a definition of curriculum with commentary on the meanings and implications of such a definition. It is equally important to give some consideration to the concept of the instructional program and to teaching, especially as it relates to instruction*

As stated earlier in this chapter, instruction (the instructional program) is a major means for implementing the curriculum. Before stating our definition of instruction, it should be made clear that the author has intentionally used the terms *instruction* and *instructional program* interchangeably. Every conceivable source in the professional literature of education as well as standard and educational dictionaries refer to instruction as a process. If instruction is a process, then all that is a part of that process might properly be referred to as an instructional program. The reader should note, however, that this serves only to explain the synonymous use of these terms but does not define it. We offer this definition of instruction:

> Instruction consists of all the decisions and activities for implementing the curriculum, including teaching and guidance, which are employed intentionally to influence the learner toward some goal or desired learning outcome.

In a fashion similar to the discussion of curriculum, some commentary on this definition is essential to its meaning. As defined here, instruction is both formal and informal. It embraces an array of decisions on what, how, and when to teach, as well as the organization of learning activities and teaching situations that comprise the instructional program. There is also an element of management to instruction simply because instruction is an organized effort, as any teacher or instructor well knows. It must be obvious in this definition that all teaching is a part of instruction—and probably the major and most significant part. However, instruction is more than teaching because it involves decisions and activities that may take place in the absence of learners and does not necessarily involve personal interaction with learners. For example, learners working at computer stations may benefit from instruction without any personal interaction with a teacher. Similarly, the teacher who decides on the sequence to follow during the year that will cover the required units in social studies is involved in instruction, but is not teaching.

---

* Eugene E. Haddan, *Evolving Instruction* (New York: Macmillan, 1970).

Combining Notions About Curriculum and Instruction

The content of Chapter 4 has thus far served primarily to define curriculum and instruction and to interpret and discuss these definitions as they are used in this text. All of this was prefatory to a more specific consideration of curriculum and instruction in the elementary school. To give some perspective to the foregoing discussion curriculum and instruction must at this point be put into a broader context to pave the way for the remainder of the chapter. One way of doing this is to employ a flow chart model that depicts and relates the concepts of curriculum and instruction.

In the flow chart (Figure 4.1) the instructional system for implementing the curriculum consists of three major means: (1) the more formal instructional program, (2) the instructional support and delivery system, and (3) the organized educative force of the school's total environment. Before turning to a discussion of the intended learning outcomes that make up the elementary school curriculum and examining all the elements of the instructional program in the elementary school, some comment on the educative force of the school's social system and the overall administrative organization of the elementary school is pertinent. As noted earlier, the instructional support and delivery system is treated in detail in Chapters 9 and 10. The third means, the organized educative force of the school's total environment, requires further explanation before proceeding further.

Elementary school pupils experience more than the transmission of subject matter, which can be defined as the methods and materials of teaching and learning that make up the more formalized instructional program of the classroom. They experience a wide range and variety of elements that are a part of the total environment of the school. In addition to their teacher and classmates they encounter and interact with other people in different roles and with different responsibilities. A janitor helps them to set up some stage scenery or yells at them to get out from under foot. A cafeteria worker shoves food at them or brings some special treats to the classroom for some child's birthday. From such experiences the children learn specific behaviors associated with different roles and how people discharge their assigned responsibilities.

Learners enter into relationships with teachers and other learners, and also experience the relationships between and among others.

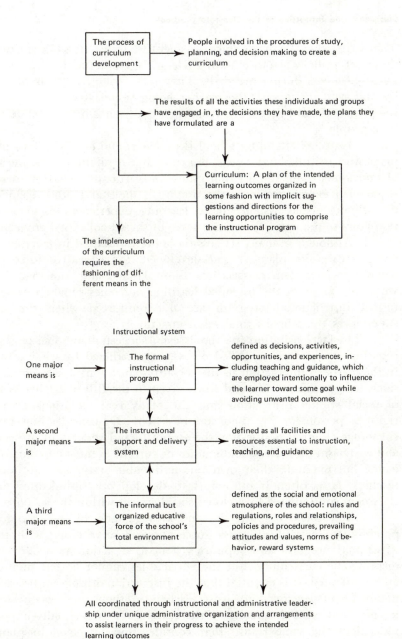

The process of curriculum development → People involved in the procedures of study, planning, and decision making to create a curriculum

The results of all the activities these individuals and groups have engaged in, the decisions they have made, the plans they have formulated are a

Curriculum: A plan of the intended learning outcomes organized in some fashion with implicit suggestions and directions for the learning opportunities to comprise the instructional program

The implementation of the curriculum requires the fashioning of different means in the

Instructional system

One major means is → The formal instructional program → defined as decisions, activities, opportunities, and experiences, including teaching and guidance, which are employed intentionally to influence the learner toward some goal while avoiding unwanted outcomes

A second major means is → The instructional support and delivery system → defined as all facilities and resources essential to instruction, teaching, and guidance

A third major means is → The informal but organized educative force of the school's total environment → defined as the social and emotional atmosphere of the school: rules and regulations, roles and relationships, policies and procedures, prevailing attitudes and values, norms of behavior, reward systems

All coordinated through instructional and administrative leadership under unique administrative organization and arrangements to assist learners in their progress to achieve the intended learning outcomes

Figure 4.1
The Instructional System for Implementing the Elementary School Curriculum.

103

They experience Tommy's embarrassment when his art work is ridiculed; they feel pride when the sixth-grade girls are recognized for helping kindergarteners during fire drill. They sense competition among teachers and sympathize with the teacher being yelled at by a parent or by the principal. And they learn from such experience how to relate to and treat people.

Learners attending school experience, and get caught up in, the prevailing attitudes and values, the rules and regulations, and the means of punishment and reward that guide and structure behavior in school. From such experience in interaction with these and other elements of the school's social system, many learning experiences occur and are testimony to the potent educative force of the school's total environment.

Although in many schools the more formalized instructional program is carefully planned and developed, the educative force of the school's social system materializes as unplanned and unmanaged. Consequently, many of the intended learning outcomes sought through the formal instructional program are not reinforced when the learner experiences the school's total environment.

In fact, visitation in schools even suggests that some of the outcomes of instruction are stifled or even contradicted by what transpires in the learner's interaction in the social organization of the school. Consider, for example, the formal study given to the Bill of Rights as a part of social studies instruction and the many real violations of pupil's rights as persons during their stay in schools. Or consider how teachers encourage children to question the authority and veracity of information and writers in their classroom studies of current events and controversial issues, but maintain their own unquestionable status and authority as teachers. How often is our effort to develop open-mindedness in the classroom contradicted by a closed social system within the school?

The social organization and arrangements of the school are a potentially powerful educative force and can serve along with the instructional program and support system as a major means for implementing the curriculum. But the curriculum cannot be left unattended and unplanned. It is essential that the instructional program be carefully planned and developed to assist learners in their progress toward the learning outcomes that make up the curriculum. It is equally important, to achieve the same result, that consideration be given to planning, fashioning, and controlling the nature and ingredients of the school's social system.

Justification of Elementary School Organization

The primary purpose of elementary school organization is to facilitate the delivery of foundational educational services and attitudes efficiently and effectively under the basic guidelines of humanistic and democratic values. Those foundational educational services and attitudes include the mastering of basic work study skills to process information in a meaningful context, being made acquainted with the general knowledge needed to interpret and understand basic social functions, helping children to function independently and in groups, providing experiences for learning to solve problems, learning how to use and cope with institutional life, and learning how to learn and values associated with learning. Without organization, the elementary school could not facilitate the delivery of the educational services outlined previously or indicate to the people served the degree to which it has fulfilled its purposes as an institution. In a real sense, the organization of the elementary school determines the extent to which it can fulfill its purposes (preparation of youth for meaningful and useful participation) as a vital institution in society.

Operationally, the specific purpose of elementary school organizations is to facilitate the learning of pupils through the pattern employed to implement the instructional program. The instructional program necessarily includes the staff, the pupils, the parents, the administration, the facilities, the curriculum, the instructional materials and resources, and the environmental (including social and emotional) setting of the school. The organization of the elementary school can be described and discussed in terms of the specific parts that comprise the instructional program. For our purposes here this would not be an acceptable approach because we are interested in the operation of the elementary school as a whole. In order to set the stage for our discussion of elementary school organization in terms of implementing the instructional program, we briefly discuss the elementary school as an organization.

The Elementary School
as an Organization[15]

Three principal elements comprise the organization of the elementary school: organizational participants, organizational goals, and organizational roles. One way to describe the elementary school's organization would be to describe in some detail the people who comprise it. Even though most of the users of the elementary school can be enumerated, it would be difficult to outline specifically the motivations of the participants, identify goals that are jointly pursued, and explain the nature of the types of interactions that characterize the participant's activity. However, it is feasible to describe the needs, resources, experiences, and personalities of those who have key roles in the instructional program.

The organizational goals of the elementary school are considered in order to formulate a description of the goals that are being pursued. This aspect of elementary school organization can be viewed in relation to the comments indicated by Cyert and MacCrimmon when they assert:

> In general, there is not a single goal but a hierarchy or interacting goals in which a particular goal may serve as an end for a lower-level goal but as a means for a higher-level goal. The goal structure itself is not sufficient to describe the organization because it indicates neither the compatibility of the organizational goals with those of the individual participants nor the operating structure by which the organization tries to achieve its goals.[16]

It is apparent that the use of organizational goals to describe the organization of the elementary school is necessary but not sufficient to provide a complete picture.

When we consider the third element employed to provide a description of elementary school organization, we are concerned with the structure of roles governing the interaction of participants and the mode of behavior required to achieve the goals of the organization. The role structure is necessarily related to the "structure of programs and constraints specifying the activities necessary at each part of the organization to achieve goals."[17] The roles that are occupied by the participants in the elementary school are shaped by the programs and constraints of the instructional experience it is expected to implement. There must be a stable element in the role structure of the elementary school if it is to withstand the constant turnover of participants. At this point one should be cautioned by the observations of Cyert and MacCrimmon when they conclude that:

> The role structure alone does not necessarily indicate which goals are being pursued, nor the future directions in which the organization is likely to move. In addition it is an inadequate description of the over-all actual behavior of the organization when particular individuals occupy the roles.[18]

Even though the role structure of the elementary school gives much insight into the patterns operating when the instructional program is implemented, it does not detail the full story in terms of describing and defining the school as an organization.

The three elements—participants, goals, and roles—that can be used to describe certain facets of organizational behavior in the elementary school are limited because, singularly, they do not reveal the interactions among them that provide an accurate account of the actual operational behavior occurring in schools. These are the interactions that comprise the implemented instructional program. In this sense, any attempt to describe elementary school organization must include a consideration of these elements and the ways in which they interact.

Even though the three elements provide a basic description of organization, a fourth element is required to understand the major determinant of organizational behavior in the school. This fourth element is the environment of the elementary school organization. It includes the social, cultural, political, legal, economic, and technological influences on the elementary school. Before a complete description of the organizational behavior in the school can be adequately presented, attention must be focused on both the organizational elements and the relevant parts of the environment.[19] Even though we do not provide here a complete description of the organizational behavior characterizing the elementary school, it is important that the reader have a broadly based view of the dimensions of the organization as a foundation for understanding the factors affecting the implementation of the instructional program.

Elementary School Organization
and the Instructional Program

Schools, especially those at the elementary level, are expected to serve functions that are explicitly and implicitly specified by the people served. In order to serve such specific functions, elementary schools must be organized to implement the implied instructional program. Whatever the organizational schema selected by a given elementary school, the organizational pattern has to perform two distinct functions: (1) it must classify pupils and move them hierarchically from a given entry level to a given exit level, and (2) it must assign all pupils to available staff. In the first instance the *vertical* organization serves the function whereas a horizontal organization serves the second function. According to Goodlad and Rehage the vertical and horizontal organization of the elementary school have been misunderstood and misrepresented in the literature. In support of their conclusions, these authors offered the following comments:

> Confusion arises from a failure to differentiate between vertical and horizontal aspects of school organization. Grading, multigrading, and nongrading are the vertical organization plans from which to choose. The horizontal pattern may be determined by grouping children homogeneously or heterogeneously, by organizing the curriculum so as to emphasize the separateness of subjects or the interrelationships among them, by having self-contained or departmentalized classrooms, or by using any one of the many possible patterns of interclass grouping.[20]

The ideas expressed by Goodlad and Rehage that apply directly to organization form the basis for outlining the particulars of organizational behavior at this school level.

The Vertical Organization
of the Elementary School

The graded school[21] represents a long-standing and generally accepted way of organizing the elementary school to facilitate the vertical progression of pupils. Figure 4.2 shows the graded structure of

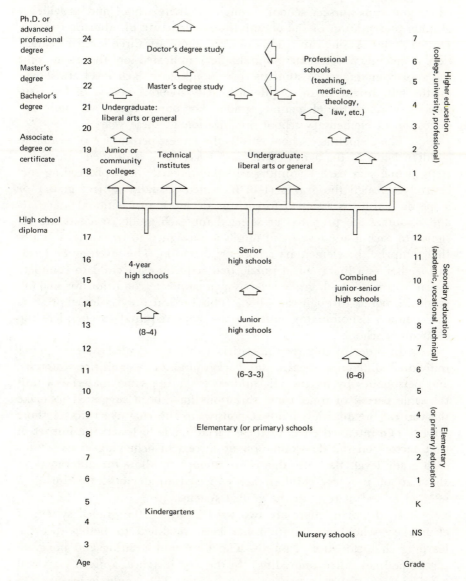

Figure 4.2

The Structure of Education in the United States. [Kenneth A. Simon and W. Vance Grant, *Digest of Educational Statistics,* 1972 ed., National Center for Educational Statistics (Washington, D.C.: U.S. Government Printing Office, 1973), p. 4.]

education from nursery school through graduate school and provides a graphic presentation of the organizational structure of education in the United States. As one can readily observe, there are three levels of education (elementary, secondary, and higher) indicated on the right, and the approximate ages of students corresponding to each level are shown on the left. In the main, pupils ordinarily spend a period of from six to eight years in the elementary grades. For our purposes we limit our discussion of elementary school organization to these years.

The elementary school enrolls the largest percentage of available children between the ages of five* and twelve and is divided into seven steps of one year each beginning with kindergarten and proceeding successively through the grades (1–6) indicated. Usually subject matter of a specific nature is assigned to each grade level; instructional materials and resources are prepared or selected for each grade; teachers are assigned to each grade level; and pupils are assigned to the various grades that comprise the elementary school organization. The seven grade levels fit together as a hierarchical puzzle that requires each child to complete a year of work at each grade level as a prerequisite condition for making vertical progress through the school. This vertical progression represents the common denominator equating the steps required to complete the elementary school.

In order to counter the criticism that the graded system ignores individual differences because of background, style, abilities, interests, and personality by having all children cover the same material within the same period of time, some variations have been suggested to make the vertical organization more responsive to the characteristics of those served. The intended effect of these variations is to lessen the impact of time factors on the determination of success in achieving goals set for each grade level. Basically this is an attempt to allow for differences in the rate of progress children are expected to demonstrate during a selected period of time in the graded system.

In the main there are two ways in which the graded system of elementary school organization has been modified to better suit the learning characteristics of pupils. These are multigrading and nongrading (sometimes called ungrading). In the first instance, a given class will contain members from two or more grades. The grade levels are not eliminated but pupils are permitted and encouraged to work at several grade levels at once, correlated with the pupil's demonstrated progress in each subject matter area. For example, a child might be working at

---

* Nursery schools in general have been totally accepted as part of the elementary school organization. However, the trend seems to be in that direction.

the fifth-grade level in arithmetic, the fourth-grade level in science, and the sixth-grade level in reading. Under multigrading, subject matter can be pursued at different grade levels by different children within the same classroom. In this way each child is allowed to vary his rate of progress across different subject matter areas in accordance with his ability and desire to handle them. Progress in this sense is determined more by the individual child than by the artifacts of the school's organization.

The second system, nongrading, involves removing grade level designations from some or all classes in a school. More precisely, the nongraded (or ungraded) elementary school is:

> A school which has no grade designations or grade level standards. In such a school pupils are reclassified frequently according to individual progress. Aspects of subject matter taught are designed for the various abilities of individual pupils. Frequently, provision is made for independent study and research by pupils as well as for permissive self-selection of problems and materials. Achievement standards vary with the rate of learning for different pupils and advancement can occur at any time.[22]

The most frequent pattern of nongraded organization in the elementary school is the nongraded primary unit and the nongraded intermediate unit. In the first instance grade labels are removed from kindergarten and the first three grades. In the second, the grade labels are removed from grades four, five, and six. The intent of nongrading—to facilitate curricular psychological and instructional strategies that provide for individual differences in a given class—heavily influences the teaching decisions made within the context of the primary and intermediate pattern of the nongraded elementary school.

The nongraded approach to elementary school organization is an attempt to mitigate against some of the negative effects of vertical (graded) pattern of organization at this level. Part of the rationale for dealing with this problem is suggested by the characteristics that manifest themselves in the graded structures of elementary school organization. The comments of Goodlad and Rehage on this point are revealing:

> In *pure* grading, the content of the instructional program and its sequential arrangement are determined by assignment of subject matter to various grade levels, by designation of instructional materials suitable for particular grade levels, and by promotion of pupils upon satisfactory completion of the work specified for each grade level.[23]

Using this description of the graded elementary school organization, there is no guarantee that the nongraded structure eliminates the existence and effects of the characteristics so indicated. At best, one might say that the organizational structure of the nongraded system recognizes the problem and attempts to deal with it within the vertical schema for elementary school organization.

The graded structure of elementary school organization is closely related to structuring the time factor as the basic consideration for shaping instructional activity. There are many requirements, expectations, and constraints that affect the allocation of time meaningfully for management and accountability. The nongraded pattern of organization is an attempt to restructure the basic and relevant units of time that are available to the school for instructional purposes. In this sense, any organizational pattern is adopted in an attempt to make sure that the available time for instruction is deployed to serve the largest number of students most efficiently and effectively.

The Horizontal Organization
of the Elementary School

Early in the discussion of elementary school organization, it was indicated that the major effect of the horizontal organizational pattern is to divide students into classes or groups and to assign available staff. Unlike the two choices (grading and ungrading) available in the vertical pattern of organization, the horizontal organizational pattern provides many alternative choices for delivery of the instructional program to students arranged in groups. The creation of horizontal class groups requires that attention be focused on *the children to be served,* the *curriculum program,* and the *characteristics* of the staff.

When one attempts to implement a horizontal pattern of elementary school organization, a decision with respect to the homogeneity or heterogeneity of the pupils slated to be divided into class groups must be considered. Focusing on curricula areas demands a consideration of whether the content will be presented in separate subjects or in various combinations of separate subjects. Consideration must be focused on assigning staff to self-contained classrooms or classrooms that are departmentalized. Table 4.2 shows some of the selection factors that must be considered in evaluating various aspects of horizontal organization.

Table 4.2

Diagram of Considerations in Formulating Horizontal Organization

Focus Priorities	Selection Factors		Major Grouping Criteria
Children	1. age 2. size 3. interest 4. ability 5. achievement 6. physical attributes	7. sex 8. experience background 9. combination of these factors 10. other factors that can be used to distinguish between children	1. homogeneity 2. heterogeneity
Curricula Areas	1. fields of knowledge 2. creative activities 3. physical activities		1. separate subjects 2. combination of various subjects
Staff	1. training 2. experience 3. interest 4. aptitude 5. personality characteristics		1. self-contained classroom 2. departmentalization

Effective elementary school organization facilitates the implementation of the instructional program by making the best use of human and material resources while contributing to the optimum development of each individual child. At times the intentions of the instructional program can be realized by skillful and thoughtful manipulation of the vertical and horizontal patterns of organization. The key concept to remember is that the organization should be changed to fit the children to be served and not to the reverse. That conclusion suggests that in order to be effective the form of organization must be sufficiently flexible to serve learners well academically, socially, and emotionally, and sufficiently structured to ensure a meaningful learning experience consistent with society's goals and expectations.

Role and Functions of the Elementary School

The elementary school* enters into the lives of children in their early impressionable ages, intentionally seeking to influence them, to foster their growth and development, and to affect their future lives. In its responsibility to educate the young, the elementary school serves three major functions:

1. It provides for the intellectual development of children.
2. It contributes to the socialization of children.
3. It fosters and develops self-awareness, self-understanding, and self-realization.

Each of these functions is inextricably related to the others and cannot be separated in the educative process. However, for purposes of discussion here, each is treated separately.

Intellectual Development

Many educators look upon the role of the elementary school in providing for the intellectual development of pupils as the school's most important and unique function. It is unique in the sense that no other community agency assumes responsibility for the intellectual development of all children. It is important in the sense that the development of rational skills and abilities is indispensable to effective citizenship and central to individual fulfillment and the achievement of a superior quality of life.

In speaking about the importance of intellectual development the Educational Policies Commission's report of 1961, *The Central Purpose of American Education,* states:

> Thus the rational powers are central to all other qualities of the human spirit. These powers flourish in a humane and morally responsible context and contribute to the entire personality. The rational powers are to the human spirit as the hub is to the wheel. These powers are indispensable to a full and worthy life. The person in whom—for

* J. Michael Palardy, ed., *Elementary School Curriculum: An Anthology of Trends and Challenges* (New York: Macmillan, 1971).

whatever reason—they are not well developed is increasingly handicapped in modern society. He may be able to satisfy minimum social standards, but he will inevitably lack his full measure of dignity because his incapacity limits his stature to less than he might otherwise attain. Only to the extent that an individual can realize his potentials, especially the development of his ability to think, can he fully achieve for himself the dignity that goes with freedom.[24]

The National Education Association Project on Instruction also assigns high priority to the school's function in providing for the intellectual development of learners. This priority is revealed in the objectives recommended for all schools throughout the nation. The National Education Association (NEA) Project publication *Deciding What to Teach* includes this statement:

> Therefore, priorities in the educational objectives need to be placed upon such ends as (a) learning how to learn, how to attack new problems, how to acquire new knowledge; (b) using rational processes and developing an abiding interest in learning; (c) exploring values in new experiences; (d) understanding concepts and generalizations; (e) competence in basic skills.[25]

As can be noted in these references, the importance of attending to the intellectual development in pupils extends beyond the emphasis historically associated with, and limited to, the "Three R's" in the elementary school of yesteryear. As can be seen, intellectual development involves pupils' growth in knowledge, skills, and thought processes.

Socialization Function

The socialization of the young is indeed a very important and complex process. Its importance and complexity require analysis and discussion from several different standpoints. First, from the standpoint of need, the society needs to maintain and perpetuate itself and to do so has established the public school enterprise to teach and guide children in the basic tenets, traditions, values, conventions, and mores of the society. In the earlier years of our preindustrial society, the socialization of the young was a fairly simple process centered in the home and focused on the universally accepted beliefs and behaviors of the society. With the advent of industrialization and major technological developments, the society has become more complex, and changes constantly. In modern-day industrial society an ever-increasing variation of acceptable alternative behaviors and beliefs exists, making the process of socialization much more difficult and complex. Socialization of the young, now a legitimate function of both the home and school, is more than just a process to perpetuate society; it seeks further to improve society, to extend and enhance the quality of life within the society. It is not just a means to enculturate youth into the status quo of the social order but seeks to develop in the young the understanding, skills, and behaviors that are essential both to social progress and their own effective functioning in a dynamic, changing social order. The needs of society to survive and progress in a rational, orderly, and controlled manner give urgency to the process of socialization and have caused the elementary school to become directly and intimately involved in the socialization of the young.

Although the needs of society constitute demands upon the individual requiring socialization and can be thought of as external dimensions of the socialization process, there are also inner dimensions. Within the individual are needs (drives) to become a social being—a socially accepted person. The need for love and affection, both giving and receiving, the need for recognition, a sense of belonging and acceptance are related to each individual's social drives, desires, and capacity for social interaction.

It is this interaction with people, events, situations, and other phenomena of social reality—these instances of social behavior that are the essence of the socialization process and contribute to social growth.

Socialization and resulting social growth begin at infancy and continue throughout maturation. At home the child learns quickly to relate to parents, friends, and siblings and to adjust his interpersonal relationships. The child also modifies and moderates his behavior in the face of these interpersonal relationships, the rules and roles of family living.

The elementary school provides young children with a new and stimulating social environment in which the socialization process continues and contributes significantly to social growth. As was true in the preschool years, the children's social behavior and growth in school is closely related to other important aspects of their total growth and development. Children's physical development becomes involved in games in competition with others or as team members where rules are made, followed, and broken and where concepts of fair play and sportsmanship are operative. The young child's early schooling puts an emphasis on language development—a major means of communication in social interaction with others. His emotions are developed and find expression through involvement with others, in reaction to social situations, and in response to people in those situations.

An examination of social behaviors characteristic of social growth and development as found in E. A. Doll's Vineland Social Maturity Scale are not only indicative of the developmental nature of social growth and the continuing process of socialization but they are also suggestive of the kind of learning environment, guidance, and learning activities that the elementary school must necessarily provide if it is to serve its socialization function effectively. Doll's list of characteristics of social growth includes the following behaviors:[26]

1. Reaching for familiar persons.
2. Demanding personal attention.
3. Playing with other children.
4. Playing cooperatively with other children.
5. Performing for others.
6. Playing simple, then more complicated games.
7. Engaging in group activities and competitions.
8. Assuming responsibilities beyond own needs.
9. Contributing to group welfare.
10. Inspiring confidence.
11. Promoting civic progress.
12. Sharing community responsibility.
13. Advancing general welfare.

In providing for the socialization of the young, the elementary school accepts and discharges an important function—one assigned the school by society and expected of it by parents. In so doing the elementary school contributes not only to social stability and progress but also to the effective functioning of children within the context of their world's social realities.

Self-Concept Development

The third major function of the elementary school emphasizes the personal development of young children. When he was head of Columbia University, the late Dwight D. Eisenhower once cautioned American educators not to become so concerned with compartmentalized knowledge, school buildings and facilities, organizational plans and schedules as to forget the primary purpose of education: the personal development of children and youth. In recent years, numerous educators and psychologists have reaffirmed and reemphasized the centrality of personal development as a major role and responsibility of early childhood and elementary education. The development of the individual as a person, those capacities and potentialities found in every human organism, is probably so important that failing to attend to the personal needs and growth of children might well deter learning and growth in other spheres of development, namely physical, social, and intellectual. Personal development is so closely related and intertwined with all other aspects of development that it dare not be neglected as a major function of the elementary school.

As a term, personal development is quite broad and conjures up many meanings and interpretations. Bruce Joyce specifies some of the alternative dimensions of development in the personal domain.[27]

1. The developing organization of the self.
2. The development of productive thinking capacity (including creativity, flexibility, ability to produce alternatives).
3. The development of personal meaning (of importance to one's inner emotional balance).
4. The development of self-teaching and problem-solving abilities.
5. The development of aesthetic capacity.
6. The development of motivation to achieve.

Because the elementary school functions to attend to any or all of these aspects, one thing is certain: the individual, his personal needs and capacities, his feelings and growth as a unique individual and personality become the central and major determinant in the total school enterprise. As Joyce states in summary:

> A school that sees its mission in the development of personal capacity will emphasize the individual in everything it does. It will try to challenge him, to free him, to teach him how to teach himself. Such a school may pay some attention to social and academic demands, but it will concentrate on the personal capacity of the individual.[28]

For the purpose of further discussion here, personal development as one of the three major functions of the elementary school is viewed as consisting of three major facets: self-awareness, self-understanding, and self-realization—all vital to healthy self-concept development in children.

Sowards and Scobey define self-concept "as that set of inferences a person makes about himself on the basis of his experiences."[29] Based on experiences, these inferences are not only what the individual thinks and feels about himself but also what others think, feel, and say about him either directly or indirectly in their behavior toward him.

The development of healthy self-concepts begins at birth, and experiences during infancy are basic to developing positive views of one's self. The young child comes to school with previously established views and feelings about himself. Sometimes these views and feelings are healthy and accurate; yet in some instances children come to school with misconceptions of themselves and with negative attitudes and feelings toward themselves. The elementary school is, for most children, their initial experience in a group setting outside the home. During the early school years the child is afforded opportunities and experiences in interaction with an increasing number of other children and adults and all the human variability they present. Such interaction is the source of new information and reactions that provide children with new views and notions about themselves. They begin to see themselves as many others see them. How others feel and behave toward them influences their feelings about themselves. They have the opportunity to test their existing self-concepts, to modify and change their views and feelings toward themselves and others.

The total learning environment of the elementary school is critical to the development of wholesome self-concepts in young learners. Children must be free to interact and relate to others in order to know how they are different from others, to learn to understand and appreciate these differences, and to accept themselves and others with all the differences they present. Children require a learning environment that invites exploration in order for them to identify their interests, to build new interests, and to learn that they share common interests with others. They need to experiment in order to learn what they know and don't know; what skills they have, do not have, and need to acquire. They need to interact and exchange ideas in order to test their ideas, to modify their thoughts, and to understand and respect the thoughts of others. They need to interact physically to gain notions of their strength, their size, and their skill. They must come to appreciate the feelings of others, as well as their own. They need to encounter others in situations where they are free to feel as they do, to express their feelings, and to check them against the feelings of others. Young learners need opportunities to explore, to experiment, to succeed, to fail, and to try again in order to gauge their personal capacities, strengths, and weaknesses. It is most important that children become aware of who they are and what they are like. They require opportunities and teacher guidance that help them understand themselves as they really are, and accept themselves for what they are. Only then are they free to become.

> A positive attitude toward self and others creates an atmosphere conducive to maturing. The child who is faced day after day with situations beyond his abilities learns to accept defeat as his lot in life. The child who is told constantly, either by word or attitude, that his efforts are not good enough, comes to discount his own abilities.
>
> The child who sees himself as capable is willing to try. The child who sees his efforts yielding results is willing to move on to harder tasks. A program which makes success possible and keeps raising sights helps to develop positive attitudes toward self, toward work, and toward others.[30]

As the elementary school functions to help children develop wholesome, positive, and accurate self-concepts, it contributes significantly to the objective of self-realization and consequently to the quality of life that learners will enjoy as contributing members of society.

Intended Learning Outcomes
for the Elementary School

Earlier in this chapter curriculum was defined as a plan of the intended learning outcomes organized in some fashion with implicit suggestions and directions for learning opportunities to comprise the instructional program. It now becomes appropriate to present those learning outcomes that make up the elementary school curriculum and form the basis for developing instructional programs. Before doing so a word of explanation is necessary. In the discussion that follows, the phrase *intended learning outcomes* is used wherever it is appropriate in preference to such terms as *goals* or *objectives*. To do so does not suggest that the author takes exception to these terms, nor does it imply that such terms cannot be used interchangeably. Rather, to do so merely emphasizes curriculum as a plan of intended learning outcomes that anticipates instruction and results as a consequence of instruction.

Over the years numerous statements indicating what children should learn during their elementary school years have been presented by individual educators, national commissions, educational foundations, and professional study groups. These presentations, variously labeled as aims or objectives most commonly assigned to the elementary school, have specified the ends sought, the behaviors to be developed and hopefully demonstrated by children as a consequence of their elementary schooling.

One example of the intended learning outcomes assigned to, and sought by, the elementary school is to be found in Havighurst's developmental tasks. These are things that every individual in our complex democratic society must learn in order to become an effective citizen and achieve success and personal satisfaction. Havighurst defines and comments on these tasks as follows:

> The tasks the individual must learn—the developmental tasks of life—are those things that constitute healthy and satisfactory growth in our society. They are the things a person must learn if he is to be judged and to judge himself to be a reasonably happy and successful person. A developmental task is a task which arises at or about a certain period in the life of the individual, successful achievement of which leads to success with later tasks, while failure leads to unhappiness in the individual, disapproval by society and difficulty with later tasks.[31]

The developmental tasks that children face during their middle childhood years come at a time (ages six to twelve) when they are enrolled in the elementary school. The elementary school program must contribute in assisting children to achieve these tasks as educational outcomes. According to Havighurst the developmental tasks of the middle childhood years are:[32]

1. Learning physical skills necessary for ordinary games.
2. Building wholesome attitudes toward oneself as a growing organism.
3. Learning to get along with age-mates.
4. Learning an appropriate masculine or feminine social role.
5. Developing fundamental skills in reading, writing, and calculating.
6. Developing concepts necessary for everyday living.
7. Developing conscience, morality, and a scale of values.
8. Achieving personal independence.
9. Developing attitudes toward social groups and institutions.

A second source of intended learning outcomes found in the NEA Project on Instruction sets forth the essential objectives of the school's program and specifies priorities in the matter of educational outcomes. A publication of the NEA Project on Instruction states:

The essential objectives of the school program must be premised on a recognition that education is a process of changing behavior and that a changing society requires that its members acquire the capacity for self-teaching and self-adaptation. Therefore, priorities in educational objectives need to be placed upon such ends as (a) knowing how to learn, how to attack new problems, how to acquire new knowledge; (b) using rational processes and developing an abiding interest in learning; (c) exploring values in new experiences; (d) understanding concepts and generalizations; (e) competence in basic skills.[33]

The NEA Project recommends that these learning outcomes be stressed in every school throughout the nation and looked upon as national objectives of public education.

The report of the NEA Project on Instruction adds this recommendation with respect to priorities in the school's program:

Priorities for the schools are the teaching of skills in reading, composition, listening, speaking (both native and foreign languages), and computation . . . ways of creative and disciplined thinking, including methods of inquiry and application of knowledge . . . competence in self-instruction and independent learning . . . fundamental understandings of the humanities and the arts, the social sciences and natural sciences and mathematics . . . appreciation and discriminating taste in literature, music and the visual arts . . . instruction in health education and physical education. Responsibilities best met by joint efforts of the school and other social agencies include development of values and ideals . . . social and civic competence . . . vocational preparation.[34]

Another basic source of intended learning outcomes that the elementary school should seek to achieve in learners is provided by the 1938 report of the Educational Policy Commission, which asserts that the major, overall objective of education is "the fullest possible development of the individual within the framework of our present industrialized democratic society. The attainment of this *end* (outcome—author's italics) is to be observed in individual behavior or conduct."[35] The Commission's report then continues with a more detailed presentation of specific learning outcomes that characterize the educated person.[36]

The Objectives of Self-Realization

The Inquiring Mind. The educated person has an appetite for learning.

Speech. The educated person can speak the mother tongue clearly.

Reading. The educated person reads the mother tongue efficiently.

Writing. The educated person writes the mother tongue effectively.

Number. The educated person solves his problems of counting and calculating.

Sight and Hearing. The educated person is skilled in listening and observing.

Health Knowledge. The educated person understands the basic facts concerning health and disease.

Health Habits. The educated person protects his own health and that of his dependents.

Public Health. The educated person works to improve the health of the community.

Recreation. The educated person is participant and spectator in many sports and other pastimes.

Intellectual Interest. The educated person has mental resources for the use of leisure.

Esthetic Interests. The educated person appreciates beauty.

Character. The educated person gives responsible direction to his own life.

The Objectives of Human Relationship

Respect for Humanity. The educated person puts human relationships first.

Friendships. The educated person enjoys a rich, sincere, and varied social life.

Cooperation. The educated person can work and play with others.

Courtesy. The educated person observes the amenities of social behavior.

Appreciation of the Home. The educated person appreciates the family as a social institution.

Conservation of the Home. The educated person conserves family ideals.

Homemaking. The educated person is skilled in homemaking.

Democracy in the Home. The educated person maintains democratic family relationships.

The Objectives of Economic Efficiency

Work. The educated producer knows the satisfaction of good workmanship.

Occupational Information. The educated producer understands the requirements and opportunities for various jobs.

Occupational Choice. The educated producer has selected his occupation.

Occupational Efficiency. The educated producer succeeds in his chosen vocation.

Occupational Adjustment. The educated producer maintains and improves his efficiency.

Occupational Appreciation. The educated producer appreciates the social value of his work.

Personal Economics. The educated consumer plans the economics of his own life.

Consumer Judgment. The educated consumer develops standards for guiding his expenditures.

Efficiency in Buying. The educated consumer is an informed and skillful buyer.

Consumer Protection. The educated consumer takes appropriate measures to safeguard his interests.

The Objectives of Civic Responsibility

Social Justice. The educated citizen is sensitive to the disparities of human circumstance.

Social Activity. The educated citizen acts to correct unsatisfactory conditions.

Social Understanding. The educated citizen seeks to understand social structures and social processes.

Critical Judgment. The educated citizen has defenses against propaganda.

Tolerance. The educated citizen respects honest differences of opinion.

Conservation. The educated citizen has a regard for the nation's resources.

Social Application of Science. The educated citizen measures scientific advance by its contribution to the general welfare.

World Citizenship. The educated citizen is a cooperating member of the world community.

Law Observance. The educated citizen respects the law.

Economic Literacy. The educated citizen is economically literate.

Political Citizenship. The educated citizen accepts his civic duties.

Devotion to Democracy. The educated citizen acts upon an unswerving loyalty to democratic ideals.

Such a comprehensive statement of outcomes that describe the educated person is not the sole responsibility of the schools, but presents the purposes of education that the schools and other educational agencies of the society must serve. Nor does the full measure of responsibility for achieving all of these learning outcomes that can be accomplished in schools fall upon the elementary school alone. The statement does, however, provide a specification of outcomes from which the elementary school can select objectives appropriate to the developmental stages and particular needs of young children and around which elementary school programs can be fashioned.

A final source of information describing educational objectives assigned to the elementary school and useful in formulating the intended learning outcomes for the school curriculum is the Russell Sage Foundation's report on Elementary School Objectives prepared for the Mid-

Century Committee on Outcomes in Elementary Education by Nolan C. Kearney. This report presents the specific obtainable objectives or outcomes of elementary schools as identified and evaluated by a distinguished group of educators and educational critics.

This comprehensive study presents nine instructional areas of the elementary school program and then specifies learning outcomes for each in four different categories of objectives:[37]

1. Knowledge and understanding.
2. Skill and competence.
3. Attitude and interest.
4. Action pattern.

Figure 4.3, a chart taken from Kearney's report, shows a cross section of the instructional areas and the four categories of objectives mentioned previously. Specific learning outcomes in the form of knowledge, skills, attitudes, and action patterns at various levels of pupil development have been identified in the study and serve to complete the blank rectangles.

Abbreviated outlines of the recommended outcomes for each of the nine instructional areas are presented because they provide a concrete basis for study, determination, and selection of the intended learning outcomes in the elementary school.

1. *Physical Development, Health, and Body Care.* Physical development, health, and body care is a broad category as compared with the narrow conception of physiology and hygiene which it has replaced in the elementary school curriculum. Today it involves both health and safety. It includes individual health and the elementary aspects of public health. It includes physical education, personal grooming, safety, sportsmanship, and an understanding of growth and maturation. . . .

2. *Individual Social and Emotional Development.* This category includes material that is commonly associated with mental health, emotional stability, and the growth of personality [with] emphasis on such goals as understanding oneself and evaluating oneself. . . . In this area there is more difficulty in pointing out basic knowledge and skills than is true in some others, since the area itself is so much one of attitudes and interests. . . .

3. *Ethical Behavior, Standards, Values.* Ethical behavior, standards, and values are related to the observance of the moral law and the civil law. This area includes the observance of much that gains validity from the customs and mores of the culture. It involves sportsmanship, kindliness, helpfulness, and the problems involved

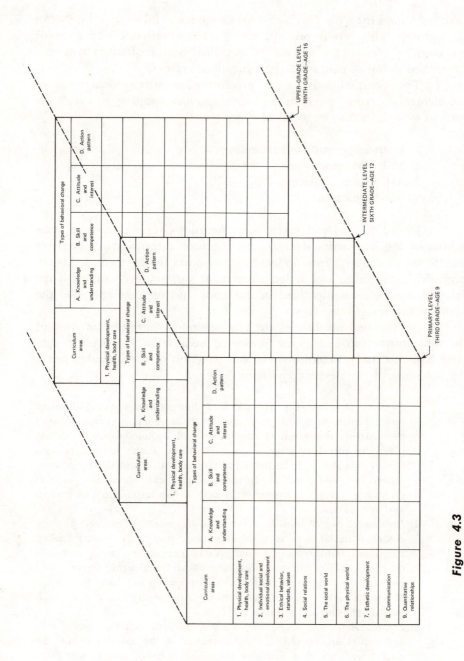

Figure 4.3

The Grid at Three Cross Sections of the Educational Continuum. [Nolan C. Kearney, *Elementary School Options* (New York: Russell Sage Foundation, 1953), p. 40.]

in living in a society with other people. It is concerned with the integrity and honesty of people. . . .

4. *Social Relations.* This . . . is devoted to the individual as a person in his personal-social relations with others, when he has to consider the needs, interests, motives, convictions, and ideals of others with whom he associates in home, community, and place of work. . . .

5. *The Social World.* This . . . considers the child in a somewhat broader social setting than does . . . social relations. Here we set the goals for the child in terms of the structure and the institutions of our culture. The behavior of the child is considered in relation to community, state, and nation. Geography in its relation to man is in this background. Civics, elementary economics, government, and the traditional American way of life come in this area. . . .

6. *The Physical World (The Natural Environment).* In this . . . attention is centered on an enlarged concept of science, and reference is made to many aspects of the child's environment. Physical science problems, as well as the science that deals with plants and animals, are emphasized. Also stressed are learning to think scientifically and the use of *methods of science* in solving problems in science and problems in everyday living. Emphasis is on thinking that associates facts and relates them in various ways to form generalizations. . . .

7. *Esthetic Development.* In this . . . emphasis is placed on esthetic appreciation and expression. Though the primary emphasis here is on art, music, and the crafts, . . . many types of artistic and creative endeavor are mentioned. The moral, the intellectual, and the emotional aspects of esthetic development are all included. . . .

8. *Communication.* This . . . covers the wide variety of means by which man communicates with man. It emphasizes the mechanical and skills aspects of reading, writing, composition, correct usage, spelling, punctuation, speaking, and listening. It includes the use of the library and of references of various kinds. It includes group skills, such as conducting and participating in meetings. It stresses the various constructive uses to which communication skills must be put, if their mastery is to be of value. . . .

9. *Quantitative Relationships.* Here we find arithmetic and the elementary aspects of algebra and geometry. Here children are introduced to a great variety of measures by which man describes in quantities the things he finds in his world. This involves the ability to analyze and solve problems on the basis of the particular problem, the information needed to solve it, and how to get the information. Emphasis is placed on giving the child an understanding of how our number system works and why, so that he will have greater competence in using numbers. Since mathematics is the language of quantity, it could be included as another means of communication, but it is so important and specialized that it is considered separately.[39]

Instruction in the Elementary School

Instruction (the instructional program) is the major means of implementing the school's curriculum. As defined earlier, instruction consists of all those decisions and activities, including teaching and guidance, that are employed intentionally to influence learners toward goals or desired learning outcomes. The curriculum as a plan of intended learning outcomes to be sought after provides the basis for deciding and determining the nature, content, and organization of the instructional program. An analysis of the intended learning outcomes is the necessary first step to instructional planning and decision making.

Instructional Planning

Planning instruction begins with an analysis of learning outcomes, either individually or in sets depending on how the outcomes are organized in the curriculum plan (see page 99–100 of this chapter). Depending on the intended learning outcomes chosen, areas or domains of instruction can be organized and designed to achieve the selected outcomes. Consider, for example, a group or set of learning outcomes specifying and emphasizing effective democratic citizenship. Several instructional areas or domains could be fashioned and designed to achieve those outcomes.

Instructional areas or domains, as used in Figure 4.4, can be viewed as an organized body of learning experiences and opportunities, which by means of teaching and guidance, pertinent materials and necessary resources, seek to develop in learners the essential knowledge, skills, attitudes, and thought processes essential to effective democratic citizenship.

In Figure 4.4 at least four areas of instruction are suggested and can be developed to contribute directly to the set of outcomes related to effective democratic citizenship.

1. School and community social problems and issues.
2. Social studies.
3. Language arts.

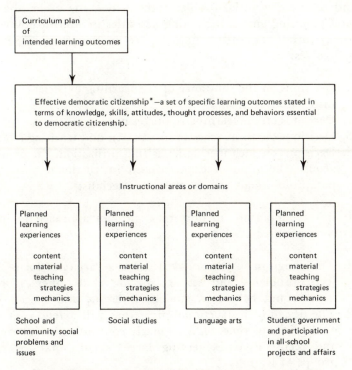

*An example of one set of specific and related learning outcomes comprising the curriculum plan.

Figure 4.4
Instructional Domains for Achieving Intended Learning Outcomes.

4. Student government and participation in all-school projects and affairs.

Each of these instructional areas provides a different set of learning experiences; each is organized differently with a different basis or focus. Over the years instruction has been organized according to the common branch subjects of the elementary school or the specific disciplines of organized knowledge such as arithmetic, science, history, and English. In the approach to instructional planning suggested by Figure 4.4, only two instructional areas have been designed according to subjects, namely social studies and language arts. The other two are organized to provide planned learning experiences in different areas. One is designed to provide learning opportunities involving study of specific school and community social problems and issues; the other, the kinds of firsthand planning and participating activities in student government and all other socially oriented action projects in the school. The actual planning involves:

1. Decisions on the substance of the learning experiences in each instructional domain.
2. Decisions on the learning resources needed.
3. Decisions on approaches to instruction and teaching strategies.
4. Decisions on such mechanics as staff utilization, size of student group, allocation of time to each instructional area, use of paraprofessionals and community specialists.

It is very important to note that such an approach to instructional planning permits:

1. The design of instructional areas on a variety of focuses: subjects, problems and issues, specific skills, themes, performances and behaviors, student interests, and special needs.
2. The design of instructional areas that will extend over different periods of time, on a regularly continuing or intermittent and recurring basis, serving large, small, total, or special groups of learners.
3. The design of instructional areas that utilize various approaches to instruction and teaching strategies as are appropriate, such as team teaching, individualized instruction, classroom learning stations, programmed instruction, large and small group instruction.

The number and variety of differently designed instructional domains relates, of course, to the range, diversity, and specificity of the intended learning outcomes. Nominally, the instructional domain can be planned and developed to provide learning opportunities that serve one or more sets of intended learning outcomes. A well-planned instructional program would then consist of a multiple of instructional domains serving multiple sets of learning outcomes.

Both flexibility and variety must essentially characterize decisions made about learning opportunities, materials and resources, instructional approaches and teaching strategies planned and developed for any instructional domain. It is virtually impossible to predetermine the absolute value of any instructional procedure and to prescribe instructional operations that are best for different learners and different learnings. Consequently, instruction (and teaching as a major component of instruction) becomes creative; experimental activities are replete with much risk taking and incomplete without a continuing assessment in relation to the learning outcomes sought in any particular instructional domain.

In recent years, much attention to individualized instruction has emphasized the adaptation of teaching methods and materials in relation to individual needs, abilities, and rates of learning. Such adaptation has usually taken place within the framework of an instructional program, predetermined and uniformly organized around subjects and subject matter. Individualization is then confined to those means that can be employed within a subject area instead of a primary provision in the planning of instructional domains. Instructional planning that results in a greater variety of instructional areas or domains offers increased opportunities and approaches for individualized instruction and learning. A limited instructional program circumscribes the learner's actions and involvement. But a comprehensive plan of instructional domains, variously designed, offers a choice of learning opportunities, methods, and materials, and other arrangements for both learners and teachers making individualized instruction more feasible and practical. A monolithic approach to planning instruction, such as the subject-matter design, limits the total learning environment and denies the many variables that need to be taken into account in planning the very dynamic and complex process of instruction.

Summary

In summary, for this chapter the elementary school curriculum constitutes a plan of the intended learning outcomes organized in some fashion. The curriculum is both intended and planned, anticipates instruction, and is implemented through the educative force of the total school environment. Although the instructional system serves as the primary vehicle for curriculum implementation, the support system of educational facilities, equipment, and materials are very vital instrumental means. Beyond this atmosphere of the school, the roles, rules, regulations, values, and attitudes that comprise the school's social system are crucial educative forces that deserve careful attention and planning similar to that afforded the instructional program.

The organization and administrative set-up in the elementary school must be established in order to plan and develop these basic means and facilitate the implementation of the curriculum.

Instruction consists of those decisions and activities intentionally employed to help learners achieve the intended learning outcomes specified by the curriculum plan. Instruction is a process in which teaching is a most significant component. Instructional planning proceeds from an analysis of the learning outcomes sought to the determination and organization of instructional areas or domains. Each of the several instructional domains consists of planned learning experiences and opportunities as well as stipulations and suggestions for learning resources, instructional procedures, and teaching strategies.

Although standard subject areas may continue to serve as the basic focus in the design of instructional areas, other focuses such as students' interests and desires, special needs of special groups, specific skills, and behaviors as well as themes and social problems and issues can be employed. Multiple bases for designing instructional domains must necessarily replace the monolithic design of subject matter if the multiplicity of learning outcomes and individual learner needs are to be served by the elementary school.

References

1. Phillip L. Hosford, *An Instructional Theory: A Beginning* (Englewood Cliffs, N.J.: Prentice-Hall, 1973), pp. 16–19.
2. George A. Beauchamp, *The Curriculum of the Elementary School* (Boston: Allyn, 1964), p. 5.
3. J. Galen Saylor and William M. Alexander, *Curriculum Planning for Modern Schools* (New York: Holt, 1966), p. 5.
4. Phillip H. Phenix, "Curriculum," in *Philosophy of Education* (New York: Holt, 1958), p. 8.
5. Mauritz Johnson, Jr., "Definitions and Models in Curriculum Theory," *Educational Theory*, 17:129 (April 1967).
6. Arthur J. Lewis and Alice Miel, *Supervision for Improved Instruction: New Challenges, New Responses* (Belmont, Cal.: Wadsworth, 1972).
7. Philip Phenix, *Philosophy of Education* (New York: Holt, 1958).
8. Mauritz Johnson, Jr., op. cit.
9. Alice Miel, "Curriculum Design and Materials—Pressure or Release?" *Childhood Education*, 44, No. 7 (1968).

10. J. Galen Saylor and William M. Alexander, op. cit.
11. Gordon Mackenzie, "Curriculum Change: Participants, Power and Processes," in Matthew B. Miles, ed., *Innovation in Education* (New York: Teachers College Press, 1974).
12. Hollis L. Caswell and Doah S. Campbell, *Curriculum Development* (New York: American Book, 1935).
13. Bruce P. Joyce, *Alternative Models of Elementary Education* (Waltham, Mass.: Ginn-Blaisdell, 1969).
14. Mauritz Johnson, Jr., op. cit.
15. Richard M. Cyert and Kenneth R. MacCrimmon, "Organizations," in *The Handbook of Social Psychology,* Gardner Lindzey and Elliot Aronson, eds., Vol. 1 (Reading, Mass.: Addison-Wesley, 1968), p. 565.
16. Ibid.
17. Ibid., p. 569.
18. Ibid.
19. Ibid.
20. John Goodlad and Kenneth Rehage, "Unscrambling the Vocabulary of School Organization," *National Education Association Journal,* 51:34–36 (Nov. 1962).
21. "Graded Schools," in *The Cyclopedia of Education: A Dictionary of Information for the Use of Teachers, School Officers, Parents and Others,* Henry Kiddle and Alexander J. Schem, eds. (New York: E. Steiger, 1877), pp. 375–377.
22. *Standard Terminology for Curriculum and Instruction in Local and State School Systems,* State Educational Records and Reports Services: Handbook VI, National Center for Educational Statistics, Washington, D.C., 1970, p. 267.
23. Goodlad and Rehage, op. cit., p. 8.
24. National Education Association, Educational Policies Commission, *The Central Purpose of American Education* (Washington, D.C.: NEA, 1961), p. 6.
25. National Education Association Project on Instruction, *Deciding What to Teach* (Washington, D.C.: NEA, 1963), p. 92.
26. E. A. Doll, "Manual of Directions," *Vineland Social Maturity Scale* (Minneapolis, Minn.: Educational Test Bureau, 1947), pp. 3–8.
27. Bruce R. Joyce, op. cit., pp. 67–68.
28. Ibid.
29. G. Wesley Sowards and Mary Margaret Scobey, *The Changing Curriculum and the Elementary School Teacher* (Belmont, Cal.: Wadsworth, 1968).

30. Arizona State University, *Design for Lifetime Learning in a Dynamic Social Structure* (Tempe, Ariz.: Bureau of Educational Research, 1968), p. 42.
31. Robert Havighurst, *Human Development and Education* (New York: Longmans, Green, 1953), p. 2.
32. Ibid., pp. 25–41.
33. NEA Project on Instruction, *Deciding What to Teach,* op. cit., p. 92.
34. Ibid.
35. NEA, Educational Policies Commission, *The Purposes of Education in American Democracy* (Washington, D.C.: NEA, 1938), p. 41.
36. Ibid., pp. 50, 72, 90, 108.
37. Nolan C. Kearney, *Elementary School Objectives, Mid-Century Committee on Outcomes in Elementary Education* (New York: Russell Sage Foundation, 1953), pp. 38–40.
38. Ibid., p. 40.
39. Ibid., pp. 52–113.

5

Developing Basic Understandings

The use of the term *basic understanding* in curriculum is rarely employed to denote a goal, describe an end product, or define an instructional intent of a teacher. The more common terminology for this area of concern includes such standards as *concepts, generalizations, principles, processes, abstractions, reasoning ability, analyzing, synthesizing,* and *evaluating*. These latter terms range in emphasis from the denoting of products (concepts) to outlining a specific process (evaluating). In most instances, the emphasis is placed on providing an adequate description and explanation of the process involved when a teacher concerns himself with these terms. Rare is the instance in curriculum where there is an attempt to relate the processes outlined to the instructional intent of the teacher. In an attempt to correct this oversight, the author has adopted the phrase *basic understanding* as an all-encompassing term for operationalizing the development and teaching of processes as they relate to the instructional program.

Basic understanding refers to the fundamental process of apprehending or grasping the meaning of events or constellations of events. When one deals with understanding he considers the inner significance of a psychic process and not just empirically determined cause-and-effect relationships. The latter phenomena contribute to basic understanding only as an integral part of the defining structure. In a real sense, then, *basic understanding* refers to the process of evolving operational thought patterns resulting from combining major approaches to processing information, problem solving, logical analysis, and so on, for creating or developing meaning from concrete or abstract experience.

135

Even though basic understanding subsumes concepts as an operationalized idea, the process cannot be dealt with apart from the nature of concepts in relation to the instructional processes employed to fulfill the mandate of society for educating youth. In this sense, some attention must be devoted to the discussion and definition of concepts before they can be considered in a system that delineates and teaches basic understandings.

Concepts: Definition and Development

Since the early 1950s, *concept* has been one of the most frequently used, misused, and misunderstood terms in curriculum literature. In part, the situation results from the concern with, and the popularization of, teaching concepts so integral to the curriculum reform movement (Huebner, 1964[1]; Fraser, 1962[2]; Goodlad, 1964[3]; Passow, 1962[4]; Goodlad, von Stoephasius, and Klein, 1966[5]; Heath, 1964[6]) of recent years. The use of concept as a primary focus in curriculum literature was further aided by writings (Bruner, Goodnow, and Austin, 1956[7]; Bruner, 1960[8] and 1966[9]; DeCocco, 1967[10]; Martorella, 1971[11]; Wilson, 1969[12]) so descriptive of the structural characteristics of content and process that were valued when the curriculum reform movement was at its height. This situation combined to make reference to concept teaching and development a direct corollary to instruction and curriculum development. Even though this helps to focus increased attention on the nature and process of developing concept formation in curriculum and instruction, problems associated with misuse and misunderstanding of the notion of concepts in theory and practice still remain.

Concern with concepts has always been a primary focus of many disciplines and this is especially true in education, philosophy, and psychology. Confusion involving the way in which concepts are defined, researched, utilized, and taught in the various disciplines abounds and it is somewhat counterproductive to efforts to deal with this content in a systematic and logically consistent manner. Part of the problem, DeCocco writes, is related to the fact that:

> there is a gap between the findings of psychologists on the conditions under which very simple "concepts" are learned in the psychological laboratory and the experiences of teachers in teaching the "for real" concepts that are contained in the curricula of the schools.[13]

There is a decided difference in the processes and difficulties involved when a college sophomore is asked to learn nonsense syllables in a laboratory setting according to a preselected pattern and when a sixth grader is asked to define *freedom* in our society in a classroom setting. Most relevant concepts are partially defined by the situational context of occurrence. Unlike the laboratory setting with controlled concept contact, the classroom offers a situational context that requires a different kind of approach to the problem of concept formation as an aid to basic understanding.

Another aspect of the problem of concept attainment is evident when one asks

> whether there is continuity, with respect to psychological "processes," between the inductive, nonverbal type of learning studied in the psychological laboratory under the guise of "concept learning" and the usually more deductive, verbal-explanatory type of teaching used in the classroom and in the typical text book material.[14]

In the first instance—inductive nonverbal type—there is much concern as to whether or not the subject can discern attributes that define a concept similar to the experimenter's notion of it. Unfortunately, the psychological and sociological noise (distractions, social interaction, background experience, spacial arrangements, and so on) and the product expectation in the typical classroom force the teacher to make use of the deductive pattern to aid concept formation. Concepts taught in classrooms are accompanied by situationally complex settings that require a different instructional process than that indicated by researchers who are attempting to show what a concept is. Identifying and denoting a concept require different instructional processes that are critical to aiding basic understanding.

Linguistic Forms for Defining Concepts

Any cursory review of the indexes to books or articles in education, psychology, and philosophy reveals a high degree of attention to the word *concept*. Across these discrete content areas of focus are a variety of ways in which *concept* is used and defined. For our purposes, many of the uses encountered are irrelevant and misleading. Too often statements referring to concepts affect all human activity. Frequently, one is faced with statements such as: The concept of a *concept* is unclear. Sometimes attention is focused on the word *concept;* at other times the focus is on the definition of *concept* or something that may be referred to and designated by the word *concept.* However, in neither of these cases suggested is there any clear notion explaining what the word (*concept*) is used to designate. This is the critical issue involved in the use of concepts as a foundation for developing basic understanding.

During the instructional process the teacher makes use of various types of information. These types of information may be classified roughly as being factual, valuational, and conceptual. How a teacher decides to deal with these types of information is suggestive of the level of basic understanding regarding single ideas or constellations of ideas that can be induced through the instructional process. The following list provides some illustrations.

1. *Factual.* What is Fred's mental age?
2. *Valuational.* Is Fred's mental age normal?
3. *Conceptual.* What is mental age? What does *mental age* mean? What is the definition of *mental age?*

The preceding list shows how words can refer to concepts. In the first two questions the words used refer to concepts even though these questions are calling for answers involving facts or values. These two questions do not require the definition of a concept (in this instance— mental age). On the other hand, the third question does require definition and delineation of the concept as a prerequisite to achieving basic understanding.

For example, if one were to suggest "Fred's mental age is twelve" as an answer to the first question in the list, the answer would be a statement about Fred and *not* about the concept of *mental age.* If an answer were provided for the second question, one would be engaged in giving a rating of Fred's mental age. Unlike the first two questions, the third one requires that the term *mental age* be dismantled, that attention be directed to the concept itself, and that the concept's elements or criterional attributes be clearly delineated. Most teachers involved in the classroom instructional process tend to make extended use of questions similar to those paralleling the first two with little attention or thought devoted to items resembling the third question. Since the third one represents a prototype of the kind of information that suggests the appropriateness of a particular teaching strategy for a selected instructional outcome, it is critical to help teachers delineate the nature and kinds of concepts available and how these concepts are related to aiding children in the development of basic understanding.

In the literature of various disciplines such as psychology, philosophy, and education, there are a number of discrete and overlapping statements that describe how the term *concept* should be used and defined. After reading from the literature of these disciplines, a list of statements describing the use or definition of a concept is shown as follows:*

1. A concept is a category.
2. A concept is a category and a set of criteria for deciding what to include or exclude from the category.
3. A class concept is a set of common reactions to objects that a subject combines in one class (equivalents of qualities).
4. A relational concept is a set of common actions different in intensity (differences as opposed to equivalences).
5. A concept is a general idea, an item in thinking that stands for a general class; it is a state in which there is a broadly generalized response.
6. Concepts are the common elements that mark off an array of objects as a class.
7. A concept is a network of inferences (drawn from trends noted and situationally determined contextual clues) by which one goes beyond a set of observed criterional properties to the class identity of the object or event and to inferences (prediction or hypothesizing) about unobserved properties of the object or event.
8. A concept is a network of inferences that are or may be set into play by an act of categorization.
9. A concept is the common form of various things, or various events—the form abstracted from all things that have it.

The statements in this list demonstrate the variety of ways in which concepts may be used and defined. They also illustrate the difficulties created when a teacher is faced with the prospect of planning a teaching strategy to help children derive basic understandings of natural, social, or theoretical phenomena that comprise the elementary school

---

* B. O. Smith and Donald E. Orlosky, "Linguistic Forms for Defining Concepts," Working Paper prepared for members of the Leadership Training Institute on Protocol Materials, Spring 1971. Reprinted by permission.

curriculum. Since these phenomena are denoted and described by the concepts assigned to them, the formulation of a teaching strategy must be preceded by a thorough knowledge of ways of describing, using, and defining concepts.

When these statements about concepts are analyzed, there is a definite set of entities, objects, or events designated by the term *concept*. The following list shows the common denominator derived from an analysis of the statements about concepts.

1. Category.
2. Category and criteria.
3. Common reactions to objects.
4. Common actions different in intensity.
5. General idea.
6. Common elements or characteristics.
7. Network of inferences.
8. Common forms.

It is obvious that any attempt to reconcile the differences in the designations shown in this list would require coverage that is likely to be both overwhelming and nonproductive. Similarly, a choice of one designation over another is equally difficult and a misrepresentation of the nature of concepts in the real world. In order to avoid the quagmire that would probably result from an attempt to reconcile differences indicated in this list and yet deal forthrightly and meaningfully with the nature of and use of concepts in developing basic understandings, it seems prudent to deal with the different *linguistic forms* that definitions of a particular concept may take. This approach appears to be the most expedient way to avoid confusion while still providing a useful and accurate framework for dealing with concepts and how they relate to developing basic understandings as a result of the instructional process.

Linguistic Forms of Concepts

From the previous section, it should be apparent that not all concepts are of the same order. As a consequence, different forms of definition are necessary to account for the variety of concepts that can be utilized by a teacher to aid children in the development of basic understanding. For the purpose of designing a teaching strategy to implement an instructional process, concepts may be defined in one of four possible forms. These four forms are: (1) classification form, (2) equivalent-expression form, (3) open-context form, and (4) conditional form.

The Classification Form

When the classification form is used to provide a definition for a concept, it requires a concept to be associated with a category and to be distinguished from other concepts by discriminating criteria. For example, a pupil behavior such as "classifying" can be distinguished from another pupil behavior such as "describing" by establishing the criteria that are essential to the act of classifying. In order to build distinguishing elements for classifying, one would have to include the criteria that the pupil "puts entities into categories," and "forms mutually exclusive categories." As additional qualifying criteria needed to distinguish "classifying" from "describing" are included, the limits of "classifying" are drawn so that differences between the two concepts are apparent and unmistakable.

The Equivalent-Expression Form

The equivalent-expression form enables one to define a concept by providing an expression that is equivalent to the word or words used to name that concept. Unlike the case with the classification form, it is not possible to develop a series of qualifying criteria for clearly defining relational concepts such as *standard score*. One can define the relational concept *standard score* by making use of the equivalent-expression form and describing it as "the ratio of the deviation of an individual's raw score from the average score of his group in relation to the standard deviation of the scores of the group" or

$$\frac{\text{raw score } (x) - \text{mean } (M)}{\text{standard deviation } (S.\,D.)}.$$

In this sense one could say that "converted raw score on a test is a standard score," or, in other words, *a converted raw score on a test is the ratio of the deviation of an individual's raw score from the average score of his group in relation to the standard deviation of the scores of the group.* The equivalent-expression form is used to define a relational concept and equivalent expressions are directly interchangeable.

The Open-Context Definition Form

When one attempts to define concepts whose definitions are imprecise because the boundaries or limits of the terms are not rigidly prescribed, the open-context definition form provides the means for establishing an operational definition for certain concepts. In too many instances, there is a temptation to avoid the definition of some concepts entirely and to consider such concepts undefinable when one is unable to determine the limits of concepts to be defined. Concepts such as well-being, equity, alienation, freedom, imperialism, and happiness are examples of loose terms that cannot be reduced to an equivalent-expression form or to a classification form without finding exceptions to the definition or restricting the definition to unreasonable limits. In such instances, it is preferable to include all the characteristics of the open-context form. A definition of a concept in this form may be stated as follows: "Happiness in an individual is characterized by smiling, being physically relaxed, expressing contentment with physical and social surroundings, describing the future with positive anticipation, and so on." The open-context form enables one to define concepts that derive their meaning in part from the situational variables related to their use. Moreover, the phenomena they denote are without boundaries that limit the range of their meaning.

The Conditional Form

The interpretation of some phenomena may vary according to the conditions that precede their occurrence. In such instances, the conditions are a part of the definition of a concept and the use of the conditional to define it is appropriate. If an individual is perspiring and trembling, it may be a normal or abnormal reaction—depending on the conditions that brought on the behavior. If the individual has just barely missed hitting a child with a car, or if the individual is just about to be introduced to a member of the opposite sex, the same behavior—perspiring and trembling—may be labeled as fear or shyness, according to the conditions preceding or accompanying the event. Some concepts can only be defined within the context of the conditions that are associated and observed.

Anxiety is a concept that can be defined in the conditional form. In order for anxiety to occur, certain conditions must be met, such as a person's being faced with a known stimulus with which he has to deal. A person facing such a stimulus may respond with apprehensive tension, uneasiness, or fear out of proportion to the known stimulus. Anxiety may be regarded as normal when it is met by constructive and protective responses. In this instance, an anxious individual would find some way of successfully coping with the danger: eliminating it or protecting himself against it. A normal handling of anxiety would also require a person to maintain his emotional equilibrium and exercise a measure of mature judgment. On the other hand, anxiety may be regarded as pathologic and the associated protectively intended and integrative responses would be limited and inadequate. Responses to anxiety in this instance are basically nonconstructive and might variously be disorganized, inappropriate, exaggerated, or ineffectual. In all of the instances suggested, a person might be exhibiting anxiety. The foregoing definition of anxiety in the conditional form provides for the circumstances in which the behaviors occur and stipulates that the combination of circumstances and individual behavior is accounted for by the concept of anxiety.

Determining Appropriate Linguistic Forms of Concepts

The preceding discussion of the nature and types of concepts available suggests that there are a variety of concepts that require a number of different patterns to appropriately identify, denote, or define. Early in this discussion we established the notions of exploring the nature of concepts and gave further support to the ideas presented by John Wilson when he writes:

> Questions of concept, then, are not questions of fact; nor are they questions of value; nor are they questions concerned with the meanings of words, or the definitions of words . . . they are concerned with the uses of words, and the criteria or principles by which those uses are determined.[15]

For the purpose of developing basic understanding through the instructional process, it should be readily apparent that procedures for defining concepts are very precise. In fact, the definition of a concept is broached primarily as a way to ascribe certain meanings* to the concept and to

---

*Clarence R. Calder, Jr., and Eleanor M. Antan, *Techniques and Activities to Stimulate Verbal Learning* (New York: Macmillan, 1970).

get others to attach the same meanings to that concept. Therefore, it becomes the task of the teacher who is defining concepts to determine the words that describe the concept and then to utilize the appropriate linguistic form to sharpen the resulting definition as a prerequisite condition to aiding youth in developing basic understanding. This situation often requires the comparison of the initial written definition of a concept with the associated linguistic form so that appropriate modifications in the initial or future operational defining statement might be made by the teacher. In a sense, the largest single instructional responsibility of the teacher in attempting to develop basic understanding is critically dependent on his ability to define operationally concepts for expectant learners.

Since the linguistic form of concepts is so intimately related to the nature of the teaching strategy developed to guide instruction, its importance should be stressed once more. It is apparent that the linguistic form most appropriate is dependent upon the nature of the concept to be defined, and it is only through writing the unique features and characteristics of a concept that the appropriate linguistic form becomes apparent. Therefore, it is essential that a teacher learn to express concepts in the most precise linguistic form possible although completeness and accuracy should not be sacrificed. In this sense, the overriding concern of a teacher involved in the definition of a concept should be the clarity with which the concepts are analyzed and the clarity with which the associated analyses are communicated to his learners. Without adequate attention to this concern, the development of basic understanding with young learners is likely to remain outside the reach and scope of the teacher and result in the thwarting of goals for him and his charges.

Techniques of Conceptual Analysis

Earlier in this chapter, attention was focused on problems and issues associated with defining and developing concepts. Now we must turn to the problem as it is more closely related to the instructional process in a given teaching strategy constructed to increase and expand the basic understanding of learners. As we approach the specific problems involved in formulating a teaching strategy and conducting an instructional process, we are confronted with a common factor permeating all the teacher's difficulties. These common difficulties are essentially failures in communication. A teacher must master the associated techniques if the communication pattern between him and his charges is to bear quality fruit.

Unfortunately, there are few, if any, fixed rules governing the analysis of concepts. Consequently, teachers will have to learn how to conduct this analysis as much *by working through the process activity* as by memorizing a set of rules. The guiding principle behind any attempt to analyze concepts includes confidence in the idea and alert attentiveness to boundaries and characteristics of the concepts under consideration. John Wilson provides an adequate summary of the situation when he asserts:

> Behind the notion of "how to analyze concepts," therefore, lies the still more general skill, "how to talk" or "how to communicate": and to employ this skill we have to learn above all to recognize and enter into the particular game which is being played. Thus the person who yields to the desire to moralize who cannot talk *about* concepts but only preach *with* them, is essentially not playing the game: it is a form of cheating. Similarly the person who insists on analyzing every single concept referred to in a statement is, so to speak, overplaying the game: like a soccer player who insists on dribbling skillfully in front of the goal when he should be taking a shot at it. To communicate, then, involves recognizing the particular game and playing it wholeheartedly.[16]

The game of analyzing concepts is a difficult but not insurmountable task to perform. The primary difficulty is related to getting teachers to play this new game and work through the resulting struggle until the idea of concept analysis is firmly entrenched. At this point, teachers should have learned to communicate in a new way that contributes directly to improving the basic understanding of learners.

Even though many of the rules governing conceptual analysis are not fixed, some general considerations must be taken into account when one attempts to participate in this type of activity. These considerations are adapted from John Wilson[17] and presented as follows:

1. *Isolating Questions of Concept.* The most difficult problem facing teachers in analysis is being able to isolate questions of concepts from other questions. Mainly, this is due to the fact that few questions deal with a concept in a pure form. Many times the teacher is faced with the problem of separating facts from values about the concept. To get over this hurdle a teacher must be able to deal with each part of the question separately and in a logically consistent way.

2. *Standard or Right Answers.* Few questions of concept have a

single, precise solution. Answers to many questions of concept are tied to the meaning the questioner attaches to his pronouncements. Therefore, the problems associated with right answers cannot be dealt with until questions of concepts are isolated in terms of facts and morality. If, then, statements or questions are appropriate at this point in the analysis, this helps the teacher to sort out the conditions that are important or essential to establishing boundaries for the concept in question. Effective communication and increased basic understanding are dependent upon the teacher's ability to distinguish the primary and central uses of a concept from the derived and borderline uses. Situational context plays a large role at this point in the analysis.

3. *Model Cases.* The use of model cases is a particularly productive way to identify a concept that is difficult to pinpoint. If a teacher can point to an instance of the concept of which he is absolutely sure, he can use it as an example from which its essential features can be derived. Model cases of a concept help the teacher to be precise in his description of distinguishing characteristics of associate concepts.

4. *Contrary Cases.* Concepts can be analyzed by finding a noninstance of their existence. This is the model case in reverse. Contrary cases can be used to illustrate characteristics that make them the opposite of concepts they are trying to portray.

5. *Related Cases.* Many concepts can only be analyzed by considering cases that are related to them. In some instances, concepts can only be understood by the relationship they share with other concepts. Constellations of concepts sometimes set the conditions for meaning associated with concepts within the network in a given situation.

6. *Borderline Cases.* There are some cases of concepts where a teacher is unsure of what should be said about them. These often involve the use of known concepts metaphorically. For example, "The candidate was *read* off by the voters." This is a borderline case of the concept of *read.* As a teacher learns to deal with borderline cases, precision is provided to identify the central criteria of true cases of a concept.

7. *Invented Cases.* If regular life experience does not provide enough naturally occurring instances that clarify a concept, cases must be invented to aid in the analysis of that concept. For example, how are the properties of water affected by

the atmosphere of Mars? When invented cases are employed, the process contributes to a better understanding of actual experience with a given concept.

8. *Social Context.* All language is associated with a social context accompanying a given set of circumstances that act to give meaning to certain concepts. One such instance might deal with the concepts employed by a politician. In such cases, concepts used have to be defined and analyzed in the context of who, where, and why statements are being made. A politician's concepts reflect both his notions of personal integrity and constituency support. Without a careful consideration of the social context of the concepts he employs, it would be impossible to attach meaning to his pronouncements.

9. *Underlying Anxiety.* Some concepts used in certain kinds of statements must be considered in relation to the mood or feelings of the person uttering them. Many thoughts are affected by feelings of insecurity and anxiety, and concepts employed during this emotional state must be considered within this concept. As anxiety levels increase with the complexity of our society, more attention must be devoted to analyzing concepts in terms of these psychological factors.

10. *Practical Results.* As indicated earlier, most conceptual questions have no "right" or "wrong" answers and as such are often misleading in a practical sense. Conceptual questions that appear to be meaningless have limited utility apart from their relationship to practical results in everyday life. When a teacher attempts to analyze questions of concept, improved communication will be facilitated if he ties his analysis to practical results.

11. *Results in Language.* Too often, attempts to delineate essential characteristics of a concept have restricted the concept too severely to convey the intended meaning in a specific case and the common meaning across a number of cases. As one examines the "results of language" in the choice of meanings or selection of delimiting criteria for concepts, it is essential that the most useful criteria be chosen for the concept to be analyzed. This step adds to the assurance that the meanings attached to a concept by the language employed conveys the clearest possible meaning of the concept under question, while enhancing its universality across cases in different situations.

As a teacher practices these techniques to analyze concepts, the process should become clearer and easier. Not all of the techniques are useful in the analysis of all cases of available concepts. Therefore, the teacher will have to exercise some judgment regarding the technique or condition that is most appropriate for initiating the analysis. It appears that a teacher would do well to apply these conceptual analysis techniques in a prescribed order so that his choices demonstrate some sort of logical progression. The suggested order of analyzing a concept would include the following processes:

1. Select *model* cases of the concept.
2. Select *contrary* cases of the concept.
3. Select *related* cases of the concept.
4. Select *borderline* cases of the concept.
5. *Invent* cases of the concept.

After a teacher has worked through each of these steps, he should have a clear picture of the concept and how it should be used to convey meaning. Then he can confidently begin to explore the *social context, the underlying anxiety, the practical results,* and the *results in language* associated with the concept under analysis. At the completion of this process, a teacher should have a firm grasp of what a concept is and how it can be used to convey meaning and aid the communication process.

Developing Basic Understanding as an Instructional Goal

Earlier in this chapter, basic understanding was defined as the process of combining significant and valid processes in terms of relevant patterns for creating or developing meaning for concrete or abstract experience. In part, we have dealt with "developing meaning" in our discussion of the nature and analysis of concepts and "combining significant and valid processes" for providing meaning for different kinds of concepts. However, we have not dealt specifically with developing basic understanding as an instructional goal. Our attention now focuses on this aspect of developing basic understanding.

Before one can deal with the relationship between basic understanding and instruction, there must be some agreement on how these terms might be usefully delineated both theoretically and pragmatically. In the former instance (basic understanding), one is concerned with "developing meaning for concrete or abstract experience" and in the latter instance (instruction) one is concerned with the "total stimulus setting within which systematic stimuli and desired responses occur."[18] The first task in setting and striving toward an instructional goal is to establish (1) what is to be understood and (2) the essential criteria required for achieving understanding. At this point the teacher must be well acquainted with the content and its unique conceptual characteristics.

Any approach to the development of understanding as an instructional goal must deal with content both as product and process. As was demonstrated in our discussion of concepts, there is a unique relationship between the process of providing meaning and the product* derived to denote concepts. The communication of this relationship represents the basis for establishing and pursuing an instructional goal. Since concepts deal with a diverse array of social and physical phenomena that require explanations that fit into different forms to communicate intended meanings, instructional goals must provide learners with experiences and patterns that enable them to acquire basic understandings necessary for adequate community valued activity and future learnings. When basic understanding becomes the primary instructional goal, the teacher's skill in conceptual analysis becomes the critical factor. Teachers cannot communicate ideas that they do not understand or the processes needed to formulate and analyze them if they lack basic understanding of the concepts involved. Therefore, a necessary first step in the establishment of an instructional goal begins with conceptual analysis so that the environmental setting and sequential procedure associated with an idea can be used to full advantage.

Sequence in Basic Understanding

When sequence is approached in terms of curriculum and instruction in the elementary school, there are two primary problem areas to be considered. First, some attention must be focused on problems of curriculum organization in relation to the establishment of continuity

---

* The concrete example of the concept that has the appropriate criterional attributes.

and integration. Second, equal attention must be given to conceptual analysis as it relates to delineation and learning. Sequence in curriculum is ordinarily restricted to concerns related to patterned ordering of content and materials for some preconceived time block. On the other hand, sequence in conceptual analysis

> . . . consists not so much in the succession of details in various areas of knowledge as in the continuity of learning steps leading toward the formation of ideas and the use of cognitive processes. This suggests a two-fold sequence for learning experiences: the sequence of ideas to be dealt with, in order of their complexity and abstractness, and the sequence of the cognitive processes in the order of increasingly demanding intellectual rigor, such as precision of analysis required or range of application expected.[19]

When a teacher attempts to classify concepts according to form, he deals with both the nature and type of the ideas under consideration. A teacher engaging in conceptual analysis is attempting to establish the appropriate sequence needed to acquire meaning through the selection of criteria and activities, and by formulating a teaching strategy to achieve basic understanding of the basic ideas to be learned. Therefore, sequence in basic understanding always involves the formulation of a teaching strategy in accord with the nature and type of ideas to be learned and the outcome expectation of the learner.

Scope in Basic Understanding

Scope in the context of developing basic understanding focuses away from the concept of "content coverage" and more toward the nature and number of required specific facts that provide the criterional attributes for concepts to be learned. As more information becomes available through the use of more sophisticated collection and analysis techniques, the problem of complexity in determining boundaries for the scope of selected content comes into play in ways heretofore not considered as integral to the instructional effort. There is also increasing concern with overspecialization and decentralization in terms of how knowledge is produced, organized, and disseminated. New knowledge developed by specialists carries with it new vocabulary and processes understood only by selected practitioners in the same area of concern.

In order to make practical use of this new knowledge, many specialists have to come together in a team effort to produce a given product. If the complexity of new knowledge limits the ability of knowledge producers to make practical use of it without consultations with other specialists, it is unlikely that a curriculum program will be able to limit the scope of such information for dissemination to youth.

It appears that the determination of the scope of the curriculum is now (and the trend indicates that it will become increasingly so) a most difficult task for curriculum specialists who are responsible for selecting relevant and current content for young learners. The prime difficulty seems to stem from the curriculum specialist's inability to decipher new knowledge and to reformulate it for dissemination to youth of different age levels and vastly diverse backgrounds. As new concepts appear on increasingly higher rungs of the knowledge ladder, the problem of scope will expand in complexity and difficulty to the point where abstractions will be required to define higher order abstractions. At this point, relevancy of knowledge becomes the prime concern of scope delineation and definition in curriculum development.

The scope of the curriculum content has a direct bearing on the basic understanding that can be derived from a study of the knowledge selected to be learned. When a given concept is selected for young learners to learn and understand, a certain number of facts, with their related constellations in contrasting or similar settings, must be learned if the learner is to acquire a basic understanding of the concept in question. The scope of the content to be studied determines the degree to which a learner can achieve a basic understanding of the concept selected for attention. For if the content fails to delineate the critical criterional attributes of the concept, it is not possible for a young inexperienced learner to acquire a basic understanding of the concept. Any focus on the achievement of basic understanding must also include the nature of learners as a prime condition for determining scope. The scope of the content must be sufficiently broad to enable learners from diverse backgrounds to grasp the basic understanding of the concepts under consideration without penalty for accidents of birth or environmental conditions. For this very reason, scope becomes a pivotal entity in helping young learners attain a basic understanding of key concepts as a result of the content that was selected and organized for presentation.

Transfer in Basic Understanding

Teaching for basic understanding involves the transfer of knowledge and learning processes directly because *what* and *how* it is learned is immediately applicable in different settings with diverse situational variables. As Travers suggests, "All teaching is based on the assumption that the immediate skills, understandings, attitudes, appreciation and other learned functions influence behavior in a diversity of subsequent situations."[20] However, transfer is not as dependent upon the assumption that knowledge will be used in new situations when instruction develops a basic understanding of the concepts being taught. When a learner achieves basic understanding, he learns both the process and the product as an interrelated whole. Basic understanding of a concept cannot be achieved apart from selecting and processing appropriate content according to a pattern that gives the intended meaning sought for the concept under consideration. As learners use this pattern it becomes a proven method for the achievement of basic understanding of selected concepts and its applicability transfers directly to other situations requiring analogous demands on one's intellectual activity.

Instructional Approaches to Effective, Efficient, and Effectant* Learning Behavior

For our discussion, an instructional approach refers to the way in which the teacher paces and moves instruction along toward an end. This notion is closely tied to the formulation of a dyadic chain (see later in this chapter) that governs the nature, type, and variety of communication patterns transpiring between the teacher and the pupil. The dyadic chain is a specific instance of the total instructional approach that remains dependent on the specific intent of the teacher and the contextual situational variables affecting the environmental setting. Under these conditions, the ultimate purpose of an instructional ap-

* A term used in Social Psychology to designate the relationship between efficiency and effectiveness.

proach is to make learning behavior more efficient, effective, and effectant.

In order to produce efficient, effective, and effectant learning behavior through the use of an instructional approach, attention must be directed to the elements of the school as a social system and to some of the structural aspects of teaching. If the school were not viewed as a social system, it would be difficult to evaluate a pupil's performance in the achievement of efficient, effective, and effectant learning behavior resulting from a given instructional approach. Likewise, the outcome of an instructional approach is dependent upon the nature of the relationship among the structural aspects of teaching such as the dyadic chain between teacher and pupil, the gap between the performance base of teacher and pupil, and the gap between the actual performance of a pupil and a preset performance standard. This latter constellation is discussed elsewhere.

Before one can deal with how an instructional approach results in efficient, effective, and effectant learning behavior, some attention must be directed toward the school as a social system. Even though many conceptual schemes employed to study "education may focus on the internal system of the classroom, the system is inevitably related to external systems and most generally to what we have called the culture, with its attendant ethos and the component values."[21] Since the school as a social system is not a central concern of this chapter, although it contributes to this particular discussion, the structural dimensions and central concepts of the schematic framework are summarized in Figure 5.1.

Even though Figure 5.1 is applicable to most human behavior in a social system, it pinpoints, specifically that: "The indicated elements of the school as a social system are not only related to each other structurally but are also related dynamically to the quality of performance in the system."[22] Since three of the basic criterion concepts of performance in a social system are effectiveness, efficiency, and effectance, we can now deal with these ideas in terms of their contribution in formulating and initiating an instructional approach.

Before we can begin to discuss the unique complexities of an instructional approach, definitions and meanings must be provided to fix efficiency, effectiveness, and effectance in a framework that enables one to deal with these ideas in relation to the purpose of the elementary school instructional efforts. In the main, *effectiveness* deals with the relationship that exists among the values (A) in the culture, the expectations (B) for roles in institutions, and the actual behavior (E) of the subject being studied. Behavior is considered effective when the correla-

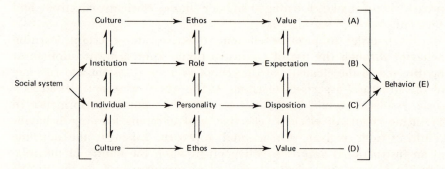

Figure 5.1

Elements of the School Social System, Showing Normative, Personal, and Cultural Dimensions of Behavior. [Reprinted by special permission from J. W. Getzels, "A Social Psychology of Education," in *The Handbook of Social Psychology,* 2nd ed., Vol. 5, Gardner Lindzey and Elliot Aronson, eds. (Reading, Mass.: Addison-Wesley, 1969).]

tion among these variables is high. When observed behavior is congruent with the values and expectations of the social system so that advances toward the system's goals are evident within the general context of adhering to cultural aspirations, the behavior is thought to be effective. In contrast, a low correlation among these variables (A, B, and E) demonstrates ineffective behavior inconsistent with the values and expectations of the social system. In the latter case, progress toward achieving the goals of the system is limited and thus fails to illuminate cultural aspirations. When we consider this idea as it relates to implementing an instructional approach, the social system of reference is the classroom and, in some instances, smaller groups within this unit. However, the conditions within a classroom still have to reflect cultural components widely accepted by people who support and use the schools.

For the most part, efficiency deals with the operational or action components of effectiveness within a social system organized to achieve prescribed goals. Specifically, efficiency deals with the relationship that exists among the subvalues (D) resulting from unique socialization experiences, the dispositions (C) of a given individual in a given environmental setting, and the actual observed behavior (E) under consideration. A high correlation among these variables (D, C, and E) is an indication that observed behavior is efficient. According to Getzels, efficient "behavior is congruent with the individual's values and dispositions, and thus fulfills his cognitive and affective needs."[23] Conversely, a low correlation among these variables indicates inefficient behavior and Getzels suggests that this type of indicator shows observed behavior to be "incongruent with the individual's values and dispositions, and thus fails to fulfill his cognitive and affective needs."[24] In planning an instructional approach, considerations related to efficiency must be directed to the individual pupil operating within the school as a social system.

Effectiveness and efficiency are essential elements in instructional planning because they focus both on the social system of the school as a whole and on the individual operating within that system. These notions operate in concert to provide a framework for devising an instructional approach within an overall teaching strategy. To some extent this is related to the nature of effectiveness and efficiency as it occurs in a social system as presented by Getzels:

> To the extent that there is discrepancy between (1) the values serving as the context for the school, with the consequent role expectations, and (2) the values available to the child for internalization, with the consequent personality dispositions, behavior may conform to the one or to the other, or to some compromise between the two. When behavior conforms to the dispositions, it appears "natural," "authentic," "pleasurable," and is forthcoming with a minimum of strain or expenditure of psychic energy: in this sense, it is efficient. But it may not fulfill the role expectations or contribute to the goals of the system— the behavior may not be effective. The child who is permitted to do just as he wishes may not necessarily learn what the school was set up for him to learn. When behavior conforms to the expectations, and there is a discrepancy between the dispositions and the expectations, the behavior seems "unnatural," "unauthentic," "painful," and is forthcoming with a maximum of strain and expenditure of psychic energy; the behavior is inefficient. But it may fulfill the role expectations and contribute to the goals of the system; in this sense, the behavior is effective. The artist or musician forced to teach against his will in order to make a living may do so exceedingly well but at great cost in personal frustration and disappointment. It is clear that it is possible for performance in the school to be effective without necessarily being efficient, and to be efficient without necessarily being effective. A critical issue in the social psychology of education is the factors making for effectiveness and efficiency, and the relation between the two in the school system.[25]

Teachers are constantly faced with demands to increase both effectiveness and efficiency in achieving the goals of the school. Unfortunately, the achievement of one quality state can retard the achievement of the other. Therefore, the teacher's choice of an instructional approach must take into account the fact that a focus on the individual pupil can add to or detract from the effectiveness and efficiency resulting from the teaching experience provided. Issues related to the impact of different instructional approaches on effectiveness and efficiency are part of the reoccurring attempts to improve and reform the effects of schooling on pupils and ultimately society. Since this is such a critical issue, we return to it later in our discussion.

In order to acquire a broader understanding of how effectiveness and efficiency are interrelated as representative "quality outputs" of the school as a social system, White, in 1959, coined the word *effectance*[26] to refer to the general relation between efficiency and effectiveness. When observed behavior is simultaneously efficient and effective, it is considered to be effectant. As the discrepancy between effectiveness and efficiency increases, observed behavior is judged to be less effectant. The primary purpose of school through the instructional approaches employed is to increase the probability that pupils will be educationally efficient and institutionally effective. Through the use of well-conceived and task-matched instructional approaches, the prime concern of the teacher must be directed toward the increased effectance of all his pupils.

Setting a goal for achieving educational effectance for the majority of pupils in a given classroom places a heavy burden on an instructional approach to "deliver" within the context of present practice and current thinking dealing with the purpose and direction of the school as a social institution. As emphases shift across technological, curricular, and sociological aspects of the elementary school experiences, greater attention is focused on either effectiveness or efficiency, thus decreasing educational effectancy. For example, pupils are judged efficient when their behavior conforms to their dispositions and appears "natural," "authentic," and "pleasurable" with minimal strain or expenditure of psychic energy. However, a primary focus on the sociological aspects of learning rarely contributes to the curricular goals of the school at the levels presently expected by the majority of the school's clientele. And, as such, schools that design their instructional approaches to correlate too highly with the individual dispositions of pupils are thought to be ineffective because they are accused of neglecting the institutional goals vital to the survival and improvement of our society. Essentially, that is the major source of detraction and criticism of the current advocates of "open education."

Another side of the coin is illuminated as one notes the outcomes of attempts to gear most instructional approaches to enhance technological and curricular components of the school experience, so prevalent in the 1950s and 1960s. As schools narrowed their focus on the "structure of knowledge," "early intellectual experience," "programmed learning," and "problem solving in experimentation," they became more effective as institutions but less efficient for individual pupils because most of the instructional approaches employed placed little or no emphasis on the dispositions of learners. This inevitably led to the charge that instructional practice ignores relevant personality variables that might be more useful as an aid to learning and application of knowledge gained. Unfortunately, this type of charge tends to make critical forces such as curriculum designers, authors, educators, professional organizations, publishers, citizen groups, governments, and foundations overreact, and causes the pendulum to swing violently in the opposite direction. As a result, attempts to chart a middle ground that might lead to greater educational effectance are thwarted.

When an instructional approach is under consideration, one must always take into account the fact that the central relationship in any school is the dyadic—that is, the reciprocal, interdependent responding between the teacher and the pupil. As the teacher designs an instructional approach to be implemented with pupils, he is always faced with the problem of trying to produce educationally effectant behavior. If the instructional approach is too closely associated with the teacher's view of institutional expectations without considering pupil dispositions, there is likely to be a gain in effective behavior at the expense of efficiency. Similarly, too much attention focused on pupil dispositions devoid of planned connection with relevant institutional expectations will increase efficiency at the expense of effectiveness. If an instructional approach is expected to help pupils acquire educational effectancy, prime concern must be focused on the planning and sequencing of effective and efficient behavior.

Problems Related to
Educational Effectance

Pupils at the same grade level in the same classroom are exposed to similar expectations. However, they are not likely to perceive the expectations uniformly. This is due, in part, to the fact that each pupil has a preset constellation of cognitive, affective, and psychomotor dispositions that tend to determine how he interprets stimuli encountered. All pupils so encumbered with such complexity of interrelated and unique dispositions will view the world and instructional stimuli from his own perspective, which will affect directly what is seen and heard, remembered and forgotten, thought and uttered, and what will be the nature of his interpersonal relationships in a given social setting.

The differences between pupils' reactions to expectations imposed by the school are critical to the selection and implementation of an appropriate instructional approach. Part of the difficulty related to selecting and implementing an instructional approach is associated with the fact that differences noted between pupils are not just a function of differences in intelligence and cognitive abilities. Often, differences in pupils' affective dispositions are much more crucial to shaping the instructional approach designed and employed. Few can deny the importance of such affective dispositions as personal preferences, individual response sets, attitudes, needs, values, drives, variable motivations, and interests. The fact that a pupil can remember intricate electronic patterns for building remote control units for model airplanes but has real difficulty memorizing a simple verse of highly rhythmic poetry is probably more indicative of his *interest* in electronics than electronic intelligence. Conversely, the pupil might be indifferent to poetry but not poetically stupid. The instructional approach selected by the teacher must take into account subtle cognitive and affective differences and interactions that combine to make each child complex and different as a prospective learner. These differences and complexities require instructional approaches designed to deal with the observed differences among pupils expected to meet institutional conditions imposed on the school by society. Therefore, the nature of pupil dispositions is at the heart of designing and implementing an instructional approach with the intent to help pupils perform according to the school's expectations.

Since personal dispositions have a decided effect on the performance of pupils in a school setting, some attention should be devoted to delineating disposition as a generic concept and indicating how the different types of dispositions affect the design, selection, and implementation of instructional approaches that are intended to alter pupil performance in predictable ways. For our purposes, interest is the key disposition in our analysis and, as such, is examined in relation to selected affective dispositions identified previously. This approach should clearly delineate the specific meaning of a disposition while highlighting the range, complexity, and the nature of such dispositions affecting pupil performance in schools. In addition, we will be in a better position to indicate the foundational knowledge required to initiate the construction of an instructional approach.

It might be profitable to begin our analysis by distinguishing between an interest and a preference. Pupils generally have a preference for arithmetic over creative writing and yet have no interest in either. In this case, it would be difficult to get them to expend a great deal of effort to learn more about one subject area than the other. Pupils often admit to a preference of one content area over another while expressing little interest in either as a fruitful way to make use of their time. From our example, we might conclude that the difference between a preference and an interest is probably associated with the fact that the former is relatively passive while the latter is inescapably dynamic. Now that we have an example of how a preference and an interest might differ operationally and have spotlighted some of the relevant critical attributes, it is easier to deal concretely with the notions presented by Getzels when he states that:

> A preference is a disposition to *receive* one object as against another; it does not induce one to *seek out* the particular for study or acquisition. In contrast, the basic nature of an interest is that it does induce one to seek out particular objects and activities.[27]

It is very easy to mistake a pupil's preference for a school activity or subject area for a direct statement or example of interest. Because this situation is probably more common than not, instructional approaches that focus on preferences rather than on interests lose the power to select, with a high degree of probability, specific experiences toward which pupils are internally and favorably disposed.

It is also true that there is a real difference between having a positive attitude toward an object and having an interest in it. It is possible to have a positive attitude toward South American Indians without having an interest in them. On the other hand, the experience of the 1960s indicates that it is possible for people to have a negative attitude about North American blacks and yet be ardently interested in them as individuals or as a group. We do not presume to suggest that pupils' attitudes will not affect what they will be able to learn about South American Indians or North American blacks. However, we do suggest that the conceptual differences between an attitude or interest as a disposition are critical to any attempt to formulate a valid instructional approach that takes these two dispositions into account. As we employ the concept, an attitude can be thought of as an enduring, learned predisposition to behave in a consistent way toward a given class of objects. In this sense, pupils are probably not driven by an attitude, although this state of emotional unrest accompanies their interests. When a teacher designs an instructional approach on the basis of expressed attitudes of pupils, it is possible to fail to tap genuine interest that provides the necessary drive required to build learning capital from existing attitudes toward objects used as content. Under these kinds of circumstances, the instructional approach employed is not likely to affect existing attitudes that control pupils' dispositions to act toward objects. The challenge to the teacher is related to being able to focus his instructional approach on pupils' attitudes in a pattern consistent with their interests.

For our purposes, it is necessary to distinguish between a drive, a need, and an interest. A study of the statement by Getzels reveals many subtle and real differences among the three dispositions. According to this author:

> A drive has its source in a specific physiological disequilibrium. An interest has its source in experience and challenges us to exert ourselves even though there is no necessity in any biological sense. Technically speaking, we may say that a drive is a function largely of our instinctual processes, an interest a function largely of our ego processes. There is a distinction also between a need and an interest, though the distinction here is more subtle. A need is a disposition or force within the organism which consistently impels him toward one type of activity as against another. Thus we may speak of an individual as having a high or a low need for achievement or for affiliation. Insofar as the source is not necessarily biological but may have its source in experience, it is distinct from a drive; insofar as it disposes the individual toward a general type of activity rather than toward a specific object or goal, it is distinct from an interest. The need for achievement may find expression in the school situation, for example, in the arts, sciences, athletics, or extracurricular activities. The need is the same; the interests are different. Against this background, we may define interest as a characteristic disposition, organized through experience, which impels an individual to seek out particular objects, activities, skills, understandings, or goals for attention and acquisition.[28]

When interests are distinguished from drives and needs in a school setting, they reveal very different points of reference for selecting and implementing an instructional approach that takes advantage of relevant individual characteristics. If a teacher wants to obtain an individual pupil's attention so that he may acquire data that directly influences observed behavior, his instructional approach must take into account the interests of the pupils so involved.

Before we turn from drawing distinctions between an interest and other dispositions, it might be particularly instructive to spotlight differences between an interest and a value. Primarily, a value can be viewed as a conception of the worth or excellence, or the degree of worth, ascribed to an object or activity, or a class thereof that influences the resulting selection of behavior. Although ascribed to the object and reacted to as if external or objective, *value* is a function of the valuing *transaction,* not the object. In this sense, interest and value are quite different as dispositions because the former disposes us toward what we *want* to do whereas the latter disposes us toward what we *ought* to do. Many conflicts between teachers and pupils emanate from the differences that are expressed by the interest and value dispositions. With this in mind, a teacher faced with the need to design or select an instructional approach would do well to take into account Getzels's comment when he states that:

> The dispositions which are brought by the various individuals into the role structure of the school tend to determine the definition of the roles, and affect not only *how much* or *how well* the learner will learn and the teacher will teach but also the *particular kind* of learning and teaching that will be done.[29]

There can be little doubt about the extent to which individual disposition should influence the nature of the instructional approach employed to affect pupil performance in a predetermined direction.

The interests and preferences of a teacher can serve as starting points for instructional planning when the content in question is optional. In the main, when a teacher is allowed to focus on content that interests him personally, he is likely to have a more intimate and thorough knowledge of relevant information that heightens his enthusiasm and makes the subject more understandable to novice learners. Since interest is a critical component in determining a teacher's enthusiasm, it plays a significant role as a motivating force for children. Children are likely to be more highly motivated by teachers who are enthusiastic than by those who have no emotional attachment to the material to be processed and learned.

The interests and preferences of teachers for certain kinds of information and subject matter content can be effectively employed to motivate children toward ideas and knowledge and processes that enable them to gain a greater understanding into some of the significant meanings and relationships associated with the information in question. Children who are exposed to knowledgeable and enthusiastic teachers are likely to learn how one's feelings toward information contribute to one's developing a basic understanding of a particular area. It is only a short step for children to learn that their interests and preferences for some content is likely to aid them in gaining a greater understanding of the subject matter because they have a favorable emotional involvement with the material to be learned. Since children are likely to value that which is of great interest to them, they profit greatly when they are exposed to teaching by teachers who deal with material parallel to personal interests and preferences.

Utilizing Products of Content and
Process for Instructional Planning

The availability of relevant and valid products determines the quality level and range of all instructional planning. All instructional planning must have a point of focus if it is to be distinguished from random or trial-and-error activity. For instructional planning, the products of content and process become points of focus to guide the construction, direction, and implementation of the results of the planning efforts. Before one can deal effectively with instructional planning centered on the products of content and process, some discussion of the meaning of relevant terms is in order.

Instructional Planning. Instructional planning is a scheme of action or an outline of a teaching strategy proposed to achieve some learning intent. Its primary function is to specify the content and processes required to achieve a basic understanding of the ideas that are to be communicated to a selected group of pupils. For our purposes, content "refers to the compendium of information which comprises the learning material for a particular course or a given grade."[30] This compendium of information usually consists of facts, concepts, ideas, laws, theories, and generalizations that are related by a predetermined arrangement of selected slices of available knowledge. Headings such as science, history, mathematics, civil war, or government may be attached to information so that the organizational structure needed to select, relate, and specify content can be completed. In summary, content can be thought of as "a rhetoric of conclusions to be transferred to the student."[31]

Process. Process is closely tied to content in that it could not exist without the presence of content to be produced, formulated, reformulated, applied, interpreted, or evaluated. Specifically, process can be thought of as referring "to all the random, or ordered, operations which can be associated with knowledge and with human activity."[32] Processes are associated with the creation, revision, utilization, and communication of knowledge. It is also possible to employ processes for guiding decision-making activity, the evaluation of outcomes and the formulation of new configurations of thought processes, methodology, and consciousness. From our discussion, it should be readily apparent that a precise description of all processes in use is not possible because they are not easily identified. However, in order to designate a process, the scheme that provides order and direction for its employment must be apparent and describable. At this point one can agree with the assertion of Parker and Rubin when they state

> that process—the cluster of diverse procedures which surround the acquisition and utilization of knowledge—is, in fact, the highest form of content . . .[33]

When we use the term *products,* it refers to the tangible symbols that represent content and process. Products are the ingredients of content and the description, picture, or image of a process. When applied to content, products are designated by such terms as *facts, concepts, ideas, laws, theories,* and *generalizations.* On the other hand, products applied to process refer to terms such as discussion, lecture, research, inference, and evaluation. It is always tricky to use products as a way to designate a process because it describes action in a "stop" position. For example, when a discussion is in progress, the process is evident. However, when one speaks of an intent to have a discussion or having had a discussion, he is describing the product of a process. This distinction is critical for instructional planning because one can only prepare for and evaluate the products of process.

Stated and Unstated Outcomes
in Instructional Planning

Instructional planning assumes that the expected outcomes of instruction can be stated and that that statement is verifiable with describable products. The most common manifestation of that expectation was evident in the widespread preoccupation of many educators with statements of behavioral objectives that characterized instruction and curriculum efforts of the 1960s. During this period, much was learned about the possibility of being able to state outcomes as the starting point for instructional planning. Part of the problem stemmed from the fact that products differ greatly according to use and content. If products are used to refer to stable information represented in a given content at a given time, then certain expected outcomes can be stated precisely. For example, one might indicate that pupils can recall a specific date and indicate why it is of historical importance to the United States and another nation directly involved. On the other hand, if one were to indicate that pupils can speculate on how the United States might have developed if the event associated with a specific date had not occurred, it would not be possible to state expected information product outcomes as a basis for instructional planning. However, the expected process outcomes that would enable pupils to demonstrate the behavior suggested in the preceding sentence can be stated.

It should be evident that certain outcomes cannot be stated because tangible products are not readily available for examination. Many important outcomes remain unstated because much relevant human behavior cannot be isolated as discrete products since they only have meaning within the situational context of their occurrence. Situational contexts that precipitate certain products cannot be replicated, duplicated, and intentionally altered for specific purposes later in time and space. Therefore, statements of expected outcomes are necessarily limited to products of content and process and cannot reflect the organic and interactive experience taking place during instruction. This suggests that instructional planning must take into account the fact that important expected outcomes can be stated or unstated. Therefore, products resulting from instruction are observed both directly and indirectly. The task of instructional planning is to ensure that both the stated and unstated expected outcomes are taken into account during actual instruction.

Explicit and Implicit Relationships in Instructional Planning

When one attempts to conduct instructional planning, some relationships necessary for understanding basic concepts and providing the climate for supportive and mutually instructive human behavior can be explicitly or implicitly described. In many instances, relationships can be explicitly stated—that is, plant growth is affected by light, water, soil conditions, and temperature, or teacher interaction with pupils should provide for the equalization of time available to each member of the group. The relationships suggested by the foregoing statements are explicit because they are stated directly and relevant data needed for instructional plannings are included.

In contrast, many important relationships can only be implicitly stated. For example, democratic participation decreases apathy among young people, or pollution is a by-product of consumption habits. The relationships suggested by these statements are implicit because they are not directly stated although they are understandable or deducible from what is stated. Instructional planning in these instances must take into account the fact that implicit relationships require a data-processing procedure that deals with the selection, nature, type, and validity of information used to explore the area of focus. Without such concern, instructional planning for dealing with implicit relationships will guide the instruction experience toward the achievement of intended goals.

Structure and Instructional Planning

The use of the term *structure* can be misleading and confusing when it is related to instructional planning. When we use the term, we refer to any enduring arrangement, grouping, pattern, or articulation of parts to form a relatively stable system or whole. Structure usually implies stability of the component parts, whereas the parts of a "gestalt" or a system alter as long as the interrelationships remain the same. Whether or not instructional planning is focused on the "whole," its "parts," or the "interrelationships" among the parts, the problem is, essentially, one of how to treat structure. Both content and process have structure that is readily discernible when purposeful organization is applied. The configuration of instructional planning is largely dependent upon how one deals with the observed structure.

If one is interested in having pupils know how a telephone works, he might approach the problem by dealing with the telephone as a whole. In this instance, he might deal with the general purpose of a telephone as an instrument that converts acoustic energy into electric energy and vice versa, how the telephone is manually operated, the proper use of the telephone for different purposes, and how the telephone affects our daily lives. Second, it is possible to study the working parts of a telephone such as the diaphragm, microphone, carbon granules, repeating coil, and telephone receiver and treat them as separate entities. As a third choice, one might study the interrelationship between the separate parts that cause them to be a telephone. Each of these approaches to the structure of telephone content affects the nature of instructional planning for teaching pupils. Many of the products of content and process require the instructional planner to make decisions regarding structure prior to the formulation of a teaching strategy because the resulting tactic is so crucial to the planning approach and goal designation.

Mediational Variables and Instructional Planning

Mediational variables are difficult to plan for but must be considered if instructional planning takes into account individual processes employed by intended learners. For our purposes, *mediational variables* refer to intervening objects or processes upon which pupil learning resulting from instruction is dependent. In other words, mediational variables are the events that intervene between the events before and after them in a chain of events. When cognition is considered, it is generally held that all knowledge is mediate: perception depends on intervening psychological processes following stimulations; other cognitive or emotional states depend on intervening associations and thought processes. With this in mind, the instructional planner must attempt to anticipate some of the mediational variables that might be engendered by the design of the resulting teaching strategy.

Some of the mediational variables that instructional planning might take into account include learning style, rate of work, experience background, familiarity with the problem, solving patterns required, application potential of the content and processes, and degree of abstraction associated with ideas. Instructional planning must take into account individual, intellectual, personality, and experience variables that influence the learning potential of pupils for whom instruction is intended. If there is no anticipation of how different pupils are likely to react to and process the content and processes to be understood, efforts of instructional planning are not likely to have much effect in the intended direction.

Instructional planning necessarily focuses on the products of content and process as a beginning point of departure. Since content and process are interrelated, the validity of a process can only be determined by the way in which it shapes content in response to a problem or question. The instructional plan determines which products apply, how they should be arranged for presentation, and how they can be most profitably processed. Even though certain products of processes cannot be tested in a school setting, the instructional plan should denote how these products might be utilized in the solution of present and future important real-life problems. It is apparent that most critical objectives in education cannot be achieved through the use of specific content and processes. However, they cannot be achieved without making appropriate use of the products of relevant content and processes, either. Instructional planning is a systematic pattern for improving the fit between the teaching strategy employed and the products of the content and processes to be taught. Hopefully, this step will make products learned in a school setting more applicable to the solution of real-life problems.

Summary

One of the primary concerns of the elementary school is to help children develop a basic understanding of ideas and concepts necessary for personal growth and satisfaction. Developing basic understandings is the focus of the instructional intent of teaching and the foundation of the instructional program.

When teachers attempt to develop basic understandings, they consider both the inner significance of a psychic process and the cause-and-effect relationships of the phenomenon being studied. Although cause-and-effect relationships do contribute to basic understanding, they are not an integral part of its structural definition. From this vantage point, basic understanding refers to the process of evolving operational thought patterns that result from combining major approaches to processing information for creating or developing meaning for concrete or abstract experience. This definition of basic understanding requires one to take a position on the nature of concepts and how they might be developed with children. It became apparent that knowing specific aspects of concepts is a necessary step toward developing basic understanding of complex phenomena. The effectiveness of the instructional program is dependent upon the care and precision with which a teacher approaches developing basic understanding consistent with the characteristics of the children to be taught.

References

1. Dwayne Huebner, ed., *A Reassessment of the Curriculum* (New York: Bureau of Publications, Teachers College, Columbia University, 1964).
2. Dorothy M. Fraser, *Current Curriculum Studies in Academic Subjects* (Washington, D.C.: NEA, 1962).
3. John I. Goodlad, *School Curriculum Reform in the United States* (New York: The Fund for the Advancement of Education, 1964).
4. A. Harry Passow, ed., *Curriculum Crossroads* (New York: Bureau of Publications, Teachers College, Columbia University, 1962).
5. John I. Goodlad, Renata von Stoephasius, and M. Frances Klein, *The Changing School Curriculum* (New York: The Fund for the Advancement of Education, 1966).
6. Robert W. Heath, ed., *New Curricula* (New York: Harper, 1964).
7. Jerome S. Bruner, Jacqueline J. Goodnow, and George A. Austin, *A Study of Thinking* (New York: Science Editions, 1956).
8. Jerome S. Bruner, *The Process of Education* (Cambridge, Mass.: Harvard U. P., 1960).
9. ———, *On Knowing* (Cambridge, Mass.: Belknap Press of Harvard U. P., 1966).
10. John P. DeCocco, ed., *The Psychology of Language, Thought and Instruction* (New York: Holt, 1967).
11. Peter H. Martorella, *Concept Learning in the Social Studies: Models for Structuring Curriculum* (Scranton, Penn.: Intext, 1971).
12. John Wilson, *Thinking with Concepts* (London: Cambridge U. P., 1969).
13. John P. DeCocco, op. cit., p. 220.
14. Ibid.
15. John Wilson, op. cit., p. 11.
16. Ibid., p. 21.
17. Ibid., pp. 23–39.

18. James B. MacDonald, ed., *Theories of Instruction* (Washington, D.C.: Association for Supervision and Curriculum Development, 1965), p. 6.
19. Hilda Taba, *Curriculum Development: Theory and Practice* (New York: Harcourt, 1962), p. 189.
20. Robert M. W. Travers, *Essentials of Learning* (New York: Macmillan, 1967), p. 234.
21. J. W. Getzels, "A Social Psychology of Education," in Gardner Lindzey and Elliot Aronson, eds., *The Handbook of Social Psychology*, Vol. V (Reading, Mass.: Addison-Wesley, 1969), p. 464.
22. Ibid.
23. Ibid., p. 465.
24. Ibid.
25. Ibid.
26. R. W. White, "Motivation Reconsidered: The Concept of Competence," *Psychological Review*, **66**:297–333 (1959).
27. J. W. Getzels, op. cit., p. 469.
28. Ibid., p. 470.
29. Ibid.
30. J. Cecil Parker and Louis J. Rubin, *Process as Content: Curriculum Design and the Application of Knowledge* (Chicago: Rand McNally, 1966), p. 1.
31. Joseph J. Schwab, "The Concept of Structure in the Subject Fields," paper presented at the 20th Annual Meeting, Council on Cooperation in Teacher Education, Washington, D.C., 1961.
32. Parker and Rubin, op. cit., p. 2.
33. Ibid., p. 1.

6

Developing Basic Skills and Intellectual Processes

One cannot effectively employ intellectual processes without having achieved mastery of, and control over, basic study skills. On the other hand, the use of intellectual processes is integral to the acquisition, development, mastery, and employment of basic study skills in any learning or activity requiring the use of knowledge as a basic element guiding action. Therein lies the dilemma. One set of functions is required to acquire and use the other set although they are conceptually different. Functionally, one explanation would classify basic study skills and intellectual processes as being part of the same domain and on a closed hierarchical and spiraled continuum. Figure 6.1 illustrates how basic study skills and intellectual processes are interrelated functionally. When one is faced with a problem, intellectual processes are stimulated to seek possible actions that could be applied to provide an adequate solution. The intellectual processes may guide a person through trial and error attempts, systematic employment of standardized procedures, or applied solutions already known. In any event, at this stage one would be employing intellectual processes in an attempt to find an acceptable solution to a problem. Once an individual has worked through a series of events focused on the solution of a problem and settled on a structured set of procedures or ideas he begins to deal with basic study skills, at least in relation to that problem. At another level, or under a different set of circumstances, basic study skills derived from the application of intellectual processes to a problem area can be employed to solve

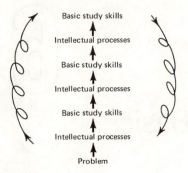

Figure 6.1
The Interrelationship Between Basic Study Skills and Intellectual Processes.

another problem that also requires the use of intellectual processes. In this sense *basic study skills* can be thought of as formalized and structured intellectual processes that one employs when using the intellect to find solutions to problems.

The connection between basic study skills and intellectual processes is confusing because as functions they have developmental stages that change across time, situations, and problem areas. Skills are developed so that the functional order of the intellectual processes one employs will lead to appropriate solutions to problems encountered. This point is ably made by Morse and McCune (1964) when they assert that:

> The importance of the development of the skill of thinking clearly and critically in the field of the social sciences can hardly be overestimated. But in mastering such a skill the learner in the field of mental abilities is in a situation parallel to that of the learner of muscular or manipulative activities. While he is learning, not the end product of his efforts but rather the process he follows is immediately significant. Proficiency will come in time *if the process is correctly mastered.* In learning to swim, for example, the speed which one may exhibit at first is less important than the efficient coordination of the parts of the body in the swimming process. A competent teacher of art also places much less weight on the first creations of his students than on the process by which they are attaining their results.[1]

Basic study skills energize and organize intellectual processes for meaningful achievement. Therefore, it is possible for basic study skills to be both the product and process of intellectual activity. In the former instance, intellectual activity outlines, specifies, and orders procedures (basic study skills) that lead to the solution of a given problem, whereas in the latter instance, intellectual activity is the process that enables one to outline, specify, and order appropriate solutions for given problems. Basic study skills and intellectual processes are both complementary and cumulative in their effects on one's ability to find meaningful solutions to real problems. This being the case,

> Study skills and critical thinking should be developed as wholes, rather than in isolated parts, and may be learned most effectively as they are to be used rather than through artificial situations. Adequately mastered, they will be of invaluable service to the maturing pupil as he continues to learn more about social relationships through his adult years.[2]

Now that we have discussed some of the interrelationships that characterize basic study skills and intellectual processes, we can devote some attention to a detailed analysis of both areas in order to delineate how these areas differ, compare, and interrelate. This is a necessary step if we are to demonstrate how basic study skills and intellectual processes operate in the instructional program at the elementary school level.

Basic Study Skills

Change has become the byword in our society. The expansion of knowledge seems to reign unchecked as rational inquiry is being utilized to further the development of technological advances and produce greater amounts of information. This tends to create a broader base line from which more varied—both in scope and number—discoveries have a higher platform from which to launch innovations. In such an atmosphere, knowledge has been and is being accumulated faster than our society can integrate it into a systematic pattern; thus we are able to disseminate adequately the knowledge we acquire to school-age youth. Yet, schools are expected to make use of vast and ever-changing amounts of knowledge to equip children to operate effectively in a society that will probably change far beyond our conception of what it might become.

It is obvious that knowledge is being expanded in breadth, depth, and quantity to the extent that it is unreasonable to consider including all the knowledge that is likely to be accumulated in a school's curriculum program. Probably, it is equally as unreasonable to think that the information taught presently in our schools will serve as an adequate foundation for later operational effectiveness with knowledge yet to be discovered. This state of affairs raises many questions as to what is considered effective education for adults of tomorrow. What criteria should be used to select content to be taught when it is taken from such an immense reservoir of available knowledge? Since it is probably unrealistic to expect children to learn all of the background information concerning knowledge they will be expected to use effectively in the future, what will be the necessary foundational skills that will enable children to make effective use of existing as well as emerging knowledge? Some possible leads toward providing answers are suggested in the following statement by Richard F. P. Salinger (1965):

> In the midst of a general knowledge explosion that gives to facts a short half-life and points out the temporal nature of our understandings, we are sobered in the recognition of the little time left to work with youngsters. This recognition and its relation to the tenor of our times immediately suggest an urgent need to be *efficient*—not in the cold sense of the term to suggest a reduction of the teaching process to the programming of learners as though they were automatons but a HUMANISTIC EFFICIENCY which recognizes we are working with people. We need an efficiency that will enable us to recognize the nature of our times, as well as the nature of the rapidly approaching future. We need an efficiency that recognizes the interdependence of the total range of man's intellectual endeavors and the rate at which things are changing—the opportunity leading to the development of functional, literate human beings.[3]

This statement suggests that the education of our youth must be made more efficient if they are to be taught to handle effectively the rapidly accumulating knowledge in the future. However, care must be taken to see that this efficiency allows for the acquisition of skills that are critical for integrating the expanded knowledge in the separate areas and that have long-range value for handling problems in the future. This requirement leaves before us the task of identifying the fundamental skills necessary to make individual children efficient in their intellectual efforts —now and in the future.

In order for fundamental* skills to be of value in children's

---

* Fundamental skills are those skills that are required to acquire other learning of a more complex nature. Use of a classification system, such as an index, a dictionary, an encyclopedia, a card catalog, and so on, to locate and use information required to complete a more complex intellectual task illustrate this concept. Fundamental skills are essential to increase the scope of learning.

intellectual efforts, some thought must be given not only to what these skills are but also to how they are related to other school activities and how the use of these skills might be transferable to intellectual tasks undertaken later in different situations. On this idea, James E. Russell (1965) comments:

> Ways must be found to develop transferable intellectual skills. Pupils must learn to apply abstract propositions to the concrete situations before them. They will have to learn some abstractions abstractly. . . . The child can learn to generalize only by generalizing, and so must be provided with large quantities of fact and experience. The route to the abstract must be for most children through the concrete.
> . . . many intellectual skills are transferable to a variety of situations. Communications skills, for example, appear to be widely transferable. The study of science or history or any discipline yields insights about reality and about man, and these insights widely influence judgments and perceptions. Transfer of knowledge and skills to new situations and reorganization in new generalizations are evident in the behavior of the thinking man. But how does he learn to make such transfers?[4]

Even though this discussion does not attempt to deal with the transferability of intellectual skills, it does treat the identification and description of these skills as a first step in linking the development of independent and operational skills needed for the type of instruction children will require in order to make effective use of knowledge as we know it to be and as it might come to be.

If one describes the fundamental skills needed to make effective use of knowledge in various content areas in different situations as being intellectual skills, one runs the risk of lumping together skills that range from higher-order thinking functions to lower-order activities needed to complete a task in any given subject area. This makes it too difficult to describe and define the skills that need to be taught to ensure effective use of content information. For this reason there is an attempt to limit the focus of our concerns to those skills that are most basic to the efficient handling of most learning tasks commonly needed in school activities. *Since these skills are fundamental, they are basic to the type of study habits children need to acquire in order to work independently with content. Therefore, they should be referred to as basic study skills because they are so essential to all school learning tasks and because they can be described in terms of specific tasks to be performed.* Because of the far-ranging nature of skills classified as basic, it is hazardous to attempt a more precise definition than the one suggested previously. However, it is our aim to make the definition more explicit when we select, classify, describe, and provide functional examples of the basic study skills that are denoted.

For our purposes, basic study skills are thought of in much the same way George Spache (1964) describes them in his work, *Reading in the Elementary School*.[5] Many skills are fundamental and basic to effective learning, problem solving, and communication but cannot be measured with objective instruments such as standardized and teacher-made tests. Basic skills such as outlining, summarizing, note taking, memorizing, rereading, preparing reports, recognizing organizational patterns, and choosing pertinent information involve a whole complex of skills that are better *evaluated* (judged qualitatively) than *measured* (assessed quantitatively). Such skills must be viewed in terms of the pattern that tends to describe essential component parts without specifying a right or wrong way of putting these parts together. Purpose and function play a large role in determining whether this group of skills has been employed properly.

Similarly, many basic study skills can be measured with objective standardized or teacher-made tests. In such instances, the products of these skills reveal the extent to which a pupil has used the skill area properly. Right and wrong answers do count and do reveal functional and operational characteristics of the pupil applying a skill to a problem area or learning situation. Basic study skills in this group include the following:

1. Dictionary Skills (meanings, spellings, syllables, alphabetical order, guide words, pronunciation).
2. Library Skills (selecting best source of information, the Dewey system, shelf location, card catalog and trays).
3. Reference Skills (parts of a book, key words, the title page of a book, encyclopedia location by volume, use of index, use of table of contents).
4. Map Reading Skills (interpretation of political, physical, product, population, rainfall maps in various combinations).
5. Reading of Graphs, Charts, and Tables (interpretation of line graphs, bar graphs, pictorial graphs, tables, and pictures of fractional parts [parts of a dollar, percentages of a whole]).

As technological advances necessitate the introduction of new curriculum programs requiring the use of independent basic study skills, it becomes increasingly evident that, as Merrifield writes, ". . . teachers must face the problem of training children whose abilities are demonstrably different in detail."[6] From many indications, the training of children must include the mastery of certain basic study skills that might conceivably aid them in handling the varied and diverse learning tasks they are asked to undertake in most school-related activities. If this is the case, a planned program for teaching the basic study skills is in order and quite necessary.

For the most part, basic study skills are not often taught systematically. Certain of these skills are taught in connection with the reading, language arts, social studies, and science programs. Others are taught in connection with instruction in the use of the library. The basic study skills are seldom considered a central or major concern in the vast majority of elementary school programs even though the need for such concern is great. As a consequence, these skills are often neglected, usually not by intent, but because they find no place in the organized curriculum. Even in places where these skills are taught directly and deliberately, it is unusual for them to be reinforced with continued or systematic practice. This makes it difficult to generalize about the contribution that basic study skills may make toward the enhancement of general achievement, general reading ability, and, consequently, use of intellectual processes in the elementary schools.

Part of the problem stems from the fact that little is known about basic study skills. Published tests attempting to measure these skills are inadequate, at least in part, because of the lack of adequate research in the area to guide their construction. Thus, there is a real need for curriculum researchers to extend knowledge in this area through the use of research studies or reports that will empirically validate the existence of basic study skills. This approach to the problem should ultimately lead to a careful description of the skills involved and to the determination of agreements and disagreements between the present literature in the area and these findings of empirical studies.

An early step in learning more about the basic study skills and their development involves exploration of how these abilities are interrelated and how they are related to other educational outcomes of high priority. This could also include factors related to abilities that are not always considered within the scope of most school evaluations. Dressel and Mayhew assert that

> the amount of progress [a child makes] is apparently dependent on the nature of the educational experience provided and varies in ways which correspond reasonably well to identifiable elements in that experience. . . .[7]

In order to determine whether the learning of basic study skills contributes to an educational experience having identifiable elements, it may be helpful to establish the fact that basic study skills are inter-related and are related to general achievement, reading ability, and academic performance in various subject areas, and general problem-solving ability.

There is also a need to establish how the interrelationships be-tween the basic study skills contribute to an understanding of how they are related to other abilities considered to be valuable educational out-comes. Dressel and Mayhew[8] assert that there is some reason to believe that a planned program in basic study skills will increase the intercorre-lation among them and that children exposed to such a program will develop an integrated ability to focus these resources upon the many school learning tasks confronting them. It follows, then, that a child who will be expected to demonstrate adequate general achievement and reading ability will need a program of study that will equip him to perform, in varying degrees, skillfully and consistently over a wide range of given tasks. If a planned and systematic study of basic study skills helps to develop a consistent ability to tackle a wide range of instruc-tional tasks, these skills should be highly intercorrelated in order to show that they may contribute jointly to the development of an inte-grated ability to achieve success in other activities of high educational value.

There are many views concerning the way in which basic study skills might be measured to ensure the emergence of flexible data about the nature of these skills. Consequently, it might prove to be a signifi-cant contribution if a theoretical framework underlying the construction of a reasonably adequate instrument could be developed for some of the basic study skills for which instruments are either inadequate or nonexistent. It should be noted in the development of such an instru-ment ". . . that particular learning situations place demands on particu-lar combinations of intellectual abilities, that these abilities are of different orders of generality in the hierarchical structure, and that all measures of abilities are measures of achievement of the appropriate order of generality."[9] Since experience has taught that the best predictor of future achievement is past achievement, we might search for a com-bination of measured basic study skills that gives the most inclusive description of the ability about which we are trying to formulate gen-eralizations. Therefore, it might be helpful to develop a theoretical framework for an instrument that gives the kinds of data necessary to collect accurate measures of, and to make generalizations about, basic study skills and higher-order related intellectual skills. Even if such an instrument is not published, the theoretical data gathered to support its construction might be of use to others doing research in this area.

If our analysis reveals the general pattern of the relationship between basic study skills and other school learned abilities, it might serve as a valuable source of data needed to improve methods of teaching in this area and to reorganize this aspect of the curriculum. Such a pattern might be suggestive of the way in which pupils make use of basic study skills to handle adequately the different content areas of the upper elementary school level. In this way, a study of basic study skills may be used for purposes of prediction and diagnosis. In the former,

> the emphasis is primarily on differences between performances of individuals or between the performance of one individual and some standard; . . . [whereas with the latter], considerable attention is paid to the analysis and description of the various characteristics or performances from task to task within one individual.[10]

Even though prediction is helpful in trying to determine how basic study skills contribute to the ability to complete successfully a wide range of learning tasks, diagnosis seems to offer more promise for intensive study of basic study skills, because it tends to locate the deficiencies and highlight factors in need of improvement. Therefore, a study of basic study skills that may help at a later date to predict achievement and to diagnose difficulties contributing to the lack of achievement has many implications for fostering efficient educational practices.

From the discussion thus far, it is evident that understanding the nature of basic study skills and how they might be related to the development of other important educational outcomes are concerns that lack the support of rigorous research and empirical substantiation. In part, the dearth of objective information about the basic study skills prompted the detailed consideration of this area in the present discussion. It is our hope that this discussion will help teachers think more critically about the nature of basic study skills and how they operate to affect every phase of the instructional process.

Children with adequate general mental ability are expected to develop to an appropriate level of competence in their general reading and achievement abilities. In order to reach a given level of accomplishment in general reading and achievement, children must be taught to focus all the skills learned in different situations within a framework that will ultimately lead to the solution of problems that are likely to be found in a wide variety of contextual settings. This notion concerning the development of general abilities in children is, for the most part, an extension into the statistical area of the concept of an integrated personality as one who has developed all abilities and who can and does bring to bear all his resources upon any task confronting him.[11]

Even though there is some support for the contention that a person with well-developed general abilities is bringing his diversely developed skills to bear in order to complete the task at hand, it has not yet been determined just how these separately developed skills contribute toward the successful completion of the total task. However, it does seem likely that the skills utilized in order to perform any general school task will be highly intercorrelated if an individual makes use of them in his efforts to fulfill stated purposes. If, in fact, skills are used to perform general tasks,

> then a program contributing to this kind of development should result in an individual who performs more consistently over a wide range of tasks. It follows that tests sampling these tasks and abilities should be more highly correlated than before.[12]

Since children have been exposed, in differing degrees, to a systematic treatment of basic study skills, any instruments used to assess these abilities among a given group will be interrelated and the degree of interrelation will probably vary according to the types of exposure that individual subjects have experienced in their previous schoolwork. However, this notion will not help us to distinguish among variations of interrelation among measures of skills and general abilities that result from individually learned approaches to the solution of general tasks, to maturation, to differences in intelligence, to differences in styles of operation, and to the way in which the data are collected. This state of affairs makes it difficult for the writer to say what the true relationship between certain basic study skills and general abilities might be. Even though there is some difficulty in trying to determine what the interrelationship between skills used in this discussion means in terms of their contribution to the improvement of general abilities, positive correlations between basic study skills and general abilities should give us some indication as to how an individual's development of skills might relate to his development of general abilities. If this relationship is established, there might be some light shed on how specific skill development might conceivably contribute to the development of an individual's general abilities. Evidence to support this idea might be suggested when the correlations between measures of different abilities are scrutinized closely to decipher any pattern that might emerge.

It should be noted that there is likely to be a positive correlation between abilities that are seemingly different if similar types of measuring instruments are used to gather data on these abilities. The nature of the measuring instruments either adds to, or detracts from, size of the correlation that exists between measures of different types of ability. When different abilities are measured with instruments that make use of similar item formats and response patterns, there is likely to be a positive correlation that is a function of the measuring technique used. This adds to the difficulty with which an investigator is faced when he attempts to furnish support for predicting positive correlations between different or related abilities. After being provided with this general explanation of why certain high and positive correlations will probably exist between measures of different or related abilities associated with basic study skills, the reader should have some basis for judging research findings in the field and for deciding some of the likely direct and supportive benefits accruing to the learning performances of pupils who have been purposely exposed to the study of selected basic skills.

A Description of Basic Study Skills

Studies concerned with providing an explanation of the nature of basic study skills are, for the most part, attempting to spell out what these skills are. Even though various authors describe similar skills differently and discuss them in dissimilar contexts, a common notion about what basic study skills are seems to be present in all of the studies encountered.

According to Spache (1963) in his work *Toward Better Reading*, basic study skills are not considered to be an array of facts and information to be studied and learned. This conclusion stems from his contention that factors inherent and evident in basic study skills are not the same components necessary for success in reading, language, and arithmetic. Thus, he concludes:

> Study skills are a reflection of academic motivation, habits of work and probably such personality traits as anxiety, compulsiveness, stability and self-confidence. . . . Academically successful students are noticeably more cautious, persistent and meticulous in their study practices, because they differ in habits of motivation rather than in knowledge of what unsuccessful students show.[13]

In this sense, personality characteristics of the learner are the cutting edge that determines what a knowledge of basic study skills will contribute to successful achievement. Even though Spache's notion about the nature of the basic study skills obviously has some empirical support, his view leaves one with the knotty problem of separating out that which is motivational from that which is knowledge of skills in the determination of factors needed for successful achievement. Applicability to most instructional purposes requires a more explicit definition of basic study skills for sound pedagogy.

In the later work, *Reading in the Elementary School*, Spache (1964)[14] seems to take a different position concerning skills for content reading than the one he took for study skills in general. The author notes the difficulties associated with reading content from textbooks and argues that effective reading ". . . in such areas as science, social science, arithmetic, health and the like . . . demands a variety of approaches, techniques, and skills. . . ."[15] Spache thus indicates that effective content-area reading requires special training at the beginning of the intermediate grade level. This leads to his conclusion that: "The major emphasis of the reading instruction [in the intermediate grades] is to be placed upon training in content skills."[16] In this work, Spache does not state that motivational factors determine the nature of the content reading skills necessary for successful reading. He explicitly suggests that the basic skills for content reading are:

1. Previewing.
2. Skimming and Scanning.
3. Reading Graphic Materials (maps and globes, charts and graphs).
4. Library Skills (general knowledge of organization and use, parts of books, reference tools).
5. Organizing and Reporting (composition skills).
6. Note Taking (summarizing, topics, sequence).
7. Critical Reading (investigating sources, recognizing author's purpose, distinguishing between opinion and fact, making inferences, forming judgments, and detecting propaganda devices).

According to Spache (1964), these skills are crucial to meaningful content, and not only can these basic skills be defined and described but pupils can definitely be trained to use them effectively.

Arthur W. Heilman (1961) defines study skills as ". . . a particular group of reading skills."[17] The list of skills this author produced is parallel to the list produced by Spache (1964). However, Heilman does present an interesting and useful point of view when he asserts that "Reading ability is a prerequisite for the development of study skills, but this ability in itself does not assure that a pupil has mastered these skills."[18] According to this author, the basic study skills are part of the activities evident in the total reading process; however, for effective instructional purposes, they have to be considered and taught as if they are essential supplements to the total reading activity.

Nila B. Smith (1963) writes that traditionally operated school programs have advocated the teaching of content subjects devoid of consideration for the development of basic study skills required in specialized areas. This author believes that teachers should make use of learning situations in the subject field that require the utilization of specialized as well as varied reading techniques.* As reading techniques that are concerned with reading skills that are effective in different subject areas are learned, there is reason to believe that the overall reading proficiency of pupils in the elementary grades will be improved greatly.

Some opposition was registered by Smith (1963) concerning the willingness of some writers to define basic study skills as habits and attitudes conducive to the most profitable use of these skills. Even though comprehension skills and speed skills in reading are extremely helpful in studying, Smith (1963)[19] believes that they do not include all of the abilities that should be considered as basic study skills. After reviewing the different concepts of what the basic study skills should entail, Smith considers it useful to characterize such skills as those

> that form an integral part of the reading process, but that are used especially when application of the content is desired. Thus concerned, study skills in reading may be broadly defined as skills used when there is intention to *do something with* the content read.[20]

Basic study skills as conceived by Smith come into play when learners are directed to apply reading material in different ways. In this sense, basic study skills are considered to be more inclusive and more broadly based for greater flexibility of application in present and in later reading tasks.

In describing the relationship between specialized study skills and general reading ability, Smith concludes

---

* In many instances, the reading techniques referred to by Smith parallel the list of basic study skills indicated earlier by Spache.

that there are unique differences in skills used in different subject-matter fields; and that while "general reading ability" is operative in all reading to a certain extent, there is also, definite need for the development of specific skills to use in the different curricular areas.[21]

According to Smith, the common basic study skills and reading skills are the skills ". . . needed in reading in all content fields . . . [and they] are common to all study situations . . . [because] we use them only when we are *studying* reading content."[22] Whenever a child reads in the content areas, he needs to:

> Select and evaluate—or pick out important parts of the text. Organize—or put together ideas that belong together. Recall what he has read—or fix it so he can bring it back when he wants it. Locate information in textbooks, reference books, and periodicals. Follow directions.[23]

For Smith, these skills make up what we refer to as the basic study skills. The specialized factors to be considered to provide flexibility and effectiveness in reading in subject areas include such things as specialized vocabulary and special patterns in the content of particular subjects. She concludes by stating

> that the development of study skills in reading presents a vast frontier to those who wish to develop more fully the ability of children to read specialized types of content for a variety of purposes.[24]

It is easily seen from this author's comments that basic study skills are activities to be performed when one attempts to approach effectively some task that requires reading. For Smith these skills can be identified and taught for practical application in activities assigned in school tasks. The need for such an approach leaves little room for opposition when one considers the type of reading activities we are demanding of our present school population at the intermediate grade level.

We have attempted to provide the reader with a broad picture of how different professional educators have characterized basic study skills. Since much of the discussion is logical rather than empirical, there was no way to decide what should be covered for all purposes. However, the requirements of instruction in various content areas do provide some guidance for including skills that may be termed "basic" to help students process information efficiently and effectively as well as contribute to their basic understanding of the ideas in question. In terms of instructional requirements, the basic study skills are library skills, dictionary skills, reference skills, map reading skills, the skills needed to read graphs and charts and use tables. Subcategories under these five basic study skills include locating sources of information, using the Dewey decimal system, locating books on shelves, and using the card catalog under library skills; finding meanings, spellings, and syllables, using alphabetical order and guide words, and finding out how words are pronounced under dictionary skills; using parts of a book such as the title page, using key words, locating encyclopedia by volume, using the index and the table of contents under reference skills; reading political, physical, population, and rainfall maps in various combinations under map-reading skills; and reading line, bar, and picture graphs, reading tables, and fractional parts ($, %) under reading graphs, charts and table skills. In some instances, use of index skills is treated in the data analysis as comprising a separate basic study skill even though it was initially included under reference skills.

Teaching Basic Study Skills

In some of the references basic study skills are referred to as reading-study skills even though the skills included are essentially the same. Arthur Heilman (1963) is one writer who makes this distinction when he speaks of teaching the basic study skills. He believes that the first step in attempting to teach basic study skills is to outline what instructional areas will be covered by the term. Based on a review of a number of sources, Heilman concludes that there is a considerable degree of overlap in areas to be included and in the way the topics should be treated. After surveying the field, Heilman concludes that:

> If the teaching of study skills is slighted or neglected in a number of classrooms, we should attempt to ascertain why this happens. One tentative hypothesis is that the literature contains relatively few concrete suggestions as to how to effectively teach these facets of reading. The general pattern is that a somewhat exhaustive list of skills will be enumerated, followed by a generalization that these are important and should be taught.[25]

From this discussion it can be easily surmised that part of the problem associated with teaching basic study skills is that there is a lack of definitive suggestions for teaching these skills as part of the instructional program at the elementary school level. In this sense, it would be unreal to expect teachers to teach* basic study skills without some notions concerning content, materials, and procedures.

Related to the problem of trying to determine how basic study skills should be taught is the problem of trying to decide which subject area to use for this task. Addressing himself to this problem, Heilman believes that many of the basic study skills are not unique to a particular subject matter area, and, as a result, these skills are not likely to be systematically taught in any subject area. Even though some areas of the elementary school curriculum such as reading and selected segments of the language arts devote time to the development and use of basic study skills, the treatment is both inadequate and frequently out of context. For example, a child who studies the use of the index in a reading workbook exercise is unlikely to be able to transfer the skill directly to using a social studies, science, or math textbook. Some basic study skills can be taught more effectively and efficiently from the texts in various content areas if pupils are expected to be able to employ the skills in solving a diverse set of problems. It should be obvious to the reader that there is some disagreement concerning the subject-matter area that will serve as raw material for developing basic study skills. There is some agreement to support the claim that these skills do not transfer readily in use from one content area to another unless they are taught within the context of the subject-matter area involved.

It is necessary to formulate specific learning experiences and concrete teaching exercises for each basic study skill from dictionary usage to choosing pertinent information. Since there is much evidence that basic study skills are developed by pupils as they are employed as a means for completing certain tasks, these skills are critical enough to the learning process to warrant systematic teaching. Because of the developmental nature of each basic study skill, teachers at different grade levels must assume the responsibility for ensuring systematic exposure to instruction in the area. Each teacher has to judge (with the help of others through professional meetings, journals, courses, and job analysis) when to introduce and teach some skills that are *new* to his pupils. Similarly, teachers must also be ready to review, reteach, and extend those skills with which pupils are already familiar. This writer advocates the direct teaching of basic study skills in each content area rather than teaching them incidentally or independently. If instruction in the use of basic study skills is not an intentional effort on the part of the teacher,

* Betty Atwell Wright, Louie Thomas Camp, William K. Stosberg, and Babette Fleming, *Elementary School Curriculum: Better Teaching Now* (New York: Macmillan, 1971).

it is doubtful that children will learn how to use these skills effectively as they attempt to process information to solve problems.

If a school employs team teaching or departmentalization, as many elementary school districts do, there is the problem of determining in which subject the basic study skills will be taught. Some authors suggest that the problem tends to resolve itself when every teacher is charged with the responsibility of teaching reading. Some writers have addressed the problem of teaching basic study skills when they suggest that every teacher must assume the responsibility for the application of these skills to the subject matter taught. This approach to basic study skills is likely to increase the precision with which pupils can productively work in various content areas independent of the teacher. As pupils become less dependent on the teacher for guidance in learning activity, they will be in positions to employ their skills for continued learning, and this will enable them to pursue meaningful life goals. Mastery of basic study skills in a variety of realistic contexts is future oriented in that it enables pupils to be independent learners and thinkers.

It becomes evident that children should be taught certain basic study skills as they relate to independent learning in specific subject-matter areas. Within this context it matters not whether a teacher is responsible for teaching all the content areas or whether he is responsible for teaching a single content area; each teacher has the responsibility for teaching the basic study skills needed for independent learning in different subject-matter areas. Children have to be taught deliberately how to learn different subjects independently when different purposes require the performance of different study tasks.

Basic study skills should be taught within the confines of an instructional strategy that helps the teacher decide how she is to function and defines the role that certain skills are to play in the study of various curriculum fields. Regardless of the type of instructional program within which teachers are expected to teach basic study skills, the decision to teach these skills is frequently optional and somewhat dependent upon whether or not the teacher recognizes the deficiencies of his pupils in that area. As a consequence, many children move on to more advanced content in later grades without having learned those skills that are essential for effective study in the different subject-matter areas. Spache (1958)[26] blames this condition partly on the fact that many teachers are untrained and unskilled in the use of the basic study skills that they are expected to teach. Even those teachers who think of themselves as specialists in a particular field do not appear to have a firm grasp of the skills required to produce, interpret, and expand knowledge in the field in question. The basic study skills in a field are more than the content of the field and require special attention (even for specialists) to employ them properly. Until this problem is adequately considered and dealt with, basic study skills will probably remain the area for effective learning of content that is critical but untaught because too many teachers lack the necessary competence and confidence to know where to place the correct emphasis.

It seems reasonable to conclude that part of the reason why basic study skills are not taught, or are poorly taught, is because of a lack of specific experience and training of the persons expected to teach them. A first step toward getting better instruction in the basic study skills in elementary schools might be to help teachers to become more aware of their own skills in this area. We can no longer afford to assume that teachers will teach that area which they have not been specifically alerted and properly trained to implement generally. No teacher can teach pupils any study skill which he himself does not know, understand, or value.

Another problem related to the teaching of basic study skills deals with the nature of the assignments used to help children gain practice in learning to make use of skills in a meaningful context. In some quarters, it is suggested that the amount of structure an assignment has tends to affect how well students retain what they learn. According to Stake (1966):

> Assignments can be structured, no doubt, by programming the materials, by instructing the student to take certain orderly steps, or by inducing the student himself to order his work. Structured assignments apparently are likely to lead to higher retention scores than nonstructured assignments.[27]

It would seem that when basic study skills are learned in a structured assignment situation there is a greater likelihood that children will retain more of what they learn about how these skills are used. This may tend to increase the probability that pupils will be able to transfer knowledge of basic study skills to different learning situations. Basic study skills must be the object of systematic instruction if the teacher expects to help pupils to become more effective and efficient learners. To do otherwise is to engage pupils in activity that is likely to be uninteresting, unrewarding, and not transferable.

Basic Study Skills and Comprehension
in Content Reading

There is a great deal of speculation by reading specialists and curriculum researchers concerning the nature of reading comprehension in both the reading of literature and reading in the content areas. Even though many notions have been expressed about what basic study skills combine to ensure adequate reading comprehension, we are still handicapped by a lack of definitive knowledge about what these skills really are and how they combine to contribute to the total reading effort when children are asked to read for different purposes in various content areas. Without this type of definitive knowledge, it is difficult to think in terms of teaching specific basic study skills that will aid in increased reading comprehension in the content fields.

In order to get at a framework within which reading comprehension in the content fields can be discussed, a theoretical basis must be formulated. Once a theoretical base is found to provide a background within which comprehension of content materials can be discussed, notions put forth by different writers should tie together in such a way that greater understanding of this area of concern is forthcoming. This idea is similar to that of Holmes and Singer (1961), as expressed in the following comments:

> *Other things being equal, then individual differences in the ability to reason about what is being read* (that is, to manipulate mentally the inflow of new ideas so that they bear a meaningful relationship to what one has already learned) *depend both upon the essential nature of the stored information and the associative logic of the conceptualizing activity—perception stimulated within the brain by the meaningfulness of the sequential input of information at the time of presentation and reception.*[28]

If reading comprehension in the content fields is viewed within the context of this notion, it is evident that children must have some knowledge of and facility with basic study skills before they can reasonably be expected to make use of them to improve their reading comprehension in the content fields. It is further suggested that the structure of basic study skills that a child is likely to need for effective content reading must be operative as he attempts to gain understanding from subject-matter content. Children should have some facility with basic study skills before they try to comprehend material in subject-matter areas. Comprehension in the content fields requires some foundational knowledge of the study skills basic to the tasks to be performed.

Some attention should be given to the fact that more than one combination or sequence of skills can be used to ensure effective outcomes. In any given reading-comprehension situation, different children are likely to mobilize dissimilar subsets of basic skills in order to accomplish identical goals.

In part this may be because of the fact that

> a student reads by integrating that characteristic hierarchy or working-system or substrata factors which will maximize the use of his strong abilities and minimize the use of his weak ones.[29]

Even when pupils are similarly trained in the use of basic study skills, all of them cannot be expected to master the skills taught to the same degree of competence. This state of affairs may be offset by the fact that children are apparently able to solve similar problems by making use of different subsets of basic skills. It is further encouraging to note that different children are able to complete similar instructional tasks by maximizing the use of those basic skills with which they seem to be particularly competent. For example, children who are particularly adept at reading graphic material might utilize this skill to glean a greater understanding from a discussion of certain ideas. On the other hand, there are children who are not very good at reading graphic material, even though they have mastered other skills (such as using numbers) that may be utilized with the same materials. In both instances children are afforded the opportunity to further their personal understanding by leaning heavily on the specific skill areas that they have mastered.

Many teachers of reading tend to agree that we have gained a great deal of knowledge concerning the nature of general reading ability because of the availability of measures of this ability. However, it should be pointed out that most of the progress we have made in the measurement of general reading ability sheds little light upon content reading at higher grade levels. This is related, in part, to the fact that skills required to read skillfully at higher grade levels are expected to be taught at lower grade levels. When this assumption is not supported in fact, difficulty in working with reading materials in content areas becomes commonplace and defies correction under current practices. It seems apparent that measures of general reading ability are more adequate for use as a quality description of the types of reading required at the primary level. However, this way of describing the quality of pupils' reading ability seems to be limited when subject-matter reading tasks at upper grade levels are considered. In considering this problem, Shores (1952) suggests that concepts of general reading ability may be somewhat too broad to be of any real help to teachers trying to teach children to be effective readers in the content fields.

However, it is within the realm of possibility that our present knowledge of general reading ability and general mental ability can be used to analyze these abilities into the skill components necessary for successful reading in the various curriculum areas.

If, as has been suggested, general reading ability is different from an ability to do effective reading in various curriculum fields, then what constitutes comprehension in either instance must be viewed in relation to the requirements of the reading task. It seems evident that ". . . comprehension cannot be more adequate than are the experiences that the reader has had in a particular area."[30] This notion concerning experience views it as being a kind of personal reality that is related to the requirements of the reading task to be performed according to the reader's purposes.

Therefore, one of the requirements for reading in the content fields is that the reader must be provided with a clear notion concerning the purpose for which he approaches curriculum areas for study. According to Shores, a reader's effectiveness in a curriculum area must be determined in relation to his purposes for reading in the area. This author states that:

> Consideration of the manner in which the reader's purpose affects his speed and comprehension leads inevitably to the conclusion that it is impossible to judge whether a reader is doing a good job or poor one until we know what the job requires in the way of reading skills.
>
> Skills have no content, except for psychologists or educators talking among themselves about the skills. Yet skills are not useful except with some content. It is obvious then that, if we would not commit the grave error of separating skills from their uses, we must teach the skills in connection with some content area.[31]

Since skills are the special abilities required to read different curricular materials for specific purposes, they should be taught in the context of their occurrence and use.

Teachers must utilize different methods of teaching specialized skills at appropriate developmental levels across curricular areas. Without such an instructional approach, the teaching of basic study skills in the content areas will continue to be mostly trial and error. There is little reason to expect teachers to make improvements in their efforts to teach reading comprehension in various content areas more effectively if basic skills are not considered an integral part of the instructional strategy.

In order to obtain a clearer picture of the possible contribution the mastery of selected basic skills makes toward effective reading comprehension in curriculum areas, some consideration must be given to what might be the relationship between rate of reading and the degree of comprehension. Even though the exact relationship between rate and comprehension in reading has not been completely substantiated, some leads suggest what the relationship might be. Some notions concerning this relationship are expressed by DeBoer and Dallmann (1960) when they indicate that although

> there is a positive correlation between rate of reading and quality of comprehension, it cannot be automatically assumed that because a person reads fast he necessarily comprehends well.[32]

There is some evidence to support these authors' contentions that faster readers are better readers if they are flexible in their approach. However, it is necessary for one to have a better understanding of what these authors mean when they refer to "flexibility of approach" if their thesis concerning the relationship between rate and quality of reading is to be supported.

In a study dealing with the relationship between reading rate and comprehension, Shores concludes that:

> Fast readers are the good readers when reading some kinds of materials for some purposes. When reading other kinds of materials for other purposes there is no relationship between speed of reading and ability to comprehend.[33]

This writer's findings seem to suggest that good readers call upon appropriate skills on the bases of the purposes set forth to guide the reading activity and the kinds and difficulty of the materials with which they are asked to work. If this is true, then, the relationship between rate variance and good comprehension is determined by the appropriateness of, and utility with, the skills selected according to the purposes of the reader and the requirements of the reading task. On the condition that DeBoer and Dallmann (1960) mean to convey a notion similar to that of Shores by their use of "flexibility of approach," there is some support for their claim that "better readers are also the faster readers" because they tend to select certain skills and vary their rate of reading according to their purposes for reading different kinds of materials.

Given this state of affairs, the relationship between rate and comprehension becomes clearer in terms of the operative skills involved.

As one begins to take a closer look at the skills basic to ensuring effective reading in the content fields, it becomes evident that a clear statement of how basic skills are distinguished as components of comprehension becomes essential. When teachers attempt to teach children in the use of skills that are basic for good comprehension in subject-matter areas, they must have a clear conception of skills that are basic for effective reading comprehension in a specific content area. The problem becomes one of providing meaning for what constitutes basic skills in reading comprehension. If understanding of this problem is to be forthcoming, basic study skills should be thought of as basic reading skills as suggested by Yoakam. According to Yoakam:

> All teachers should be able to recognize the presence or the absence of the fundamental skills in the reading of each child and should realize the necessity of dealing with deficiencies in these fundamental skills when they are recognized.[34]

This conception of basic skills in reading is useful for providing a general notion of pupils' ability to do effective reading in general, but it does not tell us how specific skills are combined to enable children to complete different reading tasks in various curriculum fields.

There seems to be a general consensus among reading specialists that a skill deficiency is associated with a specific reading task and is not general for all reading efforts. Selected basic skills that contribute to reading comprehension should be considered together with different kinds of reading tasks. This approach to viewing comprehension skills makes it possible for teachers to focus attention on those skills that, if lacking, would adversely affect pupils' performance in reading for various purposes in the content area.

Whenever one attempts to deal with reading comprehension in the content fields, some provisions must be made for indicating how the mastery of certain skills provides children with the ability to operate independently with special reading tasks. Huus (1952) addresses this idea when she states that:

> Another phase of independence in reading is that of the study skills. Basic to any real problem-solving is the understanding of how to effect a solution. Study skills, whether at Grade I or XII, include first of all the ability to grasp the main idea and the supporting details. Given this ability, the relationship among the ideas can be analyzed, and the foundation is laid. . . .[35]

It seems evident that effective reading in all curriculum areas, at least beyond the primary grades, requires the use of basic skills in reading that many pupils do not possess. Teachers must deliberately teach these skills within a context that is similar to one within which learners will be expected to operate while pursuing broader and more varied educational experiences. It is definitely not an overstatement to assert that future success in education depends a great deal on the mastery of the skills involved in "reading to learn." Since each content area has its own specialized vocabulary, unique concepts, and generalizations, special comprehension demands, differentiated use of time and space, and special requirements in setting reading rates, pupils must be exposed to those basic study skills that help them deal with differences that are evident across curricular areas.

As requirements of excellence and efficiency in learning are being heaped upon our schools and as new curriculum programs are being introduced at the elementary school level, teaching children how to make use of basic skills for effective reading in all curriculum areas becomes one of the major problems facing current educators. Just how much help will be afforded those who deal with the problem will, at least in part, be determined by how much is learned from a systematic study of the basic skills required for effective reading in the content areas. Understanding a problem is the prerequisite condition for its solution. It is obvious that more understanding about the relationship that basic skills have with regard to fostering comprehension in curriculum areas is needed. As we gain more definitive information about this area, we will be in a better position to make use of it to achieve worthwhile instructional purposes.

Materials Needed for Developing Basic Study Skills

In any program where there is an attempt to teach basic study skills, the quality of the effort will be determined in part by the availability of a variety of suitable materials. In order to determine whether or not materials are suitable for developing basic skills, one must subject available materials to the test of flexibility. If materials are used as intended, they must be judged to have the adaptability that is necessary to afford a sequential and rational approach to teaching clusters of skills found within a basic study skill. Currently, there is a trend toward the more flexible use of materials at all levels of instruction because many different types of materials are necessary to cover the range of differences in maturity, background experience, level of achievement, and ability of pupils to be taught. Therefore, materials that are meant to be used for the sequential development of basic study skills should have the appropriate variety, difficulty level, adaptability, and flexibility to make them effective in achieving intended instructional outcomes. The availability of flexible materials seems to be a key to the development of sound basic skills needed for handling content in various curriculum areas.

The very nature of the kind of reading required by some materials and purposes determines what basic skills are needed. This becomes evident when one notes that

> Material containing narrative has been repeatedly found easier to read than factual material. Conversation, characterization, and action space out details that are closely packed in expository materials. This spacing out of difficult concepts makes it possible for children to understand what would be totally incomprehensible if packed into an expository paragraph or page.[36]

When materials and purposes require the use of a wide range of basic study skills, more opportunities are afforded the teacher to give pupils training in the types of reading necessary for these materials and tasks. In order to ensure the development of skills basic to the many different kinds of reading that are likely to confront children in the future, instruction in these skills should make use of those materials with which this kind of development is possible.

Basic Study Skills and the
School Library Program

What is—and what should be—the role played by the school library program in the development of basic study skills? In some elementary schools the development of basic study skills is thought to be a part of the school's library program. On the other hand, some elementary school people believe that basic study skills should be taught in each individual classroom and that the library program should provide a type of laboratory experience in which the skills are practiced. A useful compromise may lie somewhere between these two positions. Regardless of which position a school advocates, there is general agreement with the notion that all pupils can extend and improve their basic study skills through the use of the school library.

Since children need some directed training in the use of the library and in the use of basic study skills, a school must provide experience in both areas. These skills should be taught both as part of the classroom curriculum and as a part of the school library program.

Whenever the basic study skills are primarily library skills, the development and use of a library program become essential. It is probably desirable to teach library skills in the library itself because pupils are afforded the opportunity to become acquainted with the library and its supportive advantages for completing schoolwork or learning about things of general interest. Teaching library skills in the library opens the way for a blending of theory and practice in the study and use of the library as a meaningful tool and intellectual aid.

What provisions and adjustments should teachers make in their approach to teaching basic study skills in conjunction with library skills when library facilities are lacking and librarians are unavailable? This is a perplexing problem in many elementary schools. Obviously, in this type of situation:

> Library skills have been particularly neglected because most schools have no regular course in library science (and probably should not have, since the library's true function is to supplement other classwork, not to be an end in itself).[37]

Given this situation it becomes the responsibility of the teacher to introduce children to—and motivate them to use—the school's library to obtain the information required to attain objectives outlined in the instructional strategy.

Therefore, it becomes apparent that the development of library skills is not solely dependent upon the presence of library facilities and trained librarians but rather upon the attitude the classroom teacher takes with regard to the development of these skills. Although adequate library facilities and personnel are valuable for the development of library skills, the classroom teacher remains the essential person to motivate pupils to develop and improve library skills through the employment of basic study skills.

Some curriculum workers tend to question the validity of establishing attendance unit libraries in elementary schools. They claim that book collections in elementary schools should be located in individual classrooms. Current thinking in the area seems to favor the location of library materials both in individual classrooms and in a central library within the attendance unit of an elementary school.

Mary V. Gaver (1963) sought to obtain objective evidence to justify the establishment of elementary school libraries. In her study she used six schools that fell into three categories: (1) two had only classroom book collections, (2) two had central collections, but no librarian, and (3) two had school libraries. In order to get at the evidence needed to support either category, she developed instruments for evaluating elementary school library facilities and the use children made of them in carrying out instructional tasks. This approach gave her some indication about how the presence of library facilities might be related to the types of ways children make use of them. This researcher also wanted to ascertain how the presence of library facilities contributes to the total curriculum program. To get at this problem, Gaver (1963) selected a total of 404 sixth-grade pupils who had a common measure of educational achievement at the fourth- and sixth-grade levels and were enrolled in the six schools she was studying. She found that the:

> Scope of use made of library materials was greater among schools in school library category, that pupil advancement was higher in schools with libraries; that amount of reading done by children had a direct relationship with the nature of library provision, but that school libraries seemed to have little or no bearing on either the purposes for reading or the number of interest areas reflected by reading.[38]

This study seems to support the claim that the presence of a central library collection in an elementary attendance unit contributes to the overall achievement of children. Even though this study leaves unanswered many questions concerning the exact relationship between the presence of a central library collection and the improvement of overall school achievement, it does furnish some support to the notion that the total curriculum in an elementary school is strengthened considerably with the addition and use of a central library collection.

Since the classroom teacher is the key to library instruction in the elementary school, he must attempt to teach the proper use of the library if children are to acquire this skill. Teachers must utilize texts, curricular guides, instructional goals, learners' needs, and learning experiences to discern where and how library usage may be profitably integrated into the study of content areas. Pupils must be acquainted with essential library resources if they are to make the use of the library a relevant habit for their future work and enjoyment.

Evaluation of Basic Study Skills

The quality of the teaching of basic study skills is directly related to the type and thoroughness of the process used to evaluate these learnings. When teachers attempt to learn about basic skill deficiencies by following a well-conceived evaluative process, they gain information that helps them to avoid teaching skills known to most of the children, thus permitting them to concentrate their efforts upon the apparent deficiencies. This approach to evaluation makes the teaching of basic skills more efficient and economical.

How does one proceed to evaluate basic study skills? Is a wide spread in the measured abilities of children indicative of a lack of adequate teaching of basic study skills? As we look at the evaluation of basic study skills, it becomes obvious that any program that caters to the individual needs and deficiencies of children will tend to spread the group in terms of the measured abilities. Thus, it becomes essential that:

> Evaluation . . . should be based upon a knowledge of the abilities of children, realizing that good teaching does not produce uniformity but increases diversity among children in any class or schoolroom.[39]

Even though the brighter children are likely to have greater facility with all skills than those considered to be less gifted, all children have a tendency to show different patterns of skill development. The peaks and the valleys for similar skills will differ for each child in the group. Sound evaluative procedures should pinpoint this variance in ability with skills and enable teachers to plan suitable programs for the groups involved.

Invariably, whenever one attempts to discuss or set guidelines for evaluation, he is forced to look at an assessment of relevant data with the use of tests of some sort. Since evaluation is judgmental in nature, the person who attempts to evaluate any curriculum program must collect objective data in terms of some reference point if his decisions are to be validated. In many such instances, data needed to form the foundation for evaluation are collected through the use of objective tests mainly because we expect them to tell us something about pupils, what they have learned, and what they need to learn in relation to what we have attempted to teach. When tests do not meet these expectations, judging the nature of the skills pattern possessed by pupils is risky at best. As attempts are made to evaluate the status of basic study skills as working abilities possessed by children, it becomes necessary to make use of various measures. Usually these measures are in the form of objective paper and pencil tests. These tests should be selected carefully so that the results obtained from them will provide objective data for sound evaluation. This meaningful selection pattern exists only when tests measure basic study skills in terms of the objectives that guided instruction in them.

When paper and pencil tests are used to measure basic study skills, only the verbal aspect of these skills is considered. Since children are taught basic study skills to enable them to perform certain activities with content in various curriculum areas, it is probably unsound to assume that a score obtained with a written test is fully representative of the testees' ability to make use of these skills in practical situations. In a discussion of this problem, Ryans and Frederiksen (1951) state that:

> From the standpoint of validity one of the most serious errors committed in the field of human measurement has been that which assumes the high correlation of knowledge of facts and principles on the one hand and performance on the other.
>
> Tests of information or knowledge are not, of course, to be discredited. They have an important place in education and industry for purposes of identifying certain kinds of individual differences. These tests are economical to use since they can be administered to large groups of persons and since they may be quickly and accurately scored. However, while they may provide important information about an individual's school progress, his general information background, and his knowledge of facts and principles, they often tell only part of the story. Many situations to which an individual is required to respond are very complex, and effective behavior in those situations demands something in addition to the knowledge of facts and principles.[40]

Many times children are required to make use of basic study skills in new and quite different situations. Even though they may have a thorough knowledge of the facts and principles of the skills involved, the children may not be able to bring different skills together in a complex organizational scheme that allows them to find a solution to the problem. At some stage it is essential to evaluate children's mastery of basic study skills in a performance context if one is to gain insight into how well the pupils are making use of these skills.

Since the teaching of basic study skills is based upon the assumption that children will make use of these skills to handle knowledge effectively in the future, evaluation of these skills must be ongoing and progressive as children are exposed to different tasks in various curriculum areas and at higher-grade levels. Therefore, evaluation of basic study skills must take into account the progressive development of learning experiences that pupils encounter as they proceed through school. Any attempt to appraise pupil progress in this context has to take into account the requirements dictated by the nature of the outcomes sought and the medium of instruction employed.

Basic study skills should be evaluated as children encounter tasks of different levels of difficulty so that the resulting data indicate whether the flexibility of the skills learned enable children to meet the requirements of the tasks. Continuous evaluation of basic study skills helps to determine the amount, depth, and breadth of growth fostered in the curriculum. In this manner evaluation provides an indication of how basic study skills taught at lower grades are broadened and extended as a result of later school experiences.

Intellectual Processes

Now that some background information concerning the nature and use of basic study skills in the elementary school has been presented, some attention should be focused on the nature and use of intellectual processes in elementary school instructional activity. This step is an integral part of providing background for understanding the interrelationships between basic study skills and intellectual processes and how they contribute to efficient and effective learning in the instructional program at the elementary school level. Since intellectual processes represent the intellectual functions involved in problem solving or thinking through complex situations, part of their meaning is derived from the basic study skills employed to complete the function. Therefore, at some points it might be difficult for the reader to discern differences between intellectual processes and basic study skills. This point will become clearer as we discuss intellectual processes.

One cannot begin to understand and utilize intellectual processes in the elementary school without some notion of the developmental and operational characteristics of cognitive functioning. For this background we devote some attention to the work of Piaget as discussed by John H. Flavell (1963). We do not use the original works of Piaget because much of the relevant material is not in English and is too technical for students without a background in important discipline areas. For our purposes, Flavell's discussion of Piaget's theories on the nature and development of cognitive functioning will suffice.

In order to visualize the relevance of the nature and development of cognitive functioning for understanding and utilizing intellectual processes, one might turn to Piaget's system and his study of developing intelligence in terms of *structure, function,* and *content.* According to this system, *content*

> refers to uninterpreted behavioral data themselves. Thus, when one of Piaget's subjects asserts that one object sinks because it is heavy and another sinks because it is light . . . or behaves as though time were a function of the distance an object traveled but not of its velocity . . . we witness behavioral content.[41]

In terms of our purpose, *content* can correspond to the process that takes place when pupils employ basic study skills to operationalize an intellectual process. The employment of basic study skills is the behavioral content of intellectual processes.

According to Flavell, *function* is viewed in a different and specific way by Piaget. In Piaget's system *function*

> refers to those broad characteristics of intelligent activity which hold true for all ages and which virtually define the very essence of intelligent behavior . . . [Further], intelligent activity is always an active, organized process of assimilating the new to the old and of accommodating the old to the new. Intellectual content will vary enormously from age to age in ontogenetic development, yet the general functional properties of the adaptational processes remain the same.[42]

When we refer to intellectual processes we are dealing roughly with processes suggested in Piaget's definition of function. For our purposes, intellectual processes tend to describe the intellectual and cognitive characteristics and requirements of individual pupils faced with problems to be solved in a school setting. It is our intent to help the reader to deal with the problem of how these intellectual processes might operate to impede or facilitate pupils' ability to process information and to organize experience for the completion of tasks, the achievement of personal goals, and the solution and exploration of important problems.

The last part of the puzzle of intellectual processes can be approached through the Piaget notion of *structure.* For Piaget structure refers to cognitive structures and is interposed between function and content. Using this as a point of departure, Piaget suggests that:

> Structure, like content and unlike function, does indeed change with age, and these developmental changes constitute the major object of study. . . . What are structures in Piaget's system? They are the organizational properties of intelligence, organizations created through functioning and inferable from the behavioral contents whose nature they determine. As such, Piaget speaks of them as mediators interposed between the invariant functions on the one hand and the variegated behavioral contents on the other . . .[43]

These notions have important implications for instruction in basic study skills and intellectual processes at the elementary school level because they suggest factors that might impede or facilitate pupils' attempts to learn and make use of these critical cognitive functionings. This conclusion is supported by the analysis of Flavell when he notes the example of pupils' reactions when they observe objects sinking in water. In these instances it can be concluded that:

> certain structural properties can be said to mediate or be responsible for this content. First, the child is *phenomenistic* in the sense that his cognitive structure is so organized that the surface appearances of things are overattended to; his thought is dominated by the environmental properties which strike him first and most vividly—in this case the lightness or heaviness of the object. Second, he fails to relate in a logical way successive cognitive impressions; thus heaviness and lightness are successively invoked as explanatory principles with no thought to the contradiction involved, as though the need to reconcile opposing impressions were not a characteristic of this cognitive structure. These structural properties in the sense that they determine precisely what will and will not result when a given cognizing organism attempts to adapt to a given set of external events.[44]

The structure that pupils employ to apply intellectual processes to the solution of problems determines the selection, sequencing, and deployment of basic study skills utilized. In this sense, the cognitive structures of pupils become the focal point of instructional strategy. At this point, the task of the instructional strategy is to shape the cognitive structures of pupils to foster more efficient and effective learning for solving relevant problems.

The reader should have discerned at this point how *function, content,* and *structure* are interrelated in cognitive or intellectual functioning. The various elements combine to give meaning to basic study skills and intellectual processes in both a static and dynamic context. Simply put in a general way Flavell concludes that:

. . . *function* is concerned with the manner in which any organism makes cognitive progress; *content* refers to the external behavior which tells us that functioning has occurred; and *structure* refers to the inferred organizational properties which explain why this content rather than some other content has emerged.[45]

The elements defined by Flavell are analogous to our use of intellectual processes, basic study skills, and instructional strategy. *Intellectual processes* describe the thinking and cognitive characteristics and requirements of individual pupils faced with problems to be solved in a school setting; *basic study skills* are the behavioral content of intellectual processes; and *instructional strategy* is the organizational structure that determines which, and how, basic study skills relate and contribute to the development and deployment of intellectual processes. It is apparent that the study of cognitive development as a field of study has many important and crucial parallels to improving learning through the use of an instructional strategy. This point becomes clearer when we return to a more detailed discussion of basic study skills and intellectual processes later in the chapter.

Intellectual Processes and Cognitive Organization

Another factor to be considered in intellectual process is the nature of cognitive organization. Because intellectual processes are forms of cognitive functioning, it is critical to the understanding, development, and deployment of these processes that the organization of these functions be analyzed in terms of instructional feasibility. Flavell further highlights this point when he asserts that:

Cognition, like digestion, is an organized affair. Every act of intelligence presumes some kind of intellectual structure, some sort of organization within which it proceeds. The apprehension of reality always involves multiple interrelationships among cognitive actions and among the concepts and meanings which these actions express.[46]

Although there is some doubt about all of the specific characteristics of cognitive organization, there is agreement that these specific characteristics "differ markedly from stage to stage in development."[47] The very fact that cognition is thought to be organized implies the existence of stages in its development. These stages can form the basis for developing intellectual processes through the use of instructional strategy. It is useful to remember that systems of relationships among elements of all organizations of intellectual activity can be profitably thought of as a total entity. Acts of intelligence as simple as motor movements in infancy or as complex as critical thinking in adulthood are related to a system of such acts that are part of the total system. If we think of intellectual processes as totalities, basic study skills can be thought of as systems of relationships among elements that provide behavioral reality for judging the presence and effective use of these processes. In order to develop the intellectual processes of pupils, it will be necessary to develop an instructional strategy for applying and utilizing basic study skills to solve problems requiring a definite system of thought. This is the challenge in developing intellectual processes.

Since cognitive organization is inseparable from cognitive adaptation, it is not possible to really understand the nature and use of intellectual processes without some notion of how these two cognitive functions are related. When speaking of the relationship between organization and adaptation, Piaget suggests that:

> They [organization and adaptation] are two complementary processes of a single mechanism, the first being the internal aspect of the cycle of which adaptation constitutes the external. . . . The "accord of thought with things" and the "accord of thought with itself" express this dual functional invariant of adaptation and organization. These two aspects of thought are indissociable: It is by adapting to things that thought organizes itself and it is by organizing itself that it structures things.[48]

The purpose of focusing on intellectual processes in an instructional strategy is to effect an organization and adaptation that provide interpretative order to information for the solution of problems.

When one deals with the intellectual phenomenon, he must attempt to highlight the nature and direction of movement and change. Flavell deals with this issue when he asserts that:

> Intellectual functioning, in its dynamic aspect, is also characterized by the invariant processes of *assimilation and accommodation*. An act of intelligence in which assimilation and accommodation are in balance or equilibrium constitutes an intellectual *adaptation*. Adaptation and organization are two sides of the same coin, since adaptation pre-

supposes an underlying coherence, on the one hand, and organizations are created through adaptations on the other.[49]

It appears that cognitive adaptation is both controlled by, and dependent upon, the balance between assimilation and accommodation. In the case of assimilation, there is reference "to the fact that every cognitive encounter with an environmental object necessarily involves some kind of cognitive structuring (or restructuring) of that object in accord with the nature of the organism's existing intellectual organization."[50] On the other hand, "the essence of accommodation is precisely this process of adapting oneself to the variegated requirements or demands that the world of objects imposes upon one."[51] It can be easily seen that assimilation and accommodation are dynamic aspects of intellectual processes because these processes enable pupils to adapt and adjust their thought processes to solve problems encountered.

In our discussion thus far, we have explored many elements of cognitive functioning as a way to understand the relationship between basic study skills and intellectual processes. One of the key aspects of this discussion necessarily dealt with the relationship between assimilation and accommodation and their influences on intellectual adaptation. What we have gained from our discussion is probably best stated in the summary by Flavell when he asserts that:

> the functional characteristics of the assimilatory and accommodatory mechanisms are such that the possibility of cognitive change is insured, but the magnitude of any given change is always limited. The organism adapts repeatedly, and each adaptation necessarily paves the way for its successor. Structures are not infinitely modifiable, however, and not everything which is potentially assimilable can in fact be assimilated by organism A at point X in his development. On the contrary, the subject can incorporate only those components of reality which its on-going structure can assimilate without drastic change.[52]

It is our intent to enable pupils to achieve positive and effective cognitive change by mastering the use of intellectual processes as a result of being instructed to learn and use basic study skills to solve intellectual problems. Specific suggestions concerned with how this might be brought about are presented later in the chapter.

The Structure of the Intellect

In recent years, J. P. Guilford[53] has provided us with much insight into primary mental abilities and how these abilities contribute to the structure of the intellect. Fortunately, Guilford's schema permits one to relate the primary mental abilities identified to information and activities common in the instructional process at the elementary school level. This enables us to design an instructional strategy along the lines of the structure of the intellect as proposed by Guilford. Therefore, our instructional strategy for teaching about the nature and use of intellectual processes can reflect the theoretical knowledge involving the primary mental abilities. At this point theory influences practice in a positive and verifiable way.

In his schema, "Guilford classifies and organizes the primary mental abilities according to (a) *contents* or type of information dealt with, (b) the *operations* to be performed on the information, and (c) the *products* resulting from the processing of the information."[54] Instructionally, Guilford's second classification is probably most useful from the standpoint of teaching because operations performed on the information make direct reference to major kinds of intellectual processes. The intellectual processes referred to here are:

1. *Cognition.* Those abilities associated with the discovery, recognition, or comprehension of information. This ability includes some reasoning.
2. *Memory.* Abilities involved in the retention or storage of information cognized.
3. *Divergent Production.* Abilities related to generating varied and new information from given or known and remembered information. Production of numerous diverse, unusual, unconventional answers and solutions also characterize this ability.
4. *Convergent Production.* Abilities related to the generation of new information from known and remembered information. This ability also involves the production of "right," "best," or conventional answers and solutions.
5. *Evaluation.* Abilities related to deciding about adequacy, correctness, or goodness of what is remembered or produced by thinking.

From the major intellectual processes listed and defined, many others are suggested as one attempts to approach them from an instructional mode. Some of the other intellectual processes that might be suggested as subcategories of the major ones presented by Guilford include those indicated in the list that follows. For the most part the intellectual processes shown in this list are suggestive of intellectual activities or cognitive functioning that characterize instructional activity at the elementary school level. Through the use of the intellectual processes presented, one can build an instructional strategy that operationalizes the major intellectual processes suggested by Guilford.[55]

1. Conceptualizing.
2. Generalizing.
3. Applying.
4. Inferring (extrapolating).
5. Interpreting.
6. Deducing.
7. Inducing.
8. Analyzing.
9. Synthesizing.
10. Reasoning (logical).
11. Evaluating.
12. Abstracting.
13. Organizing.
14. Classifying.
15. Comparing.
16. Contrasting.
17. Communicating.
18. Diagnosing.
19. Observing (perception).
20. Structuring.
21. Problem solving.
22. Memorizing.

There can be little doubt of the fact that Guilford's categories of thinking abilities and memory are aspects of intellectual processes or cognitive functioning crucial to various kinds of academic performance.

Using this as a foundation it is possible to expand the definition of the nature and meaning of academic performance because the various subcategories of Guilford's model (Figure 6.2) parallel specific content, intellectual processes, and activities used at the elementary school level. According to Guilford's categorization of thinking abilities, they can be thought of both in terms of their *product* (units, classes, relations, systems, transformations, and implications) and their *content* (behavioral, semantic, symbolic, or figural). For the most part, much of the attention concerning instructional strategy and curricular programs is disproportionately directed toward the *products* of thinking and not nearly enough on the *operations* and *contents* as indicated in the Guilford model. This shortcoming has to be corrected if the precision in planning instructional strategies is to result in predictable performance changes in pupils who are exposed to purposeful teaching.

Returning to Guilford's model as a frame of reference, the reader should note that each of the *intellectual processes* (operations) noted is used to deal with processing *products* in the various *contents*. For example, pupils can be taught to comprehend (cognition) units, classes, relations, systems transformations, and implications in different content (behavioral, semantic, symbolic, figural) mediums. In the case of comprehending units, one is primarily concerned with informational *items* or facts with "think" character. The comprehension of units involves the recognition of visual, auditory, and, in some instances, emotional units. In terms of instruction, this involves the recognition of word structure and knowing the meanings of words in a variety of con-

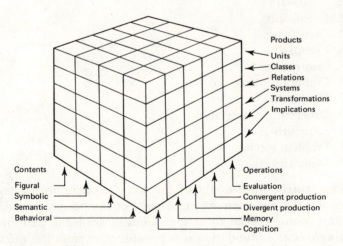

Figure 6.2

Theoretical Model for the Complete "Structure of the Intellect." [From Robert Wilson, "The Structure of the Intellect," News of NEA's Project on the Academically Talented, **2**:1 (Feb. 1961). Reprinted by permission of the National Education Association.]

texts. Instructional activity in this product area is sometimes referred to as vocabulary development.

As one moves to comprehending classes (collections of units with common properties), there is primary concern for classifying groups of objects or ideas according to criterional attributes. At this point the teacher is heavily involved in the process of concept formation as discussed earlier in Chapter 5. This is the point at which pupils learn how to use the units learned to grasp concepts that are critical to more complex thinking, learning, and applications. At the point at which teachers begin to teach pupils to use intellectual processes to understand classes of units in different contexts for a variety of purposes, they are probably at the most crucial phase of instructional activity. This is partly caused by the fact that if pupils do not learn properly to deal intellectually with units and classes, they will be unable to deal effectively with the remaining products (relations, systems, transformations, and implications) listed in the Guilford model. Even though there is no guarantee that pupils who have satisfactorily learned to deal intellectually with units and classes will automatically function effectively with the remaining products listed, it is definite that few, if any, pupils will do so without prior mastery of the intellectual processing of units and classes. This seems to be one of the keys to instructional effectiveness and developing basic understanding in pupils at the elementary school level.

The comprehension of relations (connections between units) involves helping pupils to discover relationships that exist among objects, symbols, or conceptual material when arranged according to some pattern. The application of intellectual processes such as interpreting, analyzing, synthesizing, observing, and so on can be instrumental in helping pupils to unlock the mystery of pattern that dictates a particular relationship among relevant units. In this sense, the procedures used to select and deploy appropriate intellectual processes become the key to comprehending relations.

The attempt to comprehend systems (organized structures) involves the abilities to (1) structurally arrange objects in a given space, (2) discover patterns or systems among figural, symbolic, semantic, or behavioral elements, and (3) cognize or structure a problem preparatory to solving it. The comprehension of systems is more involved than the activity suggested in being able to see simple relationships. When one goes about the business of comprehending systems, he has to deal with the organized total of a given structure. Oftentimes, this involves several simple relationships fitted together in a conceptual structure that forms the system under consideration.

The cognition of transformations (changes or redefinitions) involves the ability to form a mental image of patterns that would be possible if objects were rearranged in some way. An example would be the mental projection of a chessboard through several moves. A second ability required in the comprehension of transformation involves predictive manipulation of available data to suggest a solution to a future problem. For instance, if one were to note that each year more six-year-old children come to school knowing a greater percentage of the curricular content to be taught in first grade than came in the preceding year, and that, if the trend continues at the same rate of increase, the first-grade class in a given school in the fall of 1978 would come to school knowing 90 per cent of curricular material to be taught, then he could project the curricular program that would be required to meet the needs of the population in question. In this instance the comprehension of transformations involves being able to propose farsighted solutions to a predicted problem. If pupils are to be taught to deal intellectually with transformations, they must be instructed in the processing of data, the detection of trends, and the formulation of strategies for theoretical formulation of plausible solutions to problems gleaned from the interpretation of selected data and trends.

When pupils are asked to comprehend implications (extrapolations, such as antecedents or consequents), they are involved in an attempt to preplan or predict outcomes that might result from present conditions. In order to deal with implications, pupils must be taught to mentally select the most effective solution to a problem from among a number of alternatives. To validate the process, pupils must be expected to justify the selection of a given solution and the rejection of other possible solutions. Another aspect of comprehending implications is related to the ability to anticipate likely consequences given a particular situation and a certain arrangement of events. The comprehension of implications is heavily involved with the complexity of steps involved in reaching a goal when the environmental conditions are constantly changing. To be able to complete this kind of activity is to employ conceptual foresight.

The preceding discussion utilized the operation of cognition to indicate how it would apply to the products indicated in Guilford's model. It is possible to discuss all of the operations and intellectual processes proposed by Guilford and the writer respectively in terms of the products indicated in the model. However, it is probably not necessary to aid the understanding of the reader or to make the point attempted in this section. The point to be grasped here is that the intellect is characterized by immense richness and diversity requiring a broad range of thinking skills in conducting classroom activity. Consequently, if this classroom activity is to contribute significantly to the development of independent learners and effective citizens, more attention must be focused on mastery and application of basic study skills that ultimately lead to the development of intellectual processes necessary for intelligent human activity. To achieve this goal is to fulfill the promise of effective teaching as the primary influence in efficient and effective pupil learning.

Teaching Intellectual Processes

Instruction at the elementary school level should focus on teaching intellectual processes through the use of basic study skills. As these basic study skills are employed to process relevant content, the value of intellectual processes becomes apparent. These intellectual processes encompass most of the thought patterns required to use subject matter content to deal with problems that are important to current and future learners. The elementary school must be concerned with the teaching of intellectual processes because they form the basis for all other mental activity that will take place at a later date at higher levels of involvement to solve more complex problems. Given the significance of intellectual processes and basic study skills as an integral part of most learning activity in schools, there is a real need to examine the components involved in the teaching of these processes through the use of basic study skills with various content areas. Further, there is a need to examine the observed and assumed outcomes that result from focusing on intellectual processes as a goal in instruction.

When one attempts to teach or develop intellectual processes through the use of basic study skills to process certain content in special ways, he has to employ an appropriate teaching strategy that raises the probability of achieving the outcomes intended. In terms of our present discussion the outcomes are intellectual processes as applied in specific content areas. In order to provide a visual picture of the relationship that characterizes the teaching of intellectual processes through the use of basic study skills, a model indicating the dimensions is shown in Figure 6.3. The model presents a three-dimensional cube as a complete structural entity that is held together by the teaching strategies employed. The sides of the model consist of subject-matter content (D1), basic study skills (D2), and intellectual processes (D3). One should note that subject-matter content (D1) and basic study skills (D2) interact to

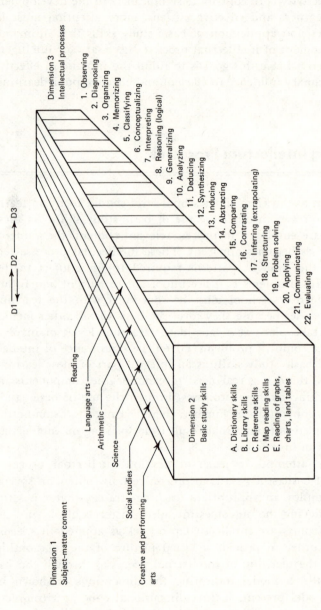

Figure 6.3

Model for Teaching Intellectual Processes Through the Use of Basic Study Skills. [Mary Jane Aschner and Charles E. Bish, eds., "Creativity—An Innovation in the Classroom," in *Productive Thinking in Education* (Washington, D.C.: National Education Association, 1968). Reprinted by permission of the National Education Association.]

Dimension 1
Subject-matter content

Creative and performing arts
Social studies
Science
Arithmetic
Language arts
Reading

Dimension 2
Basic study skills

A. Dictionary skills
B. Library skills
C. Reference skills
D. Map reading skills
E. Reading of graphs, charts, [and tables

Dimension 3
Intellectual processes

1. Observing
2. Diagnosing
3. Organizing
4. Memorizing
5. Classifying
6. Conceptualizing
7. Interpreting
8. Reasoning (logical)
9. Generalizing
10. Analyzing
11. Deducing
12. Synthesizing
13. Inducing
14. Abstracting
15. Comparing
16. Contrasting
17. Inferring (extrapolating)
18. Structuring
19. Problem solving
20. Applying
21. Communicating
22. Evaluating

D1   D2   D3

produce intellectual processes (D3) essential to solving certain kinds of problems requiring the use of structured mental abilities. The key to the functional relevance of the model is tied to the nature of the interaction between D1 and D2. In our discussion this interaction is synonymous with teaching strategies.

In order to ensure a common reference point, we have listed and provided a clarifying explanation for each of the intellectual processes in the first of these two lists that follow and basic study skills in the second.

1. *Observing (Perception)*. Directed or intentional awareness or scrutiny of particulars or facts.
2. *Diagnosing*. Classifying individuals on the basis of observed characteristics.
3. *Organizing*. Arranging data for ready reference, or in such a way as to display their relations (logical, chronological, and so on) with each other.
4. *Memorizing*. Retention, storage, reproduction of information cognized.
5. *Classifying*. Grouping objects into mutually exclusive classes, ranks, or categories.
6. *Conceptualizing*. Determining the idea that represents a number of individual instances, all of which have something in common.
7. *Interpreting*. Describing, formulating, or reformulating something in familiar terms; finding or explaining the meaning or significance of raw data.
8. *Reasoning (Logical)*. Thinking through problems by using general principles or logical forms.
9. *Generalizing*. Making a judgment that applies to all or most of a group of phenomena.
10. *Analyzing*. Breaking down complex objects, data, or behavior into smaller, more specific units.
11. *Deducing*. Proceeding from premises or propositions and attempting to derive valid conclusions therefrom.
12. *Synthesizing*. Putting data together to form a whole.
13. *Inducing*. Process by which one concludes that what is true of certain individuals or objects is true of a class, what is true of part is true of the whole class, or what is true at certain times will be true in similar circumstances at all times.
14. *Abstracting*. Characterizing any quality of something considered apart from the thing itself, or from the other qualities

with which it is associated; and pertaining to terms that refer to such a quality.

15. *Comparing.* Yielding equivalent meanings from noting characteristics of two or more sets of objects, phenomena, scores, or measures.

16. *Contrasting.* Developing heightened awareness of difference resulting from bringing together two or more items of any sort, either simultaneously or in close succession.

17. *Inferring (Extrapolating).* Using a mental process whereby, on the basis of one or more judgments, a person reaches another judgment regarded as proven or established by the former.

18. *Structuring.* Formulating any enduring arrangement, grouping, pattern, or articulation of parts to form a relatively stable system or whole.

19. *Problem Solving.* Selecting from a number of alternatives those that lead to a desired goal.

20. *Applying.* Putting or adapting items or ideas to special use to meet a particular need.

21. *Communicating.* Process whereby one system (a *source*) influences another system (a *destination*) by manipulation of the alternative signals carried in a *channel* connecting them.

22. *Evaluating.* Determining the value or relative importance of something in terms of a standard; determining the relative effectiveness of regulated conditions in furthering or hindering the attainment of present goals.

1. *Dictionary Skills.* Meanings, spellings, syllables, alphabetical order, guidewords, pronunciations, derived forms, foreign terms, etymology, synonyms and antonyms.

2. *Library Skills.* Selecting best source of information, the Dewey system, shelf location, card catalog and trays, special collections, and arrangement of the library.

3. *Reference Skills.* Parts of a book, key words, locations and organization of different sources, use of index, use of table of contents, organizing and presenting reports, note taking, outlining, content reading techniques, skimming and scanning.

4. *Map-Reading Skills.* Understanding symbols and legends; relationships in location; space and directions; time and distance; scale; comparing maps; drawing inferences; map construction; area reproduction; geographic measurement; interpretation of political, physical, product, population, rainfall, and special

maps in various combinations; demographic display and interpretation; and area relationships.

5. *Reading of Graphs, Charts, and Tables.* Interpretation and comparison of line, bar, circle, and pictorial graphs; construction and interpretation of tables; trend analysis; chronology; cartoon and picture analysis; and graphic presentation.

Use this as a starting point for formulating the teaching strategy to be employed. Concrete examples of this process are presented later in the discussion.

The model (Figure 6.3) is intended to provide the teacher with systematic analysis of classroom practices so that instructional activity results in bringing about outcomes that are intended immediately while forming the basis for practical uses in future life activity. The list of twenty-two intellectual processes indicated in Dimension 3 was devised after a survey of the structured mental operations required to successfully complete assigned activities at the elementary school level was completed. Even though the list does not include all of the possible labels that could be assigned to intellectual processes, it does encompass most of the structured mental operations that would occur in most instructional programs at the elementary school level. Since intellectual processes represent the basis for organizing and constructing an appropriate teaching strategy, teachers must be given the practice and experience required to structure and sequence basic study skills and subject-matter content in accord with the dictates of each intellectual process serving as the basis for the resulting instructional activity. This model focuses on intellectual processes as the primary concern of all instructional activity at the elementary school level even though this is the most neglected area in classroom teaching. As a consequence, we are proposing intellectual processes as the primary goals and the real ends of instructional activity at the elementary school level.

In terms of Dimension 2, the basic study skills indicated represent structured procedures needed to conduct meaningful intellectual activity at all levels of content complexity in the elementary school. These skills are employed in different ways across different problems in different content areas. Their selection, sequence, and emphasis are greatly influenced by the nature of the intellectual process to be taught, and the subject-matter content area used as the *medium* of communication. Basic study skills can be learned as an *end* as well as a means in the teaching-learning process. Therefore, it is possible to have children learn basic study skills apart from their application in teaching intellectual processes. In a few instances, this may be justified, especially if mastery of a subskill is required before one can employ the complex of skills needed to grasp a given intellectual process. However, the power of basic study skills as a means to learning structured mental operations is greatly diminished when they are learned as *ends* in themselves. At some point, there is a balance required in the teaching of basic study skills as an *end* or a *means to an end* even though quality thinking and finding relevant solutions to problems dictate that the balance be weighted in favor of *means to an end* of the continuum. Basic study skills are the building blocks for constructing structured mental operations and they should be learned in the context of their use so that pupils can get a practical "feel" of how they might be applied and adapted to the achievement of major goals of the instructional process.

Dimension 2 includes the subject-matter content that is accepted and well established as the curriculum program of the elementary school. It represents the knowledge that mankind has collected, organized, and interpreted for use in providing a type of functional order to human environments. The communication of subject-matter content remains one of the most important functions of education in our society. However, teaching subject-matter content should not be the major goal of education because it represents the results of past and present intellectual efforts of mankind in their quest to solve problems, and understand and interpret phenomena. It falls short as a means of enabling learners to deal with future problems, understandings, and interpretations that are relevant to the maintenance and improvement of meaningful societal activity. Subject matter does serve an essential role for achieving the major goal (teaching children how to think) of education because it is an integral part of the means for achieving quality thinking habits as an end. Pupils cannot be taught to think or think independently in a vacuum; therefore subject matter can be employed as the medium for developing, cultivating, practicing, and promoting relevant thinking behaviors described earlier as intellectual processes. Subject matter content can be arranged, rearranged, and processed utilizing basic study skills to control the pattern employed so that specific intellectual processes are emphasized and operationally defined. There is no way to determine whether or not the pattern employed is correct if subject-matter content is not available to serve as the standard of comparison to judge the validity of the process in question. In this sense subject-matter content serves both as the material to be taught and the standard for judging the nature of the mental operations employed to process information. Subject-matter content is the key ingredient for the employment of basic study skills to teach intellectual processes.

In order to provide the reader with concrete examples illustrating the ideas presented, an outline of some specific teaching strategies that might be employed to teach selective intellectual processes using basic study skills is presented in this section. Even though all of the details of the instructional activity cannot be covered here, we hope to provide enough information to enable teachers to get the idea and to discern how they would expand the basic example to a full-scale teaching episode. The phrases or questions that a teacher might use as cues to trigger the pattern for processing information that enables one to acquire the intellectual processes in question are discussed in the following section.

Lower-Grade Ideas

K–Second Grade: During this period, the pupils begin to cope with intellectual process (example: observing), subject-matter content (example: language arts), and basic study skills (example: dictionary skills).

Teaching Strategy: The intent of this teaching strategy is to direct the children's attention to the pattern of alphabet and to the use of this pattern in different parts of the telephone directory. A copy of the alphabet in both large- and small-case letters should be made available to each child so that the pattern of the alphabet is accessible as a guide for discerning the pattern in the directory. The teacher should select two sample sections of two different pages in a local telephone directory similar to the samples presented in Figure 6.4. Copies of the samples should be made available to each child. At this point the pupils are ready for their first instructions. The teacher should then ask pupils to note the pattern of the alphabet and how certain letters follow other letters. Pupils should be asked to note differences between small- and large-case letters. Such differences as size, shape, line, and slant of letters should be noted and discussed. The teacher should ask selected pupils such questions as "What letter comes before J and after L in the Alphabet?" One child should be directed to point to the answer in large case when he answers whereas another child might be asked to repeat the answer pointing to small-case letters. After the teacher has assured himself that pupils have adequately observed the letters in, and the pattern of, the alphabet, he should turn to the sections of the telephone directory.

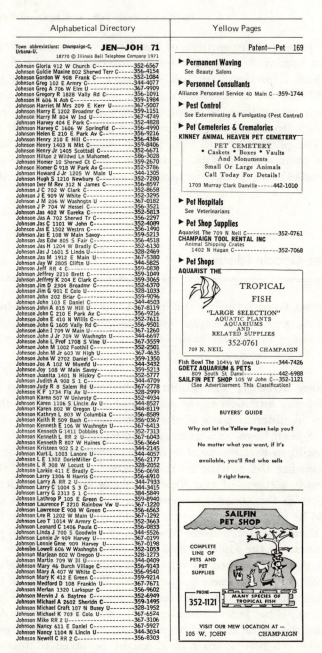

Figure 6.4

Sections from a Telephone Directory. [Illinois Bell Telephone Company for the City of Champaign-Urbana, 1971. Reprinted by permission of the Illinois Bell Telephone Company.]

Pupils should then be directed to observe the alphabetical directory section. They should be told to note JEN-JOH at the top of the page and asked why they think it was placed there. The teacher should then ask "Do you see JEN in any word in column on the left of the page?" The teacher might decide to pursue this line of questioning but it is not necessary for teaching observing. A question concerning the guide letters at the top might be asked to see if pupils have observed the pattern. Pupils' attention might then be directed to the content of the directory and they might be asked a typical question such as "Why did they place Johnson, Harry E. before Johnson, Harry M? or Johnson, Harvey before Johnson, Harvey C? or Johnson, Henry, 210 E. Hill C before Johnson, Henry, 1403 N. Mkt C?" Many variations of these questions might be employed until most pupils are able to observe the alphabetical pattern used to arrange the names in their existing order. Letter changes in the first and middle names of people might be highlighted and noted in other questions directed at the pupils. These kinds of questions should be used until most pupils have acquired the ability to scrutinize the particular features of the alphabet that determine the order and arrangement of the names listed.

When the teacher approaches the Yellow Pages section of the directory, he might ask pupils, "What kind of animals can you buy at the Aquarist Pet Shop?" or "What kind of animals can you buy at the Sailfin Pet Shop?" "Why do they list the Aquarist Pet Shop first?" Other kinds of questions can be fashioned as long as they draw pupils' attention to particular features that enable them to identify patterns and functions revelant to the material being studied.

If the teacher would like to assess how well pupils have learned to observe, he should show them different pages in the telephone directory and repeat some of the questions. The teacher might also have some pupils make a directory of the members of the class as a check on whether they are observing the relevant features required to complete this activity. Care should be taken so that pupils continue to focus on the particulars of the pattern that enables one to order things, objects, or units similar to the telephone directory. Even being able to repeat the alphabet in appropriate order is an important incremental learning. It is not the focus of this attempt to teach observing as an intellectual process. Therefore, the teacher must remember to keep pupils focused on those aspects of the lesson that help them denote or scrutinize particular attributes or facts that communicate that pupils are observing. At that point, the teacher can make some judgments involving pupils' ability to observe new phenomena in accordance with a pattern that demonstrates control over the intellectual process.

Middle-Grade Ideas

Third–Fourth Grade: Building on the skills acquired, the pupils now begin to grasp an intellectual process such as comparing, a particular subject-matter content, such as science, and a basic study skill, such as the reading of graphs, charts, and tables.

Teaching Strategy: The focus of this teaching strategy is to help pupils to elicit equivalent meanings for different kinds of cats from noting characteristics of more than one of the different members of the cat family. A chart picturing a common house cat, a pedigreed house cat, a jaguar, a lion, a cheetah, a lynx, and a mountain lion should be obtained and displayed where all the children can view them. Questions should be directed at the class in such a way that the common characteristics of the cats are readily evident. The teacher might ask: "Can you tell us something about the body shape (build) of each cat?" "Are there some things about each cat's coat that are alike?" "Do all cats have the same kind of feet and claws?" These and similar questions can be used to focus the pupils' attention on specific features that can be compared. In most instances, pupils will not be able to observe the features highlighted by the questions. Appropriate reading material must be made available so that specific information on each kind of cat can be obtained. Pupils should also be encouraged to inspect a house cat and list the characteristics called for in the questions. When the specific characteristics of the different kinds of cats have been noted, the teacher might make a chart listing this information for each cat. Pupils should be asked to note characteristics that are the same for each cat.

When attempting to denote characteristics in science, care should be taken to list those that can be validated and compared, using an agreed-upon standard measurement or description. Questions posed to help pupils develop the intellectual process of comparing should focus attention on those features that are important both to differentiating and comparing cats. This is important since some characteristics of cats are common to other mammals. In order to give the intellectual process of comparing a reasonable chance of being mastered by pupils, the focus must remain on characteristics that provide equivalent meanings for different members of the cat family. However, each definition resulting from each set of characteristics must define a cat so that the comparisons are roughly equivalent.

Fifth–Sixth Grade: The intellectual process now becomes that of inferring; social studies is used for subject-matter content; and the basic study skill is map-reading skills.

Teaching Strategy: The intent of this teaching strategy is to help pupils reach judgments on the basis of data that are suggestive of judgments based on direct observations of appropriate data. Inferring is an intellectual process requiring the use of data to draw conclusions about factors not readily associated with the phenomena of interest. In this sense, the nature and sequence of the questions are critical to the kind of inferences drawn. Attention must also be focused on the location, collection, organization, and interpretation of relevant data.

To teach inferring, a teacher might get copies of the most up-to-date travel map published by any major gas company and provide each child with a copy. The teacher should then pose a general problem to all children such as: Plan a twelve-hundred-mile trip to a given city from the pupils' present location. The trip should take approximately six days and include some sidetrips for historical sightseeing for the young children and the possibility of a variety of evening entertainment for the adults. Be sure to plan to take the most direct route, primarily over expressways, while averaging two sightseeing stops per day. No more than eight hours should be spent on the road per day and no more than two hundred miles should be covered per day. Each stopover must be in a city large enough to have at least six different motels or have at least six hundred rooms available for guests. Also there should be a choice of at least five different movies. This problem should be solved by utilizing the data presented in the travel maps.

Some of the important questions the teacher should ask include: "Where is the nearest expressway leading one in the direction of the city in question?" "What number is shown on the expressway?" "Does the expressway go through the city in question?" "If not, what are the numbers of the other expressways one would have to take to get to the city in question?" Then the teacher might instruct the pupils to list the largest cities along (or no more than ten miles away from) each of the expressways to be used to get to the designated city, and to record the approximate distance between the cities noted. Pupils should then be asked to list a number of historical sights that might be of interest to young children. Some discussion of the size (population) of a city, number of motel rooms, and number of movie houses in operation should be conducted. Pupils should relate the discussion to their own town and note the relationships that are evident. Each pupil should then be encouraged to list each of the largest cities selected and indicate their respective population statistics. The distance between each city should be noted. Then pupils should list the historical sights selected and the distances between them along the route of travel.

At this point pupils should be asked to suggest the five cities that would be used as stopover areas using the earlier criteria (size, number of motel rooms, number of movies) listed for selection. They should be asked to list the two historical sights that should be visited each day, the amount of time that can be spent at each site, and the mileage to be covered between each sightseeing and overnight stop.

In teaching pupils the process of inferring through the use of map-reading skills, the teacher should ask questions that require them to make predictions about areas on the basis of data available on maps. They should be asked to use the predictions to plan actions. As a check on the validity of their inferences, pupils might write to cities selected to ask about the number of motel rooms and movie houses in operation. Pupils might write to the states' travel bureaus or appropriate historical societies to obtain more detailed information on the sites selected for visitation. Information gained from these sources could serve as a validity check on the inferences made from data obtained from the maps. A teacher might ask many questions related to what one might expect to see in towns visited as a result of clues evident on the travel map. Care should be taken to ensure that the questions are about objects or phenomena not directly presented in map data. Questions are asked to elicit data formations that can most easily be associated with available data. In short, the questions must require pupils to infer other data configurations from data available.

It should be evident that the teaching strategy is the key element in relating the instructional program to the organized curriculum. Intellectual processes represent the goals of the instructional program and subject-matter content of the organized curriculum represents the accumulated knowledge to be processed using basic study skills. The teaching strategy is the pattern of decisions (employment and deployment of basic study skills) used in the acquisition, retention, and utilization of information in order to achieve certain objectives (intellectual processes). The pattern characterizing the teaching strategy will change as the objectives of the instructional program and the subject-matter content are altered. As a consequence, the validity of a teaching strategy is established by results—the extent to which it enables pupils to achieve the objectives of the instructional program by processing subject-matter content successfully.

One should remember that achieving the objectives of the instructional program is intimately tied to the nature of the content and the pattern used to employ basic study skills to process the content. One cannot judge whether or not pupils have acquired intended intellectual processes if content and basic study skills are unavailable for validity checks. It is necessary to use content as the standard for determining whether pupils have properly utilized basic study skills to process content for generalizing. The content resulting from the generalizing can be compared with previously validated content to determine the extent to which pupils have acquired the intellectual process. If not, flaws in the planning and implementation of the teaching strategy can be pinpointed in terms of teacher and pupil characteristics and of the use and knowledge of basic study skills. This process helps to specify how a teaching strategy relates the instructional program to the organized curriculum and how teachers help pupils acquire the intellectual processes that represent the objectives of that program.

Problem Areas Associated with Teaching Basic Study Skills and Developing Intellectual Processes

Even though it is possible to obtain general agreement concerning the value of developing intellectual processes through the use of basic study skills to process subject-matter content, there are many problem areas that tend to prevent this concern from becoming the primary focus of the instructional program. These problem areas are discussed separately so that the full range of the difficulty becomes readily apparent.

Because teaching strategies are patterns for utilizing basic study skills to process subject-matter content to achieve an objective of the instructional program, they cannot be planned completely in advance for all classes, in all situations, in all places. The designer of a teaching strategy must take into account the characteristics of the pupils to be taught (including prior knowledge of content, skills, and processes), the teaching style and relevant characteristics of the teacher, the content area, the basic study skills required (by the teacher and pupils), and the intellectual processes to be developed. Since it is not possible for teachers working under a variety of ever-changing conditions to know all of these factors in advance, educators who attempt to plan teaching strategies for others make certain assumptions about the nature of the factors involved. An example is the preplanned unit approach to teaching.

When the preplanned unit is used as a teaching strategy, there is a focus on a grade level, an attempt to be comprehensive in content coverage, an assumption that the teacher understands the purpose and content of the unit, an attempt to teach basic study skills as content, and a tendency to view instructional outcomes in terms of observed behavior. Most of the assumptions underlying preplanned units for all teachers violate the basic conditions and dynamic qualities of teaching strategy because they are not tailored to dynamic requirements and conditions of a specific teaching/learning situation. In this sense, a teaching strategy can only be formulated with regard to a specific objective (or group of objectives) of a given instructional program while taking into account relevant pupil and teacher characteristics, the basic study skills to be employed, the specific subject-matter content to be processed, and the special conditions affecting the teacher's intent in this particular situation.

Even with the obvious advantages of having teachers formulate their own teaching strategies in accordance with select objectives under unique conditions, it is unrealistic to expect all teachers to do so. This is primarily related to the fact that most teachers are not specifically trained to conduct this activity; it is too time consuming considering how much is expected of today's elementary schoolteachers, it requires teachers to master relevant intellectual processes and the skills that can be used to develop them, and the teacher is limited in the amount of subject-matter content that he can supervise pupils in covering. For all of these and other reasons, elementary schoolteachers are not likely to formulate all the teaching strategies they hope to use in the instructional program across the various content areas. However, it is important for them to learn how to do that, so that they may become more competent and systematic in their adaptation, use, and adoption of teaching strategies planned by others without specific information relevant to a given class.

Instructional Materials

Instructional materials usually suggest basic study skills required to achieve the objectives of a given lesson. However, they do not suggest the use and patterning of these skills to practice and master intellectual processes. In most instances, instructional materials are organized in accord with the hierarchical and taxonomic structure of subject-matter content and, as such, encourage teachers to instruct and pupils to learn the material in relation to its organization. This situation causes teachers to focus on the products of intellectual processes rather than on the mental operations they represent. If instructional materials are to contribute more directly to the development of intellectual processes, more attention must be given to the way in which they are organized. The organization of instructional materials often determines the goals of instruction and, as such, tends to focus the instructional program too narrowly for meaningful generalizations across other problem areas.

When one attempts to develop intellectual processes via the use of basic study skills to process subject-matter content, there is a need for instructional materials that are focused at an appropriate level of difficulty while maintaining clarity. Too often instructional materials introduce and increase *difficulty* by adding special vocabulary that represents unique conceptual understandings but reduce *clarity* because the learner is not furnished with data to indicate how these conceptual understandings were derived. In the development of intellectual processes difficulty should be related to the increased complexity associated with locating, sorting, organizing, interpreting, and presenting relevant data paralleling specific mental operations. Clarity at this point is associated with the ease with which additional information can be meaningfully processed to yield a variety of mental operations. Instructional materials can effectively deal with difficulty and clarity to the extent that appropriate supportive data underlying complex conceptual understandings are made available to the pupils for individual processing.

Providing for Individual Differences

One of the supreme challenges of developing intellectual processes through the use of basic study skills is to provide for individual differences of pupils at different stages and levels in their mastery and use of the skills and processes in question. This situation is further complicated by the fact that many different levels of understanding are associated with intellectual processes because as mental operations they can be continually refined to meet different situations at different times. It is possible for pupils to learn to infer at a very low level utilizing one basic study skill area. At the same time, another pupil may acquire and extend the same intellectual process at a higher level utilizing a number of basic study skills. The task in providing for individual differences is to select basic study skills that pupils can use to develop specific intellectual processes. Different pupils should be encouraged to utilize different basic study skills to learn similar intellectual processes so that all students can develop important mental operations while taking different routes to success.

Introducing Basic Study Skills Systematically

It is probably a good idea to introduce and teach some of the basic study skills systematically so that pupils are better able to use them to process basic information according to some designated pattern. In some instances the skills should be learned by rote through the use of meaningful drill and practice on real informational problems. For example, it would facilitate the development of map-reading ability if pupils were encouraged to take imaginary trips by using travel maps to reconstruct the mental experience. As pupils read the legend, determine distances between specific points, locate points of interest, and note differences in scale, they will be getting the necessary drill and practice that will improve their ability to process this kind of information when they are attempting to learn certain intellectual processes.

Even though basic study skills should be introduced systematically, they should be taught, as much as possible, within the functional context of the different subject-matter areas. Certain basic study skills are employed differently in different subject-matter areas and require special treatment to develop intellectual processes with certain kinds of information. For example, selecting the best source of information for each subject-matter area will differ according to the purposes of the activity. Even though there are some common elements of this skill associated with different subject-matter areas, some of the critical elements remain unique to the content area in question when employed for certain purposes.

Basic study skills can be classified in general categories but they are usually employed as specific subskills. For example, dictionary skills cover all of the general class of activities associated with the use of the dictionary, but when this class of skills is employed to solve a particular problem it is presented in terms of meanings, spellings, alphabetical order, and so on. When a teacher attempts to help pupils learn intellectual processes, he is primarily engaged in guiding pupils in the use of specific skills within a general class of skills. Therefore, specific subskills of the different basic study skills areas become the focal point of processing information to learn a given intellectual process.

In this chapter we have discussed the nature of basic study skills and intellectual processes. We indicated that we believe that the development of intellectual processes is the prime purpose of elementary education. We also suggested that the proper employment and deployment of basic study skills to process subject-matter content will enable pupils to develop the intellectual processes that are the objectives of a given instructional program. In order to properly implement an instructional program that yields intended objectives, the teaching strategy designed and utilized must reflect a pattern that increases the probability of success. It then could be concluded that an appropriate teaching strategy guiding the instructional program enables pupils to pattern basic study skills for processing subject-matter content to develop important intellectual processes.

Summary

The development of intellectual processes is interrelated with the mastery of, and control over, basic study skills. Intellectual processes are necessary to acquire basic study skills, and basic study skills are essential to the effective employment of intellectual processes. Even though intellectual processes and basic study skills are conceptually different, one set of functions is required to acquire and use the other set. Basic study skills and intellectual processes are interrelated functionally. One of the primary tasks of the elementary school is to help children learn how to utilize these two sets of functions to improve the process of solving problems that offer different degrees of familiarity in relation to previous experience. Children must be helped to see the relationship between intellectual processes and basic study skills and how they combine to contribute to their ability to pursue personal interests and to solve problems of importance to them. This idea is at the heart of the selection, organization, processing, and development of content utilized to conduct the instructional program. As a consequence, the attention given intellectual processes and basic study skills by teachers is likely to influence greatly the direction, impact, and effectiveness of the instructional program of the elementary school.

References

1. H. T. Morse and G. H. McCune, "Selected Items for the Testing of Study Skills and Critical Thinking," Washington, D.C.: National Council for the Social Sciences, Bull. No. 15, 4th ed., 1964, pp. 3–4.
2. Ibid., p. 4.
3. R. F. P. Salinger, "Humanistic Efficiency," An Appendix to a Proposal to the National Science Foundation for Support of the School Science Curriculum Project, July 1965, p. 2.
4. J. E. Russell, *Change and Challenge in American Education* (Boston: Houghton, 1965), pp. 25–26.
5. G. Spache, *Reading in the Elementary School* (Boston: Allyn, 1964).
6. P. R. Merrifield, "Trends in the Measurement of Special Abilities," *Review of Educational Research,* 35:30 (Feb. 1965).
7. P. L. Dressel and L. B. Mayhew, *General Education, Explorations in Evaluation* (Washington, D.C.: American Council on Education, 1957), p. 244.
8. Ibid., p. 249.
9. W. G. Findley, "Ability and Performance," in *Proceedings of the 1963 Invitational Conference on Testing Problems* (Princeton: Educational Testing Service, 1964), p. 107.
10. G. C. Helmstadter, *Principles of Psychological Measurement* (New York: Appleton, 1964), p. 7.
11. Dressel and Mayhew, op. cit., p. 249.
12. Ibid.
13. G. Spache, *Toward Better Reading* (Champaign, Ill.: Garrard, 1963), p. 335.
14. G. Spache, *Reading in the Elementary School.*
15. Ibid., p. 198.
16. Ibid., p. 199.
17. A. W. Heilman, *Principles and Practices of Teaching Reading* (Columbus, Ohio: Merril, 1961), p. 286.
18. Ibid., p. 288.
19. N. B. Smith, *Reading Instruction for Today's Children* (Englewood Cliffs, N.J.: Prentice-Hall, 1963).
20. Ibid., p. 307.
21. Ibid., p. 309.
22. Ibid., p. 313.
23. Ibid.

24. Ibid., p. 315.

25. A. W. Heilman, "Teaching the Reading Study Skills," in Albert J. Mazurkiewicz, ed., *Reading, Learning, and the Curriculum*, Proceedings of the 1963 Lehigh University Twelfth Annual Reading Conference (Bethlehem, Pa.: The Bureau of Educational Services, 1963), p. 42.

26. G. Spache, "Types and Purposes of Reading in Various Curriculum Fields," *The Reading Teacher*, 2:158–164 (Feb. 1958).

27. R. E. Stake, "Activity, Novelty and Structure in Study-Hall Assignments," *American Educational Research Journal*, 3:11–12 (Jan. 1966).

28. J. A. Holmes and H. Singer, *The Substrata-Factor Theory: Substrata-Factor Differences Underlying Reading Ability in Known-Groups at the High School Level* (Berkeley, Cal.: Mimeographed at the University of California, 1961), p. 5.

29. Ibid., p. 305.

30. J. H. Shores, "Importance, Timeliness, and Challenge of the Conference Theme," in William S. Gray, ed., *Improving Reading in All Curriculum Areas*, Supplementary Education Monographs (Chicago: U. of Chicago, 1952), pp. 3–4.

31. Ibid., p. 4.

32. J. J. DeBoer and M. Dallmann, *The Teaching of Reading* (New York: Holt, 1960), p. 118.

33. J. H. Shores, "Are Fast Readers the Best Readers?—A Second Report," *Elementary English*, 38:244–245 (April 1961).

34. G. A. Yoakam, "How to Cope with Deficiencies in Basic Reading Skills That Block Progress in Learning Activities," in William S. Gray, ed., *Improving Reading in All Curriculum Areas*, op. cit., p. 71.

35. H. Huus, "Basic Instruction in Reading and the Promotion of Reading Interests," in William S. Gray, ed., *Improving Reading in All Curriculum Areas*, op. cit., p. 111.

36. G. A. Yoakam, "The Reading-Study Approach to Printed Materials," *The Reading Teacher*, 2:147 (Feb. 1958).

37. J. E. Berry and W. Mercer, "Developing Library Skills: Every Teacher's Responsibility," *Education*, 78:81 (Oct. 1957).

38. M. V. Gaver, "Effectiveness of Centralized Library Service in Elementary Schools (Phase 1)," in *Research in Reading for the Middle Grades* (Washington, D.C.: Department of Health, Education and Welfare, 1963), p. 54.

39. Office of Education, *Implications for Elementary Education*, Follow-up on the 1960 White House Conference on Children and Youth

(Washington, D.C.: Department of Health, Education and Welfare, 1961), p. 23.

40. D. G. Ryans and N. Frederiksen, "Performance Tests of Educational Achievement," in E. F. Lindquist, ed., *Educational Measurement* (Washington, D.C.: American Council on Education, 1951), pp. 455–493.

41. J. H. Flavell, *The Developmental Psychology of Jean Piaget* (New York: Van Nostrand, 1963), p. 17.

42. Ibid.

43. Ibid.

44. Ibid., p. 18.

45. Ibid.

46. Ibid., p. 46.

47. Ibid., pp. 46–47.

48. J. Piaget, *The Origins of Intelligence in Children* (New York: International Universities Press), 1952, pp. 7–8.

49. Flavell, op. cit., p. 47.

50. Ibid., p. 48.

51. Ibid.

52. Ibid., p. 50.

53. J. P. Guilford, "Three Faces of Intellect," *American Psychologist*, 14:469–479 (1959).

54. R. Wilson, "The Structure of the Intellect," in Mary Jane Aschner and Charles E. Bish, eds., *Productive Thinking in Education* (Washington, D.C.: NEA), 1965.

55. Guilford, op. cit.

7

Influencing Pupils' Attitudes and Values

Curriculum and instruction in the elementary school are primarily concerned with influencing pupils' attitudes and values in a direction deemed desirable by the adults of their society. In this sense there is no such thing as an amoral curriculum. The curriculum of the elementary school represents a value orientation that formalizes the beliefs and behaviors that characterize the social systems of the culture. Instructional processes must develop and focus the attitudes of the young so that they learn how and why they should accept the value orientations that are central to the social systems of the culture. Therefore, the elementary school curriculum can be thought of as the values of culture that adults expect youth to learn and accept, and instruction as the means for shaping the attitudes of youth, so that the vast majority of them will achieve the expected value orientations to maintain and extend the general welfare of the society in question.

In this chapter we hope to discuss the general area of attitudes and values in the context of the elementary school program. If we are to accomplish our intent we must show the relationship between the personal characteristics (attitudes and values) of students, and the program (curriculum and instruction) component of the elementary school. Only then can we justify attempts to influence pupils' attitudes and values in the elementary school grades. This is the basic intent of the ideas presented in this section.

Justification for Influencing Pupils' Attitudes and Values in the Elementary School

Consistently, from the beginning of our public schools, one of the major purposes of the American elementary school has been education for democratic citizenship and individual dignity and development. Accordingly, one of the main intents of the elementary school is to enable youth to enhance the general welfare through the pursuit of individual welfare. Elementary education is the beginning stage of a formal and systematic socialization process geared to maintain and extend the reach and effectiveness of social systems that comprise the society. In his classical work, *Democracy and Education*, Dewey acknowledged education's socialization function when he made the following assertion:

> Since education is a social process, and there are many kinds of societies, a criterion for educational criticism and construction implies a *particular* social ideal. The two points selected by which to measure the worth of a form of social life are the extent to which the interests of a group are shared by all its members, and the fullness and freedom with which it interacts with other groups. An undesirable society, in other words, is one which internally and externally sets up barriers to free intercourse and communication of experience. A society which makes provision for participation in its good of all its members on equal terms and which secures flexible readjustment of its institutions through interaction of the different forms of associated life is in so far democratic. Such a society must have a type of education which gives individuals a personal interest in social relationships and control, and the habits of mind which secure social changes without introducing disorder.[1]

Careful examination of Dewey's comments suggests that education shaped by "a particular social ideal" is an expression of the values of the society in question. Therefore, all education is concerned with teaching the young the values of the society. This is at least one justification for making the conscious influencing of pupils' attitudes and values a legitimate concern of the elementary school.

Another justification is related to the associated survival consequences. The attitudes and values of a society preserve past experiences so that future members are spared the energy, the mistakes, and the expenditure of time spent by earlier generations to discover and rediscover many of the simplest relationships required just to attain the basic needs to sustain life. This point is made even more pointedly by Bontrager when he states that:

> . . . we cannot obtain the materials for the next meal without drawing on the knowledge of preceding generations. The peas that we now buy in a can were among the agricultural plants in ancient Merinde in 4400 B.C. "Wrapped up" in that can of peas are many forms of knowledge passed on through the verbal environment in the early dawn of history: knowledge of fire, the calendar, agriculture, metallurgy, food preservation, the wheel, the plow, systems of transportation. This knowledge has accumulated through the ages.[2]

The attitudes and values held by members of a society contain many ideas and bits of information that are critical for the survival, maintenance, and extension of that society. The elementary school is charged with part of the responsibility for seeing to it that children are exposed to those attitudes and values that represent the unbroken link to those ideas and procedures that are required to maintain our democratic society.

Attitudes and values that characterized the early existence of our society are harmful to today's societal requirements. Superstitions, prejudices, and misinformation keep many people in our society from utilizing what is known to improve their personal lives and functioning which would contribute greatly to the general welfare. A superstitious notion can keep many whole groups of people from utilizing a needed resource because they believe it to be sacred. Some Indian tribes still believe that certain geographical landmarks are sacred and, therefore, should not be disturbed by the presence of man. Even if the area offered the possibility of contributing measurably to their physical existence and conditions, many of the Indians would not consider disturbing these sacred land areas. In this and similar instances the nonsurvival value systems persist to affect, negatively, some aspects of present-day social activity. The same can be said of prejudices and misinformation. The persistence of nonsurvival value systems must also be a major concern of the elementary school.

In conclusion, the justification for systematically influencing the attitudes and values of elementary school pupils toward a social policy is dictated by members of society and the cultural traditions they embrace. However, in order for the elementary school to select those attitudes and values that should become the focus of experiences that each child is expected to have, there must be clear statements of social policy that specifically and operationally define the democratic ideals to be taught. According to Bontrager, clear

. . . statements of the social policy to which we are committed in the basic documents: The Declaration of Independence, the Constitution of the United States, and the Constitutions of the various states, all of which are in correspondence with the Federal Constitution. In these documents we find stated the social policy, the value generalizations, to which we are at least verbally committed. In broad outline, our verbal commitments assert that we value the general welfare (an interest in the other fellow), respect for the moral rights and feelings of others, freedom of expression, the consent of the governed, the right to be confronted by one's accusers, peaceful methods of settling controversy, the principle that one is innocent until proven guilty, the responsibility of the individual for maintaining his liberties and the liberties of others, respect for differences, and an appetite for learning as the only ultimate guarantee of the liberties we cherish.[3]

From this statement it is clear that certain attitudes and values are basic to the instructional concern of the elementary school. The ultimate justification for selecting and teaching such attitudes and values is dictated by the social policy that characterizes our democratic society. In this sense, the elementary school is the first step in a long series planned to shape the thought and behavior of youth in a mold that is consistent with our democratic way of life.

The Relationship Between Attitudes and Values

The relationship between attitudes and values has been the subject of much discourse over the years. This discourse has been pursued along two major lines of inquiry. One suggests that a value should be defined as a broader attitude. When attitudes and values are dealt with in terms of this notion, they are considered as part of a continuum of four concepts—opinion, attitude, interest, and value. These concepts represent successive points along a single continuum. Any attempt to understand attitudes and values within the context of the four concepts outlined in terms of the single continuum must demonstrate how one concept is related to the one next to it. Since this approach does not allow for all the complexity of interrelationships suggested by the concepts individually, the resulting conceptualization of the relationship between attitudes and values appears to be of little interest to researchers at the present time.

A second line of inquiry that thinks of values as components of attitudes characterizes the phenomena in terms of their interrelationships. When thought of in this context, one accepts the following conclusion:

> An attitude toward a state of affairs is defined as a composite of the valence (positive or negative) of all the values or goals to which that state of affairs is perceived to have positive or negative instrumentality.[4]

The conceptualization of the relationship between attitudes and values implied by this notion views personal experience and exposure as major components in determining how one should think of these constructs. Since this conclusion has been discovered or rediscovered by many researchers in the area, it appears that this explanation of the relationship between attitudes and values offers more for our discussion of these ideas in terms of the elementary school.

At the elementary school level the relationship between attitudes and values should exercise great influence on the operational procedures of teachers working with different students in a classroom. Since one of the primary jobs of teaching is to shape pupils' attitudes in a desirable direction while meeting the expectations of the elementary school, teachers must learn to make use of the value or goal orientations of the pupils as the starting point for systematic attitude development. Because of the interlocking complex relationship between attitudes and values, the nature of the influence teachers can exert on the development of pupil attitudes is very closely tied to their ability to understand and utilize the value and goal orientations of those to be taught. If pupils fail to perceive an operational and personally acceptable connection between the attitudes they are expected to develop and acquire, the values or goals held by pupils will not permit them to alter their attitudes in ways sought by the teacher. Any successful attempt to develop attitudes of elementary school pupils in a certain direction is dependent upon the success with which the techniques employed achieve the appropriate match with the value structure of the pupils involved.

The Nature of Attitudes

A number of definitions of attitudes[5, 6, 7, and 8] have been collected and reviewed in recent years. Many of the definitions that were available precipitated major issues that had and still have considerable empirical and conceptual consequences. Since our purpose is more concerned with the conceptual aspects of attitudes rather than the empirical aspects, we do not attempt to deal with many of the issues suggested by differences associated with delineating definitions. For our purposes, we utilize the definition of an attitude proposed by Allport (1935) and dicussed by McGuire.

> An attitude . . . has at least five aspects: (1) it is a mental and neural state (2) of readiness to respond, (3) organized (4) through experience, (5) exerting a directive and/or dynamic influence on behavior.[9]

The complexity of this definition is associated with the many ways in which an attitude might be defined resulting from the method of inquiry used or the variables selected for study. The definition itself provides us with a convenient framework for relating definitional endeavors associated with attitudes to the specific concerns of the elementary school. We can now turn to a discussion of the five factors that define an attitude and how these factors relate to the intentions of the elementary school in this area.

The Mental and Neural State
Factor in Attitude Development

When an attitude is thought of in terms of a mental and neural state, a decision has been made to define attitude as an abstract mediating concept tied to antecedent conditions as the basis of providing meaning for observed behaviors. The use of mental and neural states to define an attitude creates considerable ambivalence between the phenomenological and the physiological. In the first instance (phenomenological) attitudes are viewed as being determined by the phenomena of experience rather than by external, objective, physically described reality. The use of a person's perceptions is also extensive from a phenomenological perspective. In the second instance (physiological) attitudes are viewed as being determined by the physical states (body functions) of the person considered. Here selected physiological measures are employed to infer some type of behavior associated with various feeling states and to determine the intensity of such feelings. The reader should note that in both instances (phenomenological and physiological), attitude is not treated as a directly defined entity that accounts for the consequent behavior observed.

When an attitude is defined in mental and neural terms at the elementary school level, emphasis is placed on the value and nature of antecedent conditions (life experiences and physiological characteristics) that determine the observed behavior of children in the classroom and the school. Viewed from this standpoint, an elementary schoolteacher who wished to influence the attitudes of children would have to have a thorough knowledge and understanding of their experience backgrounds and relevant demographic factors, and some indications of their physical conditions (conditions such as rest, health, nutrition, well-being, and so on). It is assumed that a teacher with access to this specific background information can better understand the attitudes that currently shape the in-school behavior of children. In addition, this information can be used to decide the direction that attitude development should take and the techniques that should be employed to complete the job. The mental and neural definitional approach to attitudes is one of the primary ways used to conceptualize the elementary school's role in influencing pupils' attitudes at this level.

The Readiness to Respond Factor in Attitude Development

A considerable difference of opinion exists as to whether or not an attitude should be defined in terms of a response or readiness to respond. Many of the researchers in the area are found at both extreme ends of—and along—the response-readiness to respond continuum as a way of defining an attitude. Professionals on the "response" end of the continuum prefer a direct operational definition to determine what phenomena should be selected and observed. On the other hand, professionals on the "readiness to respond" end of the continuum prefer to define attitudes as theoretical constructs that may only be indirectly related to overt responses. Technically those in the former group (response) are called positivists and those in the latter group (readiness to respond) are called mediationists. If the elementary schoolteacher is interested in utilizing the perspectives of professionals in these two groups, it might be helpful to view attitudes in terms of gradations between the two positions. These five gradations include definitional approaches that (1) deal directly with the relationships between the antecedents and consequents, (2) deal with the relationships between paradigmatic antecedents (establishment of a fundamental antecedent from which all other antecedents derive meaning) and paradigmatic consequents (establishment of a fundamental consequent from which all other consequents derive meaning), (3) deal with a mediating construct tied into socially observable reality at both ends in terms of antecedent conditions that lead to it and consequents that follow from it, (4) deal with assuming the presence of mediating constructs on both the antecedent and consequent sides, and (5) deal with the interactions among antecedents and the relationship between the interactions among consequents.

The elementary school can utilize the "readiness to respond" definitional approach to understand attitudes as a way to influence the attitudes of the pupils. Using this approach, the elementary schoolteacher might depend heavily on observations of responses that pupils have to the various phenomena encountered in the classroom. The teacher may treat these observed responses as a direct reflection of pupils' attitudes. Teachers using this approach make their judgments about the nature of pupils' attitudes on the basis of the kinds of responses they observe. On the other hand, elementary schoolteachers may approach the influencing of pupils' attitudes by observing overt responses and attributing them to causes apart from the observed act. When this occurs, teachers have to assume that observed responses are caused by factors that are antecedents. In this context, the sources of attitudes are inferred from what the pupils do under varying conditions. These two ways of viewing the nature of attitudes that children exhibit at the elementary school level have profound consequences for determining how teachers will set out to influence pupils' attitudes.

The Organizational Factor in Attitude Development

The organizational factor in attitude development refers to the extent to which attitudes are "organized." There are two separate ways to view attitudes as being organized. The first is concerned with whether a single attitude contains components with a certain characteristic structure. The components of attitudes fall into two major categories: instrumentality-value analysis and knowing-feeling-acting analysis. The first category of attitude components, instrumentality-value analysis, defines attitude toward an object . . . "as a composite of the perceived instrumentality of the object to the person's goals, weighted by his evaluation of those goals."[10] Although this is an interesting way to view attitudes in relation to the elementary school experience, the instrumentality-value analysis approach is difficult to implement as part of the instructional process at this school level. The instrumentality-value approach probably is best thought of as an aid to helping teachers gain a better understanding of the nature of attitudes. The resulting information might be utilized to influence elementary school pupils' attitudes in a desirable direction through the instructional process.

The second category of attitude components, knowing-feeling-acting analysis, offers the greatest potential for direct utilization to influence pupils' attitudes in the elementary school. Other terms have been and are being used in literature to describe the subparts of this category as cognitive (knowing), affective (feeling), and conative (acting). Since the elementary school is charged directly with the responsibility of teaching knowledge, contributing to positive emotional development, and shaping behavior responses, the knowing-feeling-acting analysis of attitudes is directly applicable to the program of the elementary school. With this in mind, our discussion of the cognitive, affective, and conative aspects of attitudes will provide just enough detail to let our readers know what is intended when applied to instructional practice in the elementary school.

> The *cognitive* component of attitudes (also called the perceptual, informational, or stereotypic component) refers to how the attitude object is perceived, its conceptual connotation—it is the "stereotype" the person has of the attitude object (to use the somewhat pejorative term popularly used in discussions of ethnic attitudes).[11]

It is apparent from this description that the cognitive component of an attitude consists of the beliefs of the individual about the object. For example, a pupil's attitude toward eating meat may include his understanding of nutrition, his knowledge of nutrition related to sickness, his beliefs about the strengthening characteristics of meat, and his conception of himself as a physical being. In this sense, the most critical cognitions incorporated in the attitude system are evaluative beliefs that involve the assignment of attributions such as bad or good, positive or negative, favorable or unfavorable, and desirable or undesirable qualities to the particular object. It is also possible that the cognitive component includes the beliefs of pupils about the appropriate and inappropriate ways of responding to an object. In terms of influencing pupils' attitudes, the elementary school probably does its most effective job in the cognitive area. At this level pupils are taught accepted practice, traditions, procedures, content, and acceptable social patterns, and this serves as the knowledge base for developing their attitudes toward information and learning, with themselves as learners and individuals, and others in a variety of group settings. This knowledge will shape much of the pupils' disposition toward these classes of objects throughout their lives. The correctness and relevancy of knowledge pupils gain toward fundamental objects in a child's development are critical ingredients in influencing pupils' attitudes at the elementary school level. In this sense, what a child learns early is a critical determinant of what he is able to learn later. Early knowledge shapes how children will approach various key objects later in life.

The second component of an attitude in this analysis area is the affective component. According to McGuire:

> The *affective* component of attitude (also called the feeling or the emotional component) deals with the person's feelings of liking or disliking about the object of the attitude.[12]

Since this is primarily the evaluative component of an attitude, some thinkers in the area feel that this is the central focus of what an attitude is. This kind of thinking leads to the conclusion that the cognitive component is the content that is used to shape the affective component and the affective component determines the specific nature of the conative component. The cognitive and conative components can be thought of as serving the development and use of the affective component of attitudes. There is little doubt that the affective component of an attitude refers to the emotions pupils might attach to the objects in question. If pupils feel that an object is pleasing or displeasing, they like or dislike it. It is this very quality of emotional loading that gives pupils' attitudes their insistent, excitable, motivating character. If a child is a Boy Scout, he feels friendly toward Scouts from other countries, he likes scouting techniques that are unique to various countries, and he follows international scouting with avid interest. Children's attitudes at elementary school level are influenced in great degree by relevant affective components of their experiences and knowledge background. Therefore, if teachers are expected to influence pupils' attitudes in a certain direction, the instructional processes that teachers employ should concentrate on the affective aspects of pupils' personality development.

The third component of attitudes that should be considered here is the conative component. McGuire indicates that:

> The *conative* (action, behavioral) component of attitude refers to the person's gross behavioral tendencies regarding the object.[13]

Since the behavioral tendencies of elementary school pupils toward significant objects in the classroom or school can be observed directly, the conative component of an attitude can be a valuable area of concern for the teacher. Because the action tendency (conative) component of an attitude includes all of the behavioral readinesses associated with the attitude, teachers can anticipate some actions of children by knowing their attitudes toward certain objects. Therefore, if a pupil holds a positive attitude toward a given object, he will be disposed to approach or help or reward or support the object. On the other hand, a pupil who holds a negative attitude will be disposed to avoid or harm or punish or destroy the object. Therefore, if a black pupil has a favorable attitude toward white pupils, he will have a tendency to seek them out, to accept them as friends, to treat them as equals. However, if a black pupil is antiwhite, he will have a tendency to avoid white pupils, to reject them as friends, to withhold help, and to treat them as inferior persons. The teacher of elementary school age pupils must be alert to the actions of his pupils toward objects (human and nonhuman) that comprise their classroom or school experience if he wants to gain some insight into attitudes that influence the observed activity. The actions of pupils are a good place to start to understand some of the attitudes influencing that behavior. The other side of the coin suggests that the teacher might be able to discern how the attitudes he has tried to develop are reflected in pupil actions. In either instance, the conative component of attitudes is and should be a prime concern of elementary school teachers because it allows the teachers to obtain a measure of the attitudes in which they have an interest. Pupil actions are the ultimate expression of their attitudes.

The Experience Factor in Attitude Development

There is much agreement and evidence to suggest that attitudes are learned through experience. In terms of the elementary school experience, many of the pupils' attitudes are shaped during this time of their life and school experience. It is crucial to the total development of pupils that their elementary school experiences introduce, develop, and implement attitudes that are consistent with social expectations. If this is not an integral part of pupils' systematic elementary school experience, attitudes will be acquired, but the teacher will not be likely to know if these attitudes are in the direction intended. Teachers who want to influence the attitudes of elementary school pupils must structure the experiences so that this will occur in an expected social direction.

Directive and Dynamic Factors
in Attitude Development

Our last major consideration in this discussion deals with whether attitudes are dynamic as well as directive. If attitudes are considered directive, they guide a pupil's existing level of energy toward one behavioral outlet rather than another, or toward a given target, while excluding others. This directive view of attitudes suggests that specific objects are the most probable focus of a given pupil's attitudes. Another view of attitudes suggests that they are dynamic because they determine the absolute level of energy expressed by pupils while, at the same time, they determine the expression channel of the energy noted. In short, the dynamic quality of attitudes determines the extent of involvement and activity that pupils will direct toward the objects of their attitudes. For the elementary school, the dynamic view of attitudes appears to be the focal point of concern. Most elementary schoolteachers would like to motivate pupils toward a given target with the enthusiasm and activity required to be successful. This is the ultimate goal of the elementary school in its attempt to influence pupils' attitudes toward desirable ends.

Attitudes and the Program
of the Elementary School

In the last few pages we have discussed some of the different aspects of attitudes and their development and related them to instructional activity at the elementary school level. The different aspects of attitudes presented offer a number of opportunities for systematically influencing the attitudes of pupils through the elementary school program. Even though there was not a specific attempt to provide the reader with instructional techniques and processes for developing different attitudes, we did try to present a sufficiently broad picture of the nature of attitudes in hopes that increased understanding of the area will lead to better practice. Another reason for taking the approach we did is associated with some feeling that elementary schools should limit the range of consciously conceived program to influence pupils' attitudes. Therefore, any systematic program of attitude development or alteration is met with suspicion and opposition. This is one reason why specific suggestions for influencing pupils' attitudes by utilizing a given instructional program or process and achieving widespread agreement supporting the action are difficult to make. Therefore, our approach to attitudes in the elementary school program is restricted to improving the reader's understanding of attitudes and their development. It is our hope that this improved understanding will be reflected in all attempts to realize the conception of the elementary school.

Values in the Elementary School

Values are the worth or excellence, or the degree of worth, ascribed to an object or activity or a class thereof. Individuals are influenced by and tend to accept as their wants and goals the values shared by members of their reference groups and, less directly, the values of their larger society. What is "desirable" in an individual's life tends to become the "desired." Therefore, the self-esteem of most men is based on the pursuit and achievement of goals that reflect reference (and sometimes a larger group) group values. The priority placed by the individual on the goals in terms of importance is determined by the extent to which they are representative of the dominant values of his group. Even though values are ascribed to an object (goals sought) and therefore are reacted to as if these objects are external or objective, values are a function of the valuing transaction, not the object. The approach to values in the program of the elementary school is focused on the transactions and processes that determine what pupils will value in the school setting.

Earlier in the chapter, we discussed the relationship between attitudes and values and how they were related to the elementary school program. It was concluded that values are probably a broadened attitude resulting from an individual's experience with certain objects in different settings. Therefore, the *process of attitude development* is intimately tied to *valuing transactions,* and to affect one process is to affect the other. The attitude structure of an individual is determined by his response to objects under varying conditions, and the values an individual develops are the results of placing some type of worth on objects encountered. Without the development of attitudes in relation to objects, it is unlikely that an individual will value these objects.

The values of a society or reference group do change, primarily because of the actions of individuals. Individuals do not copy perfectly the values of their respective groups. This, in part, accounts for the individual's acquisition of new values and goals as the dominant force in his life. The achievement of these new goals will often have profound effects on the social reality of his and other groups. This is possible because the complexity of our society dictates that individuals are likely to be members of groups that may be in conflict with one another. If the individual in such a predicament is to achieve internal harmony with himself, he has to synthesize conflicting values and formulate a new set of values that are appropriate to the situation as he sees it. It is possible and highly probable that this new value will be accepted by other members of the society. Through this process society is changed while the continuity with widely accepted traditional values is maintained. When the elementary school sets out to affect values, either through the study of existing values or by the derivation of new sets of values that accommodate and extend traditional values, it serves a necessary and vital role in helping pupils acquire values that are consistent with living in America and in a democratic society. Knowledge and understanding of the traditional values of our society help pupils to deal with their American heritage and to decide what approaches are suitable for altering these values in a democratic system.

Elementary school-age children must be taught—and have a reasonable understanding of—the notion that the values of a society do change, and that they change as a result of the actions of individuals. This concept is the key to understanding what it means to be a member of a democratic society. As we consider the values of individuals in terms of group membership, it should be noted that the individual tends to accept the values of his reference groups as his goals and he makes judgments about the extent of his achievements and success in terms of the degree of accomplishment of group-defined goals. In this instance, the level of achievement conceived or perceived by the individual defines for him whether his efforts are "successful" or "unsuccessful" or whether he is "virtuous" or "evil." The point to be made here relates to helping pupils establish levels of achievement in terms of values that are important to them personally and to the society in general.

One of the tasks of the elementary school in the area of pupil acquisition and study of values is assisting them to set acceptable levels of achievement of these goals. There are at least four sets of factors to be considered if elementary schoolchildren are to be helped to devise systematic procedures for determining acceptable levels of achievements associated with the study and pursuit of values (goals). The four sets of factors of reference are (1) understanding personal capacities and limitations, (2) judging the attainability of levels of achievement, (3) relating to personal histories of success and failure, and (4) status of individuals in reference groups. Each of these factors is discussed in relation to the program of the elementary school.

Understanding Personal Capacities and Limitations

In our society, children will try to attain a number of goals. These goals are representative of the values that encourage children to seek one direction over another. One of the tasks of the elementary school is to help pupils understand how to set levels of achievement with respect to goals that are consistent with their personal capacities and limitations. For example, most elementary school pupils will aspire to achieve mastery of content or processes that are being taught. However, only a few of the pupils in a given class have the capacity to do so given the reality of limitation in the available time, the complexity of the content to be covered, and the experience background of the learners. Children must be helped to set a level of achievement for themselves that takes into account their personal capacities and limitations. Therefore, different children can feel that they have realized their goals at levels of achievement consistent with a valid assessment of their personal capacities and limitations. Success can be experienced at different levels of achievement for each pupil.

Judging the Attainability of Levels of Achievement

Elementary school pupils need help in setting realistic goals for themselves. This is not to imply that children should limit their range and scope to the possibilities that seem apparent within their own reference group. If this were the case, many children from certain backgrounds would not aspire to achieve goals that are consistent with the values of some other reference group that may be more attractive in terms of the larger society. When a pupil is asked to judge the attainability of a goal for himself, he is being asked to consider himself eligible for the pursuit of goals that are valued by other groups. The important point here is that the elementary school must help children to pursue values that may be beyond their personal experience but are considered to be of great worth in the general society.

Relating to Personal Histories of Success and Failure

The success and failure history of children in the elementary grades can be helpful in assisting each pupil to set goals for himself. If a pupil has been successful in the past, then he can be encouraged to set higher levels of achievement in the pursuit of traditional goals or new goals. This notion also implies that those pupils with a history of failure will be helped to set levels of achievement that will enable them to experience a degree of success as they pursue goals. The personal history of success and failure of pupils is a prime consideration in the level of achievement that should be set when they pursue well-defined goals. Without this knowledge of individual pupils' backgrounds, it is not possible to relate each child's effort to the level of achievement associated with judging himself to be successful.

Status of Individuals in Reference Groups

The goals that pupils will select to pursue might well be determined by their status in the reference groups whose values they ascribe to. Since an evaluation of the self, like any other evaluation, requires a comparison with something else, the elementary school pupil is likely to compare himself with other pupils of his reference group. Pupils who perceive themselves as having high status in their reference group are more likely to overestimate what their future performance will be, whereas pupils of low status are likely to underestimate their future performance. Most times these estimates from the high and low status pupils are unrelated to their actual abilities. It is important that the status of individual pupils in their reference groups does not adversely affect how they set levels of achievement. Pupils should set levels of achievement for the pursuit of goals that are consistent with their talents and their personal preferences. The elementary school should help all pupils, regardless of the status they hold in their respective reference groups, to set levels of achievement that are consistent with their individual talents and motivation toward the specific goal in question. In this way the elementary school makes equality of opportunity an operational reality.

Attitudes and Values in the Elementary School Program

In the first part of this chapter, we discussed some of the different factors associated with attitudes and values and how these factors were generally related to the program of the elementary school. Now we discuss the specific issues related to attitudes and values resulting from the implementation and operation of the elementary school program. Traditions and practices at the elementary school level provide support for different attitudes and values as different activities are completed by pupils. It is important to look at the elementary school in relation to attitudes and values that result from the administration and expectations of its program. This enables one to decide the nature of the attitudes and values that are being shaped and to make judgments about those that should be taught as part of the school's responsibility. The remainder of this chapter is devoted to these issues.

Cooperation and Competition

Cooperation and competition are two values with which the elementary school must deal. At times these two values are at odds with each other and often in conflict with values of other community agencies and cultural units. There are instances wherein cooperation should be given precedence over competition as a value and in other instances the reverse is the case. The task of the elementary school is to determine when either or both of the values should be stressed, and what areas of the program are most appropriate for the task. Research comparing cooperation and competition in classroom situations suggests that the amount of learning achieved using either value as a focus is not significantly different.[14] When groups of children were asked to perform under cooperative and competitive conditions, the cooperative group was superior in coordinated effort, diversity of contribution per member, achievement pressure, and attentiveness to their classmates. This finding suggests that the advantages of cooperation over competition are apparent in certain areas. It remains the job of the elementary school to see that its pupils are exposed to cooperative and competitive values under the right conditions.

It matters not whether one feels that cooperation should be emphasized as a value over competition or vice versa because both values are intimate parts of the American way of life. In terms of decision making that affects groups, cooperation is a value that makes the democratic process a reality. On the other hand, achieving distinction as an individual usually involves focusing on competition as the value to guide one's actions. Both values make it possible for the American way of life to continue to serve both individual and group needs within the framework of a democratic society.

When activities are planned for elementary schoolchildren, they are likely to be in either a cooperative or competitive framework. When the competitive framework is emphasized, pupils may be competing with their previous performance, with a preset standard, with other children, or with an idea. However, competition acts as a powerful motivating force when utilized in appropriate situations. The problem to avoid when using competition as a motivating force is that of putting a pupil in a situation wherein he has no chance to be successful (he is overmatched) and where the resulting failure will be taken as a personal shortcoming rather than a misapplication of his talents. At that point competition will become a negative value because it makes an individual feel unworthy as a person.

A similar case could be made for a cooperative framework being used in the elementary school. The cooperative framework is especially useful when pupils are expected to work with others in achieving group and individual goals, to build confidence in their ability to work in group situations, to listen to the views of others, and to make compromises that are reasonable. However, too much emphasis on cooperation can lead to uncritical conformity and personal compromise of one's views. There has to be a balance in the extent to which pupils accept the cooperative framework as a primary value in all school activities.

In conclusion, cooperation and competition are values that affect most activities engaged in by elementary school pupils. Both values are important to the personal and social development of children in a democratic society. It is the task of the elementary school to see that these two values are employed appropriately in different situations with different kinds of problems. In addition to their psychological and social value to the program of the elementary school, these values help pupils operationalize life in a democratic society.

Attitudes and Values in Major Elementary School Functions

If one considers the major functions of the elementary school in terms of teaching attitudes and values, it is possible to outline what the relationship between functions, attitudes, and values might be. Earlier we discussed the relationship between attitudes and values and concluded that values can be thought of as higher order attitudes that are goals— the "good" of the society. The characterization of the relationship between attitudes and values provides us with a way to approach elementary school functions. The major functions of the elementary school are intellectual, social, and self-concept development. These functions are the values of the school, in particular, and the society in general. As elementary school pupils are provided with a complex array of experiences, they learn to value these functions as worthy goals to be sought. These functions are the values for elementary school pupils.

If major functions are the values of the elementary school, then those feelings, dispositions, and motivations toward specific and operational aspects of those functions are the attitudes. In this sense, attitudes help children attach significant worth to functions of the elementary school. When we consider the intellectual function, there are attitudes that are consonant with it. One such attitude is a respect for facts and knowledge. This attitude is a requirement for pursuing the intellectual function in the elementary school. A second attitude consonant with this function is respect for the views of others. At times, one's intellectual understanding can only be extended when the opinions of others are solicited and accepted. A third attitude consonant with the intellectual function is open-mindedness. The pursuit of the intellectual as a value requires that pupils feel that they must be open-minded about all data that might be relevant to a problem under study. A fourth attitude consonant with the intellectual function is critical honesty. Critical honesty enables pupils to consider evidence that is inconsistent with present knowledge but related to the problems under consideration. One other attitude consonant with the intellectual function is acceptance of systematic study as a useful pattern for solving problems. The acceptance of systematic study helps the pupil to perceive the intellectual function as a value.

The second major function, socialization, has attitudes that are consonant with this value. One such attitude consistent with this function is adherence to democratic ideals. When children believe and act in terms of the democratic ideals, the socialization function of the elementary school is being appropriately pursued. A second attitude consonant with the socialization function is positive response to cultural and ethnic differences. Without this attitude, the elementary school would not be doing an effective job in completing its socialization function in concert with societal expectations. A third attitude consonant with the socialization function is acceptance of change. Since change is such an integral part of American and world society, this attitude tends to socialize children to deal effectively with a continuing aspect of their lives. A fourth attitude consonant with the socialization function is tolerance for ambiguity and uncertainty. The complexity of our society breeds ambiguity and uncertainty, and pupils must develop a workable tolerance for this occurrence if they are to be socialized for effective participation in daily living. A fifth attitude consonant with the socialization function is individual development. An individual's feelings about his personal development is a vital part of the socialization experience for all children in our society. One other attitude that is consonant with the socialization function of the elementary school is belief in meaningful group interaction. In our society, meaningful group interaction is necessary to carry on many of our basic social functions. This, in part, explains why belief in meaningful group interaction helps to fulfill the socialization function of the elementary school.

The self-concept development function of the elementary school requires children to develop certain attitudes if this function is to leave a positive impression on each child. One of the attitudes consonant with the self-concept development function is a feeling of self-respect. Having a feeling of self-respect contributes to the enhancement of the elementary school's ability to realize the self-concept development function. A second attitude consonant with this function is belief in self-direction. If pupils do not believe in self-direction they are unlikely to achieve a positive self-concept. A third attitude associated with the self-concept development function is a belief in self-evaluation. When a child believes in self-evaluation he makes judgments about himself, which helps the elementary school fulfill its self-concept development function. One other attitude consistent with this function is a belief in self-improvement. Self-improvement is a vital part of the development of one's self-concept because it enables the child to make changes consistent with his perception of the values involved.

The elementary school emphasizes the attitudes related to its major functions so that pupils' feelings, beliefs, and motivations are consistent with the values implied. Without such an emphasis on the development and extension of such attitudes in pupils, the elementary school would probably be unable to carry out its functions as a social institution. In this sense, the relationship between attitudes and values is a real and vital one in the conduct and effectiveness of the program of the elementary school.

The Teacher's Role in Teaching Attitudes and Values

There are many who believe that although teachers shape some of the attitudes of pupils as they complete school requirements and interact with others, they cannot teach children values. However, there is some evidence that the way a teacher characterizes his role can be quite influential in teaching certain values. That is the course to take if teachers are to learn to reconcile what they verbally profess to believe and their actions in the classroom. The consistency between teachers' actions and beliefs can have a profound effect on the values of the pupils they teach. Since this is the case, each teacher must take his role as a shaper of values seriously and deal with it accordingly.

When we consider the teaching of values to elementary school pupils, little reliance can be placed on the belief that values can be transmitted by commandment. For example, a teacher can have children read and learn the Declaration of Independence and yet violate everything the document stands for in his treatment of pupils. Teachers can deny the democratic right of pupils to participate in classroom decisions. Through daily actions, teachers can demonstrate arrogance in favor of their opinions and disrespect for the beliefs of others. Teachers can deny freedom of expression and hand out questionable punishment on the basis of hearsay in violation of the ideas of "due process" expressed in both the Declaration of Independence and the Constitution of the United States. Teachers can present one-sided views of historical events and current affairs and expect their pupils to believe and accept their explanations of reality. Teachers can also communicate to students the idea that their statements concerning a phenomenon are complete and should be taken as a total explanation in time and space. Teachers can teach pupils about hypocrisy when their actions are inconsistent with their statements of beliefs. When teachers choose to do some of the things indicated previously, they teach children that their actions can differ from those ideals that form the basic structure of our society. In effect, they teach children not to value the ideals for individual and group behavior expressed in our basic documents such as the Declaration of Independence and the Constitution of the United States.

Values are taught by the teachers' actions in social situations and by the attitudes they express in completing activities that involve children. Children tend to imitate the actions of adult models in real-life situations and not the verbal explanations of these acts if the verbal responses are inconsistent with observed actions. The observed actions of teachers teach children what to value. If a teacher wants pupils to value certain behaviors in our society, he must demonstrate those values in his actions. The verbal expression of values is not sufficient to teach children to judge them worthy of personal consideration for belief and use.

Unfortunately, too many teachers and other adults important in children's lives have failed to present children with models of behavior that act out value generalizations valid for our times and consistent with our stated beliefs about the nature of a democratic society. It is crucial for the total positive education of children that the daily behavior interactions of teachers reflect their acceptance of the primary values of society that enable individuals and groups to profitably interact as human beings carrying out needed social functions. The list that follows shows some of the teacher behaviors that would be required to facilitate the teaching of values to elementary school pupils. It is also suggestive of the attitudes that should guide teachers' behavior if the value orientation that pupils are expected to have is to be realized. The main point to be made is that the modeling behavior of teachers is likely to do more in teaching values than the verbal descriptions of what should be valued could ever be expected to do. Any attempt to teach elementary school pupils attitudes and values must focus on the role model that teachers demonstrate in their daily classroom activities. The shaping of pupils' values is the result of the nature of the actual human interactions they experience as opposed to learning the forward statement characterizing the nature of these human interactions. The best of both worlds would have pupils exposed to human interactions that are consistent with the expected values of our society. However, the teaching of values must have appropriate human interaction as the main ingredient if pupils' values are to be shaped in a predictable direction.

The behaviors required by teachers in order to teach certain values are described in the following list of value areas.

1. *Examination of Personal Values.* Teachers must act as models for examining, testing, and revising values consistent with personal and societal beliefs.

2. *Examination of Historical Values.* Teachers should become aware of the origins of different systems of value and their own system of value.

3. *Justification of Value Choices.* Teachers should help children sort out value systems that influence the behavior of some individuals so that they are not automatically accepted or rejected without critical consideration. This acceptance or rejection applies to old and new values in a given society.

4. *Acceptance of Content and Knowledge.* Teachers should help pupils learn to value knowledge through perception resulting from the teachers' demonstrated attitude toward learning as a value to pursue. The emphasis must be on the models teachers present as users of knowledge to carry out meaningful social functions including critical thinking.

5. *Acceptance of Individuals.* Teachers must behave in such a way that demonstrates their belief that every individual is important. The models teachers present determine the extent to which children see themselves as worthwhile and others as possessing equal worth as human beings.

6. *Acceptance of Differences.* Teachers should place a high value through their actions on differences characterizing individuals. Children must be shown that differences between individuals can make contributions to their own lives.

7. *Acceptance of the Importance of Unity.* Teachers should demonstrate through their actions that unity between individuals and groups on many critical issues is basic to the future advancement of our society.

8. *Acceptance of Self-Direction.* Teachers should help children to learn through precept by providing opportunities for them to participate in decision making.

9. *Acceptance of Changing Conditions.* Teachers should demonstrate through their actions how to tolerate some discomfort when dealing with school activities. The school experiences planned for children should also enable them to view themselves and their universe as an integral part of a dynamic, constantly changing relationship.

10. *Acceptance of Knowledge and Experience Limitation.* Teachers should help children become aware of the factors operating in the environment that may be unknown to them. The actions of teachers should help children conclude that knowledge cannot explain all the phenomena operating in a given environmental setting.

11. *Acceptance of Individual Actions.* Teachers should help chil-

dren place a high value on the actions or deeds of individuals as opposed to their expressions of intent. Teachers' model behavior in the school will have a great influence on pupils' acceptance of this value.

12. *Acceptance of Truth.* Teachers should act so that pupils can conclude that the value of truth is critical in all of human experience. The interaction between individuals in conducting social functions is dependent on truth to be most effective for all who will be affected. Teachers must practice techniques for determining truth in different areas if children are to learn the value of truth in human activity.

Other Influences on Pupils' Attitudes and Values

Other influences affect the attitudes and values of pupils in the elementary school. One such influence is the teacher's personality. When the basic personality characteristics of a given teacher match a pupil's conception of what a teacher should be like, his attitudes toward his teacher, himself, and others are affected in a given direction as he interacts in the school environment. Also this personal experience influences the choices that this pupil makes in terms of what he will value as part of his school experience. If, on the other hand, the teacher's personality characteristic is inconsistent with a pupil's conception of what a teacher should be like, another set of attitudes might come into play to shape this child's value orientation in a different direction. In both instances the teacher's personality exerts a profound influence over the attitudes and values of pupils who are served by the elementary school. The nature of the quality of human interaction in a given classroom with certain children resulting from a given teacher's personality will determine the developmental direction of attitudes and values possessed by those served. This should be an added incentive for taking teacher personality into account as preparation for systematically influencing the attitudes and values of elementary school pupils.

The peer society of elementary school pupils will exert undue influence on the attitudes and values of children if the teacher does not counteract the trend through her actions. The peer society of pupils can be a positive influence if the rules governing their actions are consistent with the attitudes and values that society expects children to acquire. The peer society of pupils should not be allowed to violate the values that are the expected goals of our society by encouraging children to develop attitudes that lower their estimates of themselves and others. In terms of developing acceptable attitudes and values affecting meaningful and necessary human interactions, the peer society of pupils must be considered as a force that can aid or hinder the achievement of appropriate behaviors in this general area. The elementary school should try to enlist the aid of the peer society of pupils to develop appropriate attitudes and values whenever possible and should deflate the influence of peers when it appears to be working against individuals and groups in the classroom and the school.

Influencing the attitudes and values of pupils in the elementary school is an expectation that is difficult to realize but critical to the survival of our democratic society. Although we lack all the specific knowledge required to get the job done, we must continue to work toward the goal of shaping pupil behavior in a direction that enhances the individual and general welfare within the context of a democratic society. Part of being able to accomplish this goal is related to the extent that the elementary school can influence the attitudes and values of its pupils in a desirable direction. This is, and continues to be, an important area of concern for the elementary school.

Summary

This chapter has been concerned with the attitudes and values of children as they relate to curriculum and instruction in the elementary school. It is apparent that any curriculum selection and implementation is based on sets of beliefs and behaviors that characterize social systems of the culture. The teacher's task is to utilize instructional processes to develop and focus the attitudes of the young so that they learn how and why they should accept the value orientations that are central to the social systems of the culture. In this sense the curriculum of the elementary school can be thought of as being representative of the values of the culture that the majority of adults expect youth to share, to learn, and to accept. Instruction in the elementary school is seen as the means for shaping the attitudes of youth that enable the vast majority of them to achieve the expected value orientations necessary for the maintenance and extension of the general welfare of our society. In short, this chapter attempted to show the relationship between the personal characteristics (attitudes and values) of students, and the program (curriculum and instruction) components of the elementary school. To the extent that the purpose of the chapter was achieved, the case or justification for influencing pupils' attitudes and values in the elementary school grades should have been made evident to the reader.

References

1. John Dewey, *Democracy and Education* (New York: Macmillan, 1916), p. 99.
2. Michael Belok, O. R. Bontrager, Howard C. Oswalt, Mary S. Morris, and E. A. Erickson, *Approaches to Values in Education* (Dubuque, Iowa: Brown, 1966), p. 9.
3. Ibid., p. 14.
4. William J. McGuire, "The Nature of Attitudes and Attitude Change," in Gardner Lindzey and Elliot Aronson, eds., *The Handbook of Social Psychology*, Vol. III (Reading, Mass.: Addison-Wesley, 1969), p. 151.
5. E. Nelson, "Attitudes," *Journal of General Psychology*, 21:367–436 (1939).
6. D. T. Campbell, *The Generality of Social Attitudes*, Doctoral Dissertation, University of California, Berkeley, Cal., 1947.
7. M. L. DeFleur and F. R. Westie, "Attitude as a Scientific Concept," *Social Forces*, 42:17–31 (1963).
8. G. W. Allport, "Attitudes," in C. Murchison, ed., *Handbook of Social Psychology* (Worcester, Mass.: Clark U. P., 1935), pp. 798–884.
9. McGuire, op. cit., p. 142.
10. Ibid., p. 153.
11. Ibid., p. 155.
12. Ibid.
13. Ibid., p. 156.
14. Morton Deutsch, "The Effects of Cooperation and Competition on Group Process," in D. Cartwright and A. Zander, eds., *Group Dynamics Research and Theory*, 2nd ed. (Evanston, Ill.: Row, Peterson, 1953), pp. 414–448.

8

Classroom Teaching: Diagnosis and Strategies

Classroom teaching requires a close coordination among situational analysis, prescription, presentation, and application. This, in effect, represents the total system for implementing diagnostic approaches and formulating strategies for classroom teaching. Teaching strategies and diagnostic approaches must always complement each other if a teacher is to elicit a predictable response from the learner even if the intended product* is itself a variable, that is, critical thinking or aesthetic appreciation. A teacher has to make decisions in prescribing, contriving, simulating, and organizing the kinds of content, techniques, media aids, and activities that foster effective learning. These decisions are appropriate in proportion to the quality of feedback obtained from the diagnostic approach employed to set the stage for instruction. Hence, the teaching strategy a teacher employs is dependent upon his approach to diagnosis and his ability to design instructional activities suggested by the accumulated data.

* Responses children make during an instructional sequence are outcomes that are, in fact, products of the experience. Specific instructional moves by teachers are made to produce certain responses from pupils. Since these responses are the concrete evidence of the influence of instruction, these responses are the products of instruction. Because pupil responses vary in quantity, magnitude, or in some qualitative aspect, they cannot be seen as a specific outcome for a specific instructional stimulus. In this sense, pupil responses (or products) may be considered as a specific outcome or as a variable.

When a teacher employs a diagnostic approach, his primary goal is to generate comparisons that may be interpreted with the aid of a conceived or perceived standard. This standard of comparison may be either implicit or explicit; however, it must have a tangible quality and quantity for the teacher if he plans a teaching strategy on the basis of the results generated from his diagnostic approach. Any diagnostic tool employed by a teacher is intended to provide the data that are required for analysis. After the data are collected, the standard selected for comparison determines the type of the interpretations required to guide the formulation of a teaching strategy suggested by the conclusions drawn from the data.

The task of a teaching strategy is to pattern teaching behaviors sequentially, consciously, and systematically to accommodate crucial instructional variables. A teaching strategy is probably most effective when the product sought is identifiable and not attributable to conditions and evaluative comparisons that are both ambiguous and tentative. When one attempts to employ a teaching strategy, consideration must be given to the kind of content to be taught, the objectives to be achieved, the differences among learners (both as individuals and groups), the nature and conditions of the learning process, the personal style of the teacher, and the institutional and environmental setting of the school. The formulation and application of a teaching strategy should not be focused too narrowly on observable products, for a narrow focus at this stage in the total instructional schema would mediate effectively against the acquisition of incidental learnings (intellectual processes, basic skills, standard procedures) that are essential to pupils' future learning possibilities. In any given teaching strategy, each of these considerations will have a varying degree of influence on the conduct of the instructional pattern employed at any given time, but all of them must be considered in the planning stage of a teaching episode.

The Nature of Instruction and Related Terms

Before one can properly discuss how diagnosis and strategy formulation relate to classroom teaching, some position must be assumed regarding the nature of instruction and some of its component parts. There is much confusion in the literature[1] when distinctions are attempted in defining curriculum, instruction, and teaching. In many instances, definitions for the three terms are used interchangeably within the same source and across sources. This confusion of terms makes a systematic discussion of diagnosis and strategy formulation as it relates to an instructional pattern extremely difficult, if not impossible. For our purposes "curriculum is a structured series of intended learning outcomes."[2] Curriculum is concerned with ends and, as such, prescribes the results of instruction. In this sense, curriculum is not concerned with the means of achieving results as some authors suggest.

Instruction is the interaction situation among pupil, teacher, media, and the environmental setting. It can be further thought of as "the total stimulus setting within which systematic stimuli and desired responses occur. . . ."[3] Instruction differs from curriculum in that the former outlines what the learner must do while the latter dictates the intended material to be learned.

Even though teaching is essential to providing operational meaning to curriculum and instruction, it differs in significant ways. Teaching is "any interpersonal influence aimed at changing the ways in which other persons can or will behave."[4] This definition of teaching is restricted to influences aimed at a person's perceptual and cognitive processes and to responses between people. Basically, as Turner suggests: "Teaching is dyadic . . . , i.e., involves reciprocal, interdependent responding between at least two people."[5] The interpersonal relationship is the distinguishing characteristic of the way teaching should be defined. This distinction becomes more crucial as one deals with diagnosis as the starting point for formulating a strategy for implementing an instructional pattern.

When one discusses curriculum, instruction, and teaching, some stance must be taken with regard to strategy, method, and procedure. Unfortunately, the literature in education often uses these terms interchangeably or one term has been used as a replacement for the other, owing to the "fad" in vogue at the time of its use. This confusion makes it difficult to describe the nature of instruction with any accuracy at a given level or in terms of sequential development. Therefore, it is necessary to distinguish among the three terms so that their meaning is clear and more precise.

According to Bruner and others:

> A strategy refers to a pattern of decisions in the acquisition, retention, and utilization of information that serves to meet certain objectives, i.e., to insure certain forms of outcome and to insure against certain others.[6]

It should be noted that attention is given to both the negative and positive contingencies as defining characteristics of a strategy. In this sense, there is an uncertainty that accompanies a strategy because this definition acknowledges the fact that certain objectives are pursued through a maze of uncharted factors* and problems. Therefore, a strategy should permit one to proceed toward a set objective in spite of the unknown problems likely to be encountered. In summary, when one employs a strategy, he is interested in (1) attaining an objective using a minimum number of encounters with essential elements, (2) sorting out of irrelevant data using appropriate test procedures, (3) minimizing cognitive and affective interference that might increase the strain on inference and recall capacity, and (4) minimizing the number of incorrect categorizations (increase efficiency and effectiveness) experienced in processing data.

As we are using the idea, a strategy refers to a conscious plan for achieving an instructional objective through the use of selective information. The extent to which a teacher is conscious of his teaching strategy is directly related to his knowledge of how learners are specifically affected by his actions. In this sense, the test of a strategy is the result that pupils demonstrate in their patterns of learning and responses. For example, a pattern for getting children to learn problem solving can be a teaching strategy as long as the four factors discussed in the previous paragraph are dealt with.

Method is a systematic way of dealing with facts and concepts. It can be thought of as an adopted pattern for dealing with content. Some examples are the inductive or deductive method of reasoning, the lecture method, or the inquiry method of teaching. In either instance the general pattern determines the manner of selecting and organizing the specific techniques required to implement the method. This is associated with the fact that a method has a specific arrangement and sequence of parts that require the use of specific techniques to implement it. The use and deployment of techniques determine whether a given method has been implemented as defined and intended. Implementation of a method requires a teacher to develop his activities in great detail. Before a teacher can implement a method, he must have the prerequisite skills to operationally define and develop it. In this sense, before trying to utilize a given method of instruction, the teacher must set forth an entire course of action in detail.

The concept of procedure refers to the manner of controlling all the relevant conditions in order to elicit a given response or to elicit it

---

* Factors refer to characteristics of the learners, teachers teaching procedures, content, and types of learning sought. As these factors are combined in the many combinations that are possible, they present different problems for planning strategy.

in varying strengths and frequencies. The procedure specifies the actions of the teacher that cannot be completely determined in advance and acts as a guide for choosing and organizing the teacher's activities as they may be dictated by the situational variables of the setting and the learners. For example, the way a teacher works with a selected group of pupils through the use of different kinds of questions is suggestive of the procedure employed to implement part of a teaching strategy. Since specific ways of working with a selected group of pupils on particular concerns have to be determined, the contextual feedback prior to planning is not realistic or possible. Therefore, the teacher must apply appropriate procedures geared to deal with learning problems that occur as he works with the pupils. In order to develop effective procedures, a teacher must have a vast repertoire of methods and a command of the techniques required to choose activities that are appropriate to pupil needs at any specified time.

If one were to consider teaching as being on a continuum, strategy deals primarily with the pretutorial components, procedure deals with the tutorial components, and method employs aspects of both the pretutorial and tutorial components. The following diagram illustrates the notion just described.

Pretutorial |————————————————————| Tutorial
               Strategy————→Method————→Procedure

The critical decision point for the teacher occurs when he considers the nature and extent of this strategy. It is at this point that he formulates his objectives and outlines his plan for achieving them with a set of pupils in mind. Only after a strategy has been outlined can the necessary methods and procedures be selected and utilized. Without a strategy it is almost impossible to focus methods and procedures on desirable ends that operationalize the intents of teaching. This concept of teaching suggests that the planning and decision making comprising the pretutorial stage of teaching is critical to the total act and that method and procedure are necessarily guided by the strategy formulated. The dynamic aspects of this idea are shown in Figure 8.1.

Figure 8.1 shows the flow of the component parts of a teaching episode. It is interesting to note that the teacher is acting in all the components but one—activity. During the activity stage the learner performs a specified set of actions or skills that are the result of the teacher's actions at each of the previous stages in the teaching episode. Since the distance from the formulation of the teaching strategy and the activity stage is so vast, many problems of continuity and predictable relation-

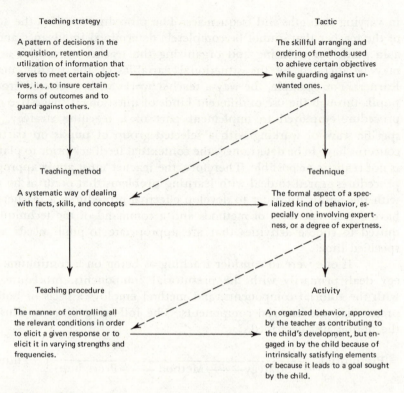

Figure 8.1
The Flow of the Component Parts of a Teaching Episode.

ships abound. This is the point where a number of questions related to the relevancy* of activities performed by learners are raised. If a teacher is unable to justify what he has children do in terms of his teaching strategy, he cannot demonstrate that his actions are structured, system-

---

* Questions about the relevancy of activities that the teacher has selected to enable pupils to achieve the objectives outlined in this strategy are usually raised in relation to interests and preferences of pupils and the value orientation of parents. In some quarters there is strong support for pupils and parents being allowed more of a say in the selection of activities to be performed. According to this argument, activities have greater relevancy in the lives of children when they are selected in concert with their interests and preferences. Not only will such activities have greater meaning in the life of the child but he will be more highly motivated toward the completion of the activities. Even though this is a valid alternative in many respects, it does not speak well of the need for activities to provide pupils with experiences that enable them to achieve objectives outlined in the strategy.

atic, and goal directed. At this point, questions involving aspects of accountability are brought to bear in a most significant way.

As one studies Figure 8.1, he should note that there is a hierarchical relationship involving strategy, method, and procedure. The teaching strategy determines both the method and procedure in general, but the specific procedure to be employed is determined by the conditions of the selected method, the environmental setting, the characteristics of the learner, and the interactional conditions of the exchange. Even though method and procedure have a logical relationship to the teaching strategy, they do not, in a linear sense, follow a completely predictable course of development when they are implemented as part of the tutorial phase of the teaching act. Most of the confusion that surrounds any systematic discussion of teaching occurs at this point.

Noting the horizontal relationships shown in Figure 8.1, the functions on the right are what the teacher does to define operationally the implied purpose of the concepts shown on the left. A teaching strategy becomes a reality when appropriate tactics are formulated, developed, and implemented. Similarly, the techniques employed by teachers determine whether or not a given method can be successfully and effectively used as part of a teaching episode. In this scheme, activity is not analogous to teaching procedure in the same sense that tactic and technique are analogous to teaching strategy and method, respectively. However, there are many similar criterional attributes (specific characteristics that denote a concept) that permit the parallel comparison. Since the activity performed by the learner is in fact determined by the teacher,* it suggests that this is what the teacher would do to operationally define his teaching procedure. In effect, then, the activity of the learner should parallel the activity of the teacher having similar goals. Even though activity is suggestive of learner response, it is clearly tied to teacher expectation and, as such, represents what she would do under similar circumstances.

One last point concerning Figure 8.1: The broken lines between tactic and teaching method, and technique and teaching procedure should be explained. These lines indicate that under special conditions

---

* This idea is not in opposition to the notion that self-directed learning on the part of learners is not a viable educational objective. However, the position does speak directly to the issue of teacher's responsibility to see to it that all activities engaged in by pupils make a positive contribution to the achievement of sought objectives. Since self-directed learning might very well be one of those objectives in specific instances, the teacher is justified in permitting pupils to choose some activities to pursue. However, the ultimate responsibility for the selection of appropriate activities belongs to the teacher.

the actions on the right are unique cases of the concepts of reference on the left. When a tactic becomes standardized and is employed similarly in different situations, it in fact becomes a method. Similarly, when a technique is mastered to the degree that its use in certain situations elicits predictable responses, it is a special case of a teaching procedure. An example of tactic that becomes a method is the administration of a battery of tests individually using the same tests in the same sequence in the same environmental setting as a prerequisite to teaching subject matter. On the other hand, a technique becomes a teaching procedure when the learner is asked to observe the activity of an expert in order to perform a certain activity (the intern in many professions learns many of his techniques in this fashion). It should be noted that the distinctions indicated become more important as one attempts to understand the nature of the teaching act as a systematic, logical, and interpretable human activity.

Initiating the Teaching Strategy: Diagnosis

The teaching strategy employed defines the curriculum for presentation; the implementation of a teaching strategy initiates the instructional program. The nature of that program, therefore, is dependent upon the precision of the teaching strategy utilized. A teaching strategy is, and should be, the end product of diagnosis. The characteristics of the diagnosis may include the total range of approaches available and different degrees of precision in its application. However, the primary goal of diagnosis* at any level involving teaching is to specify the nature of the gap between a performance standard and the judged performance of a learner. The performance standards may be prescribed by forces beyond the control and influence of the teacher or they may be arbitrarily set by each teacher according to situational variables or other criteria. No matter how these performance standards are set, they have to be present before diagnosis can take place. The judgment of performance of a learner may be arbitrary, formal or informal, structured or unstructured, subjective or objective, general or specific within a specific, well-defined topical area, across a number of related topics, or

---

* Our use of diagnosis here refers to methods by which pupils are classified on the basis of facts relevant to their school progress.

related to general information. Even though the options for diagnosis are far reaching, it must outline the nature of the gap between a performance standard and the judged performance of a learner if the results of the diagnosis are to be used as bases for formulating a teaching strategy.

Even though our reference to diagnosis is in terms of a classroom teaching context, the concept is also applicable to other levels of the schooling process. When diagnosis is employed at the system and school levels, the relationship between a performance standard and the judged performance of learners is not as clear-cut, but the ultimate purpose of the act of diagnosing still has validity. Ultimately, all activities related to schooling must be judged in relation to their contribution to closing the gap between expectations and judged outcomes evident in the performance of the pupils. Since we are not directly concerned with diagnosis outside the classroom in relation to formulating teaching strategies at this point, we confine our discussion to this primary focus.

Teachers have a vast array of meaningful and effective diagnostic approaches from which to choose as they work with diverse groups, pursuing a variety of goals* in different subject-matter areas. This range of diagnostic possibilities is a mixed blessing because it requires the teacher to select approaches that are appropriate. Unfortunately, too few teachers have acquired the techniques necessary to match the appropriate diagnostic approach to the problem when it involves the setting, the content, the learner, and their interaction. Even though it is not feasible to deal with acquainting the teacher with all of the crucial elements of sound diagnosis in this volume, there are many excellent sources[7,8,9,10,11,12,13,14,15] that provide the sound procedures and skills required to employ effective diagnostic techniques.

In many instances these sources deal primarily with defining and analyzing diagnosis as a process, whereas in other instances, the sources focus on the identification and application of diagnostic procedures. Some sources combine both ends of the continuum implied previously as they discuss the nature and use of diagnosis in teaching. It is our belief that the professional teacher must understand the complete range of issues related to diagnosis if these procedures are to be appropriately incorporated into the teaching strategy that is ultimately formulated and employed.

In a real sense, diagnosis in teaching is a special case of evaluation as suggested in the following statement:

---

* Norman E. Gronlund, *Stating Behavioral Objectives for Classroom Instruction* (New York: Macmillan, 1970).

Like all forms of evaluation, diagnosis involves a valuing, determination, description, and classification of some aspect of student behavior.[16]

There are, however, essential differences between diagnosis and evaluation when applied to teaching and learning, or more descriptively, the process of instruction. When diagnosis is related to the process of instruction the purpose is twofold:

> . . . either to place the student properly at the outset of instruction or to discover the underlying causes of deficiencies in student learning as instruction unfolds . . .[17]

Both purposes of diagnosis are essential to formulating an appropriate teaching strategy for achieving the goals resulting from the employment of an instructional process.

When diagnosis is used as the initiating phase in the instructional process, its primary function is placement. In this sense, it helps to focus the act of instruction by pinpointing an appropriate starting point for learners as members of a group or as individuals. At this point, diagnosis might take several distinct forms, each having different implications for planning an overall teaching strategy. Therefore, it is critical to planning a teaching strategy that a teacher be clear as to whether he is using diagnosis in one (or a combination thereof) of three ways,

> to determine whether or not a student possesses certain entry behaviors or skills judged to be prerequisite to the attainment of the objectives of the planned unit . . . to establish whether the student already has mastery over the objectives of a unit or course, thereby allowing him to enroll in a more advanced program . . . [or] to classify students according to certain characteristics, such as interest, personality, background, aptitude, skill, and prior instructional history, hypothesized or known to be related to a particular teaching strategy or instructional method.[18]

Each of the three ways of using diagnosis has different consequences for planning a teaching strategy to deal with the relevant characteristics of children that are revealed. In the first instance, determination of the existence of prerequisite skills, the strategy employed would have to take into account problems of novice learners who would be expected to achieve objectives requiring the use of specific skills. The second instance of diagnosis, prior mastery of objectives to be attained, determines the strategy to be formulated to guide students in the selection of content and processes. The selected content and processes help pupils do things of greater worth and utility than would be the case through repeated coverage of known material and processes that employ the same patterns of involvement. The use of the third instance of diagnosis, classification of students according to selected characteristics, is probably the most central to the formulation of a teaching strategy, because this approach furnishes information on the prospective learners' present characteristics that can be associated directly with objectives to be sought. Owing to the nature of the observed relationship between learner characteristics and specified objectives, the specific pattern of the teaching strategy can be shaped to raise considerably the probability of learner success in achieving intended outcomes. Any deliberate, systematic approach to diagnosing relevant pupil characteristics provides the necessary data required to plan a realistic, meaningful, efficient, and effective teaching strategy.

Techniques for Determining Individuals Who Have Specific Learning Difficulties

In a most general way, techniques employed to detect specific difficulties or deficiencies should be administered to a group if one is concerned with the formulation of a classroom teaching strategy. At this level, the purpose of diagnosis deals with grouping. Grouping here refers both to rearranging the children within the class and rearranging knowledges and deficiences in learning by type and similarities. The former case of grouping refers to the way the teacher might arrange children for instruction and the latter case refers to the content with which he will be dealing with each group. In most instances, the two forms of grouping are very closely related. On the other hand, they may be separate as the teacher focuses away from academic concerns, that is, interests, creativity, and appreciations.

The most common label attached to this phase of diagnosis is "survey." It can be initiated through the use of the general achievement test that is either teacher or commercially constructed. It involves an item-by-item analysis of the error patterns noted for different groups of children in a given class. At this point, a teacher also notes the kinds of responses that different groups achieve correctly. From this information he begins to formulate a general teaching strategy.

The teaching strategy results from the teacher's interpretation of the group pattern noted during the survey phase of diagnosis. In order to supplement the written results noted, he may want to ask questions of the class as a whole to discern whether or not the results obtained via written tests are representative of the pupils' understanding. This is how the teacher begins to refine his teaching strategy by strengthening his validity criterion—product results. During this phase, he may also want to look at records of past performances indicated for the group testing. Now the teacher is ready to consider what methods would be most productive in alleviating the pattern of deficient learning noted and how these methods might be best arranged to achieve the defined goal—the standard of expectation.

The next step involves determining whether or not the tentative selection of methods to be coordinated in the teaching strategy is appropriate for the general deficiencies noted during the survey of the group's achievement pattern. This is the point at which more detailed information is required if the teacher is to add precision to his planning the overall teaching strategy. Before he can proceed, information involving the achievement patterns of each individual child will be needed. This is the point where individual diagnostic techniques[19] must be employed. Individual diagnosis is necessary to pinpoint more accurately the true pattern of achievement in a specific area on a selected topic that was suggested during the survey phase. The objective now is to learn more about the true nature of the learning deficiency, that is, lack of appropriate facts, need for certain skills, misunderstanding of key concepts and certain relationships. Once this information is obtained, the teacher is in a better position to rearrange the grouping of children for instruction that was suggested by the results of the initial survey. In some instances the teacher may want to decrease the size of the group and in others, he may want to do the reverse. He is likely to plan for regrouping children both in terms of their strengths and their weaknesses; however, his most significant move at this point would be to formulate a rationale for the inclusion and exclusion of methods selected to help the learners in question. At the conclusion of this process, much of the formal aspect of the formulation of a teaching strategy is complete, at least as a thought process.

The employment of individual diagnostic techniques provides information both for the selection and arrangement of methods and the selection and sequencing of procedures. In order to alleviate the specific deficiency noted for each child and for the group, the teacher now must formulate procedures that are applicable to his subjects. At this point he begins to plan the activities and the specific practices children will utilize as they attempt to correct their individual deficiencies. It is also at this point that the teacher specifies his plans to orchestrate the activities of learners both as individuals and in groups. This is the point at which the content is selected and organized for the learners and a standard of expectation formulated.

After the teacher has designed the activities that the children are to complete, he is now ready to refine his techniques. The refinement of his techniques at this point will determine the quality and nature of the procedure required to monitor the learners' activity patterns. The teacher must be sure to relate the activity to the strategy or to make adjustments in the overall strategy to accommodate the requirements of the standard of expectation. Care should be taken, however, not to focus the teaching strategy too narrowly on observable products, for a narrow focus at this point might tend to mediate against the acquisition of incidental learnings (intellectual processes, basic skills) that may ultimately prove to be more essential to the child's future learning than the product standard (test scores) used to judge his performance on a given activity. In this sense, the teaching strategy must always remain broad enough to encompass valuable learning outcomes not specifically detailed in the activities to be performed by the learners.

Diagnosis, as we have discussed, initiates the total instructional process. It gives focus to the teaching act as it relates to selection of the content, instructional pattern, and the activities engaged in by the children. In addition, diagnosis functions to provide corrective feedback for the instructional process. In this sense, diagnosis provides the teacher with information at each stage concerning the nature of progress achieved in relation to a teaching strategy. Diagnosis is also, ultimately, the mechanism that determines whether or not a teaching strategy achieved the goal for which it was formulated. At this level, diagnosis is serving both a formative and summative function for monitoring the flow of the learning process and assessing both the quality and quantity of the results.

When diagnosis serves a formative function it is employed primarily at the activity stage. Its primary function is to monitor the pattern of learning experienced by each child as he completes activities related to removing a learning deficiency noted earlier through diagnosis. If one were to use the language of programmed instruction, it would be classified as "branching," for it directs the pattern of instruction that should be employed for each learner as he moves toward the completion of an activity. At the end of each activity, diagnosis tells the teacher whether or not the child should be recycled back through the activity, should move on to the next activity, should redo parts of the activity, or should complete directly related activities. In a real sense, diagnosis at this level determines the sequence of the instructional process for any given child according to his measured performance compared with a standard of expectation.

The summative function of diagnosis deals with the pattern of achievement noted after the activities formulated to achieve certain objectives have been completed. In some instances it may be a compilation of the results of formative diagnosis at the end of each activity in a given set or it may be a sampling of components excerpted from all the activities completed by a learner in a given set. The results of summative diagnosis can be used to judge the adequacy of a technique employed in a given method and also to provide first-level information regarding the adequacy of the total teaching strategy. Since the teaching strategy involves outcomes that are broader than those that can be taken into account in some forms of summative diagnosis, judging its adequacy* on this information alone probably is unwarranted and often leads to misinterpretation of effects.

Postulated and Empirical Findings
Related to Instruction

It is important to note the tendency for a conflict between conclusions generated through postulation and those resulting from empirical data. This is inherent in the way that learning occurs; some things are known through the logical relationships to associated phenomena—postulation—and other things are known by testing and/or measuring relationships that produce a predictive pattern—empirical data. When the teacher deals with the performance of a learner compared with the preset standard, he is working in the empirical realm of knowing. When he attempts to discern the interest level, the attitude, or the child's appreciation of the activity, he is dealing with knowledge that has to be postulated. The latter outcomes cannot be directly observed or measured.

* Adequacy here refers to the extent that the summative diagnosis considers all of the specific outcomes suggested by the objectives guiding the total teaching strategy employed. Those specific outcomes of objectives that are not taken into account in a particular summative diagnosis should be known to the user of the results so that the available data are not used to infer notions about all learnings resulting from a given teaching strategy. When summative diagnosis is used to make a conclusive statement about the effects of a total teaching strategy in the pursuit of specific and varied objectives, the reader should not be led to conclude that the indicated data explain all facets and outcomes of the experience in question.

Even though the postulated truths may be most critical to the child's ability to complete an activity, it offers unpredictable interference to the teacher who is attempting to judge the adequacy of his teaching strategy.

Postulated truth plays a critical role in judging the total teaching act for it offers an acceptable pattern for making comments about the strategy employed. However, at the operational level of teaching (use of methods and procedures), empirical data are essential to formulating judgments about the worth and validity of formal instructional activity. When judgments about teaching are being made, postulated and empirical truths complement each other and address different aspects of the teaching act. Empirical data suggest how aspects of the teaching act work in accordance with an expectation standard and defined population and a given setting. Postulated information organizes empirical, personality, and social expectations in a pattern that attempts to describe the worth of the total teaching act. Both approaches to judging the teaching act have to be employed to adequately evaluate the classroom teaching.

Instructional Contact Time: The Critical Variable in Student Performance

Any diagnosis of student performance as a basis for formulating a teaching strategy for instruction must deal with temporal variables associated with school learning. *Time* is the key element, the swing variable, in determining the quantity and quality of all instructional activity conducted in the school. There can be no valid and effective diagnosis of learning problems and planning of teaching strategies without taking time into account. Since this chapter deals with classroom teaching, the discussion of time as a variable will be limited to the instructional aspects of the problem to be highlighted. As a consequence, most of our discussion deals with *instructional contact time* as it influences classroom teaching activity and student performance.

Recently, much attention has been focused on time as a crucial variable in determining the learning achievement outcomes resulting from instruction. Many of the important research studies dealing with this area of concern were reviewed by Rodgers[20] and are not repeated here in detail. For our purposes, it might be useful to discuss briefly the model most frequently used to denote the influences of time variations upon effective learning of school-related tasks. The model of reference was proposed by John B. Carroll[21] and is best characterized by the notion that the degree of learning is considered to be a function of the ratio of time actually spent *in* learning to the time needed *to* learn.

Explicitly, Carroll's model suggests that time spent in learning is defined by a combination of the following: (a) the time allowed for learning; (b) the length of time in which the learner is willing to persevere; and (c) the amount of time needed to learn. The values representing the time spent and the time needed are the numerator and the denominator, respectively, in the ratio mentioned earlier. It should be noted that the time needed to learn may be extended by poor quality of instruction, by the work styles and process habits of the learner, and by the inability of the learner to understand and follow instructions. One of the assumptions of Carroll's model is that if a learner were allowed sufficient time for learning and is willing to persevere as long as necessary, he would achieve perfect learning. In its most succinct form, the formal explication of Carroll's model is:

$$\text{Degrees of Learning} = f\left(\frac{\text{time actually spent}}{\text{time needed}}\right)$$

Even though Carroll's model offers a convenient way of describing time as a variable in learning and achievement, it suffers from a lack of basic data to be manipulated in the formula. Since there has been no determination of the amount of time required to learn specific information by a given individual or group, measures of time needed to complete certain learnings must be made. However, *the collection of these time measures should take into account the fact that different individuals as well as groups of individuals complete the same job at different rates even when motivation is held somewhat constant.* Unquestionably, time is a critical element in school learning and achievement although it is difficult to pinpoint the relationship between its qualitative and quantitative aspects. Therefore, the problem for the practitioner is to use effectively the quantitative aspects of time to understand and predict how its qualitative aspects might be brought into play to influence learning in a desirable direction.

A few studies demonstrate effective and practical use of some aspects of Carroll's model as it relates to classroom learning. Several of these studies have pointed out significant factors in considering time in the classroom learning context. In one such study, Shores[22] attempted to establish whether fast readers were the best readers and concluded that there is a definite and predictable relationship between what is learned and the time involved in processing information. Shores's study further demonstrated how the injection of different purposes for completing tasks acts to affect the relationship between time and learning. This work by Shores proved to be significant for two reasons: (1) he established the relationship between *what is learned and the time involved in processing information,* and (2) he demonstrated that *purpose affects the relationship between time and learning outcome.* Both of these findings have great utility when dealing with issues related to classroom teaching.

In another study, Bugelski[23] attempted to define a learning trial empirically by focusing attention on the various temporal factors in learning such as exposure time per item, interitem interval, intertrial interval, and total learning time. Bugelski's findings suggest that the total learning time is a significant variable to consider in at least some kinds of learning. He further suggests that the practice of breaking up a learning session into blocks of time and labeling these blocks "trials" is probably a questionable activity when trying to discern what *subjects are actually learning or doing.* When Bugelski's findings are considered in terms of classroom teaching, there is a suggestion that a more parsimonious and useful index description of learning is probable if *time,* rather than a *number of trials* involved, is used as the sequencing variable determining instructional activity. The teacher who uses the temporal character of instructional activity as a prime aspect of the planning and executing of the teaching strategy to be employed to teach a certain objective is in a better position to compare two different learning trials in terms of a single criterion or variable (time). This would represent a real departure from the instructional practice of increasing the number of trials (repetitions) as a way to improve or increase learning and achievement. Rethinking the temporal aspects of instructional activity is likely to alter drastically the configuration of classroom teaching both in form and substance.

Another researcher, Sjogren,[24] attempted to fix the temporal aspects of instructional activity by measuring the degree of learning resulting from the study of an instructional program *one time* to discern if such an activity were significantly related to the *ratio of time taken to time needed* for the study of the program. Sjogren's data suggest that *time ratios have a significant linear relationship with measures of learning (including standardized achievement tests) and aptitude.* These findings are important because they tend to reinforce the notion that instructional sequencing should build on the idea of encouraging learners to take as much time as is needed, in accordance with their individual aptitudes for the subject matter in question, for mastery.

Another variable for consideration suggested by Sjogren's work is associated with values attached to the subject matter itself. For example, students may be helped to learn, more quickly, subject matter that might be more valuable for later learning or broader application. This raises the question of whether time spent on learning more difficult or less useful content might be better employed to learn information of greater value. This issue has to be dealt with in the context of the total teaching strategy formulated and implemented. The appropriate use of a pupil's time is a value that should be taken into account in one overall instructional plan.

Another important temporal aspect of instructional activity was explored by Jester and Travers[25] when they studied the effects of various presentation patterns on the comprehension of speeded speech by tracing two conditions of increasing and decreasing speed. The major conclusion that was drawn from this study suggests that maximum learning occurs when the rate of presentation nears the optimum level required by the learner for mastery. A teaching strategy for classroom instruction must take into account the pacing of learners in terms of expected performance. In the same vein as the Jester and Travers study, Kress and Gropper[26] set out to determine how externally controlled pace setting affected the accommodation of individual differences to pacing requirements associated with selected achievement tasks. Their findings suggest that achievement scores tend to decline as the tempo increases and that the mean performance is highest when characteristically fast students work under a fast fixed tempo, and when characteristically slow students work under a slow fixed tempo. It is evident that the rate set by the teacher for an activity has far-reaching effects on achievement and must be taken into account in the formulation of any teaching strategy.

In some research conducted by Rodgers,[27] the findings suggest that there is a very definite relationship between rate variation and modes of instructional presentation. His basic conclusions are indicated as follows:

1. The method of presentation affects the rate variation of pupils when they are asked to perform related tasks.
2. Pupils with different operative rate patterns will show different achievement outcomes when exposed to different modes of presentation.
3. The rate of work is the best predictor of gain in achievement if the method of presentation is flexible (fast workers will be superior achievers).
4. The rate at which learners complete the criterion test can be used to predict performance when the mode of presentation is used as a variable.

The interaction between time and instructional presentation modes and the effects of time on achievement patterns is definite enough to be considered a significant condition to be noted as part of the overall teaching strategies.

If the reality of classroom teaching strategies and their relation to the use and organization of temporal factors is to be adequately considered, some attention must be devoted to time influences associated with the effects of group size on the quality of the student-teacher interactions. For illustrative purposes, focus is placed on the most common types of student-teacher interactions such as the single student teacher, the small-group teacher, the whole-class teacher, and the selected-class-group teacher relationships.

In formulating a teaching strategy, the type of interaction a teacher has with children is largely affected by the amount of time that is available for the planned activity. If the planned activity calls for interactions between the teacher and individuals (twenty-five in number) within a fifty-minute time period, he is faced with several alternatives. First, the teacher might allow two minutes for each child to participate and interact with him or a few of his classmates. There are many readily apparent shortcomings to this strategy. For instance, two minutes per child leaves no time for the teacher to initiate the activity, interact with the student, expand on ideas presented, correct misinterpretations and misunderstandings, allow flexibility of response patterns (some student may have much to contribute whereas others may have nothing to contribute to the topic being discussed), or randomly select students to participate. When a teacher's instructional presentation is faced with so many limitations, opportunity to deal with unplanned but significant interactions is seriously curtailed or nearly impossible. From the example provided, it is obvious that any attempt to assign strict time periods across individuals during a classroom interaction activity is likely to restrict the spontaneity and creative interest value of the learning process of the whole class. Even though the teacher must be conscious of time available to achieve a particular goal, it is self-defeating to become prescriptive to the point of destroying the natural flow of interacting among children as the catalyst for more insightful and shared learning experiences.

When time is considered in a classroom group learning context, the group, rather than the individuals, becomes the focal point of concern. The *quality of time use rather than the quantity of time allocation* should guide both the preactive and interactive phase of the instructional process. Time allocation is much more crucial to the activity of individuals assigned a given learning task to complete and/or master. The quality factor in the latter instance deals primarily with the motivational aspects associated with individual effort. The teacher is always faced with the need to balance quality and quantity considerations in the allocation and management of time across situations, groups, individuals, and expectations as a justification for his activities.

In classroom teaching the quality of time problem always creates a dilemma involving the *coverage of material* and *learning a significant process*. If a teacher focuses on the former, specific time allocation will be critical to determining the amount of material that can be covered reasonably well by a majority of the class members. In the latter instance, the amount of time allocated will be subordinated to the quality of the experience as related to the purpose and objective as judged by the teacher.

In part, this is true because:

> The difference in elapsed time between individuals and groups in problem solving would seem to be dependent on a number of additional factors, including the nature of the problem, the measure of elapsed time used, the criterion used in terminating problem-solving activity (for example, attaining correct solution, majority vote, consensus, etc.) and the amount of conflict both within and among individuals. There are undoubtedly conditions in which group decision making is "ruled out" because of time constraints.[28]

When a teacher plans and executes a teaching strategy involving the class as a contributing factor in the learning experience, he must be prepared to be flexible in his allocation of time and favor the quality of the product as the ultimate criterion for the justification of the total man hours (for the children and the teacher) involved in the instructional activity. There is evidence to support the notion[29] that the probability of a class's being able to arrive at a correct or acceptable solution is higher than would be the case for individuals working on the problem alone. However, this increased probability of success is achieved only after a substantially greater investment in man hours. In short, it takes much more time for a class to solve a problem and the teacher must decide if the investment yields adequate returns.

Instructional Contact Time
and Achievement Outcomes

Instructional Contact Time is the actual time the teacher employs to instruct a class in clearly identified content related tasks. This is the period in which the teacher's intent is to change class members' behavior in a specified direction both in quality and quantity, and class members are aware of his intent. ICT requires both the specification of objectives within a defined period of time and the measurement of achievement resulting from the experience as a quality check on the effect of the teacher-pupil interaction. The quality of a teacher's ICT provides direct evidence related to his responsibility to the school system, the children, the parents, and the community.

In order to make use of ICT as a viable measure of teaching quality, it must be employed as part of a formula to determine an index of Achievement Growth (AG). This index should provide evidence that a teacher used the time available to achieve certain objectives while taking into account relevant factors that tend to influence AG. To compute the AG index, the following formula is utilized:

$$\text{Achievement Growth} = \frac{\dfrac{\text{Grade Level Achieved}}{\text{Grade Level Expected}}}{\dfrac{\text{Instructional Contact Time}}{\text{Instructional Time Allotted}}}$$

This formula is based on the fact that if a child spends one hour per day studying subject matter area, the ICT available theoretically is one hundred eighty hours per year. It is expected that each child will receive one hundred eighty hours of ICT during the school year in a given subject-matter area. However, many unavoidable conditions work against every child's being able to experience maximum number of hours of ICT with a given teacher. Therefore, this state of affairs must be reflected and accounted for when the index for describing AG is computed. In short, the teacher needs to know how different revelant factors associated with ICT tend to affect AG.

Using the formula, it is possible to compute a crude index as a measure of performance by taking into account both the amount of time spent and the performance achieved. In order to explain better how the index operates, some examples may contribute to the clarity of this discussion.

$$AG = \frac{\dfrac{GLA}{GLE}}{\dfrac{ICT}{ITA}}$$

Example 1: $AG = \dfrac{\dfrac{5.9}{5.9}}{\dfrac{180 \text{ hrs.}}{180 \text{ hrs.}}} \qquad \dfrac{1}{1} = 1$

Example 2: $AG = \dfrac{\dfrac{5.9}{6.9}}{\dfrac{160 \text{ hrs.}}{180 \text{ hrs.}}} = \dfrac{.86}{.89} = .97$

Example 3: $AG = \dfrac{\dfrac{5.4}{3.9}}{\dfrac{160 \text{ hrs.}}{180 \text{ hrs.}}} = \dfrac{1.38}{.89} = 1.56$

Example 4: $AG = \dfrac{\dfrac{5.4}{6.9}}{\dfrac{180 \text{ hrs.}}{180 \text{ hrs.}}} = \dfrac{.78}{1} = .78$

Example 5: $AG = \dfrac{\dfrac{5.4}{3.9}}{\dfrac{180 \text{ hrs.}}{180 \text{ hrs.}}} = \dfrac{1.38}{1} = 1.38$

Example 6: $AG = \dfrac{\dfrac{6.2}{4.9}}{\dfrac{150 \text{ hrs.}}{180 \text{ hrs.}}} = \dfrac{1.26}{.83} = 1.52$

The reader should note that the size of the index (AG) is a function of the relationship between the time allotted and the instructional contact time experience as it relates to the grade level (achievement test scores) achieved and the grade level expected.

The first example reflects the fact that given one hundred eighty hours of instruction time available, a child can be expected to achieve (5th month of grade five) a score of 5.9 if an achievement test is given to him at the end of the school year. (It is also assumed* that the same child

---

* Any casual reading of educational literature in this area suggests that this assumption is probably unwarranted.

achieved a score of 5.0 at the beginning of the school year.) If the instructional contact time equals the time allotted and the measured grade level achieved is less than expected, the growth in achievement will equal 1. On the other hand, when instructional contact time and grade-level achievement is less than expected (see Example 2), the index shows that growth in achievement is less than 1 and below the level expected. The reader should note, however, that AG index is dependent upon the ratios indicated in the numerator and denominator and that if the ratio between ICT and ITA varied proportionately, the index would still be 1. The pattern shown in Examples 3 and 5 demonstrates the change in the index when the grade level achieved is greater than expected even though the instructional contact time experienced is less than or equal to the instructional time allotted. The size of the index is greater in Example 3 than in Example 5 because the increase in achievement was similar to or less than ICT.

One of the advantages of employing this pattern is related to the fact that growth in achievement can be discussed in relation to some of the relevant realities of the instructional environment. Similarly, the formula allows substitution (scores from teacher made tests) of several different kinds of quantitative data according to the needs of the instructional pattern employed. If a pattern that determines growth in achievement while taking time into account as a variable were to be employed by every teacher, it would contribute greatly to the making of consistent and objective decisions concerning the quality of instructional contact time spent in the classroom. This state of affairs should contribute greatly to improved precision in judging both the quality and effects of a particular teaching strategy employed in a given subject-matter field requiring an identifiable product performance as an outcome. When a teacher becomes conscious of how effectively he has spent his time in trying to achieve a specific instructional objective, he has discovered how to improve and judge some aspects of the quality of his efforts. Since every teacher is expected to operate within a specified period of time the way in which he uses his allotted time is a critical determinant of his effectiveness as a teacher. This is added support for teachers to pay greater attention to temporal variables affecting their interaction with pupils in the classroom.

Summary

In this chapter, the writer explored some of the factors in making diagnosis and formulating strategies as they relate to classroom teaching. Teaching strategies and diagnostic approaches were shown as complementing each other for the purpose of eliciting predictable responses from learners. In part, the problem is related to the confusion in the literature involving the many unsubstantiated explanations about the nature and definition of diagnosis and strategy as they contribute to classroom teaching activity. As a result of this situation, the relationship between strategy, method, and procedure as they relate to classroom teaching were clarified. It was concluded that the actual relationship between these components of instructional activity is critical to formulating a total classroom teaching strategy to decide where and how to begin, and to judge the effectiveness of the efforts.

Diagnosis as a pattern for initiating the teaching strategy to be employed was discussed as was the setting of performance standards as the critical element in completing the diagnosis that would, in turn, become the foundational base for formulating the teaching strategy. Some specific techniques of diagnosis were discussed and related to classroom teaching activities.

The latter part of the chapter was devoted to a discussion of instructional contact time as a variable in instructional activity and student performance. Some of the influences of time on classroom teaching were noted and discussed in relation to the complexity of the environmental setting of the classroom. A way to evaluate the quality of ICT by computing an index of growth in achievement by associating time with achievement variables was investigated. Finally, the manner in which time variables might become a critical aspect of evaluating instructional quality within prescribed and realistic temporal frameworks, was demonstrated.

References

1. James B. MacDonald and Robert R. Leeper, *Theories of Instruction* (Washington, D.C.: Association of Supervision and Curriculum Development, NEA, 1965), p. 2.

2. Mauritz Johnson, Jr., "Definitions and Models in Curriculum Theory," *Educational Theory,* **17**:127–140 (April 1967).
3. James B. MacDonald, op. cit., p. 6.
4. N. L. Gage, "Paradigms for Research on Teaching," *Handbook of Research on Teachers* (Chicago: Rand McNally, 1963), p. 96.
5. Richard L. Turner, "Conceptual Foundations of Research in Teacher Education," in B. Othanel Smith, ed., *Research in Teacher Education* (Englewood Cliffs, N.J.: Prentice-Hall, 1971), p. 12.
6. Jerome S. Bruner, Jacqueline J. Goodnow, and George A. Austin, *A Study of Thinking* (New York: Science Editions, 1962), p. 54.
7. H. O. Berg, ed., *Evaluation in the Social Studies, Thirty-fifth Yearbook of the National Council for the Social Studies* (Washington, D.C.: National Council for the Social Studies, 1965).
8. Robert L. Ebel, *Measuring Educational Achievement* (Englewood Cliffs, N.J.: Prentice-Hall, 1965).
9. Benjamin S. Bloom, J. Thomas Hastings, George F. Madaus, *Handbook on Formative and Summative Evaluation of Student Learning* (New York: McGraw-Hill, 1971).
10. Norman E. Gronlund, *Measurement and Evaluation in Teaching* (New York: Macmillan, 1965).
11. William D. Hedges, *Evaluation in the Elementary School* (New York: Holt, 1969).
12. Robert F. Megen and Peter Pipe, *Analyzing Performance Problems or "You Really Oughta Wann"* (Belmont, Cal.: Fearon, 1970).
13. Arthur G. Storey, *The Measurement of Classroom Learning* (Chicago: Science Research Associates, 1970).
14. Eugene J. Webb, Donald T. Campbell, Richard D. Schwartz, Lee Sechrest, *Unobtrusive Measures: Nonreactive Research in the Social Sciences* (Chicago: Rand McNally, 1970).
15. Fred T. Wilhelms, ed., *Evaluation as Feedback and Guide* (Washington, D.C.: ASCD, NEA, 1967).
16. Bloom, et al., op. cit., p. 87.
17. Ibid.
18. Ibid.
19. Guy L. Bond and Miles A. Tinker, *Reading Difficulties and Their Diagnosis and Correction* (New York: Appleton, 1957).
20. Frederick A. Rodgers, "Influences of Time Variations on Learning and Achievement," *Educational Leadership,* **27**:101–105 (Oct. 1969).
21. John B. Carroll, "A Model of School Learning," *Teachers College Record,* 64:723–733 (May 1963).
22. J. Harlan Shores, "Are Fast Readers the Best Readers?—A Second Report," *Elementary English,* **38**:236–245 (April 1961).

23. B. R. Bugelski, "Presentation Time, Total Time and Mediation in Paired-Associated Learning," *Journal of Experimental Psychology*, **63**:409–412 (1962).

24. Douglas D. Sjogren, "Achievement as a Function of Time," *American Educational Research Journal*, **4**:337–343 (Nov. 1967).

25. R. E. Jester and R. M. W. Travers, "The Effect of Various Presentation Patterns on the Comprehension of Speeded Speech," *American Educational Research Journal*, **4**:353–360 (Nov. 1967).

26. Gerard C. Kress, Jr., and George L. Gropper, "A Comparison of Two Strategies for Individualizing Fixed-Paced Programmed Instruction," *American Educational Research Journal*, **3**:273–280 (Nov. 1966).

27. Frederick A. Rodgers, "Gain in Programmed and Flexible Presentations," *The Elementary School Journal*, **68**:312–324 (March 1968).

28. Victor H. Vroom, "Industrial Social Psychology," in Gardner Lindzey and Elliot Aronson, eds., *The Handbook of Social Psychology*, Vol. V (Reading, Mass.: Addison-Wesley, 1969), p. 228.

29. Ibid., p. 229.

9

Instructional Materials and Resources

In previous chapters we delineated the components of the instructional program. In addition to explaining and interpreting the mutually exclusive properties of these components, we also described how these components and their respective subcomponents are interrelated both logically and conceptually. For the most part we dealt primarily with the most general aspects of, and influences on, classroom teaching at the elementary school level. We now, therefore, turn our attention to the primary vehicle—materials and resources—for delivering the instructional program.

For our purposes, *instructional program* refers to "the totality of the curriculum and its implementation through direct instruction and other means."[1] It is important to note how we are employing instructional program as a concept because it determines how materials and resources will be viewed in a generic sense. Before we can meaningfully discuss materials and resources in a generic sense, it is necessary to carefully delineate the boundaries of curriculum in terms of its use in our definition of instructional program. For our purposes,

> The *curriculum* is considered to encompass the instructional activities planned and provided for pupils by the school or school system. The curriculum, therefore, is the planned interaction of pupils with instructional *content,* instructional *resources,* and instructional *processes* for the attainment of educational objectives.[2]

It should be apparent that the instructional program is theoretically and structurally tied to the curriculum and the way in which it is implemented and that materials and resources play a pivotal role in that implementation.

Instructional Materials and Resources and the Instructional Program

Some distinction between instructional *materials* and instructional *resources* must be made before the manner in which these elements are related and interrelated with the instructional program can be discussed. *Instructional materials are the means by which a learner comes in contact with ideas, values, and concepts represented in a given body of subject-matter content.* Although instructional materials* encompass subject-matter content, they go beyond the scope of knowledge organized in accordance with the dictates of the disciplines in question because they deal with packaging of knowledge for use with a selected group of learners and teachers in a variety of settings. The production of instructional materials is governed by rules that are broader than the subject-matter content utilized and the medium of communication employed. Instructional materials take into consideration the subject matter, the learner, the instructional intent, the teacher, and the setting for presentation. Instructional materials cover such things as textbooks, films, filmstrips, television tapes, games, audio tapes, models, charts, graphs, maps, transparencies, displays, pictures, transcriptions, guidebooks and resource people. The primary purpose of all instructional materials is to enhance the ability of students to achieve effective and efficient learning. Any analysis of instructional materials must be done in the context of the relationship and interrelationships of three basic components: subject-matter content, treatment of subject-matter content, and planned instructional outcomes of students.

The primary concern of instructional materials in teaching must relate to the intended cognitive processes to be generated in, among, and across a given set of individuals. The generation of intended cognitive processes among and across individuals is dependent upon the efficiency of the communication characterizing the interactions experienced by all participants in a given instructional network. The specific role of a given instructional material for affecting the cognitive processes in a

---

* Carlton W. H. Erickson and David H. Curl, *Fundamentals of Teaching with Audiovisual Technology,* 2nd ed. (New York: Macmillan, 1972).

prescribed way is best explained by the use of Runkel's[3] notion of *colinearity*. In general the notion of colinearity suggests that when the cognitive space of each of the communicators does not proceed along the same dimension, communication among them is impaired. Efficient communication occurs when a number of individuals order a given set of stimulus items (facts, concepts, generalizations, judgments, beliefs, opinions, or attitudes along the same dimension). Accordingly, the task of instructional materials is to order the intentional cognitive processes of learners along dimensional lines consistent with the purpose or instructional objective guiding the intellectual activity in question. When instructional materials fail to give the intended dimensionality to the cognitive processes of learners, they do not communicate effectively the message and experience sought by the teacher. At that point a given instructional material's utility for the intended purpose becomes questionable.

The contents of instructional materials are not limited to topical events and as such often reflect societal values, norms of behavior, and traditional perspectives for interpreting the environment and life experiences of the characters employed as examples. It is reasonable to conclude that instructional materials contribute greatly to the transmission of culture to new learners and to the acculturation of experienced learners. Little imaginative effort is required to appreciate the dependence of schools and other institutions engaged in teaching on instructional materials to communicate the complex of skills, attitudes, and emotions required to adequately transmit, culturally, vital and potent ideas to youth. In the main, instructional materials should present new objects and ideas that engage and activate an "empathetic capacity" (the ability to see oneself in the other fellow's situation or one-to-one identification with a referent) while simulating the development of this capacity. A learner's horizons are expanded and new incentives generated as he is able to imagine playing the life roles portrayed in instructional materials. To the extent that an individual learner can conceive of himself as fulfilling a social function suggested, whether implicitly or explicitly by instructional materials, he is provided with the "psychic mobility" required to make learning meaningful and real. Without instructional materials knowledge of many social functions would be unavailable to many youth because of the restriction this situation would place on the universe of vicarious experience. One of the significant roles of instructional materials is the accurate substitution of vicarious experiences for real-life experiences that are the social functions that maintain and enhance the quality and variety of life in our society.

Another way to conceptualize instructional materials is in terms of their easy and ready availability to all learners. In this sense, instructional materials can be thought of as an organized means of reaching large numbers of diverse kinds of learners quickly and efficiently. This characterization of instructional materials is at best ambiguous for speed, efficiency, and the size and heterogeneity of the intended user are relative matters. Similarly, there is no attempt to deal with the quality, effectiveness, possible emotional impact of instructional materials, and technical aspects of packaging, encoding, decoding, and disseminating. Before educators can be expected to be able to deal with these issues affecting instructional materials, some attention must be devoted to the specific concerns suggested previously.

A related problem for the educator is associated with the fact that there is no satisfactory or theoretically derived schema available for categorizing the effects of instructional materials. The literature ([1], [3], [4], [5], and [6]) is filled with claims about the apparent value of a multimedia approach largely based on the rationale suggested by points made by Petersen when she asserts:

> In summary, the multimedia approach is widely accepted today because it (1) helps to make learning a vital, meaningful, and firsthand experience and (2) helps to provide a wide range of learning experiences suited to learners of greatly varying abilities. It is, in short, an integral, vital, and necessary component of what we believe today constitutes sound educational practice.[4]

Coupled with this claim is another notion offered by Dale in his "Cone of Experience" when he suggests that instructional materials can be placed on a flexible continuum from direct experience to pure abstraction. A good example of Dale's "Cone" as modified by Sowards and Scobey (pictured in Figure 9.1) shows how it is theorized that learners are expected to move from active to passive participation as the experience changes from concrete to abstract.

All of these claims about the possible effects of instructional materials on learners appear to be reasonable as a starting point for providing a general schema for categorization. However, this still leaves the educator with the knotty problem of trying to determine how to classify instructional materials in accordance with variables that are directly associated with the instructional programs. These variables represent the dimensions that can provide a framework for an empirical organization of the effects of instructional materials on learning under different conditions.

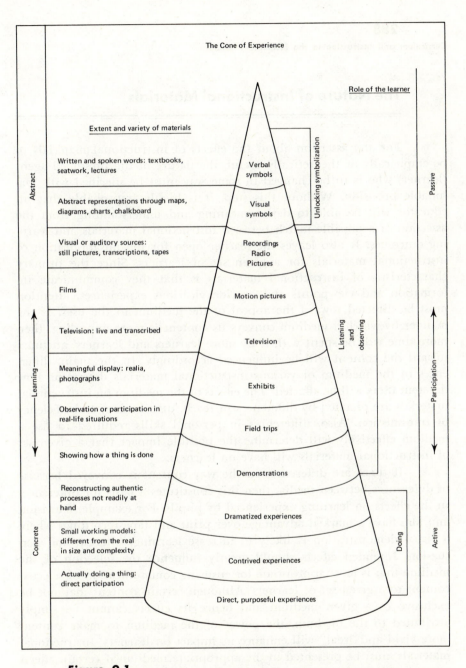

Figure 9.1
The Cone of Experience. [G. W. Sowards and M. M. Scobey, *The Changing Curriculum and the Elementary Teacher* (Belmont, Cal.: Wadsworth, 1961), p. 445. As adapted from Edgar Dale, *Audio-Visual Methods in Teaching*, revised ed. (New York: Dryden Press, 1956), p. 43, copyright © 1954, Holt, Rinehart & Winston, Inc. Used by permission of the publishers.]

The Nature of Instructional Materials

For any assertion about the effects of instructional materials to be empirically or theoretically useful, the nature of the presumed agent (learner) who is to be changed in some way must be specified with reasonable precision. Without this step, it is highly improbable that an educator will be able to derive meaning and understanding from the assertion of a possible match between instructional materials and learning outcomes. It also leaves the teacher open for the misapplication of instructional materials for a given set of learners. Since the primary characteristic of instructional materials is that they communicate information and viewpoints and provide vicarious experiences, attention must be directed toward the appeal of the medium to the user. If the manner by which a medium conveys its content is more appealing, then more time will be spent with it by more learners and learners' attitudes toward the content will be influenced accordingly. In the main, differences in the medium of various instructional materials determine how different users will be affected. The effects of the medium on instructional materials are dictated by differences in reach, distribution, and efficiency of transmission. Also, differences in personal skills required to use a medium effectively will determine the possible impact that a given set of instructional materials will have on learners.

If there are differences in the way content is conveyed because of differences between media, then this constitutes a basis for differences in the effects on learning experienced by pupils. For example, television and film have a marked advantage over print and tape recordings where a visual demonstration is likely to increase learning, interest, and persuasion. Intended effects should greatly influence the selection of the medium that is most appropriate for ensuring communication of selected content to a given set of learners. Although certain content may not be exclusive to a given medium and hence its effects cannot be simply attributed to the medium, the power of the medium to make content more vivid and "real" will enhance its impact on learners. Instructional materials must be presented in the appropriate medium if certain effects are to be forthcoming with young learners.

At this point, some attention should be devoted to the discussion of instructional resources as a generic idea. *Instructional resources* is a broad term for denoting instructional staff members, instructional support services, community resources, location of instruction, facilities, equipment, and supplies required to conduct the instructional program. These factors affect the instruction program because they set the stage and describe the environmental setting in which instruction is to occur. The nature and effects of the instructional program are largely determined by the shape of the configuration of instructional resources. A short description of the generic areas of instructional resources should enable the reader to visualize why these factors are so critical to the delivery of the instructional program.

Instructional Staff. This term refers to the identified general characteristics of the instructional staff and the conditions under which it works. Among these characteristics are preparation (formal and informal), experience, certification status, assignments, and teaching load or pupil load.

Instructional Support Services. This term refers to the broad areas of services supporting instruction such as resource services for pupils, pupil personnel services, and services for instructional staff. Services for pupils include the school library and audiovisual services that make instructional resources directly available to pupils. Pupil personnel services refer to guidance, health, school psychologist, audiology, speech pathology, attendance, and school social work services that are concerned with the total welfare of pupils. Services for instructional staff incorporate such things as library, audiovisual, and instructional supervision services and provisions for in-service education, which provide materials, guidance, and other assistance to teachers and other members of the instructional staff. Among factors to be considered concerning each of these broad service areas are appropriateness, accessibility, adequacy, frequency of use, and effectiveness of management.

Community Resources. These include the facilities, agencies, businesses, and persons outside the schools in the community that may be used, or are used, by the schools for their educative values, for example, theaters, parks, playgrounds, libraries, art galleries, museums, zoos, planetariums, botanical gardens, universities, churches, Scouts and other youth groups, service clubs, social service agencies, industries, and individuals, including representatives of various occupational groups, cultural groups, and civic organizations.

Location of Instruction. This concept includes activities of directing and managing an operation—of the school system or school—related to instruction, curriculum improvement, and instructional services.

It also includes the scheduling of pupils and staff into classes and services. The manner in which the administrators, other staff members, and resources are organized for the administration of the school system or school, or of an instructional service provided by the system or school, is also included under this category.

Facilities. This term refers to the appropriateness, quantities, adequacy, accessibility, and frequency of use of various types of facilities (buildings and grounds) including built-in equipment.

Equipment. This term refers to the appropriateness, quantities, adequacy, accessibility, and frequency of use of the various types of portable equipment (audiovisual aids, and so on) including library books.

Supplies. This term refers to the appropriateness, quantities, adequacy, accessibility, and frequency of use of the various types of materials, including paper and other expendable items.

The brief descriptions of the generic areas characterizing instructional resources should provide the reader with a general overview of the factors that must be considered here to aid the development of the instructional program.

Even though all of these factors are important to the delivery of the instructional program, the classroom teacher's primary concern is with community resources, equipment, facilities, and supplies when he makes plans to use instructional resources. The other instructional resources discussed are treated by classroom teachers as factors outside the domain of their personal instructional planning. This point should be kept in mind when we discuss the use of instructional resources in the instructional program.

The Relationship of Materials and Resources to the Instructional Program

Earlier in this chapter *instructional program* was defined as referring to the totality of the curriculum and its implementation through direct instruction and other means. In order to deal with the instructional program as thus defined it is necessary to determine the meaning intended for curriculum. In our earlier discussion curriculum was indicated as being the planned interaction of pupils with instructional content, instructional resources, and instructional processes for the attainment of educational objectives. It follows then that the instructional program embraces all of the intentions of the curriculum and the means for reaching the objectives indicated by those intentions.

In schools, *instructional content* is operationally defined by available instructional materials. Several factors have been considered (both serially and in combination) in the construction of these instructional materials. In some instances, the medium of presentation dictates which of the factors guiding the construction of instructional materials is to receive the most emphasis. In that sense, educational objectives are partly determined by the nature of the instructional materials available.

Instructional resources define operationally what is available for use by the teacher that falls outside his direct and sole control. These resources are brought into play to supplement or expand the experiences provided learners through the use of instructional materials. Instructional materials and resources are related to the instructional program because they define operationally what is to be manipulated by the teacher as he interacts with pupils for the attainment of educational objectives. Without instructional materials and resources there could not be an instructional program because there would be no basis for the teacher and pupil to interact for the attainment of publicly determined educational objectives. In short, instructional materials and resources are the fundamental units of the instructional program and, as such, help to determine the extent of the relationship such a program may have on a given set of learners.

The Influence of Materials and Resources on Instruction

Generically, instruction can be thought of as "any specifiable means of controlling or manipulating a sequence of events to produce modifications of behavior through learning."[6] Instructional materials and resources are "specifiable events" that can be employed by teachers modifying the behavior of pupils through learning. As the means or tools available to teachers for modifying behavior, instructional materials and resources exert a powerful influence on the type of instruction that pupils receive. The instructional process employed by a teacher is shaped by the materials and resources that are available to him for working with a particular group of children. Even though a teacher may alter the impact of the materials and resources through the use of different teaching techniques, it is difficult to overcome the influence of the available materials and resources because they control the nature of the learner's involvement. Because of the fact that the learner's involvement is guided by available materials and resources, the teacher's instructional approaches are shaped accordingly. The key to understanding the nature of instruction is, therefore, tied to the shape of instructional materials and resources. It is also essential that instructional materials be reliable and current so that pupils are not taught facts and ideas that scholars have found to be invalid, distorted, or untrue.

The Effects of Teaching Strategy on the Use of Instructional Materials and Resources

In Chapter 5 we discussed the nature of teaching strategy and how it relates to the instructional program. At that time it was concluded that teaching strategy as an idea can be summarized into the following components:

1. An attempt to have learners achieve an objective using a minimum number of encounters with essential elements.
2. An attempt to sort out irrelevant data using appropriate test procedures.
3. An attempt to minimize cognitive and affective interference that might increase the strain on inference and recall capacity.
4. An attempt to minimize the number of incorrect categorizations (increase efficiency and effectiveness) experienced in processing data.

The employment of a teaching strategy must include all of these components to be complete in terms of our earlier discussion. It can be readily observed that any teaching strategy defined by the list of components will have definite effects on the use of materials and resources in the instructional program. Our attention here is directed toward describing the nature of materials and resources when they are viewed within the context of the teaching strategy employed.

No matter how broad the conceptualization of a given set of instructional materials, or how complex the instructional resources, they cannot be substituted for, or made synonymous with, a teaching strategy. Even though there are many instructional materials and resources* that are advertised and presented as a complete teaching strategy requiring a teacher or adult only as a guide and helper, they still fail to meet the criteria that define a teaching strategy. Although it is possible for instructional materials and resources to be used to achieve an objective, there is no way to determine *a priori* and arbitrarily the minimum number of encounters with essential elements that different children using these sources should have. Instructional materials and resources can be designed to seek out some irrelevant data using appropriate test procedures, but not all, because tests are designed to sample knowledge and understanding of selected information. A given test procedure is unlikely to cover all of the aspects of the data that are crucial to the development and the focus of a given set of instructional materials and resources designed for a prescribed purpose. Instructional materials cannot be designed and resources cannot be selected to minimize cognitive and affective interference that might increase the strain on inference and recall capacity. The effects of instructional materials and resources on the cognitive and affective experience of a variety of young people of different backgrounds can only be presumed in their design and selection and the nature of their influence on the inference and recall capacity of different young people cannot be predicted without controlled and purposeful intervention. Instructional materials and resources cannot be designed or selected to minimize the number of incorrect categorizations experienced by different youth processing data under a variety of conditions. Although programmed materials are an attempt to satisfy this criterion, the linearity and step size of the approach does not ensure correct categorizations by the different variety of children who use them. Instructional resources do not come as close to meeting this criterion of a teaching strategy.

From this discussion it should be apparent that instructional materials and resources alone do not satisfy the criteria that define a teaching strategy. However, it is possible to use instructional materials and resources to operationalize and conduct a teaching strategy. At best,

---

* It should be noted that an expert or specialist used as a resource can in fact formulate and utilize a teaching strategy in a particular presentation to a given group of students. In that sense a resource person can be thought of as embodying a teaching strategy.

instructional materials and resources can be employed as methods and procedures that are skillfully arranged and ordered to achieve certain objectives and to guard against unwanted ones. Instructional materials and resources are the elements that are manipulated to complete a given teaching strategy. It should be clear from this discussion that a teaching strategy is a process that takes into account situational variables that define the nature of the task precisely and provide the basis for adjusting the students' experiences so that they will be consistent with the intended outcome sought. In this sense, the teaching strategy employed determines how instructional materials and resources are to be used with learners to achieve a prescribed end without unintended side effects. Materials and resources are the *means* of an instructional process and not its *ends*. This conclusion must guide the decision making of all teachers who expect to affect the learning experience of young people, in the intended direction while they are teaching them, and to foster meaningful life experiences for the future.

Instructional Materials and Resources and Flexibility of Teaching Strategy

Instructional materials and resources aid the teacher in the successful completion of a teaching strategy in several important ways. First, they expand the instructional contact time of the teacher with individual pupils. It will be recalled from the discussion of instructional contact time (ICT) in Chapter 5, that ICT is the actual time the teacher employs to instruct a class or its individual members in clearly identified content-related tasks. As indicated earlier, if the time allocated daily for teaching major ideas in a given content area were divided among the children equally, the ICT available to each child would be too little to matter very much. Instructional materials and resources help the teacher to deal with the ICT problem because they can be employed or organized to systematically and effectively deal with the facts, skills, and concepts considered to be crucial to the individual pupil's achievement of the intended outcomes of a teaching strategy. With the use of instructional materials and resources to present ideas and content for some pupils to interact and practice with, the materials become teacher "substitutes," "extensions," or "supports" for the acquisition of facts, skills, and ultimately, the concepts needed to demonstrate mastery of understanding that teachers utilize to determine the degree of success that pupils experience resulting from a particular teaching strategy. The use of instructional materials and resources enables the teacher to expand his ICT because there is less demand for him to make direct contact with each student to ensure similar exposure to a well-defined specific aspect of a total instructional experience.

Second, instructional materials and resources enable teachers to take advantage of the different styles of learning that different pupils exhibit. Since instructional materials and resources range from direct, purposeful experiences to verbal symbols (see Figure 9.1), they take into account all of the known ways in which youth learn. It is also possible to combine various levels of concrete and abstract experience to make a given set of materials or resources more acceptable to, and effective for, pupils who employ different learning styles to learn similar information. The form of packaging of instructional materials and resources also allows learners to employ a number of different sensory receivers (sight, listening, touch, smell) to acquire a more complete picture or understanding of a concept or idea. There can be an instructional material or resource that will aid any learner in the acquisition of concepts no matter which learning style or combination thereof he uses. The problem becomes one of selection and matching rather than one of availability.

Third, instructional materials and resources enable teachers to plan, design, and construct methods and procedures to be manipulated and orchestrated in the conduct of the teaching strategy. In order to achieve specific objectives (see Chapter 5), methods and procedures have to be carefully planned so that there is an increased probability that the resulting interaction experience between teacher and learner will yield intended results. Another way to view the problem is to note that the same facts and skills, organized and sequenced differently, define concepts that are quite different. For example, demographic statistical data can be used to describe the stability and cohesiveness of a community, and the same data can be rearranged or analyzed in smaller data units to demonstrate how the community is in a constant state of flux. Can a community be static and dynamic at the same time, using the same set of data to justify either conclusion? The answer is yes, and one justification is in part related to how facts and skills are organized and sequenced to define or describe concepts. Since instructional materials and resources are prearranged facts and skills to denote specific concepts, they tend to operationalize methods and procedures employed by the teacher in formulating and conducting a given teaching strategy.

Fourth, instructional materials and resources offer the opportunity of combining ideas that could not be otherwise mentally related.

For example, erosion and its various forms is a concept that can be taught strictly as a verbal experience. But a picture showing the different effects of different kinds of erosion on similar and dissimilar land forms combines the ideas that would be difficult for an immature learner to visualize mentally. Once the pictures of the different facets of erosion are brought to the attention of the young learner, his concept of erosion becomes a "mental reality" based on being able to see the total relationship as a whole. Many examples of this type suggest that instructional materials and resources enable learners to see relationships as a "whole" that cannot be conceptualized by "part-by-part" seriation. The formulation and conduct of a particular teaching strategy are dependent on the ability to make relevant comparisons and combinations of data and life experiences to define and denote a concept.

Fifth, instructional materials and resources offer the opportunity for some direct experience when possible and for meaningful vicarious experience when it is not possible or practical for learners to participate directly. Without the meaningful vicarious experience of quality instructional materials and resources, many of the basic concepts underlying critical social functions that young people must learn would not be available to large numbers of students. In such an instance, most young people would be limited to experience with social functions that touch them personally in carrying out their daily activities. This situation would decrease greatly any choice a student might want to exercise over his personal decision to participate in a given social function that is unavailable in his real-life experience. Instructional materials and resources fill this void and expand meaningful vicarious life experiences.

Selecting Instructional Materials and Resources

The school is primarily concerned with the development of each student's basic understanding. This concern is realized by students through the learning and acquisition of knowledge and information and the formation of concepts and generalizations. Knowledge and information needed by students to formulate concepts and generalizations are communicated largely through the use of instructional materials and resources. As a consequence, the materials and resources selected are critical to determining the nature of the instructional processes required and the clarity and sequence appropriateness of the ideas that are to be used by a selected group of students to learn concepts and generalizations that are essential to fostering certain basic understandings of a given reality. This point is further elaborated by Barnes when he states that:

> Instructional materials greatly influence the quality of these learnings [information, concepts and generalizations]. This ideational quality is pervasive in nearly all learning activities common to schools; it is represented by the meaning of numbers in arithmetic, the relationship of facts in history and geography, the principles of biology and physics, the scientific aspects of the culture, the development of taste in the arts, the recognition of style in physical education, the perception of affective elements in literature, and many others.[7]

Since instructional materials and resources determine the nature and extent of the kind of basic understanding that students are likely to develop, it is essential that the strategy employed to select these materials and resources reflect both the instructional intent and the target learner in a given situation. The development and employment of criteria for selecting appropriate instructional materials and resources become the critical factor in determining the effectiveness and efficiency of instruction.

There is an infinite variety of basic understandings in a number of subject-matter fields that teachers are expected to help students grasp within a given period of time. For each of these basic understandings there is a multitude of instructional materials and resources varying in complexity and purported effectiveness in terms of a given teacher's instructional intent. Since there is no one teacher who knows all of the basic understandings that should be developed and the instructional materials and resources that could be utilized, it is difficult, if not impossible, for teachers to make rational choices suggested by the intent of the instructional experience. This situation makes it very difficult for teachers to plan an instructional strategy for enabling students to acquire a selected basic understanding. In order to alleviate the problem, some comprehensive scheme for selecting instructional materials and resources to ensure outcomes suggested by the teaching strategy employed must be formulated as a guide.

Any discussion of the use of instructional materials and resources in teaching should include the verbal reality* of all such materials and resources. Even though this aspect of the problem is not covered in de-

---

* An excellent discussion of the role of verbal meanings as it relates to instructional materials is presented by Fred P. Barnes in his chapter entitled, "Instructional Materials and Curriculum Decisions."[8]

tail here, some points should be given to provide clarity and purpose to the following discussion. We accept the notion that the vast majority of instructional materials and resources require the use of verbalizations to communicate the intended messages. Whether these verbalizations are written or spoken, their primary purpose is to communicate ideas in the form of information, concepts, or generalizations that explain or re-create reality that may or may not be personally accessible to a given learner. In this sense, the verbal characteristics of instructional materials and resources must be a prime consideration in any selection strategy.

Instructional materials and resources can be classified in accordance with the extensional and intentional meanings suggested by the verbal arrangements of the words used to describe the phenomenon under consideration. Extensional meanings refer to meanings for which words represent a one-to-one correspondence factor. For instance, a comment such as "Billy lives at 702 Arlington Court," has extensional content because a check of the site confirms the fact of residence and, therefore, the words correspond with reality. On the other hand, intentional meanings are representative meanings because they refer mainly to ideas or abstractions about reality that may not be directly observed. An example of intentional meaning may be gleaned from such a comment as "American citizens feel the spirit of democracy." There is no way that one can establish this assertion empirically even though many people believe and act as if this were possible. Making use of intentional meanings, it is possible to utilize one's imagination to explore meaningful relationships to communicate ideas that, though they cannot be empirically validated, still facilitate understanding of phenomena classified in different realms of knowledge.

A Schema for Selecting Instructional Materials and Resources

Instruction was defined in Chapter 8 as the interaction situation among pupil, teacher, media,* and the environmental setting. The instructional program thus consisted of strategies, methods, procedures, processes, resources, and structures that organize the interactions of the components of instruction to achieve the intended outcomes. Referring

---

* Used in its broadest sense to refer to any means, agency, or instrumentality employed to communicate ideas.

to the list on page 262 in Chapter 8, it should be readily apparent that instructional materials and resources are central to any teaching strategy that might be proposed. When one notes that the interaction phase of the teaching/learning couplet (technique/activity) always involves the teacher and the student with some form of instructional material or resources, the critical nature of materials and resources in being able to conduct school learning experiences becomes evident. Teaching techniques define or describe how a teacher (or substitute) utilizes given instructional materials and resources to operationalize parts of a teaching strategy, and learning activities define or describe how students utilize instructional materials and resources to realize, through practice and direct experience, goals set for them in the teaching strategy. In both instances, instructional materials and resources must be manipulated in some way before a given teaching strategy can successfully have the intended effects on learners. Now that the critical nature of instructional materials and resources has been established, the problem of selection can be put into a meaningful perspective.

In Figure 9.2, an instructional materials stairway suggests the beginnings of the formulation of a schema for selecting instructional materials and resources. The stairway indicates the different levels that can govern the arrangement of instructional materials and resources. Each of the levels indicated determines the extent of the basic understanding that learners might derive from the use of instructional materials and resources. The levels may be thought of as being on a continuum from concrete to abstract or direct to vicarious experiences. The aim of a sound teaching strategy would be directed toward helping learners to proceed from one point (concrete) on the continuum to a more complex point (abstraction). Different kinds of instructional materials and resources enable learners to move along this continuum and to gain mastery over basic understandings at the level of meaning under consideration.

One criterion that should guide the selection of instructional materials and resources is "their specific ability to promote the learning of concepts at certain levels of abstraction."[9] When a teacher employs this criterion to select instructional materials and resources, he must have some notion of the possible effects of different media on learning. For example, taking a trip to the Smithsonian Institution is a less abstract experience than hearing a lecture or reading a pamphlet about the Institution. Dramatizing an event in history is less abstract than reading about the same event. There are advantages and limitations accompanying the use of instructional materials and resources focused at different levels of abstraction, and their effectiveness is somewhat determined by

Start reading from the bottom UP

Levels of instructional materials	Example	Psychological processes in learning	The process of abstracting
V. Symbolic materials verbal and visual symbols as found in textbooks, encyclopedias, formulas used in mathematics and the sciences, musical scores, etc.	V. Consulting textbooks, reference books and encyclopedias to gain knowledge on the changing condition of the atmosphere which surrounds the earth.	V. Systematic generalization including awareness of "knowing," reflective thinking, mature ingenuity, etc.	V. The object or experience at an extremely high level of abstraction omitting almost all reference to the original characteristics.
IV. Pictorial materials experiences with flat pictures, motion pictures, television, maps, charts, graphs, radio, recordings, etc.	IV. Learning to read weather maps prepared by the U.S. Weather Bureau, and weather charts and maps published in local newspaper.	IV. Verbalization and symbolization including understandings, appreciations, extension of ideas already in process of formulation, etc.	IV. The object or experience portrayed. Still fewer characteristics selected for attention and more are left out.
III. Manipulative materials experiences with models, machines, instruments, laboratory-type objects, art media, constructional equipment, aquaria, collages, dramatizations, sociodrama, exhibits, chalkboards, etc.	III. Use of aneroid barometer, anemometer, and wind vane at school to make own predictions.	III. Exploration and discovery including study, location of talents and abilities, practice, development of skills, etc.	III. The object or experience selected for study. Certain characteristics are seen as important and others are left out.
II. Reality materials first-hand experiences with real objects in their complex, usual settings; field trips, work-experiences, school "stores," etc.	II. Trip to the local television station to observe "weather man" prepare for next broadcast.	II. Readiness including drives, needs, interests, sets, etc.	II. The object or experience recognized and named. The name is not the object; it merely stands for the object and omits many characteristics of the object.
I. The enormous world of things and ideas consisting of the biological universe, the physical universe, and the social-psychological universe. Qualities (indicated by irregular lines) include anything in the natural universe, all man's social inventions and ways of living. Characteristics are infinite and everchanging. This is the *dynamic* level.	I. Interest in the problem of weather predictions. How are storm warnings determined? How is fair weather foreseen? How far ahead can weather be predicted? Characteristics (indicated by irregular lines) are many and changing.	I. The learner's psychological state in a learning situation, according to scientific inference. Characteristics at this level (represented by irregular lines) include goal-seeking and tension-reducing behavior, and a complex of acts, such as motor, verbal, emotional, and attitudinal responses.	I. The object or experience in the "chance" world. Characteristics of the object or experience at this level (indicated by irregular lines) are complex and ever-changing.

Figure 9.2

Instructional Materials Stairway. [Fred P. Barnes, "Instructional Materials and Curriculum Decisions," in Merle M. Ohlsen, ed., *Modern Methods in Elementary Education* (New York: Holt, 1959), p. 121.]

the concepts to be understood and the background of experience of the target group. Given the nature of the constellation of personality and experience characteristic of individual students and the variety of learning styles they possess, the degree of abstraction inherent in a given set of materials and resources will have differential effects on different students. Even though all students will not react in the same way to materials and resources of varying degrees of abstraction, it is generally agreed that the majority of them are likely to increase their basic understanding of a particular concept at higher levels of abstraction if they have been afforded meaningful experiences with the same concept at the lower levels. A student's ability to understand new concepts or more complex levels of known concepts is largely dependent upon the nature of his past experiences.

In many instances it is more economical in terms of resources and time to utilize, initially, materials and resources that are classified at a higher level of abstraction than those designated as "reality materials." Similarly it might be feasible to initiate a particular teaching strategy utilizing materials and resources classified at a high level of abstraction and move down to lower levels of abstraction to ensure a broader learning experience. In both cases, however, the decision must be made by the teacher as he operationalizes the teaching strategy to fit the learning conditions suggested by a given group of students.

At this point, the reader should return to the Instructional Materials Stairway and observe the steps (II–V) that ascend in abstraction from direct, concrete, first-hand learning experiences and objects to symbols that represent objects or personal experience. As one ponders the arrangement of information in the Materials Stairway, it is easy to agree with the conclusion drawn by Barnes when he asserts:

> It is neither possible nor desirable to attempt to replicate, for study in the school environment, the infinity of life situations as they are encountered in the actual world. Rather, the school can best be understood as a *simplified and controlled* environment for the study of life and its adjuncts. As we have seen, concepts learned in the school are abstractions of reality, and the school, in a real sense, represents an abstraction of life (i.e., certain characteristics are selected for our purposes, and others are left out). It would be absurd to suppose that all real-life objects or materials could be imported into the school, or that children could be transported to many actual scenes of real-life happenings.[10]

Instructional materials and resources are "representative" segments of real life that are selected for study. As these segments are encountered at higher grade levels, more details are added, more complexity becomes apparent, and more instances of the same phenomenon are observed under different conditions. This enables the learner to develop and handle higher levels of abstraction of a given concept studied in the hierarchy sequence. The learner is broadening his basic understanding of a concept that should equip him to deal with that concept more effectively in real-life situations. At this point the learner has acquired the transportable skill—the ability to form higher level abstractions of a concept. Appropriate instructional materials and resources allow the teacher to help his students to deal with parts of the life experience in a systematic and rational way so that they may be exposed to basic understandings necessary to deal with chance activities and experiences.

Reality Materials

According to the stairway, reality materials represent the first level of abstraction. Even though the materials at this level are abstracted from the real world, their close association with the senses (taste, touch, sound, smell, and sight) ensures their continuance as part of that world. When a child is asked to learn from reality materials, his efforts are active oriented, his experiences are personally forceful, direct and alive. In short, as one who is affected by the total environment, the learner is totally involved in the learning activity. Reality materials afford students the opportunity to have realistic experiences that contribute to greater understanding by the systematic building concepts. An additional contribution of reality materials is associated with the notion that they serve to validate a learner's mastery of concepts introduced at higher levels of abstraction. Criteria for selecting instructional materials at the reality level include those shown in Table 9.1.

Manipulative Materials

The next step on the stairway is concerned with *manipulative materials*. These materials are closely related to reality materials because they are tangible and require the active participation of the learner. Manipulative materials have the added advantage of making it possible

Table 9.1
Instructional Materials at the Reality Level

Criteria	Examples of Materials and Resources
1. The materials and resources enable the learner to *observe* and *study* social functions conducted by a variety of people in different settings.	Provide field trips, interviews, and guest speakers.
2. The materials and resources enable the learner to construct an environment or activity that provides needed goods and services in the class or school.	Plan and initiate a school store, publish a newsletter or newspaper, make a model of the local area.
3. The materials and resources enable the learner to participate in the processes that comprise the school's environment.	Participate in a class election of officers, serve on committees, serve as an assistant to a staff member.

for students to be able to have a simulated experience with objects or events that would be either unmanageable or inaccessible in the real world. In this sense, manipulative materials differ in size and complexity from the event or object they represent. Oftentimes young children need to study an event or object that, in real life, is too large, too small, too obscure, or too dangerous to be dealt with directly. In these instances manipulative materials can serve as an edited version or model of the real-life object or event that is reduced or advanced in scale to improve the teacher's chances for achieving instructional purposes. Because manipulative materials are under the direct control of the user, they are readily adapted to classroom use. Criteria for selecting instructional materials and resources at the manipulative materials level include those shown in Table 9.2.

Pictorial Materials

Pictorial materials generally include and exclude some of the sensory impressions that are characteristic of the levels II and III shown in the stairway. These materials also take into account some of the sensory impressions that characterize level V in the stairway. The primary focus of pictorial materials is to communicate well-defined and

Table 9.2

Instructional Materials at the Manipulative Level

Criteria	Examples of Materials and Resources
1. The materials and resources enable the learner to visualize explanations given by the teacher or in some kind of written source.	Demonstrations, chalkboard, apparatus (stove, sink, food, glassware, chemicals, and so on), feltboards or flannelboards.
2. The materials and resources enable the learner to display or observe the products of schoolwork.	Exhibits, displays, bulletin boards, plays, loan exhibits, puppetry, sociodrama, role playing, posters, charts, museum (classroom), tackboard.
3. The materials and resources enable the learner to rearrange raw reality for meaningful presentation and understanding.	Models, mock-ups, objects (souvenirs, relics, coins, stamps, tools, and so on), specimens.

refined concepts selected to present ideas in accordance with a preconceived pattern. In this sense their greatest value may be to aid students in the refinement of ideas that were formed earlier. Pictorial materials involve students passively or as spectators and observers and often do not require overt participation or direct intervention as is the case with manipulative materials. This factor of pictorial materials is not necessarily bad because these kinds of materials enable students to maintain a personal detachment from the concepts under consideration. At this point students can participate in a more rational and intellectual consideration of the concept portrayed in the pictorial materials. Not only is a "picture worth a thousand words" but it also can serve to summarize what the thousand words mean and aid the learner in broadening his understanding. Criteria for selecting instructional materials and resources at the pictorial materials level include those shown in Table 9.3.

Symbolic Materials

Symbolic materials are at the highest level of abstraction in the stairway. They include both visual and verbal symbols that extend meaning and understanding for the concepts and generalizations learned

Table 9.3
Instructional Materials at the Pictorial Level

Criteria	Examples of Materials and Resources
1. The materials and resources enable the learner to visualize highly abstract "pictures" of areas, locations, quantitative data, institutional organization, sequences of events, and ingredients in products and processes.	Charts, maps, globes, and graphs.
2. The materials and resources enable the learner to visualize a reality at a given moment within a selected context.	Photographs, illustrations, stereographs, slides, filmstrips, and microprojection.
3. The materials and resources enable the learner to recreate visually an experience from a verbal description.	Radio programs, recordings.
4. The materials and resources enable the learner to study visually and auditorily processes and events that occur over time in their natural state.	Motion pictures, television (this medium can be utilized to record and to report separate events).

earlier. Developing basic understanding is the mastery of the process of deriving meaning from personal experience and much of that meaning is derived from the symbolic and abstract world of experience. With symbolic materials students can deal with abstract thinking at both higher and lower levels, manipulate problems imaginatively, utilize procedures to make certain predictions, restructure mental images, and exercise creative imagination. In order to accomplish any of these, students have to learn to use visual and verbal symbols effectively and efficiently. Criteria for selecting instructional materials and resources at the symbolic level include those shown in Table 9.4.

In the preceding paragraphs, we have outlined some criteria that might be employed to select instructional materials and resources. It was noted that materials and resources can be classified roughly according to the level of abstraction they represented and that criteria for selecting materials and resources will differ within each category. With some types of instructional materials and resources, it is difficult to determine the level of abstraction they represent apart from the way a teacher intends to use them with children. For example, an oil burning lamp might be presented as a manipulative material representing light production. However, if the teacher focuses on the design of the lamp as a medium for supporting the required burning while maximizing light output, or discusses the relationship between oxygen flow and the neces-

Table 9.4
Instructional Materials at the Symbolic Level

Criteria	Examples of Materials and Resources
1. The materials and resources enable the learner to reconstruct reality by interpreting symbols that represent it.	Flat maps, chalkboards, sketches, cartoons, comic strips, diagrams, charts, graphs.
2. The materials and resources enable the learner to derive meaning from verbal symbols.	Textbooks, workbooks, flash cards, worksheets, word lists, magazines, and newspapers.

sary burning required, or relates heat to light, he is dealing with some of the highest levels of abstraction. This latter notion is an important point to remember as a general concern in the selection of instructional materials and resources. In selecting an instructional material or resource, the teacher should consider which one is best suited for a given instructional intent. The teacher and his choice of teaching strategy is the critical determinant of appropriate instructional materials and resources. Therefore, the apparent degree of abstraction possessed by a given instructional material or resource is best thought of as a major determinant of the techniques utilized with different children but not the sole factor in determining which one should be selected to achieve a certain level of understanding with young learners.

Evaluating Instructional Materials and Resources

Any use of instructional materials and resources must necessarily focus on the student requirements for acquiring concepts essential to developing basic understanding. Ultimately this is the primary basis for judging appropriateness and effectiveness. Our discussion of evaluating instructional materials and resources proceeds within the context of this general notion. Specifically, the approach to evaluation is guided by consideration of eight critical topics.

Accuracy of Conceptual Presentation

In addition to presenting inaccurate information, some instructional materials and resources distort reality and provide students with faulty conceptions. Pictures in textbooks of tenements in urban ghettos or skyscrapers in commercial districts may cause students from rural and suburban schools to conclude that only the poor reside in the city whereas the rich work there. It will, therefore, be difficult for these students to visualize families who are similar to their own residing in the city. Materials and resources can also produce a distorted impression such as when they depict the state of Illinois as being topographically flat and primarily devoted to the growth of corn and soybeans. This picture of Illinois, however, does not take into account the rolling topography that characterizes the northern and southern parts of the state and that the primary work is nonagricultural in different parts of the state. In both of these instances the materials and resources are inappropriate samples of the variety of human organization and activity they claim to represent. A teacher using these materials and resources must always be aware of the possibility of distortion when use extends beyond their range. This same concern for distortion in instructional materials and resources applies when they represent a period of time that is not related to the reality required for appropriate understanding. It should be evident that materials and resources that do not provide an accurate picture of the concepts they are expected to present do not help students develop meaningful basic understanding.

The Match of Materials and Learning Tasks

The learning tasks and objectives to be pursued by students are determined by information and concepts to be learned to foster understanding in a desirable direction. One of the purposes of instructional materials and resources is to facilitate the successful completion of selected learning tasks. In this sense, instructional materials and resources are useful to the extent that they enable learners to complete, successfully, learning tasks. Even though a given set of materials and resources may be of high quality and great interest, they may not be the appropriate match for the learning task under consideration. Therefore, specific materials and resources must be judged in relation to how well they match the learning task that enables a given group of students to achieve an intended outcome.

The Match of Materials and
Learner Characteristics

One of the difficult problems facing teachers is the need to match materials and resources to the maturity level, intellectual capability, and background experience of learners. Oftentimes there are excellent materials and resources for teaching a particular concept, which are, however, inappropriate for the particular group of learners being taught. The inappropriateness may be related to the medium, the complexity (or lack of it), or the interest level of the content. In short, we are concerned here with whether or not the instructional materials and resources are appropriate for the learners who display a particular set of characteristics. Since determining the appropriateness of materials and resources is largely a matter of judgment, a teacher must formulate criteria and standards for judging this quality in terms of the observed learner characteristics.

The Technical and Physical Characteristics
of Materials and Resources

Even though teachers can formulate and utilize criteria for judging the technical and physical quality of materials and resources, they are not likely to be competent to judge them beyond superficial and surface factors that may not adequately detail the critical characteristics affecting their effective use with learners. Therefore, it would be unwise for teachers to rely solely on their own judgments in these areas. Fortunately, there are many excellent sources that may be utilized by the teacher to aid him in making judgments about the technical and physical quality of instructional materials and resources. One such source is the Educational Products Information Exchange (EPIE). EPIE is probably the most valuable source available for making certain educational judgments about the appropriateness of all types of instructional materials, resources, and systems. Specifically, the intent of EPIE is best characterized when it suggests that this service should be:

> envisioned as a cooperative venture among professionals in all segments of the educational world, established to collect, codify, and disseminate dependable information on all types of educational materials, equipment, and systems. Information would be gotten from users as to how products performed, from producers as to what the products were

about, from analysts trained to describe the content and pedagogical base of the materials. Information would be gathered in light of "instructional settings"—detailed descriptions of the environments in which products had been used or for which they had been designed—so that recipients of information would have understood bases for comparison among products. Up-to-date lists and descriptions of products too new to make user reports feasible would always be maintained, and producers would be encouraged to introduce into the system, just as soon as progress warranted it, information about products which they were planning to put on the market.

All this information, systematically and impartially collected, would be sifted, matched up, codified, and summarized in a form which would provide a sound basis for the decisionmaker to make a judgment. The collecting and disseminating agency, or exchange, would maintain a policy of open discussion of its procedures and practices and would seek the counsel and cooperation of individuals and of industry and education associations whose activities were related to it.[11]

To date, EPIE has conducted its activities in accordance with this description and has published some of the most useful reports on instructional materials, resources, and systems utilizing criteria appropriate for making the necessary judgments of technical and educational quality. Any teacher would profit greatly and improve the validity of his judgments if he consulted EPIE Products Reports prior to making certain decisions about the technical and physical characteristics of instructional materials and resources. This source is also invaluable for making certain educational quality judgments. Most EPIE reports suggest other sources that might be employed to evaluate the quality of instructional materials and resources.

Adequacy of Instructions and Teacher Guides

Instructional materials and resources must be accompanied by clear and precise instructions detailing how they should be used. It is not expected that all such materials and resources will have specific instructions unless they have been prepared to facilitate a particular learning task. In such an instance, the teacher must know explicitly the intent of the instructional materials and resources and how the pattern of use is related to that intent. All of this information should be a part of the teacher's guide accompanying the instructional materials and resources.

In some instances, short descriptions of the content and concepts portrayed in the materials would be most helpful in helping a teacher to formulate his teaching strategy. These descriptions can alert the teacher to special problems to plan for or to special conditions required to make the materials more meaningful to the learners. Descriptions of materials also help to orient teachers when they have not had the opportunity to preview the materials they will be using. Because specific instructions on the use of materials can be so critical to the learning outcomes experienced by students, teachers should consider developing their own instructions and descriptions when the producer of the materials fails to do so. Instruction that proceeds according to such a guide is likely to have a greater intended impact.

Contributions to Critical Thinking

Instructional materials and resources should enable students to do critical thinking about issues associated with the information or concepts covered. In order to accomplish this, instructional materials and resources must not be so tightly programmed that they only present a single point of view based on a biased selection of supporting data. On the other hand, materials and resources with no conceptual direction are likely to be useless in helping students to acquire intended basic understanding. There must be a balance between too much or too little programming of instructional materials and resources if critical thinking is to be encouraged among students. Materials and resources must be able to point to a reasonable conclusion that describes a sound explanation of a series of related events without forcing students to accept that conclusion unquestioningly. Similarly, materials and resources should enable students to make alternate choices of data and interpretations of them without doing violence to the reality they represent. When materials and resources provide this kind of flexibility for fostering students' intellectual explorations while enabling them to acquire the intended basic understanding, they have contributed to aiding students to engage in critical thinking. When materials and resources help students raise important and significant questions, they have personalized learning for individuals and enhanced the value of critical thought as an appropriate part of human activity.

Fostering Positive Group Interaction

In a democracy, attention must be directed toward the effects of instructional materials and resources on moral values and personal attitudes of students. Content that gives an unflattering and derogatory picture of others is not in keeping with the respect for the dignity of individuals that is central to democratic thought and action. Teachers have a responsibility to ensure that the incidental learnings project values that provide continued reinforcement for enhancing the dignity of individuals in a democratic society. To ensure this outcome, teachers must be aware of the type of group interactions that the materials and resources suggest and encourage students to practice.

Economic Realities

In the final analysis, instructional materials and resources must meet the challenge of economic reality. Another way of stating the same idea would be to inquire about the extent to which instructional materials and resources are worth the time, expense, and effort required to locate, select, and utilize them with students. Teachers are always faced with the decision as to whether a less costly experience might not serve students just as well. Ultimately, all costs factors (time, expense, and effort) must be judged in terms of the critical nature of the ideas to be learned and the extent to which students learned what was intended. If what is to be learned is of low power as an idea, then any materials used to teach such ideas might be too costly. On the other hand, the high cost of instructional materials and resources is justified when students are able to learn important ideas that enable them to acquire the intended basic understanding. The direction of all instructional materials and resources should be improved understanding at the lowest possible cost.

Articulating Materials and Resources with the Teaching Strategy

Whenever any teacher considers materials and resources for use with students, the nature and extent of the teaching strategy to be employed must also be considered. It is relatively easy for a producer to design materials and resources to minimize technical media problems while dealing little, if at all, with how they correlate with, or increase the effectiveness of, the teaching strategy guiding instruction. This phenomenon places a heavy burden upon the teacher-user to adapt materials and resources to the tactical requirements of the teaching strategy selected. This problem is likely to exist as long as teachers design teaching strategies and require materials and resources. As long as teaching strategies are formulated with present goals in mind, and materials and resources are planned with no knowledge of those specific goals, the quality of the match between the two worlds will be left solely to the creative and intellectual skills of the teacher-user. As a consequence, there is a high risk that most instructional materials and resources do not fit a teaching strategy that might be selected by a given teacher, and as such are subject to misuse or being inappropriate. All teachers must face this problem when they attempt to use instructional materials and resources to put into operation a teaching strategy that yields understanding as students learn to deal effectively with selected concepts and information.

An Expanded Concept of Library Facilities in the Elementary School: The Instructional Materials Center

We are being confronted with dramatic and sometimes turbulent change that presents the general citizenry with a rapid array of novel and critically important situations that force alterations in crucial social functions within increasingly short spans of time. Forces of change are evident in the rapid growth of populations around the world; the accelerated rate of urbanization experienced by both the have and have-not nations; the development and extension of science and technology on an international scale; the alteration, elimination, and creation of a variety of specialized occupational classifications; the growth and development of multinational corporations; the modification of role expectations for family, church, school, and government as basic institutions; the ideological conflict between dominant political systems; the influence of small nation states on the major nation states in specialized areas; the increasing interdependence of nations for economic survival and vitality; the diminishing energy sources; the shift in the ease of and means for transportation and communication; the rise in world literacy rates; the growing influence of youth and formerly excluded groups on the political decision-making machinery; and the rising expectations of disadvantaged people at home and abroad. All of these changes tend to influence profoundly the elementary school curriculum programs and practices both in scope and direction, probably because all of the problem areas indicated are linked in some critical way to the availability, validity, and appropriateness of information that people have access to on a regular basis. It is strongly implied that the elementary school has to begin to help young people deal with this critical information if the quality of life experiences of the general citizenry is to be maintained and extended more broadly over a longer period of time.

Although these changes appear to involve modifications in our artifacts, they are primarily reflective of the role that man's mind and knowledge are beginning to play in guiding and shaping human affairs. Man's mental efforts are constantly being directed toward rational inquiry and empirical validation that imply the use of logic and evidence (knowledge) for the purposes of imagination, classification, generalization, evaluation, comparison, analysis, synthesis, deduction, and inference. This spirit of rational inquiry and empirical validation has given rise to the development of changes in the organizational structure and methods of developing and presenting new curricula at the elementary school level. As a result, elementary schools around the country are implementing curriculum programs that differ greatly from traditional conceptions surrounding the traditional subject areas. As changes concerned with altering school curricula areas are included in the total program, all resources and facilities* that are earmarked for enhancing and enriching the instructional efforts at the elementary school level must be changed conceptually to meet requirements of newly initiated innovations. The elementary school library, being an integral part of the instructional program at this level, is no exception in its requirement of responsiveness to the pressures of change and, as such, it must be conceptually returned to its rightful place in the total instructional scheme.

Elementary school libraries can be viewed according to a number of schemes. Any chosen scheme will place emphasis on different aspects of library facilities in accordance with the perceived purposes of the elementary schools that they are expected to serve. In this discussion, library facilities are viewed in relation to their ability to serve an elementary school curriculum that places stress on problem-solving activities; application of processes and knowledge to the solution of real problems; individualization of instruction, matching learning tasks to student learning styles, and obtaining or developing a wide variety of materials for the newly introduced programs in science, mathematics, foreign lan-

* Carlton W. H. Erickson, *Administering Instructional Media Programs* (New York: Macmillan, 1968).

guages, language arts, social studies, career education, consumer education, and environmental education.

This concept of the elementary school library has expanded to include provisions for the storage of audiovisual materials and equipment as well as furnishing adequate work space for using available materials while providing shelving for printed materials. With this inclusive view of library facilities at the elementary school level, there is a need for redefining the personnel needs in terms of the expected role to be played by the staff. Using this frame of reference to structure this view of the elementary school library facilities according to the requirements brought on by rapidity of change in our society and the nature of the new curriculum programs, these facilities are discussed as they relate to accessibility and flexibility and as they contribute to efficiency and economy in instructional programs.

Library Facilities for Elementary Schools

A library facility for an elementary school can be organized according to the type of unit it is to serve. In terms of the instructional program at this level, the organizational units used to view library facilities are the separate elementary school (attendance center), the local educational agency (school system), and the individual classrooms. This approach to the analysis of elementary school library facilities focuses on the instructional problems and requirements growing out of relevant demographic characteristics of the groups of students to be served.

The Elementary School Library

The library in the elementary school must help to facilitate the conduct of the instructional program. In this context, the elementary school library is an instructional space designed, or adapted, as a place for study, research, reflection, and reading, and for the custody, circulation, and administration of a collection of books, manuscripts, and periodicals kept for the use of the student body and school staff, but not for sale. Study carrels (wet and dry), audiovisual storage, and other service areas (production, repair, experimentation) opening into, and serving as adjuncts to, a particular library are considered parts of the elementary school library area. When elementary school library services and audiovisual services are located in the same instructional space, this space frequently is referred to as an *instructional materials center*. Audiovisual areas that do not open into, and are not adjuncts of, the elementary school library are generally considered under the audio-visual room category. One concept of the elementary school library is consistent with the instructional materials center concept of the facility. The requirements of the elementary school library facility are discussed under the general headings of location, size, design, flexibility in use, accessibility, instructional materials, and staff.

Location

The elementary school library should be located near the center of the school building. Its location should not encourage teachers who have classrooms in close proximity to the inside entrance to feel that the library is their personal possession and, as such, an enrichment corner for their classrooms. On the other hand, the location of the elementary school library should not discourage teachers who have classrooms far away from the inside entrance from using the library. In short, the frequency of use made of the library facilities by individual teachers should be dictated by the requirements of the learning activities and not by distance of their classroom from the library.

If it is possible to use the elementary school library during after-school hours, on weekends, or during summer vacation, the library should be located on the ground floor and have a separate outside entrance. It is especially important that elementary school libraries be located away from the gymnasium, playgrounds, and utility rooms for extracurricular activities (music, shop, and so on) that may produce considerable and distracting noises. Libraries should be located where expansion (by removing the walls of adjoining rooms) is not thwarted as changes in instructional outlook and increases in enrollment call for more space.

Audiovisual areas within the library should be located so that noise does not interfere with the quieter library areas. Users should be able to reach these areas from corridors that do not require them to go through the reading rooms. When elementary school libraries are found in geographic areas with a considerable amount of warm climate during the school year, out-of-door reading areas may be profitably used.

Size

The school's enrollment should determine the size and the nature and extent of the library's collection of materials. If elementary school libraries are planned to include audiovisual materials, and they should be, their size will increase in proportion to the variety of nonprint materials included and the way they are to be used by pupils and teachers. The size of the reading room in an elementary school library should provide for a minimum number of students at a given time, while assuring at least thirty square feet per reader. The size of the minimum number to be contained in any given school's library reading space should be determined by the school's program and what it expects the library to contribute to the total instructional program. However, in some quarters it is believed that the size of the reading room should be based on enrollment, seating 10 to 15 per cent of the enrolled students in schools having more than five hundred and fifty pupils, and forty-five to fifty-five pupils in schools with enrollments of two hundred to five hundred and fifty pupils. Either plan for determining the size of the reading room is acceptable as long as thirty square feet per reader is allowed and there is at least enough space to seat an entire class.

Design

The spatial relationships and shape of the elementary school library should be determined by its functional qualities in achieving present instructional purposes. Materials included in a library should be joined together in places for their use in adding mileage to the learning activity being experienced. The arrangement of the elementary school library should route the flow of traffic from the entrance to keys that help locate the materials being sought and to reading zones or work areas. Service areas that give information and active assistance to pupils should be strategically located for maximum use and minimum distraction to readers. The arrangement of the library should allow an adequate number of open zones for general use, smaller areas for small-group use, and private enclosures for individual use. Elementary school libraries should provide for a variety of spaces and models for different types of learning activities and for different types of personalities of the learners involved.

Flexibility in Use

Flexibility must be a key factor in planning elementary school libraries. At this level, libraries must adapt easily to changes in enrollment, in educational program, in teaching methods, and in communication media. Therefore, it is essential that the school's instructional program dictate the facilities to be included in the library. Some facilities and materials that might be included in a functional elementary school library with an expanded view of elementary school curriculum are:

1. A reading room with shelves for at least three fourths of the book collection and additional shelves for current magazines, reference books, and pictures. The reading room may also include carrels, some of which should be located away from the reading room to ensure more privacy for individual study.
2. The library should provide space for teachers' professional materials. This space might also be used for the storage of materials and equipment.
3. A conference room shoud be provided for small groups of pupils or teachers working on projects or reports. The room should probably open off the reading room and contain one long table, enough chairs for eight or ten persons, a small chalkboard, a bulletin board, and one standard shelving unit. It should be properly equipped to use various types of electrical equipment.
4. A room should be provided for storytelling and informal group discussion, furnished with equipment and furniture to ensure a relaxed atmosphere.
5. The library should provide a place for *teachers* and *pupils* to review and view films, filmstrips, and slides, and to listen to phonograph records and tape recordings. It might be necessary to provide a few individual listening booths within this room so that a variety of similar activities could be carried on at the same time. Because of its location and the equipment to be used, this room should be soundproof and constructed so that it can be darkened. The listening and viewing room should be adjacent to the audiovisual storage space.
6. Storage area for audiovisual materials and equipment should be made available in the library. This area should house equipment such as mechanical copying machines, microfilm readers, mobile phonocarts, projectors, record players, and tape recorders, and have a work counter. How much audiovisual storage area should be allotted in any given elementary school library will depend on the amount of this type of material to be administered in the library.
7. The school library should include an area for preparing in-

struction materials, the reproduction of printed materials, and the production of transparencies and overlays, slides, models, and other materials closely related to individual interests and not readily available from commercial sources. The area should include the materials and storage space necessary to complete adequately the job for which the room was intended.

8. The librarian in an elementary school should have her own office when the size of the school warrants it. If the size of the school makes this prohibitive, a special corner should be made available for the librarian's private use.

9. A workroom should be provided in the elementary school library for the library staff as well as for the pupils. The library staff can use the workroom for the technical processing of books and other materials, and the pupils can use the area for constructing individual, group, or class projects. The equipment should allow for an easy fulfillment of construction activities common to the elementary school.

10. Libraries in attendance units should house all of the print and nonprint materials needed to carry out the instructional program of the unit in question. They should also include print and nonprint materials that are used infrequently by any given teacher and can be profitably shared by many teachers. Enrichment materials should be housed in the same library. In some instances, it might be feasible to store textbooks and supplementary textbooks in the school library.

Even though it is a commonly held belief that flexibility in the use of the library should be determined by the curriculum and instructional program, it is evident from the list of specific facilities that flexibility in the use of the elementary school library is also a direct function of the variety in nature and design of facilities available. When elementary school libraries are well planned, certain facilities must be included to ensure maximum instructional flexibility even if they are not used in this way. It is good to have the facilities that are needed when educational innovation and expansion call for them. This is reason enough to plan elementary school libraries for adequate flexibility over a wide range of learning activities—now and in the future.

Accessibility

The elementary school library should be accessible to individuals needing to use it. Administrative decisions (such as using the library for a study hall) should not hinder the library from being a functionally related part of the instructional program. Keeping in focus the purpose of the elementary school library, decisions should make it always accessible to both teachers and pupils in their efforts to meet the learning demands of a broad instructional program. Library decisions should not in any way restrict the stimulation of independent study and research activities by teachers and pupils. The accessibility of a school library to its users can determine the part it will play in enriching, enhancing, and improving the school's instructional program.

Print and Nonprint Instructional Materials

The elementary school library should include both print and nonprint materials. If a library is to be well equipped to correlate with the expanded instruction and curriculum program at this level, it must have as part of its regular collection these instructional materials: books, filmstrips, maps, motion pictures, pamphlets, periodicals, phonograph records, slides, and tapes, as well as the equipment necessary to use them. This type of arrangement tends to locate print and nonprint materials in the same area and, as such, contributes to more efficient use of all types of materials.

When print and nonprint materials are located in the same area, more people are likely to use the facilities because they have more reasons for going to the area. Learning can be made more efficient because a variety of materials can be selected for a given activity in a place where it can be demonstrated how these materials are related. This arrangement contributes to the quality and effectiveness of teaching while improving the economic possibilities by saving searching and previewing time and by concentrating staff in a central location. Libraries that include print and nonprint materials become centers for instructional advice and resources and contribute more to the flexibility and efficiency of instructional programs.

Staff

The person trained primarily as a librarian or as an audiovisual materials specialist is not fully trained to handle the needs of an elementary school library as it is conceived in this discussion. Since the library is conceived as part of an instructional program, the staff should be committed primarily to enhancing the instructional program in the elementary school. Therefore, the library staff should have a wide background of knowledge of the elementary school curriculum and some of the learning activities that individual teachers use to teach this curriculum. Using this knowledge of the elementary school curriculum as a background, the library staff will be able to select, preview, evaluate, introduce, present, and suggest print and nonprint materials to individual teachers who are pursuing different purposes in their instruction. In addition to their knowledge of how print and nonprint materials are related to the instructional program, the elementary school librarian must know print and nonprint materials from the standpoint of classification, storage, cost, quality, appropriateness, new developments, and final location of materials. In short, the elementary school librarian is a resource person who is expected to aid individual teachers and pupils in carrying out the goals of the instructional program through the efficient and independent use and production of print and nonprint materials.

Staff responsibilities in elementary school libraries should be determined by the number of personnel available for any given unit. Every library in an attendance unit should have a staff member who serves as a resource person in print and nonprint materials as these relate to the instructional program. This means that the staff in individual attendance units must be acquainted thoroughly with the available print and nonprint materials and how these materials might be used to carry out the learning activities required by the instructional program. Not only is the staff personnel in the attendance units expected to have substantial knowledge about the print and nonprint materials now included in the unit but they are expected to select, study, and integrate new materials into the instructional program.

The responsibility allotted to individual staff members connected with elementary school libraries will be determined largely by the number of staff working in the unit. As the size of the staff increases, the tasks associated with operating the library can be divided according to the instructional program needs of the school being served. The responsibilities expected of the elementary school library staff should be divided to achieve a balance between the efficient use of presently held print and nonprint materials and the integration of new materials as they are made available. Staff duties should be divided to achieve this balance in the most efficient manner.

It should be apparent from this discussion that the elementary school library is the critical resource affecting the facility with which teachers can implement an effective and efficient instructional program. The school library cannot be replaced by classroom or system-wide libraries for a number of important instructional and logistical reasons. In the former instance, students in a given classroom will not need to use the same print and nonprint materials at the same time. It would be wasteful to deny others the use of materials not being used in individual classrooms and to detract from meaningful activity by moving these materials from classroom to classroom. In addition, there would be a tendency to unnecessarily duplicate holdings and thus lower the efficient use of available space for construction and storage. On the other hand, a system-wide library presents too many administrative and logistical problems to be either effective or efficient for implementing the instructional program. It would make the exploration of certain problem areas or topics difficult if not impossible because teachers would have to know all of their needs in advance. This is not always possible or desirable. Similarly, individual students could not conduct independent study and research over a wide range of topics without severe loss of time and needed guidance from the teacher. For these and other reasons, individual classroom and system-wide libraries must be supplemental to the efficient implementation of the instructional program.

The System-Wide Library

The library for a school system should be an instructional materials resource center. Print and nonprint materials that are not commonly used to carry out instructional programs in individual attendance units, but may be used by individual teachers with special interests, should be housed here. These special interests might deal with personal hobbies, art, music, dance, outdoor activities, and arts and crafts. The system library might be used to supplement library holdings in individual attendance units. In some instances, the system library might be used to distribute new materials and announcements about them to personnel in libraries located in individual attendance units. For the most part, the system library should include those print and nonprint materials and special collections that might help to enhance and enrich instructional programs throughout the system. These materials should be the type that are not used in all schools at the same time and, therefore, lend themselves to a sharing scheme.

The staff at the system library level serve as resource personnel for the attendance unit staff. Coordination, implementation, and dissemination of information should be the prime responsibility of staff in the system-wide library facility. The central staff can be of service to the staff located in the attendance unit by aiding them in the acquisition of new skills, learning about new materials, and relieving them of unnecessary bookkeeping chores for the central office.

The relationship between the system-wide library and the instructional program at the elementary school level is dependent on the sensitivity of the respective staffs to the needs and requirements evident in both instances. Ultimately, all library resources must be judged by their effects on the total instructional program. Given this expectation, these resources must be designed and deployed to enhance the effectiveness of the instructional program. Knowledge and understanding of the instructional program are essential in order to achieve this state of affairs.

The Classroom Library

Library materials needed to carry out the daily routine instructional activities should be included in all classrooms. Therefore, materials in individual classrooms should be those that are frequently required to complete basic daily learning tasks required to conduct the instructional program. In order to deal effectively with the instructional demands of a given elementary class, each classroom should be provided with a reading table and at least one bookcase large enough to accommodate from fifty to one hundred books. There should be at least one file cabinet to store nonprint materials. The classroom collection of print and nonprint materials should be a *changing collection*. The teacher should assume the responsibility, with some assistance and advice from his students and the school librarian, for changing the classroom collection or any part of it as children have completed reading and research activities and specific learning tasks suggested by selected content areas. This temporary classroom collection serves as an on-the-spot reservoir that provides the necessary breadth and depth of content for conducting some instructional learning tasks, facilitates recreational reading for students during free time periods, and supplies the teacher with a varied selection of materials to match with the relevant characteristics of the pupils to be taught.

Some reference materials should be thought of as part of the permanent collection of materials in the classroom. Those materials include such items as dictionaries, sets of encyclopedias, atlases, special indexes, almanacs, and how-to-do-it-type books. For the most part, these reference materials can be employed repeatedly across a number of learning tasks to achieve goals specified in different content areas. In addition, continued practice with reference materials has the potential for aiding learning in the future because the skills and habits learned are highly transferable to intellectual pursuits in other settings—both real and contrived.

The Instructional Materials Center's Role in Implementing the Teaching Strategy

The traditional concept of a library has been expanded to take into account the availability and use of different kinds of media to aid children in the effective and efficient completion and mastery of meaningful learning tasks. This expanded concept of the school library is popularly known as the Instructional Materials Center (IMC). Even though the school IMC is the major resource needed to conduct the instructional program, it is evident that the classroom and system-wide collections of print and nonprint materials are a critical supplement to the IMC's offerings. And as such, these three types of library services have to be considered as interdependent partners in providing comprehensive instructional materials and resources required to conduct the instructional program.

There is a critical relationship between the IMC and the implementation of a teaching strategy. In an earlier discussion in Chapter 5, teaching strategy was defined as "a pattern of decisions in the acquisition, retention, and utilization of information that serves to meet certain objectives, that is, to ensure certain forms of outcomes and to guard against others." The teaching strategy is primarily a description of the processes to be employed to utilize the collections in the IMC to put the instructional program into operation. To the extent that the IMC is limited, the teaching strategy will also be limited even though a given teaching strategy might facilitate more learning than the available resources suggest. The main point here is the recognition that the basis for formulating and implementing a teaching strategy starts with the IMC. The range and scope of instructional planning must be consistent with the availability of appropriate materials and resources housed in the IMC. When the available collections in the IMC are unknown, formulating a teaching strategy is both meaningless and basically unproductive. Therefore, the formulation and implementation of a teaching strategy begins in the IMC.

The IMC and Classroom Management

Even though a thorough discussion of classroom management might be helpful to the reader, it is not within the scope of this present discussion. However, Johnson and Bany have done an excellent job in discussing classroom management in their book *Classroom Management: Theory and Skill Training*. This book is well worth the time for a student of teaching and its problems. For our discussion, the issues of interest can be covered by utilizing the comments indicated by Johnson and Bany when they assert that:

> The management aspect of teaching involves establishing and maintaining an internal environment which encourages the release of human potential, and which enables children working together in classroom groups to perform effectively and efficiently to attain educational objectives. In other words, it is the management dimension of teaching that makes it possible for individuals to make their own best contributions to achieve and attain educational goals. Clearly, teachers cannot perform in this dimension if they do not know what functions are needed to develop this environment, or understand the many factors which affect this area of operations.[12]

The way in which these authors discuss classroom management is closely related to the discussion of teaching tactics presented in Chapter 5. Accordingly, a teaching tactic was defined as *the skillful arranging and ordering of methods and procedures used to achieve certain objectives while guarding against unwanted ones.* Classroom management includes the implementation of the teaching tactic.

Before one can relate classroom management problems to the use of the IMC, some specific indication of the nature of these problems is necessary. Johnson and Bany provide us with some insight in the following comments:

Hundreds of descriptions of classroom management problems, which in one way or another affect the learning and instructional processes, are unmanageable. Although the sources of management problems differ, outward manifestations of behavior are limited in number. Children talk at inappropriate times, they delay work processes, engage in disputes and conflicts, react with indifference and lack of interest, and fail to follow prescribed procedures. They quarrel, fight, resist, protest, and fail to cooperate. Of course, many class groups exhibit such behavior to a very limited degree, but when management problems occur, they are concerned with one or more of the problems described.[13]

A quick look at some of the classroom management problems indicated by Johnson and Bany suggests that student use of the IMC presents the teacher with a number of control problems if the learning experience is to be meaningful to a large number of learners. The effective and efficient use of the IMC is directly tied to a teacher's classroom management skills. If a teacher is unable to control the behavior of students, the IMC fails to provide students with the kind of learning environment intended for learners. Self-discipline is necessary for a meaningful exploration of an enriched environment.

The IMC and Teacher Preparation

In addition to acquiring skills for doing critical reading, teachers must spend time and a great deal of effort in practicing the skills and procedures, and perfecting the techniques required to use specialized print and nonprint materials. Teachers should be aware of all the types of reference materials that can be profitably used by their students. It is necessary to know specifically what the intended use of each instructional resource is and the exact steps a user should follow to properly use a particular resource. For example, a teacher should know the different types of dictionaries that are available and should be able to use selected dictionaries according to the suggested pattern of the publisher. A teacher who has not learned to use a dictionary correctly, or read a map or atlas, cannot teach students to use these resources properly. In short, teachers must prepare themselves to use the actual print and nonprint materials contained in the IMC if they expect to be proficient in utilizing these resources to effectively and efficiently implement the instructional program. To ensure this, teachers must be helped to acquire the skill and experience associated with the appropriate use of available print and nonprint materials in the IMC.

Integrating New Technology into the Instructional Program

One of the persistent problems facing any instructional effort is associated with how to integrate new technology into the instructional program. As new technology is formulated and designed for facilitating learning tasks, teachers redesign some of their teaching strategies in order to accommodate the suggested innovation. In some instances the new technology is a definite procedural and conceptual improvement over technology presently employed to implement the instructional program. However, too often the new technology tries to be too many things to too many people and loses power in terms of adaptability to specific learning problems presented to selected students. It is also evident that much of the new technology is constructed with an instructional design as its basis that may be inconsistent with the instructional design presently employed by the teacher. Problems associated with lack of knowledge of availability, evidence of effectiveness, and unwanted side effects with selected groups of learners, as well as with skill in operating the associated machinery and insufficient time to properly study new technology make integrating new technology into the ongoing instructional program a particularly tough problem for teachers. This being the case, it is possible that the technology needed to achieve a given result with a selected group of students is available but unknown to, or out of the reach of, the teacher. It is not enough to have a firm grasp of the nature of the instructional program to make the proper decisions needed to integrate new technology. A thorough knowledge of the new technology and how it might relate to the instructional program is a first step to any meaningful integration experience.

Summary

In this chapter we described analytically how instructional materials and resources relate to the instructional program of the elementary school. The instructional program of the elementary school is theoretically and structurally tied to the curriculum and the way it is implemented. Implementation of the instructional program is dependent to a large extent on the nature of the materials and resources available to the pupils and teachers. Instructional materials are broader than the subject-matter content of the organized knowledge field from which it was taken because they also deal with the packaging of knowledge for use with a selected group of learners and teachers in different settings. Instructional materials are governed by rules that extend beyond the criteria guiding subject-matter content utilized and the medium of communication employed. A systematic study of instructional materials suggests that they encompass the subject matter, the learner, the instructional intent, the teacher, and the setting for presentation.

Instructional materials are intended to order the intentional cognitive processes of learners along dimensional lines that are consistent with the purpose or instructional objective guiding the intellectual activity in question. In order to accomplish this intent, instructional materials must accurately substitute vicarious experiences for real-life experiences that represent the social functions that maintain and enhance the quality of life. Instructional resources supplement or expand the experiences provided to learners through the use of instructional materials and often fall outside the teacher's direct and sole control. Instructional materials and resources are related to the instructional program because they define operationally what is to be manipulated by the teacher as he interacts with pupils for the attainment of educational objectives. Without instructional materials and resources there could not be an instructional program because there would be no basis for the teacher and pupil to interact for the attainment of publicly determined educational objectives. In short, instructional materials and resources are the fundamental units of the instructional program and, as such, help to determine the extent of the relationship such a program is likely to have with a given set of learners.

References

1. John F. Putnam and W. Dale Chismore, eds., *Standard Terminology for Curriculum and Instruction in Local and State School Systems,* State Educational Records and Report Series, Handbook IV (Washington, D.C.: Department of Health, Education and Welfare, National Center for Educational Statistics, 1970), p. 3.
2. Ibid.
3. P. J. Runkel, "Cognitive Similarity in Facilitating Communication," *Sociometry,* **19**:178–191 (1956).

4. Dorothy G. Petersen, *The Elementary School Teacher* (New York: Appleton, 1964), p. 407.
5. G. W. Sowards and M. M. Scobey, *The Changing Curriculum and the Elementary Teacher* (Belmont, Cal.: Wadsworth, 1961), p. 445. As adapted from Edgar Dale, *Audio-Visual Methods in Teaching,* rev. ed. (New York: Dryden Press, 1956), p. 43, copyright 1954, Holt, Rinehart & Winston, Inc.
6. A. A. Lumsdaine, "Instruments and Media of Instruction," in N. L. Gage, ed., *Handbook of Research on Teaching* (Chicago: Rand McNally, 1963), p. 584.
7. Fred P. Barnes, "Instructional Materials and Curriculum Decisions," in Merle M. Ohlsen, ed., *Modern Methods in Elementary Education* (New York: Holt, 1959), p. 112.
8. Ibid., pp. 111–146.
9. Ibid., p. 122.
10. Ibid.
11. "The EPIE Forum," *Educational Products Information Exchange Institute,* 1:1 (Sept. 1967).
12. Louis V. Johnson and Mary A. Bany, *Classroom Management: Theory and Skill Training* (New York: Macmillan, 1970), p. 44.
13. Ibid., p. 45.

The Professional
Staff of the
Elementary School

The professional staff of the elementary school includes the principal, supervisors, special teachers (art, music, physical education, and so on), teachers, teacher-interns, teacher associates, teacher assistants, and teacher aides. All of these staff roles are considered professional in the sense that those who fill them share the responsibility for providing a well-rounded instructional experience for elementary schoolchildren. The key professional staff role in the elementary school is the classroom teacher. All other staff performing professional activity serve as the supporting cast for the classroom teacher. Since this is the case, our primary focus is on the classroom teacher and how other members of the staff complement him in providing a meaningful instructional experience for all the students.

Any attempt to discuss the professional staff of the elementary school must take into account certain categories that tend to describe and define it in functional terms and as it relates to the instructional program. These categories include the purpose of the elementary school, the characteristics of its pupils, the requirements of the related learning tasks, the nature of the instructional setting, the expectations of the public, and the perception of the teacher. Each of the categories has a number of operational subparts that may vary in significance from one situation to another. For example, in some communities, emphasis is placed on the elementary school's purpose to prepare children for learning what is taught at the next highest level of schooling, whereas in other communities this would not be emphasized greatly. The possible combinations of emphasis on the subparts of major categories is unlimited across instructional settings. However, the general characteristic of each category seems to be similar across all settings characterizing the elementary school, that is, most elementary schools try to avoid extreme positions on any of the categories. It is these general characteristics of categories that enables us to provide a framework for discussing the professional staff of the elementary school.

Evaluating the Quality of the Professional Staff

In order to evaluate the quality of the professional staff, one must establish the nature of the expectations that define the associated roles. The role expectations must be dealt with to the extent possible, in terms of the instructional environment that serves as the setting for fulfilling those roles. To accomplish this task, the elementary school-teacher is discussed using the categories indicated earlier. All other members of the professional staff of the elementary school are discussed in terms of the individual classroom teacher. It is our intent to establish a base line for evaluating the professional staff of the elementary school. Our concern with evaluating this staff closely parallels that expressed by Barzun in his work *Teacher in America*. According to this author's conclusion, an evaluation of professional staff might be described as follows:

> Hence tomorrow's problem will not be to get teachers but to recognize the good ones and not discourage them before they have done their stint. In an age of big words and little work, any liberal profession takes some sticking to, not only in order to succeed, but in order to keep faith with oneself. Teaching is such a profession. Why does it exist and what is it like? The public thinks it knows from its own experience of school. Ideally, teaching is ever the same, but teachers have changed since the days when aged Headmasters reminisced in mellow volumes, and the question I must really answer is what is teaching like now?[1]

That is precisely the question we propose to answer in this section.

The Elementary School as a
Guide for Staff Evaluation

Before any position on the evaluation of the professional staff at the elementary school level can be taken, it is necessary to provide a conceptualization of the expected educational experience that is unique and common at this level in the educational hierarchy. This step provides a description of an environmental setting that enables us to pinpoint relevant boundaries for formulating criteria and setting standards for making judgments about the products of the elementary school experience. Without such a conceptualization of the elementary school, evaluation of the professional staff would have little meaning in terms of the role expectations at this level of involvement. In an effort to conceptualize the elementary school, Russell suggests that:

> The elementary school is the basis of all education. It must therefore be the school where the first steps toward rationality are taken.[2]

It is at the elementary school level that a child's emotional and rational skills for successfully completing learning tasks are developed and nurtured. At this point children learn about the necessity of schooling as a critical component in life experience. To learn and to accept the necessity of school is to value education as an integral part of life experience and to develop a healthy respect for the dimension it brings toward the enrichment of the human experience.

The elementary school is basically a training ground for initiating, developing, and extending the rationality of young children. Rationality is fostered in the main by a series of informal and formal interactions between teachers and pupils, pupils and pupils, pupils and content, pupils and activities, and pupils and experiences. The character, shape, nature, and results of the rationality developed by individual pupils will vary widely because no two learners will experience the exact same program at the elementary school level. Given this state of affairs, rationality at the elementary school level cannot be narrowly conceived or prescribed. In order to be meaningful, rationality at the elementary school level must be considered within the context of children's positive acceptance of the setting as a congenial place to be and work, and in terms of the characteristics that are unique to the elementary school. The unique characteristics of this level of educational experience provide a specific point-by-point description of the daily operation and conceptualization of the elementary school. A brief discussion of these characteristics should orient the reader to the environmental setting that influences the requirements and responsibilities of the professional staff in the elementary school.

Developmental Impact

The elementary school exerts the greatest impact on the intellectual, emotional, and social development of children of any school in the educational hierarchy. This situation results from the fact that the elementary school deals with children who are at the most impressionable stage in their development, that much of the content is new to them, and that the event of schooling represents a major experience or adventure in their lives. These factors give the elementary school a tremendous advantage because it represents for most children their first full-scale experience with systematic learning in an institutional setting over an extended period of time. In addition, the year spent at the kindergarten level represents approximately one fifth of the entire time the average child having this experience has been alive. Contrast this with the year the average child spends at the twelfth-grade level, the accumulated educational experience (twelve years) makes this particular school experience one thirteenth of his formal schooling and less than one eighteenth of his life existence and, as such, has much less impact on his personal development. In short, the tenth-, eleventh-, and twelfth-grade levels represent approximately the same percentage of time in the school experience that the year spent at the kindergarten level represents in the entire life existence of the learner. The three grade levels represent 25 per cent of a student's school experience whereas the year spent in kindergarten represents 20 per cent of the time the child has been alive. Another way to visualize this whole problem was masterfully suggested in the following comments by Jackson:

> Thus if a student never misses a day during the year, he spends a little more than one thousand hours under the care and tutelage of teachers. If he has attended kindergarten and was reasonably regular in his attendance during the grades, he will have logged a little more than seven thousand classroom hours by the time he is ready for the junior high school.
>
> The magnitude of 7,000 hours spread over six or seven years of a child's life is difficult to comprehend. On the other hand, when placed beside the total number of hours the child has lived during these years it is not very great—slightly more than one-tenth of his life during the

time in question, about one-third of his hours of sleep during that period. On the other hand, aside from sleeping, and perhaps playing, there is no other activity that occupies as much of the child's time as that involved in attending school. Apart from the bedroom (where he has his eyes closed most of the time) there is no single enclosure in which he spends a longer time than he does in the classroom. From the age of six onward he is a more familiar sight to his teacher than to his father, and possibly even his mother.[3]

It is easy to see by this example that the elementary school is virtually the whole of the society for a child outside the home. In terms of demands on the use of the child's time, the school may have an edge on the home. There is little doubt that the elementary school as an agency purposely designed to influence young children has a decided opportunity to impress profoundly their intellectual, emotional, and social development. In this respect the elementary school is probably the most influential institution in the life experience of children.

Foundation for Learning

The elementary school is responsible for teaching the basic skills of communication and computation that provide the foundation for all later learning. Since all rational inquiry is dependent on the development of the skill and knowledge foundations, the elementary school's pivotal role in determining the shape of the rational processes children will acquire is readily apparent and significant. Through the proper learning and interaction of basic skills and knowledge in selected content areas, children at the elementary school level become oriented to the major divisions of ideas about the human experience. The pattern set by the elementary school's efforts to provide children with a foundation for learning important intellectual ideas will determine the extent to which these children will be able to extract practical and personal meaning from the subject-matter environment that characterizes school and life experience as they get older.

The elementary school also provides children with a socialization experience that determines how they think and feel about themselves in groups. In this sense the elementary school provides the foundation for the development of a child's self-concept. Since the self-concept a child acquires is so critical to his future success, this characteristic of the elementary school is quite influential in determining how children are likely to interact in other institutional and group settings in later life. At the elementary school level a child can learn how to learn, and learn that he can learn independently and with a degree of satisfaction that encourages later learning. By the same token, a child can learn that he cannot learn generally or selectively across certain subject-matter areas and can convince himself that learning is difficult and distasteful.

During their elementary school experience children learn social skills that can only be acquired in this kind of setting. It is during this experience that children begin to compare and contrast themselves with others of their age over a number of learning tasks and activities. Children learn to compete, to succeed, to fail, to work with others and independently, and to perceive themselves as members of a group during their elementary school experience. This is the beginning of acquiring a sense of place in the society. In this sense the elementary school plays a critical role in building the total social foundation requirement of children and, as such, helps to determine how children will live out their social existence in the institutional settings that define our society.

Universality

The elementary school is, for all practical purposes, the only universal school experience available to all the nation's children. This conclusion is supported by data presented in the *Digest of Educational Statistics* for 1972, which provides the following data:

> Specifically, the following percentages of the school age population are estimated to be enrolled: Of the 5-year-olds (the usual kindergarten age), 84 percent; 6- to 13-year-olds (grades one to eight), 99 percent; 14- to 17-year-olds (grades nine to 12), 94 percent; and 18- to 24-year-olds (college age), 30 percent.[4]

Almost every child in the United States has, and avails himself of, the opportunity to attend an elementary school. Even though universal education is fast becoming the case at higher levels of education, it is only a fact at the elementary school level. This fact gives the elementary school a unique position in the total experience of all American children. As the universal school, the elementary school is a part of every child's personal experience.

Process Orientation

The elementary school is primarily and of necessity oriented toward teaching children processes as opposed to heavy concentrations of substantive knowledge. Even though subject-matter content is basic material used to help children acquire rational processes, the elementary school does not focus on this knowledge as the end result of its mission. The elementary school is alone in its orientation toward teaching children processes over substantive knowledge and, as such, is easily distinguished by this characteristic.

Critical Role

The elementary school plays such a critical role in the lives of children because failure at this level usually means failure at subsequent levels in school or in life experience. If the elementary school is not successful in its essential functions, then the children who use it will have deficiencies that adversely affect their performance throughout life. These deficiencies are not as likely to be overcome if they persist throughout children's developmental years. This is ample support for trying to ensure the continued success of the elementary school experience for all children.

Criteria and Standards

The criteria and standards for judging the effectiveness of the elementary school cannot be formulated from school experiences external to its primary focus. Standards that are set for judging the success of schooling at other levels are inappropriate for judging the products and outcomes of the elementary school. Since the elementary school is unique as an experience for young children, criteria and standards for judging that experience must evolve from, or be based on, the intent and requirements of the educational experience sought. The needs and practices of the schools at higher levels should not determine what children should study and learn in the elementary school. Just because young children can learn certain intellectual content earlier is no justification for requiring them to do so. In the final analysis, the elementary school's criteria and standards for judging its efforts must focus on the nature of its mission as an institution charged with the responsibility of orienting young people to the processes and foundation skills of human activity. This mission must form the basis for determining the criteria and standards for judging the elementary school.

We have discussed some unique characteristics of the elementary school as a starting point for evaluating its professional staff. Even though these comments are suggestive, they cannot, and probably should not, be prescriptive. For our purposes, the reader should have acquired a feel for the critical role that the elementary school plays in the lives of children because of its unique characteristics. This orientation is important for considering the requirements expected of the professional staff who are asked to carry out the mission of the elementary school. Russell furnishes us with an appropriate summary of our discussion in the following comments:

> The modern elementary school seeks greater intellectual resources for individual study, recognizing the diversity required to satisfy many children's needs: books, films, field trips, simulated model situations, plays, exercises—in short many different mediums to insure increased involvement by individuals in getting experiences which feed individual growth.
>
> The school is also greatly concerned with the motivation of its pupils, recognizing that the child's learning is a function of his motivation. Thus the school is engaged in a self-conscious search for an atmosphere of congeniality. It is a school in which every child present senses the respect for him, irrespective of his background or his color or his religion; he is recognized for the human promise that he is.[5]

Cooperative Teacher Education: A Meaningful Partnership of Public School Systems and Universities

This section is based on the premise that the public school system and the teacher education institutions should cooperatively train teachers and staff for the elementary school. Until now the teacher training institutions have had the primary responsibility for training teachers and staff who conduct the professional tasks of the instructional program in the elementary school. In recent years serious questions about the validity of having teachers receive training in programs conceived, conducted, appraised, and controlled entirely by a teacher education institution without adequate participation by professional educators who work in the public schools have arisen. This situation has led to the continued separation of theory and practice as a general way in which to view the education of teachers. Theory is thought to be the contribution of higher educational institutions, and practice is thought to be the contribution of experience gained from working with children in classrooms. Increasingly, professional educators from both ends of the theory-practice continuum agree that a rational way to bring the two areas together as an organic whole for educating teachers for effective instruction in tomorrow's classrooms is a critical step in tailoring the school experience to foster appropriate individual development and to meet the needs of society. This is possible if teacher education institutions and public school systems assume cooperative responsibility for the education of elementary schoolteachers.

Before one can propose a cooperative teacher education training program for elementary schoolteachers, it is necessary to provide a general notion of what is expected of these teachers at this level. In this respect, the following statement by Conant seems to be an appropriate descriptive match when he asserts:

> Clearly, whether [elementary school] teachers of the future are to teach all subjects in a self-contained classroom or are to be specialists teaching only one subject throughout the grades is profoundly significant in considering the education these teachers are to receive. What one needs is a reliable crystal, for prophecy must precede planning. My guess is that, in spite of all the talk about the importance of specialists in the elementary school, *self-contained classrooms will continue to be the dominant pattern for kindergarten and the first three grades during the next ten years.* During these years, however, there will be *an increasing tendency to use specialists in grades four through six.* It follows, then, that teachers for kindergarten and the first three grades must be prepared as generalists capable of handling all the subjects appropriate for these early childhood years. Their repertoire of skills must include special competence in the teaching of reading. Because of the variety of patterns of classroom organization likely to be encountered in grades four through six, the teacher for these grades also is advised to have familiarity with a variety of subjects. But, since the demand for specialization is increasing, the teacher of these grades should also possess depth in a single subject or combination of related subjects taught in the elementary school.[6]

Conant's general description of the instructional requirements facing the majority of elementary schoolteachers is still an accurate picture of general expectations at this level. In the main, most teacher education institutions that train elementary schoolteachers have changed their programs to conform to the requirements suggested by the recommendations made by Conant in *The Education of American Teachers.** For our purposes it is unnecessary to describe and justify a particular teacher education program for elementary schoolteachers because that approach usually

* Anyone interested in background information on teacher education programs will find this book very helpful.

leans too heavily on factors that do not include the classroom teacher and his supporting staff in their natural setting of operation as would be the case in a cooperative program in teacher education. Most educators concede that higher education institutions are best equipped to offer prerequisite educational experiences in general studies or special areas of concentration that are unavailable in the public schools. These areas can readily serve as the basis for separating mutually exclusive domains of the two institutions in terms of educating elementary school-teachers. However, the domains of these two institutions converge when professional educational experiences of teachers are considered. This is the case because it is widely believed (and generally accepted) that "laboratory experiences" in "real" classroom settings will substantially increase the meaning, acceptance, and effectiveness of professional (education, methods) educational experiences in preparing teachers to implement effectively and efficiently the instructional program of the elementary school. It is at this point that a cooperative teacher education experience becomes a necessary requirement if the expectations of both the teacher education institution and the public school system are to be met.

A proposal for teacher education institutions and public school systems to cooperate in providing the professional education experiences for teachers is not new to most educators. The form of cooperation that is most familiar to professional educators is suggested by Conant's description of an appropriate practice teaching experience in the following comments:

> I have already presented my case for requiring all teachers to prove their competence during a period of practice teaching. Such practice teaching is to be done in close cooperation with the school board and under conditions approved by state officials; the university or college professor responsible is to be the clinical professor. He is to be responsible for arranging the teaching experience and together with the cooperating teacher for assessing the competence of the student.[7]

This notion of cooperation falls short of the requirements of a cooperative teacher education program because of one role it expects university or college staff to play with adequate input from the professional staff of the public school and its constituency. In the first place, the casting of the university or college staff person in the role of a "clinical professor" suggests that he operate under the following conditions:

1. He is able to observe specific behaviors and infer specific traits that foster understanding of an individual's actions or characteristics in a given situation.

2. In addition to a description of observed behaviors, he is to suggest remediation for deficiencies detected.
3. His intuitive judgment can be substituted for measurement.
4. He can intuitively integrate measurement findings with direct observation.
5. He can summarize and evaluate a complex interaction of human behaviors related to the successful completion of learning tasks in different subject areas.
6. He can recommend specific actions that will qualitatively alter the interrelationships and learning outcomes of future educational experiences.

Even though most educators agree that being able to employ these skills would probably contribute significantly toward improving the instructional programs in the elementary school, few believe that a university or college staff person could perform these skills with the necessary competence across different classrooms, student teachers, and public school staff. Most professional educators have come to believe that those skills can only be demonstrated by a trained person who works daily with children in classrooms in a variety of situations. It is believed that without this continued experience requirement, there is little possibility that a teacher trainer will be able to be a "clinical professor" for prospective teachers. Given this view, increasing numbers of professional educators believe that public school teachers would be the logical choice as clinical professors for training prospective teachers.

Another aspect of this teacher-training issue is associated with the suggestion that the university or college staff be responsible for arranging the teaching experience and, if they are to be responsible for arranging teacher experience, assess the competence of the student teachers together with the cooperating teacher. According to this line of thinking, competence should be assessed in relation to the relevance of the instructional intent and the total development of the learners expected. Therefore, the teaching experience that prospective teachers should have can best be determined by those who have intimate knowledge of the task expectations presented by young learners in classroom settings. Again, this is an argument for the public school teacher to take the teaching role in providing teacher training experiences.

This analogy referring to student teaching is similar (with minor variations) to other professional experiences such as methods courses in education. For the most part, professional educators believe that these courses should be taught in laboratory settings and that public school teachers should have the greatest influence over their development and implementation. In keeping with this view of the training requirements for prospective teachers, cooperative teacher education means that the university or college staff will cooperate with the professional staff of the elementary school in providing the professional education experiences for prospective teachers.

It appears that there is a power struggle on between the "outside expert" and the professional staff of the elementary school for the right to provide the primary professional educational experience for the prospective teacher. Past attempts to provide this professional educational experience cooperatively have been heavily weighted toward the desires of the "outside expert." Presently there is a widespread acceptance of the idea that the professional staff of the elementary school should direct the professional educational experience of prospective teachers in classrooms and other school settings. This notion changes the focus from "in cooperation with" to "cooperative" with the professional staff of the elementary school, which determines the teaching and learning experiences prospective teachers should have before they are given the responsibility of planning and conducting the instructional program of a group of children.

Cooperative Teacher Education

Values and quality experiences can be gained from substantive involvement of the professional staff of the elementary school in the education of prospective teachers—the cooperative approach—as contrasted with a situation in which the university or college staff dictates the nature of the professional training experience—the expert approach. Our discussion suggests that these approaches are on opposite ends of the teacher training continuum as they are presently practiced in most schools. The former approach has the total involvement of the professional staff of the elementary school (cooperative) and the latter mostly excludes the professional staff when the professional training experience is being formulated and developed (expert). These two extremes in teacher education are presently in open warfare in an increasing number of places. Even though the ultimate goal—more effective and competent educators—of the two positions is the same, the payoff in educational gains is likely to differ widely over time.

One of the promising patterns geared to foster cooperative teacher education is the teacher center concept. As Stephen Bailey described it:

> Teacher centers are just what the term implies: local physical facilities
> and self-improvement programs organized and run by the teachers

themselves for purposes of upgrading educational performance. Their primary function is to make possible a review of existing curricula and other educational practices by groups of teachers and to encourage teacher attempts to bring about changes.[8]

Viewed in the context of cooperative teacher education, teacher centers could represent a fundamental change in teacher and pupil performance for three important reasons:

1. The improvement of professional teacher education is dependent on the basic involvement and direction of teachers charged with the responsibility of delivering the instructional program.
2. Teachers are not likely to perform in a certain way because an expert tells them to do so.
3. Teachers are likely to take attempts to train them seriously only when they are responsible for defining their own educational problems, delineating their own needs, and receiving help on their own terms and turf.

The reasons outlined suggest that cooperative teacher education requires teachers to provide the necessary leadership in determining the nature of valid professional teacher training. The author's analysis of different approaches to teacher training leads to the conclusion that teacher centers can serve as the base setting for a cooperative teacher education program. Now we can turn our attention to how the professional staff of the elementary school might cooperate with teacher education institutions in training preservice and in-service teachers.

Cooperative teacher education aims at increasing opportunities for teacher growth in the most realistic and accessible laboratory available—the school itself—as opposed to carrying out the professional training function in substitute settings provided by schools of education. The latter approach tends to pursue skills, knowledge, and attitudes that enhance theoretical instruction rather than the processes and skills to be employed in the natural habitat of teaching: the school. This change in the training environment provides an opportunity for the teacher to learn his professional skills in the actual work setting with its rituals, expectations, constraints, opportunities, and incentives in proper dynamic perspective. Since this kind of environmental setting is a replica of the milieu of a teacher's professional life, the skills obtained can be practiced in the context of their continued use in providing educational experiences for youth. The schools are the ultimate simulated training environment wherein prospective and practicing teachers can learn and practice behaviors, tactics, techniques, and procedures that enable them to select and process information, manipulate materials, utilize and teach a complex of skills to achieve instructional goals and influence student learning in a desirable direction. The schools are the only laboratory wherein teachers can have these experiences in the context of their expected use and deployment.

All teacher education programs should have as their primary goal the modification of teacher performance for the purpose of improving student learning while adhering to actions that are consistent with society's cherished values. For our purposes, *teacher performance refers to actions that relate to specified objectives that guide the display of a teacher's professional behavioral patterns to influence student learning through specific instruction.* A teacher's performance can be observed, assessed, and evaluated in relation to accepted procedures for handling certain ideas in different subject-matter areas, under a variety of conditions, and with children of different experience backgrounds. However, the construction of that program must be built partly on the nature of the role of situational variables (for example, complexity and nature of subject matter, background and ability of teachers, background and ability of students to be served, logistical support systems, certification requirements and standards, expectations of community members, and social demands to be made on graduates) employed to determine criteria and standards to judge teacher performance during their preservice and in-service experiences. Because many of the situational variables involve knowledge that can only be gained as a result of the practice of teaching, in-service teachers should contribute greatly to the formulation, implementation, and evaluation of teacher education programs. Accordingly, cooperative teacher education appears to be the pattern that will ensure the greatest input of in-service teachers in influencing the direction of teacher education.

In the main, cooperative teacher education must be a system that permits interested parties to act as equal partners. Insofar as the education of teachers is concerned, the interested parties include the university, public school personnel, parents, community leaders and members, and students. The problem facing such a program is related to how these interested parties are dealt into the pattern to be employed for providing the educational experience to prospective and practicing teachers. This approach to teacher education assumes that educational theory and practice are not separate entities. As a consequence, practicum opportunities become basic to the conduct of a teacher education program. The validity of that practicum experience increases when public school personnel are permitted to provide the realistic opportunities that become the integral part in the development of a teacher education program. When public school personnel play an integral role in the formulation and delivery of a teacher education program, there is a greater probability that work reality will influence teachers from the very beginning. This should more closely correlate training with the role teachers are expected to play as they work with students.

The nature and form of a cooperative teacher education program must be based on how one conceptualizes the elementary school. This enables the designer of such a program to gear the experiences to the requirements of the elementary school. In planning a cooperative teacher education program, it should be noted that our society, with its democratic tradition as a setting for the elementary school, implies a commitment to the values and principles of democracy, a democratic environment, and democratic procedures. Even though the practice of democracy is in rapid transition—consistent with and away from the ideal at the same time—the elementary school must help children learn to accept and practice the basic tenets of our democratic state.

Since Americans have a basic commitment to universal education for all citizens, universal education implies that the primary role of the elementary school is that of general education for all children. This school must provide the foundation for "learning how to learn" and learning what is important to learn. As part of this general education function, the elementary school is expected to complete three major functions: (1) the intellectual function, (2) the socialization function, and (3) the self-concept development function. In fulfilling the general education role and in discharging these three major functions, the elementary school must be committed to providing for equal educational opportunity, all aspects of positive and meaningful human development, cooperative working relationships with the home and other community agencies, and an environmental setting that enables children to learn acceptable ways of social interaction and self-development. In short, the major concerns of the elementary school should include the following:

1. The personality and attitude development of young children in individual and group situations.
2. The personal and social problems that children face individually and in groups.
3. The daily pressures upon children.
4. The fullest possible development of the intellectual and creative abilities of each child.

5. The nourishment and development of children's appetites for learning.
6. The nature of children's relation with, and the influence of, peer society.

These concerns form the bases for any cooperative teacher education program because they represent the broad categories of demands that face teachers in the elementary schools. Therefore, the program that provides these teachers with basic training should enable them to deal effectively with the basic concerns of the elementary school.

Supervision in Cooperative Teacher Education

Supervision as a professional role in American schools has meant anything from a "teacher of teachers" to an "inspector" of teachers and programs, to "change agent" for instructional programs, to "constructor" of new programs for selected groups of teachers and students, and to a consultative relationship to interested parties in the educational enterprise. In the consultative relationship, the role of supervision is based on a peer relationship that can be aborted by either person at any time when either of them feels that progress toward a specified goal is lacking. Supervision today implies a "working with" people relationship that is judged in relation to task completion rather than the authority position of the supervisor. This style and new role of supervision is uniquely suited to the requirements of cooperative teacher education because it is attuned to the realities of providing for input from all interested parties in the education of teachers.

As teachers organize into unions and invoke sanctions through the use of collective negotiations to define and protect the professional status of teachers, the role of the supervisor is shaped in ways that cannot be easily influenced by him. When teachers negotiate directly with the sources of revenue and legal control—the school board, the state legislature, or the governor—supervisors are expected to manage conditions and policy resulting from agreements that they had little, if any, influence in determining. This situation in effect changes the role of supervision to that of a consultative relationship because of the requirement to work on problems identified and formulated by others. Cooperative teacher education recognizes that the problems of teaching should be defined by practicing teachers who should have a great deal to say about the training of those proposed as prospective members of their ranks. The new role of supervision fits the changing role of teachers and teacher training programs that is evident in cooperative teacher education programs.

It should be noted that cooperative teacher education places a heavy premium on an apprentice type of on-the-job training for prospective teachers with practicing teachers in real classrooms. It is basically an antitheoretical stance that assumes that the classroom teacher can provide the prospective teacher with the necessary practice experiences essential for learning to teach pupils over a given period of time. In this sense, the classroom teacher becomes the supervisor of pedagogical skills learned and practiced, the definer of the appropriate instructional climate and setting, the manager of situational variables utilized for instructional purposes, and the evaluator of teaching competence. If the classroom teacher assumes all of these critical roles in the education of prospective teachers, the role of the "official" supervisor is reduced to one of working with others who do the actual supervision of educational functions. Therefore, the consultative relationship of the supervisor to the interested parties in the educational enterprise seems to be both appropriate and necessary in a cooperative teacher education program.

The supervisor's role in cooperative teacher education cannot be altogether clear until the division of labor implied by instructional roles as prescribed in negotiated contracts, the use of paraprofessional staff, and the role of the classroom teacher as a teacher trainer are rationalized in terms of the expectations of the educational enterprise. Until the situation defining staff functions in the educational process has become a stable and understandable entity, the role of supervision in cooperative teacher education will remain general and unclear. However, the cooperative role of supervision will be vital in helping to determine what the shape of the roles of the professional staff should be.

Academic Credentials and Instructional Competence

The relationship between licensing teachers and their functional competence over a long period of time is a continuing concern of any teacher education program. The search for ways to make academic credentials reflect and contribute to the instructional competence is relentless and foremost in the minds of those who are responsible for accounting for delivery of services to children in schools. Since the classroom teacher is the biggest factor in the delivery of educational service, the procedure for admitting and certifying the competence of new members to the teachers' ranks must be of continuing concern to those responsible for the education of teachers.

When cooperative teacher education programs are considered, the intent is to make the determination of the competence of teachers subject to the test administered in actual classroom settings. In short, competence in teaching is the result of a competence-based teacher education program that utilizes actual classroom situations as the setting for training. In this sense, cooperative teacher education can be thought of as a competence-based program of licensing prospective teachers.

For our purposes, competence in teacher education is *sufficient ability, skill, or fitness to do the tasks one must do.* In the instruction of children, this presents at least three major problem areas: (1) What knowledge, skills, and processes should every teacher master?, (2) When should this knowledge, skills, and processes be employed by the teacher to achieve a specific instructional intent?, and (3) What should be the criteria used to determine whether a given candidate can successfully complete a given instructional task? None of the foregoing questions have been answered with the precision necessary to build a teacher education program that ensures a highly predictable outcome for the majority of those trained. However, the question of criteria is at the heart of the problem of licensing educational personnel. Without a satisfactory answer to this problem, it is of little consequence to consider the value of any teacher education program as the means of certifying the competence of prospective teachers as a basis for licensing them for permanent professional practice. The answer to the criterional question is well covered by the criteria proposed by Turner:[9]

1. Academic proficiency.
2. Ability to perform skills and behaviors deemed essential to teaching.
3. Ability to produce changes in pupil behavior.

Academic proficiency as the first-level criterion is the lowest level currently affecting the majority of teacher education programs. Primarily, it requires that each candidate meet a specified level of academic achievement in courses within selected subject-matter areas. Typically, this level can be reached by attaining a bachelor's degree that required the specified courses suggested for certification. The acceptable evidence for judging whether the candidate has met the condition of the criterion consists of presenting a transcript from an accredited institution or testimony by an official of the institution that the requirements have been satisfied. There are many variations of the theme related to meeting the conditions indicated by the first-level criterion. One such variation is the completion of a five-year program or a master's degree as a condition for licensure. Other variations insist that the training program must be approved by the licensing authority before graduates can obtain a license. The form of the variation guiding the application of this criterion level doesn't matter; it is the record furnished by the university authorities that serves as the supporting evidence for an applicant's request for a license to practice. This approach operationally completes the assumption that academic proficiency is highly correlated with instructional competence resulting in increased student achievement. In this case, the question of whether the candidate can demonstratively perform the required instructional tasks any better as a result of college preparation is never considered. This situation, in part, has led many professional educators to consider the merits of cooperative teacher education as a means of lessening the dependence on the assumption that academic proficiency makes teachers perform their instructional tasks more effectively.

The second-level criterion actually deals with three components: (1) it prescribes skills that a teacher must be able to perform (in some instances the level of performance is indicated); (2) it requires that teachers be able to talk technically about teaching and learning, and (3) it specifies that a teacher exhibit appropriate affective behavior. This absence of specific course requirements and academic hours of credit (subject-matter field excepted) as a basis for certification is conspicuous in terms of this criterion. With the exception of the discipline a candidate is to teach, questions about other courses and the accompanying evaluation (grades) are mostly nonexistent with this second-level criterion. The judgment of a candidate's teaching ability at this level is made on the basis of his observed behavior with children in the classroom setting, of feedback from parents and students resulting from interviews, of comments made by colleagues, and of evaluations of success in other professionally related activities. Specifically, there is much concern with things such as whether the candidate can explain complex phenomena clearly to young children, can outline correct procedures for accomplishing set goals, can make meaningful instructional decisions while interacting with the class, can help children deal with their emotional problems, can complete instructional planning that is related to short- and long-term outcome expectations, can make judgments of student progress to determine the specific assistance required for individual growth requirements, and can express a social position that is consistent with our democratic ideals and expresses real concern for positive human development. This criterion is also concerned with a candidate's ability to analyze the teaching act in technical terms (self-concept, ego development, frustration, regression, conceptual development, basic skills, information processing, and so on) that foster meaningful communication with other professionals. Finally, this criterion is concerned with whether candidates can effectively and correctly deal with difficult encounters with interested parties in the educational enterprise in terms of objectivity and rationality. Supporters of this criterion believe that teachers who have met these conditions have received appropriate professional training.

The Cooperative Teacher Education Program (CTEP) embraces the second criterion level in its approach to training teachers. This type of program accepts the schools as the single most important setting and practicing teachers as the most important judges of skills and competence required for effective instruction. In addition, the CTEP accepts all interested parties in the educational enterprise as equal partners in outlining appropriate training experiences required for teachers to do an acceptable job in completing meaningful instructional tasks with children. Operationally, the CTEP is closely akin to competence-based teacher education programs that are discussed briefly later in this chapter.

The third criterion level—ability to produce changes in pupil behavior—is the most rigorous for judging whether or not a candidate is to be admitted to the profession and awarded a license to practice. This is the level of performance most people would like to see prospective teachers attain because it requires that the candidate's instructional behavior directly produce an acceptable level of student learning given specified conditions within a specified period of time. This growth in student learning is not to be limited to cognitive achievement but is to include progress made in affective development. Because of certain moral and technical limitations associated with getting reliable and valid assessments of these types of student outcomes, this criterion remains beyond our present grasp but is hopefully within our reach. When teacher education is able to reach consistently the third criterion level in judging who will receive a license to teach, we will have achieved the status of a true profession and tie training directly to the expected outcome of schooling—predictable changes in student behavior resulting from intentional instruction.

Competence-Based Teacher Education (CBTE)

During the past decade there has been a quiet though persistent evolution in teacher education under the rubric of performance-based teacher education. Since about 1970 this evolution has moved at a quickened pace as evidenced by the number of teacher-training institutions formulating and initiating performance-based teacher education programs. Similarly, the teacher certification agencies in a growing number of states require teachers to complete their training in a performance-based program as a condition for being certified as a teacher in the public schools. These and related developments in teacher and other professional organizations suggest that CBTE is likely to become and remain a permanent part of the American educational scene.

The support for the growth and development of CBTE has been generated, in part, by the general trends toward the use of the systems approach in social activity and public demand for accountability in public institutions. Coupled with general dissatisfaction among many professional educators with present approaches to teacher education, the trend toward CBTE has found an acceptance that is rarely associated with the introduction of new educational approaches. The speed with which CBTE has been accepted outside and within the ranks of professional educators has encouraged the adoption of these programs without a careful consideration of the possible consequences that might result from such an approach to the education of teachers. Now that CBTE has become entrenched on a large enough scale to expose the intricacies of its approach to training and its effects on the educational process, it is possible to analyze it critically in terms of general and specific learner and instructional demands. With this as background the writer focuses on CBTE in terms of learning and instructional demands of all students.

In the main, CBTE is characterized by at least five essential elements. These are:

1. The public statement of specific behavioral objectives in terms of the teaching competencies to be demonstrated.
2. The public statement of criteria and standards employed to assess competencies at prescribed mastery levels.
3. The prime evidence for assessment based on the performance of prospective teachers.

4. The dependence of the individual student program rate on demonstrated competency.
5. The development and evaluation of specific competencies are facilitated by the instructional program.

Accordingly, CBTE is characterized by the (1) individualization and personalization of instruction, (2) use of feedback to guide the learning experience of prospective teachers, (3) systematic program approach, (4) emphasis on the exit requirements for certifying competence, (5) division of instruction into modular units, and (6) student accountability for their performance in a teacher preparation program. Combining the essential elements and the resulting characteristics of CBTE, a picture emerges that can be critically viewed and analyzed to take into account other outcomes that are expected of the educational enterprise. One such expectation deals with the effective and efficient education of all students within a social context that supports and extends a healthy individual emotional outlook and enhances the extension of democratic principles to serve all members of our society. The writer judges CBTE in the spirit of this statement.

Areas of Concern

When one focuses on the essential elements and the resulting characteristics of CBTE, many areas of concern for the education of youth become apparent. CBTE as a teacher preparation approach has as its prime concern the training of personnel who are competent intellectually, academically, emotionally, and socially to help young people acquire knowledge and attitudes needed to contribute to and compete in our democratic society. In this sense, CBTE—like all teacher education programs—must prepare teachers who have the skills required to shape the learning behavior of youth consistent with our democratic way of life and the requirements for meeting the basic needs of our society. CBTE has to be judged in relation to its ability to deal with the product expectation of all teacher education programs.

The first concern with CBTE and its effects on the education of students is the precise definition of teaching roles and behavioral objectives in which teachers are expected to become competent. Research in teacher education has presented us with a confused and sometimes conflicting set of teacher characteristics that are used as the basis for defining a teacher's role. Some of these characteristics focus on the teacher's behavior as a person and as an information processer, whereas others focus on situational variables and student performance outcomes as the appropriate basis for defining teaching roles. Current specific problems related to teacher role definition acknowledge the importance of identifying teaching characteristics by employing different methodological and theoretical approaches. Consequently, there is no way of deciding which approach provides the best analysis of the teaching act that could serve as a basis for describing and defining the role required of teachers instructing minority group students. This situation is understandable when one considers that the ultimate criterion for judging good teaching results from one's value orientation. As long as different value orientations have to be accommodated in the schools, the role definition of good teaching remains an open and public issue.

Unfortunately, the proponents of CBTE have defined too narrowly those who should pass judgment on the nature of good teaching. In the main, proponents of CBTE have based their role definition of good teaching and the behavior objectives prospective teachers should demonstrate on the thinking of a few educators who have spent considerable time and effort experiencing, thinking, researching, and writing in the area of teacher education. There is little evidence that consideration for the concerns and preferences of the clients (children and their parents) has influenced the thrust of CBTE to date. This represents a serious omission because it changes the value placed on the judgments of different interest groups associated with the schools. In this sense, CBTE represents some negation of gains parents supposedly acquired in having a voice in the determination of policy affecting the education of their children.

During the 1960s, parents argued and fought for the right to help determine the goals of educational practice that were so critical to the type of school experience their children were to receive. The parents' concerns also covered the nature of the training experience that would be critical to the success of prospective teachers with their children. After many hard-fought battles the concept of parental input into the decision-making activity affecting their children's educational experience has been generally accepted as a valuable addition to the wisdom employed to guide school activity. CBTE appears, in fact, to have ignored the principle of parental involvement in decision making by restricting the range of judgment sources for defining appropriate teacher roles and specifying behavioral objectives that prospective teachers are to master. This raises critical questions such as "Who shall be judge?" "What is evidence?" "Is the evidence admissible?" "What are appropriate criteria and standards for admissible evidence?" and "What sanctions are to be employed when deviations are noted?" CBTE places entirely too much emphasis on the quantitative judgments of professional educators as opposed to the qualitative judgments of those (parents and students) to be served. Using this as a basis for the preparation of teachers sets back progress that has been made toward expanding the number, quality, and experience backgrounds of judges so that the *evidence* of teaching quality is admissible as valid data for clients to judge the quality of educational experience delivered by the schools*. Without this consideration, CBTE returns to a pattern of professional educators deciding what values are important in teaching behavior. If the rights to this kind of decision making are not granted to representatives of the ultimate recipients of CBTE by its proponents, an unacceptable pattern of educational practice is likely to be perpetuated. Judgments of "good" or "effective" teaching are, as yet, too value laden to risk the exclusion of those served when teacher education programs are being formulated, implemented, and evaluated. Should CBTE continue to ignore this reality, it will sow the seeds for its eventual demise. Unfortunately, irreversible damage will have been done to those who attempted to follow a trend without a critical analysis of the possible consequences.

The second area of concern with CBTE and all students deals with the emphasis on individualization, personalization, and the division of the content and behaviors to be learned and demonstrated with a preset level of acceptable competence into modular units. With the present quasireligious fervor suffusing the advocacy of individualized instruction as the predominant instructional mode, this writer will risk being labeled sacrilegious by asserting that this method is inappropriate for prospective teachers. Since individualization of learning experiences is one of the cornerstones of CBTE, some attention should be directed at analyzing some of the possible consequences resulting from placing too great an emphasis on this mode of instruction. In the main, individualization of instruction in CBTE provides for rates of speed appropriate to the individuals from widely differing backgrounds and purposes, and for instruction that is highly person- and situation-specific. In addition, it allows the student to select, direct, and evaluate parts of his program, report his own educational opportunity, and plan ahead for his own growth and development. On the surface, individualization of instruction in CBTE appears to be a mode of pedagogy that encompasses all of the positives of individual learning. A closer look, however, reveals some

---

* A more complete discussion of the nature of evidence in education is now being developed by Robert L. Wolf, an assistant professor in education at Indiana University, Bloomington, Indiana. His insight into this area has aided me greatly in considering this topic.

disturbing realities. Teaching is primarily a group activity because there must be some type of interaction between at least two people. Learning to teach probably requires group interaction to provide a reasonable degree of authenticity and understanding of concepts in teaching that can only be explained and described in a group context. For example, the concept of classroom control cannot be demonstrated by a prospective teacher through a prepared individualized program since a "control" situation is specific and defined by the group characteristics involved. In teacher training a prospective teacher might be able to learn and demonstrate knowledge of *the rules of teaching behavior through an individualized program, but mastery of many teaching concepts requries learning in a group context.*

Another problem with the individualization of instruction in CBTE and training teachers to work with a wide variety of students with different backgrounds is the requirement that a great deal of attention be paid to affective factors in teaching when working with them. Teachers must be able to relate to students of different background experiences as people worthy of respect, and a quality program of instructional experience is necessary. Evidence suggests that teachers who are successful in this have mastered the affective areas of the teaching act to an extent that selected groups of students feel a bond and a respect that enable them to achieve more than would have been the case if the teacher did not have these skills. The mastery of affective skills needed to teach certain kinds of students requires learning to take place in a special, situation-specific context. For example, a white middle-class teacher who was socialized completely in an all-white small-town community from birth to adulthood cannot learn to relate to black children from poor urban areas in a preplanned individualized program of instruction. There is no way of knowing beforehand what attitudes a prospective teacher from such a background needs to revise and in what direction. It is probably erroneous to assume that all white teachers from such a background have the same attitudes toward a specific group of black children. Similarly, it is equally erroneous to assume that all white trainees have similar dispositions toward learning to deal with the affective areas of teaching. It is extremely unlikely that concepts describing the affective components of the teaching act can be taught on an individualized basis because of the requirements of group interaction to determine what skills the prospective teacher needs to develop. Since affective factors appear to be critical to the effective teaching of some students, the emphasis on individualized instruction in CBTE does not appear to offer a reasonable alternative to present teacher education programs.

The personalization of training suggested by CBTE appears to ask the prospective teacher to choose modes of learning and activities in accordance with his personal preference. On the surface, one could conclude that this heightens interest and involvement because of the greater match between the task to be accomplished and the use of techniques that are personally satisfying. This approach neglects the use of different methodologies that are unique to the development and understanding of knowledge in specific content areas. This latter notion requires the effective teacher to master a repertoire of methodologies appropriate to learning and understanding concepts in a number of different content areas even if some of the methodologies are not personally satisfying. A professional teacher has the responsibility to learn methods of teaching and learning that transcend personal preferences. If CBTE fails to adhere to this standard of competency, it has precipitated the ultimate barrier to the personalization of teacher development. Skills in teaching are beyond the personal preferences of those who aspire to teach. A teacher's training should open new vistas for prospective teachers by exposing them to new possibilities for enhancing the teaching/learning experience.

The fragmentation of instruction into modular units is another characteristic of CBTE that is not necessarily conducive to training prospective teachers to work with all students. For CBTE a module is a set of learning activities (with objectives, prerequisites, preassessment, instructional activities, postassessment, and remediation) intended to facilitate the student's acquisition and demonstration of a particular competency. According to the evidence, dividing instruction into modules is likely to contribute more to the learning of the person who constructed the module than the person who uses it as a learning device. This conclusion is supported by the findings from tutoring experiences involving disadvantaged students at different age levels. When low-achieving high-school disadvantaged students were asked to tutor low-achieving elementary school disadvantaged students in reading, the high-school students gained in their own ability to read. In effect, the results indicate that the tutor made greater gains than the individual receiving the instruction in this particular teaching experience. When prospective teachers are asked to acquire and demonstrate knowledge of teaching through the use of modules, there is considerable doubt as to whether the student gains what the author intended and, as such, learns to perform without mastering the critical assumptions underlying the learning activity. It might be more useful if CBTE were to provide minority students with an effective educational experience and have prospective teachers write modules outlining learning activities that will enable one to acquire and demonstrate a particular competency. There would be a greater probability of mastery than would be the case if the same student were asked to study a module constructed by someone else. This notion should be considered by the proponents of CBTE especially as it relates to the preparation of teachers who will work in a number of different environmental settings.

Another area of concern for CBTE involves the demonstration of teaching roles. This is a particularly critical consideration because of the apparent focus on the performance of teaching competencies with little emphasis on academic competencies. There is almost universal agreement that many students are extremely deficient in the skills and knowledge necessary to understand new ideas that contribute to personal development through independent learning experiences. Any teacher faced with such children has to be proficient in the methodology of teaching, the skills associated with processing information in a particular content area, and the knowledge of the subject matter serving as the medium of communication. When a teacher attempts to work with some students, it is absolutely necessary that he be able to explain a concept in a variety of ways utilizing examples and analogies appropriate both to the conceptual development of the content and the experience background of the learner. There is little doubt that in these instances teachers must have academic mastery over the prerequisite skills and content they employ to communicate with these students.

According to the notions concerning demonstrated teaching competencies expressed in CBTE, too little attention is paid to the demonstration of academic competence in content areas intended to be used with students. By way of example, it is possible for a prospective teacher in a CBTE program to demonstrate mastery of ten steps of reading maps and still fail to utilize a map properly in a teaching situation. For instance, to learn to read a map does not necessarily enable a teacher to infer associated factors and other significant relationships. Further, mastering the steps of reading a map does not ensure a teacher's ability to help students to visualize the reality that a symbol represents on a particular map. The major point is that competence in a particular skill cannot be demonstrated in a short time span and without considerable effort on the part of the learner to master the skill in question. *Real competence requires a perfect match between talent and the task to be performed and many, many long hours of dedicated practice.* The use of competence as a defining characteristic for outcomes resulting from experiences gained in a CBTE program is either an overstatement of the products or an understatement of its real meaning. The present description of teaching competence employed by CBTE would produce teachers who are ill prepared to deal with the academic competencies required to teach all students effectively.

The final area of concern with CBTE deals with the motivation necessary to get any student to expend the effort required to learn effectively. Even though the proponents of CBTE do not deal directly with student motivation as a factor in the demonstrated performance of teachers, it is at the foundation of any attempt to teach certain children. According to the rationale of CBTE, a prospective teacher can acquire skills of motivating students and demonstrate his teaching competence in the area. Teaching competence in the area of student motivation cannot be demonstrated apart from reference to a particular child in a particular situation. Students are internally motivated to learn all sorts of materials for their own reasons. Some children are motivated to learn by peer approval, teacher approval, parental approval, personal desires to excel, the need to impress a significant person, or many factors that remain undetectable. The point here is that the teacher cannot demonstrate competence in motivating students in a vacuum. In regard to the relationship between teaching and student motivation, the teacher can be characterized in terms of a good offensive lineman on a football team. The really good offensive lineman avoids direct contact to move the defensive lineman against the latter's direction of movement. The offensive lineman's solution is to discern the direction in which the defensive lineman is headed and to provide the necessary force to keep him going a little bit faster and a bit farther than he intended to go. A teacher must be able to determine the direction chosen by the learners and apply the necessary push to keep them going a little bit faster and a bit farther than they had dreamed or intended. The CBTE pattern does not enable teachers to learn firsthand the critical role that the internal motivations of students play in their own learning. CBTE appears to assume that skills of student motivation can be learned, thus perceiving an affective state as external to the learner. It is questionable that the CBTE pattern can help prospective teachers demonstrate teaching competence in student motivation apart from actual practice with real children.

CBTE is a good idea if its application is limited to a scope commensurate with the areas that the approach covers adequately. The major shortcoming of CBTE is revealed when it is pushed as a total program for the education and preparation of teachers. Like all specific cures for specific ills, the misapplication of the remedy is likely to cause patients to fail to seek an appropriate cure that is readily available in other places. CBTE comes dangerously close to being advocated as a cure for all our educational and instructional ills resulting from the preparation of educational personnel. This is an unfortunate development for all children who will be taught by teachers so narrowly trained, but it is particularly disastrous for selected groups of students who require teaching competence that is more broadly based. The preparation of teachers is still a value-laden activity because there are conflicting notions regarding what constitutes "good" or "effective" teaching. CBTE will not resolve the issues associated with this problem and will probably do a disservice if the approach causes educators to belittle the importance of value conflicts reflected in present teacher education programs. It is entirely possible that the vitality of our democratic society results from our constant search for, and use of, different perspectives for interpreting the values guiding the selection and presentation of knowledge to young people. To the extent that CBTE fails to honor this tradition, we run the risk of overlooking important new developments that enhance the human condition. This is not an appropriate outcome of any teacher education program. To the extent that the cooperative teacher education program is able to avoid some of the pitfalls of the CBTE, it will prepare teachers who are suited to the changing conditions affecting instruction in today's schools.

The Paraprofessional and the Teacher in the Elementary School

In recent years, many of the urban area schools (especially those in the inner city) increasingly serve students who are primarily members of minority groups and predominately poor and disadvantaged in many areas of social function. As minority members of the society became the major clients in inner-city school systems, their traditions and behavior patterns became the dominant force in determining the shape of emotional and social climate characterizing the ongoing interactions in the schools. Since many of the schools were staffed by members of the majority group citywide, conflict between the new majority clients in inner-city schools and the old majority staff created a condition that reduced communication, militated against understanding, and created widespread distrust that made normal instructional activity rare if not nonexistent. The two-headed monster of poverty and background differences triggered the move toward establishing the paraprofessional as a permanent fixture on the American educational scene.

The use of paraprofessionals in schools was intended to alleviate many problems that were related both indirectly and directly to the purpose of the elementary school. Specifically, these problems were highlighted and defined as a result of certain forces that placed a different set of concerns with a variety of environmental conditions into the sphere of the elementary school. Some of these forces were as follows:

> The gap between expanded needs for school services and the availability of professional personnel to meet these needs reached critical proportions in the late sixties;
>
> New dimensions in educational concepts and technology required a more complex role for teachers;
>
> Heightened awareness of the special learning needs of young children, and a developing insight into the communication blocks that often exist between middle-class professionals and disadvantaged children called for closer linkage of school and community;
>
> The plight of the undereducated person, unable to compete in an increasingly automated society pointed to the need for a new entry level to careers of human service with opportunity for upward mobility on the job;
>
> Finally, and most importantly, new resources became available to school systems through OEO, MDTA, Title I of ESEA, the Nelson-Scheuer Amendment to the Poverty Act, and the Javits-Kennedy Act for Impacted Areas, all of which provided Federal funds for the employment of low-income persons who lacked the traditional certification for education.[10]

A careful study of these forces reveals that many of them were outside the usual concern of the elementary school in terms of an accepted responsibility for which it was accountable. This list suggests that the elementary school was expected to assume the responsibility for recruiting professional personnel, redefining teacher roles, relating the school's program more closely to the clients served in the community, providing jobs and advancement opportunities for the unemployed local people, and responding to outside requests to make room for different professional types. All of this was to be accomplished with the aid of paraprofessionals who would be added to the elementary staff.

In addition to dividing professional responsibilities so that paraprofessionals could become members of the professional instructional staff, the elementary school was expected to provide continued employment and job advancement opportunities for a group that heretofore would not have been included in the career ladder. This focus on career development for paraprofessionals was largely the result of a book by

Pearl and Riessman.[11] The "New Careers Movement" that was suggested leads to the conclusion that:

> This is a movement to recognize and establish new qualifications for careers in the human services so that economically and educationally disadvantaged persons have the opportunity for upward mobility in careers instead of frustrating dead-end jobs of a menial nature. This career concept is one of the essentially innovative components of the current thrust toward the utilization of paraprofessionals in the public service, which has captured the imagination of many seminal thinkers in American education.[12]

The inclusion of the career development notion as part of conceptualization of the paraprofessional role in the elementary school essentially altered the professional role of the classroom teacher who traditionally had total responsibility for the instructional program. This fact makes the discussion of the relationship between the paraprofessional and the classroom teacher critical to understanding how these two roles may combine to provide the most effective instructional program possible.

In order to discuss the relationship between the paraprofessional and the teacher, some notion about the hierarchical relationship between the various types of paraprofessionals and teachers would be helpful. This relationship is highlighted in the stages of career development of paraprofessionals suggested in Table 10.1:

Table 10.1
Possible Stages in Career Development of Auxiliaries

1. Aide such as	Illustrative Functions	Training Suggested
General school aide	Clerical, monitorial, custodial duties	Brief orientation period (2 or 3 weeks) in human development, social relations, and the school's goals and procedures, as well as some basic skill training
Lunchroom aide	Serving and preparation of food, monitorial duties	
Teacher aide	Helping teacher in classroom, as needed	
Family worker or aide	Appointments, escorting, and related duties	
Counselor aide	Clerical, receptionist, and related duties	No specified preschooling required
Library aide	Helping with cataloging and distribution of books	

Table 10.1 (*cont.*)

2. Assistant such as	Illustrative Functions	Training Suggested
Teacher assistant	More relationship to instructional process	High school diploma or equivalent; one year's in-service training or one year in college with practicum
Family assistant	Home visits and organizing parent meetings	
Counselor assistant	More work with records, listening to children sent from class to counselor's office because they are disrupting class	Both can be on a work-study basis while working as an aide
Library assistant	More work with pupils in selecting books and reading to them	

3. Associate such as	Illustrative Functions	Training Suggested
Teacher associate	More responsibility with less supervision by the professional	A.A. degree from two-year college or two-year special program in a four-year college
Home-school associate		
Counselor associate		
Library associate		Both can be on work-study basis while working as an assistant
Social work associate		

4. Teacher-intern such as	Illustrative Functions	Training Suggested
Student teacher	Duties very similar to those of associate but with more involvement in diagnosis and planning	B.A. or B.S. degree and enrollment in a college of teacher education or other institution which offers a program leading to certification
Student home-school coordinator		
Student counselor		

5. Teacher

Source: Garda W. Bowman and Gordon J. Klopf, *New Careers and Roles in the American School* (New York: Bank Street College of Education, 1968), p. 21. By permission of Bank Street College of Education.

Given the fact that role descriptions suggested by the illustrative functions in the chart for paraprofessionals in Table 10.1 (aides, assistants, and associates) provide a composite description of a teacher's duties with the exception of diagnosis, planning, and instruction, it is difficult to differentiate responsibilities unique to each group. The range of the paraprofessional's role is dependent upon his training and the personal preference of the teacher involved. Therefore, any discussion of the relationship that should exist between these two groups would have to be general. The situation-specific application of the general comments about this relationship will be dependent on the conditions facing a professional staff in a particular instructional setting. In the main the operational relationship between paraprofessionals and teachers should be based on the following factors:

1. A mutual agreement is needed between the two parties in terms of the role to be played by the paraprofessional.
2. There should be mutual agreement on the functions that have high priority in terms of pupil-related items.
3. Task-oriented activities should be specified and adequately described in terms of expectations and specific responsibility.
4. The teacher should review the role description and expectation of the paraprofessional frequently to reflect changes that may have occurred through their operational approaches to classroom activity.
5. The teacher should evaluate a paraprofessional's ability to perform a variety of instructional tasks prior to asking him to perform them with children in the classroom.
6. The teacher must communicate the extent of his responsibility that must remain under his direct control, supervision, and implementation.
7. The lines of authority for different types of decisions affecting classroom activity should be clearly spelled out to avoid conflicting directions to students.
8. Joint planning of all activities is essential if the paraprofessional is expected to complement the teacher in terms of total professional responsibility.

These factors represent areas that must be dealt with systematically if the relationship between paraprofessionals and teachers is to contribute to a meaningful educational experience for the students to be served. The main concern must be directed toward a coordinated effort that strengthens the joint offerings of the paraprofessional and teacher to an extent greater than the sum of what they could offer individually. In short, the paraprofessional and the teacher must be an instructional team with a single goal—providing the best educational experience for their students.

Summary

The professional staff of the elementary school shares the responsibility for providing a well-rounded instructional experience for elementary school children. The key professional staff role in the elementary school is that of the classroom teacher. Accordingly, all other staff performing professional activity serve as the supporting cast for the classroom teacher. Our primary focus centered on classroom teachers and how other members of the staff complement them in their efforts to provide meaningful instructional experiences for all of their students. The professional staff of the elementary school was discussed in terms of certain categories such as the purpose of the elementary school, the characteristics of the children to be served, the requirements of related learning tasks, the nature of the instructional setting, the expectations of the public, and the perceptions of the teachers. Each of the major categories served as a framework for discussing the professional staff of the elementary school. This approach enabled us to cover many of the aspects of the elementary school's function as they relate to the professional staff responsible for implementing the instructional program.

References

1. Jacques Barzun, *Teacher in America* (Garden City, N.Y.: Doubleday, 1954), pp. 16–17.
2. James E. Russell, *Change and Challenge in American Education* (Boston: Houghton, 1965), p. 51.
3. Philip W. Jackson, *Life in Classrooms* (New York: Holt, 1968), p. 5.
4. Department of Health, Education, and Welfare, *Digest of Educational Statistics* (Washington, D.C.: National Center for Educational Statistics, 1973), p. 1.
5. Russell, op. cit., pp. 54–55.
6. James B. Conant, *The Education of American Teachers* (New York: McGraw-Hill, 1963), pp. 147–148.
7. Ibid., pp. 161–162.
8. Stephen K. Bailey, "Teachers' Centers: A British First," *Phi Delta Kappan,* 53:146–149 (Nov. 1971).

9. Richard Turner, "Levels of Criteria," Appendix A, in Benjamin Rosner, et al., *The Power of Competency-based Teacher Education* (Washington, D.C.: Department of Health, Education and Welfare, Office of Education, Committee on National Program Priorities in Teacher Education, 1971), Project No. 1–0475.

10. Garda W. Bowman and Gordon J. Klopf, *New Careers and Roles in the American School* (New York: Bank Street College of Education, 1968).

11. Arthur Pearl and Frank Riessman, *New Careers for the Poor: The Nonprofessional in Human Services* (New York: Free Press, 1965).

12. Bowman and Klopf, op. cit., p. 6.

A Critical Look Ahead

At the present time the elementary school is faced with many challenges. Some of these challenges are historical in nature, some are related to societal conditions, some are related to the environmental settings within which schools must operate, some are the result of technological changes and advances, and some are dictated by the requirements of changing lifestyles. Even though there is some question about the major source of influence focused on the elementary school and its programs, there is little doubt that there is an influence or complex of influences directed at the elementary school determining its present activity and shaping its future course. In this chapter we look at some of these major influences and suggest some of the areas that are likely to be the central concerns of the elementary school in the very near future.

Developing Foundational Skills in the Elementary School

The elementary school is likely to continue to be held accountable for developing foundational skills required to "learn how to learn." This school will still be expected to help children acquire the foundational skills of communication and computation required to successfully complete rational processes needed to process information effectively and efficiently. Introducing children to certain types of knowledge foundations will still be a central focus of the elementary school but in a slightly different form. As media techniques are improved, the subject matter of coverage continues to expand, and opportunities to view replicas (wild-life parks, museums, exhibits, and so on) become more commonplace, the selection of foundational knowledge will have to be more systematic and tailored to the experiences and needs of the children in question. What is knowledge orientation for some children is unwarranted repetition for others.

The establishment of a knowledge foundation for elementary schoolchildren may cut across present subject lines in ways that are quite different. Even though the future teacher is likely to make use of existing knowledge areas such as social studies, science, arithmetic, and literature, these areas may not adhere to subject-matter boundaries as was and still is the case at this level. Orientation to foundational knowledge in the future is likely to focus more on problems and life studies that require an interdisciplinary approach. Foundational knowledge in this latter sense will be closely tied to the nature of the area to be studied. Another way to state it might be to think of children being taught the types of knowledge that help one find solutions to problems clustered in major subgroups. In this sense, exposing students to foundational knowledge in the future elementary school is likely to be more functional, with a definite focus on reality and basic human needs—physical, social, and emotional.

The elementary school is likely to continue to be the prime institution that provides the foundation for the child's self-concept and group orientation. It is still very likely that the elementary school will play a major role in determining the degree of acceptance each child will have toward certain systematic ways of processing information, thinking about problems, and selecting knowledge that is worthwhile for certain purposes. The elementary school is likely to continue as the primary institution where children will be able to learn about themselves in relation to age mates with different personalities and backgrounds. Developing foundational skills that enable children to formulate social sensitivity in terms of their own individuality in the society is likely to continue to be an important function of the elementary school in this area of concern.

The development of foundational skills in the future elementary school cannot be considered in isolation from the child's total educational experience. Acquiring an adequate foundation in skills is dependent upon the attitudes and values and the knowledge and the opportunities that children are afforded to practice skills to be learned in meaningful and realistic settings. The resulting performance will determine the extent to which children are likely to acquire the foundational skills in question. The shape and nature of the foundational skills that should be taught in tomorrow's elementary school will be determined by the particulars and requirements that comprise its environmental setting for individuals and society. In any event, the foundational skills taught will have to have promise in helping children solve current social problems and to plan for handling problems that will emerge as a result of the rapidity of change experienced in society that calls for major changes in our social functions. And the elementary school is still likely to have the major responsibility for teaching the foundational skills required to meet challenges implied in this discussion.

Providing for the General Education of Young Children

The elementary school will continue to provide for the general education of the children it serves. However, its general education function is likely to be altered to take into account the expanding opportunities that children will have for acquiring general education outside of the school. The new general education function of the elementary school must have a greater focus on utilizing the specialistic knowledge to solve general problems resulting from rapid changes occurring in our society. This generalistic approach to knowledge will be expected to help children deal with the fragmentation associated with the production of knowledge. In this sense, general education in the future elementary school will help children become more adept at utilizing fragmented knowledge to focus on the reality of their lives and the lives of others.

General education in the elementary school has the aiding of young children to think critically as one of its goals. Critical thinking[1] is the primary aim of general education. Critical thinking is here used to refer to "a point of view toward problems and their solutions and a way of thinking about basic problems faced by mankind."[2] The conception of critical thinking suggested by this definition assumes that the notion will be allocated a central position in formulating the curriculum and the accompanying instructional processes employed to teach children.

If general education in the elementary school is to foster the development of critical thinking skills, children must be helped to approach a particular knowledge area in an integrated rather than a compartmentalized fashion. This view is very ably expressed in the following comments:

> In the field of communication all aspects—reading, writing, listening, speaking—involve or should involve thinking and may be approached in this way rather than as discrete elements. The act of writing, consisting of formulating a problem, exploring it, and reaching a conclusion would thus be viewed as having much in common with giving a speech. Although the medium is different, the problems of choice of words, adapting to the audience, and ordering the presentation, are similar.[3]

Critical thinking skills are needed to arrange information so that solutions to real problems can be found. The general education program in the elementary school will provide the type of content required to develop and utilize critical thinking skills. The elementary school of the future must have a general education program that offers the relevant content required to develop and extend the critical thinking skills needed to solve current problems.

It matters not whether one believes that the fundamental purpose of an elementary school

> . . . is the inculcation of moral and spiritual values, the transmission of knowledge, the development of traits of citizenship, the preparation of individuals for adult life, or the development of intellectual keenness, critical thinking must play a major role. To all save the most doctrinaire of religious sectarians there is a willingness, even a demand, that rational methods of inquiry be used in all fields of human activity, including religion. In American democracy there exists the hope that its values and traditions be subjected to constant scrutiny so that those who accept them do so reasonably and not by blind faith. Knowledge acquired without reason becomes a mere jumble of facts and not the essential instruments of an educated man. The techniques by which knowledge can be effectively utilized are those involved in critical thinking.[4]

The general education program of the future elementary school must take into account the nature of critical thinking that is required to deal with problems that are not readily predictable. The appropriateness of the general education program for tomorrow's elementary school will be dependent on how well it helps children respond to the following questions related to aspects of critical thinking. These questions are presented below in major groups.

Group I: How much information is required for critical thinking in some problem areas? What information should children explore and remember? How should certain types of information be processed and presented? How should different kinds of knowledge be stored, ordered, summarized, and screened?

Group II: How should existing knowledge be used to solve perceived, real, and predictable problems? How should information be retrieved to foster and/or further critical thinking? How do different indicators of knowledge relate to critical thinking?

Group III: How can knowledge produced by specialists be made available to the general population? How does one make learning a continuous activity in the regular lives of children? How do we make new knowledge affect the actions and attitudes of children toward positive ends?

The general education program must enable tomorrow's teachers and students to find answers to these questions as an outcome of their elementary school experience.

Rural, Urban, and Suburban Concerns

During the course of the elementary school's existence the nature of the community it served has exerted a profound influence on its program and the extent of its influence in the lives of the children it served. The community setting of the elementary school changes in relation to salient demographic and geographic factors. Yet the elementary school is expected to provide a program that helps pupils learn knowledge and processes that will take them beyond the boundaries of their community experiences. The mobility patterns of the population in the United States will dictate many different community problems for the elementary schools in the future. The staff of the elementary school needs to consider what the changing scene within which the school will operate will be like and begin to plan its programs accordingly.

The elementary school in the rural community will continue to be faced with the problem of making the population of the school into a cohesive unit. Children who live in rural areas are likely to be transported longer distances to school because fewer elementary school-age children will be living close to each other. In order to maintain a certain school population size in rural areas, children will have to be collected from a wider geographic area. This will increase the percentage of children who have not known each other before and cannot get together in after-school activities. The situation increases the task of the school regarding the building of a student body that is cohesive and whole: a student body that supports individual members and provides an atmosphere that encourages friendships outside of the school's physical boundaries. The elementary school in rural areas will continue to have to attempt to build an integrated student body under most difficult conditions. The rural elementary school will not be able to count on the after-school group experiences of its pupils to reinforce the attitudes and values learned during the regular school day.

When the future rural elementary schools are faced with the problem of teaching group-related skills, processes, and understandings, they will have to seek ways of achieving these goals during the school day. This continues to have profound implications for the programs of the rural elementary school.

The elementary school in the urban community will continue to be faced with a pupil population that is poor and composed mostly of members of minority groups. The surrounding folkways and mores of the community will continue to challenge the validity of the content being taught in the elementary school. Most of the problems facing teachers in the urban elementary school will be brought into the schools from the homes, and at present the school has few if any adequate means to cope with the problems. The urban scene experienced by most pupils will exert a powerful counterforce to the elementary school program and its staff. Urban pupils are likely to continue to be ill-prepared for doing the level of work expected and to have very little incentive for making the necessary changes.

Given the very nature of the present urban community, the elementary schools serving these areas have an awesome responsibility for countering the negative effects of a pervasive community and home experience. The urban elementary school cannot afford to fail to provide pupils with the foundational experiences that make it possible for them to begin to take advantage of available opportunities. With the high mobility pattern experienced in most urban elementary schools, it will be necessary for these schools to do a better job at coordinating their programs to maintain the consistency of learning experience required to build useful and meaningful foundational skills and understandings. There is likely to be a greater need for one urban elementary school to provide a total positive experience for its pupils if it is to be expected to deal effectively with the problems that are thrust upon its pupils by the community environment. The urban elementary school of the future cannot be successful if it fails to help children receive the full benefit of its program in spite of the many problems associated with its surrounding community.

The suburban elementary school of the future will continue to deal with large numbers of children that come mostly from one social class or live in communities with a small range of socioeconomic differences. Suburban children are likely to continue to be dominated by their mothers in their upbringing and social activities. This domination by the mothers will continue to influence the kinds of pressures that will be brought to bear upon the elementary school to provide a program that is preferred by selected groups of parents. Suburban communities are likely to continue to offer social contacts that are circumscribed and controlled by parents. The difficulty children face in being unable to move about freely over a wide geographic area places suburban parents in a unique position to control their children's movements by controlling their transportation. Given this general problem, suburban children will continue to remain largely isolated from children who have very different backgrounds and share values based on a different set of circumstances.

The suburban elementary school will continue to have the problem of helping its children to respect others with different kinds of life conditions and to develop ways of interacting with each other. Children who attend these schools will have a difficult time relating to children who do not share their experiences or values. This same case could be made for children who attend rural and urban schools, but there seems to be at least one critical difference when applied to suburban children. The parents of suburban children usually earn high incomes, work in influential jobs, and control resources and social patterns. Since suburban children are likely to be afforded greater opportunities as adults to influence major social functions affecting most people, it is crucial that these children be helped to become more socially aware. The suburban elementary school has to do this job for its children if it is to become a common experience for these pupils. If the suburban elementary school fails to help its children learn to accept and work with those who are less fortunate and have different background experiences, it will not fulfill its responsibility as a servant of a democratic society. If many of our future leaders and intellectuals are allowed to grow up socially isolated, our society will be in grave danger of becoming less democratic and thus less humane. The suburban elementary school can be of great assistance in helping its children deal with the issues involved.

The setting of the elementary school is likely to continue to exert a profound effect on the program it offers. Rural, urban, and suburban communities offer different kinds of challenges to the elementary school. However, all elementary schools in a variety of community settings are expected to provide their children with the necessary experiences they will need to serve as productive and happy members of our democratic society. Different community settings dictate the alterations that have to be made in the elementary school's program to ensure a balanced experience for the children. If tomorrow's elementary schools fail to adapt their programs to the requirements of their community setting, they will provide a school experience that is truly elementary for children with different experiences and talents who are expected to become cooperative members of the same democratic society.

Orientation Toward Meaningful Work Activities

As our society becomes more complex and major institutions become larger in size and influence and are more interrelated, human activity becomes specialized into more selective parts to conduct basic social functions. Specialization of human activity into selective parts for carrying on the basic social functions of our society defines the nature of work for individuals presently and in the future. Since part of the major responsibility of the elementary school is and remains the preparation of youth for productive activity in the society, the orientation of pupils to the world of work becomes a major concern in their school experience. Orientation to the world of work tends to provide pupils with the tangible and useful evidence for major parts of the program of the elementary school because the program of the elementary school is supposed to help pupils learn about the major functions of our society and how these functions relate to their lives and the lives of others past, present, and future.

The conduct of the major social functions of our society is a work activity for some people in our society. Whether we are discussing construction activities, artistic works, voluntary efforts, personal hobbies, or travel experiences, we are concerned with work activity for someone. In that sense, one cannot discuss the social functions carried on in the society apart from the work required to complete the implied and explicit activities that accompany them. The world of work is intimately tied to all of the social functions required to maintain and improve our society. Therefore, the elementary school has a real stake in helping children grasp the relationship between its curriculum program and the social functions of society. One way to do this is to associate the curriculum program with the world of work.

Career education has gained the attention of professional educators and laymen alike who feel that the schools have not done such a good job in exposing students to the various occupational opportunities available for people who possess certain kinds of skills. A large part of the justification for greater focus on career education in the schools stems from the fact that 1,737,602 (59 per cent) of the 2,944,000 1971 high-school graduates are enrolled in an institution of higher education.[5] More than half of the high-school graduates were attending institutions of higher education whereas the occupational opportunities were expanding faster in areas that do not require college degrees. In effect, this meant that more and more of our young students were acquiring training and education for occupational positions that were nonexistent whereas occupational positions that needed filling were going begging. Also, many of these positions were as attractive in terms of salary and job satisfaction as those that required college degrees. Career education was thought of as a way of informing students about the present and future availability of occupational positions and the skill requirements for filling these positions. Because of the direct relationship implied between occupational positions and prospective workers, career education is seen as being most appropriate for students who are above the elementary school-age level. However, the number of reasons why this kind of information might be made a more integral part of the program of the elementary school is increasing. The first reason is related to the fact that occupational interests might be shaped early in the school experience of most children, and these interests are limited to those occupational fields that are readily recognized by most people. Since the range of occupational positions in various categories that can be known by young learners is so limited, they restrict their choices too severely in terms of their personal interests and talents. A second reason is associated with the need for young children to see a real connection between information and procedures for processing it, and how they relate to the world of work. Many times young children have a tendency to see work only in terms of physical exertion rather than as mental or emotional activity. A third reason is associated with the fact that as many as 50 per cent of the high-school students in some urban areas drop out prior to graduation. Many of these dropouts will be seeking employment with little understanding of the expectations of training and personal characteristics needed for a number of occupational positions that might be available. As long as the possibility exists that as many as half of the high school students in some areas will not have the benefit of an orientation to the world of work if the elementary school fails to deal with the problem, it becomes a prime responsibility to give some attention to the problem in the program of the elementary school.

Orientation to the world of work is likely to become a primary concern of the elementary school because it offers a way to make the program more relevant to the pupils served. It is not likely that this orientation to the world of work will take the form of a course or unit in career education because it is competing for valuable time that is already too limited by the many demands being made of the elementary school at present—demands that are likely to increase in the future. At the elementary school level, orientation to the world of work is likely to focus on the generic qualities of work.[6] According to the argument put forth by J. M. Slater, mankind must perform individually or collectively the following generic work functions to maintain a viable society:

1. Sustain themselves, including their everyday commerce with other people.
2. Marshal man's resources, including the intellectual as well as those which reside in nature.
3. Produce goods.

As society becomes more complex, the carrying out of these work functions requires the effective communication of discrete occupational skills and information required to pursue certain aspects of the generic work functions in question. Also there is a greater need for coordinated collective action. Collective action needed to complete the tasks implied by generic work functions include man-made arrangements (systems) that require three kinds of human input (or functions) to assume success. These human inputs or functions are associated with the following areas:

1. Conceptualization (planning and designing).
2. Implementation (operating and conducting).
3. General services, including maintenance (routine attending and delivering).

Since all jobs to which men aspire, or are assigned, fall into these functional categories, they serve as the basis for dealing with the accompanying issues and information in the programs of the elementary school.

The elementary schoolchild must be introduced to the world of work in relation to the regular curriculum program of the elementary school. It is the responsibility of the elementary schoolteacher to see to it that both *the methods of processing information and the type of information employed* are viewed by pupils in terms of their relationship to the world of work. Even though this is likely to be done at the generic quality of work level, it is a necessary beginning for orienting pupils to the functional world that they will inherit as adults. If the elementary school is successful in its attempt to orient pupils to the world of work, there is likely to be a vast improvement in the ability of young adults to make more meaningful occupational choices for themselves and society's general welfare. This role of the elementary school is likely to grow in importance as occupational roles proliferate to meet the challenges of an increasingly complex society. Orientation to the world of work is likely to achieve a continuing place in the program of the elementary school.

Styles of Curriculum Development

In the immediate future, the program of the elementary school will be approached in terms of styles of, rather than models of, development. Styles of curriculum development refer to "sets of related characteristics about the way curricular change is organized, which fit together with something of the consistency and coherence."[7] *Styles,* as the term is used here, refers to idiosyncratic patterns employed to put into operation choices and assumptions involving social, political, and educational values. Accordingly, a style of curriculum development is a particular pattern selected to organize curriculum reform to reflect different sets of values. *Styles,* in this sense, is contrasted with *models* as applied to the curriculum-development process. A model of curriculum development refers to the notion of engineering and design in terms of a quasiscientific social science approach to organizing curriculum. Conversely, the language of the arts dominates the thinking about style as a way of organizing curriculum. Basic to the latter way of thinking are techniques of perception and analysis for combining significant events or factors.

The elementary school's program of the future will be approached stylistically from time to time. The styles of curriculum development will be called different things and given different descriptions according to the preference of the curriculum designer. These styles of curriculum development might carry such names as "open" style, "informal" style, "humanistic" style, "creative" style, "instrumental" style, "individualistic" style, "training" style, or "growth" style, and so on. The choice of names given to depict styles of curriculum development is unimportant; all of the styles put forth will purport to make the value choices that determine how the curriculum will be organized. The question raised by the styles of curriculum development that will be proposed for the elementary school is: Does the curriculum program that results from a particular style of curriculum development enable pupils to achieve the goals that operationally define the conception of the elementary school in a democratic society? That is the question that will ultimately decide what, if any, effects different styles of curriculum development will have on the program of the elementary school.

New Developments and Educational Constants

New technology in terms of instructional materials and resources, teaching techniques, and organizational strategies will continue to be available to the elementary school. These new developments slated for the elementary school will have to be implemented while, at the same time, some of the primary constants that characterize the elementary school experience will have to be taken into account. One such educational constant is the teacher-pupil relationship. The elementary school will continue to value a teacher-pupil relationship that enhances the positive emotional and intellectual development of children. Any new development that impedes the development of a meaningful teacher-pupil relationship is not likely to be acceptable to professionals and laymen alike. A second educational constant characterizing the elementary school is the expectation that pupils will learn to process information. New developments will be judged in terms of the ease with which they facilitate the processing of information and how they help children to understand that process. A third educational constant is the matter of chronological age and grouping. The fourth educational constant of concern here deals with the provision of quantitative (or validated systematically collected data) measures of pupil performance. New developments that make provision for yielding quantitative measures of pupil performance will meet with a great deal of opposition. Although the writer acknowledges the many fallacies associated with quantitative measures of pupil performance, these measures represent, and will probably continue to represent, a type of quality check on the efforts of the elementary school to provide pupils with foundational skills. New developments in the elementary school must take the problems of measuring pupil performance quantitatively as an educational constant that will continue to be part of the elementary school.

The Elementary School in the Year 2000

The elementary school reflects now what it will be or can become in the future. This idea was suggested in the Summer 1967 issue of *Daedalus,* "Toward the Year 2000: Work in Progress." As one writer commented, "The future is not an overarching leap into the distance: it begins in the present."[8] As we attempt to project the elementary school to the year 2000, we must not forget that the present conception of that school will dictate the nature and focus of that institution in the future. Many of the goals of the present elementary school will not change even though the means may be vastly different and the need for the achievement of certain goals will be greater.

If one attempts to predict what a given institution will be like in American society in the year 2000, he might begin by trying to describe in general terms some of the trends that are appearing on the scene and are likely to characterize societal existence in the not-too-distant future. One such description is offered by Daniel Bell when he comments:

> More and more we are becoming a "communal society" in which the public sector has a greater importance and in which the goods and services of the society—those affecting cities, education, medical care, and the environment—will increasingly have to be purchased jointly. Hence, the problem of social choice and individual values—the question of how to reconcile conflicting individual desires through the political mechanism rather than the market—becomes a potential source of discord.[9]

The elementary school will be expected to help children learn to cope with the new conditions of society suggested by this passage. Teaching children the values of democracy and the processes of a democratic society will become a necessary expectation for the survival of our society; at the same time, the maintenance of harmony and a respect for individual rights will also be expected. When political action begins to determine, increasingly, how decisions are to be made involving all phases of basic social functions, the effective practice of democracy by the majority of our citizens becomes a minimum standard for judging the extent to which the elementary school is preparing children to live in our society as it is evolving.

The elementary school of the year 2000 will have to prepare children to renew their education for entering new careers several times during a lifetime. The foundational skills taught in the elementary school must equip students to "learn to learn" new information that may be packaged in many different ways. Children must learn to select information to solve specific problems that may need different solutions in relation to intended use. Critical thinking skills will be required to perform many of the activities, and the elementary school will be expected to see that these skills are taught to all students, at least to some degree.

Another problem of great magnitude that will face the elementary school in the year 2000 is the accumulation and transmission of information. As techniques advance for storing, retrieving, reproducing, and transmitting information, the need to teach children how to handle these systems effectively becomes critical. In too many instances, the elementary school has not taught the majority of its pupils to use modern library resources. This failure to be able to use library and other storage-retrieval facilities in the future will hamper the learning opportunities of pupils to an extent that might negatively affect their ability to learn to participate in conducting major social functions in our society. The ability to handle multipackaged information will be a basic requirement for tomorrow's adults and the elementary school will have to assume the major responsibility for helping pupils in this area.

The future elementary school will be judged by the extent to which it helps most of its pupils acquire the "elements" of learning and living in a democratic society. If the elementary school fails to provide pupils with foundational skills that enable each child to reach the limits of individual development while contributing his equal share to the general welfare, it does not live up to its expectations and become what it is conceptualized to be. Failure of the elementary school to fulfill its conception for the majority of children in our society makes it difficult to maintain a viable, democratic way of life that is consistent with the desires of our citizens to live the good life in harmony with our environment and with each other. Even though the problem is great and the expectations are high, past accomplishments suggest that the future elementary school is equal to the task.

Summary

The future of the elementary school is tied to its history, social conditions, environmental setting, changes and advances in technology, and the requirements of changing lifestyles. There is no way of determining which of these factors exert the major influence on the shape and direction of the elementary school even though there is little doubt that they combine to affect the present activity and future course of the elementary school. In this chapter we outlined a few of the major influences affecting the present and future program of the elementary school so that educators might think more critically about the role of, and the demands on, the present and future elementary school.

Our discussion suggested that the elementary school has been, is, and continues to be concerned with developing foundational skills, providing for general education, demographic factors experienced by those served, orientation to work, patterns of curriculum development, effects of innovations and evolving social patterns. These concerns determine the present role of the elementary school and set the course for what it can become in the future. As one gains experience in viewing the elementary school in terms of the concerns as outlined, he should broaden his understanding of the concept of what the elementary school is.

References

1. Paul L. Dressel and Lewis B. Mayhew, *General Education: Explorations in Evaluation* (Washington, D.C.: American Council on Education, 1954), p. 273.
2. Ibid.
3. Ibid., p. 274.
4. Ibid., pp. 277–278.
5. *Digest of Educational Statistics,* 1972 Edition (Washington, D.C.: Department of Health, Education and Welfare, 1973), pp. 55 and 69.
6. J. M. Slater, Unpublished Paper, "The Process of Career Education Student Learning and Staff Involvement" (Spring 1974), p. 5. Vocational and Technical Education Department of the University of Illinois.

7. *Styles of Curriculum Development,* Centre for Educational Research and Innovation, Director of Information, Organization for Economic Co-operation and Development, 2, rue Andre-Pascal, 75775 Paris Cedex 16, France, p. 7.

8. Daniel Bell, "The Year 2000—The Trajectory of an Idea," *Daedalus,* **96:**645 (Summer 1967).

9. Ibid.

Index

Page numbers in *italic* refer to references at the end of chapters.
n. refers to names in footnotes or figure captions.
Page numbers in **bold type** indicate table or figure.